KOINONIA

KOINONIA

Spiritual and
Theological Growth
of the Religious Community

Fabio Ciardi, O.M.I.

New City Press

Published in the United States by New City Press
202 Cardinal Rd., Hyde Park, NY 12538
www.newcitypress.com
©2001 New City, London (English translation)

Translated from the original Italian
Koinonia: itinerario teologico-spirituale della spiritualità religiosa
© Città Nuova, Rome, Italy

Cover design by Nick Cianfarani

Library of Congress Cataloging-in-Publication Data:
Ciardi, Fabio, 1948-
   Koinonia : spiritual and theological growth of the religious community / Fabio Ciardi.
       p. cm.
   Includes bibliographical references.
   ISBN 1-56548-145-3
   1. Monastic and religious life--History--20th century. 2. Monasticism and religious
orders--History--20th century. I. Title

BX2385 .C4513 2000
255--dc21   00-060941

Printed in Canada

Contents

PART THREE
THEOLOGICAL REFLECTION

PART FOUR
THE DAILY JOURNEY

Introduction

In the history of the Church and society, religious communities have been a source of renewal, spiritual energy, creativity and response to the demands of the time. The beginnings of the monastic movement were an urgent call to the whole Church to return to the radicalism of the gospel, while, as a challenge to the Roman Empire, the monastic movement also had a clear social influence. Throughout the Middle Ages, the Benedictine Order and its numerous reforms could not avoid a heavy involvement in civil and religious rebirth. The same happened with the mendicant movement, whose inspiration of the masses centred on the ideals of the Gospel. Less striking but no less influential were the later movements such as the *Devotio Moderna*, the orders founded in the Reformation and Counter-Reformation periods, and the congregations of the eighteenth and nineteenth centuries. The history of the consecrated life can be seen as a series of interventions by the Holy Spirit, who unceasingly guides his Church into a better understanding and fulfilment of the Word of God. In every age the Word of God responds to humanity's hopes and speaks through the founders of religious communities, the instruments of the Spirit.[1]

Today the religious life is troubled by uncertainties and crises, especially in the West. Does it still have a specific role to play in the Church and the world? Can it still act as the leaven of the Gospel in society, in accordance with God's plan? Can it still answer the needs and questions of people today? If these needs have until now been met with an adequate response, we can assume that the Spirit has his answer prepared for today's needs also.

In fact, there is today a widespread yearning experienced by the whole of humanity: a yearning for a profound identity; for freedom, liberty from all forms of servitude, and a legitimate autonomy; for independence and, at the same time, for a true and authentic communion; for cosmic reconciliation and universal peace; for unity at every level from the family to the planet. To this new and most urgent sign of our times, the Church can offer a decisive and effective response.

Longing for Unity: A Sign of the Times

Like any other age, our time displays apparently contradictory tendencies. On the one hand, there is the quest for autonomy; on the other, the search for unity.

The international events which are themselves taking place before our eyes today, and in which we play a part, seem laden with drama and hope. The collapse of the Berlin Wall and the swift and systematic dismantling of the Iron Curtain demonstrated the demand for communion. These were sudden and unexpected rays of hope which were immediately clouded by an alarming reawakening of nationalism and the tragic developments in Romania. The hope of a 'new world order', which seemed just around the corner, was followed by the atrocities of the Gulf War and the tragedy of the Kurds. Sudden upheavals, increasing difficulties and the erection of fresh walls have hampered efforts to build a common European home.

The demand for independence is dismembering states and driving people into new groupings. The Soviet empire has disintegrated and, driven by nationalism, embarked on a laborious quest for new ethnic balances. The two peoples of Czechoslovakia, different in history and culture, have divided into separate states. Yugoslavia has fragmented in an explosion of ethnic conflicts. The same upheavals affect other European countries, from Spain and Italy to Ireland. Their turmoil is perhaps less dramatic, but it is no less urgent. The balancing of autonomy and unity is the problem in Europe.

With the Eastern and Western blocs no longer opposed, the gulf between the North and the South has been deepened and thrown into relief. New waves of migration, and the consolidation of earlier movement from North Africa, are affecting western Europe; fences are being erected between rich and poor; racial, cultural and religious divisions are resurfacing. We are all aware of the new phenomena of violence and terrorism, the continuing use of torture, and unjust and illegitimate forms of repression.

Within our society itself there is a growing unease, which a recent Vatican document has clearly defined as

> a destruction of traditional social structures, cultural movements and traditional systems of values - caused by industrialization, urbanization, migrations, the rapid development of systems of

communication, completely rational technocratic systems, etc. - leaves many individuals bewildered, uprooted, insecure and, as a result, vulnerable ... [Many people] feel ill at ease with themselves [crises of identity], the future [unemployment, the threat of nuclear war] ... They are suffering from a loss of direction, a lack of orientation, of participation in decisions, of real answers to their real problems. They experience fear because of manifold forms of violence, conflict and hostility; fear of an ecological disaster, of a nuclear holocaust and a nuclear war; of social conflicts and of manipulation. They feel frustrated, uprooted, without hearth or home, without protection; with nowhere to turn to, and without hope; and consequently without motivation, alone at home, at school, at work, in the university, in the city; lost in anonymity and isolation, relegated to the fringes of society, alienated, in other words, they belong nowhere, they feel they are not understood, that they are betrayed, oppressed, alienated, unimportant, not listened to, rejected, not taken seriously.[2]

In the age of communications, human beings are experiencing as never before a complete inability to communicate.

Alongside this progressive social dissolution, there is an undeniable and growing need for a new system of values and a new ordering of society that will better satisfy the demands of the human spirit. In the midst of today's tensions and divisions we can perceive, as John Paul II pointed out,

an unmistakable desire on the part of men of good will and of true Christians to mend what is broken, to heal wounds, to restore, at all levels, an essential unity. Such a desire is combined in many with a veritable nostalgia for reconciliation ... The desire for a sincere and consistent reconciliation is, without the shadow of a doubt, a fundamental motive force in our society, the reflection, as it were, of an irrepressible will for peace, the more vigorously so, paradoxical though it may be, the more perilous are the very causes of division.[3]

Paradoxically, the longing for communion seems to be in direct proportion to the reality of the divisions which humanity experiences today.

The desire for autonomy and the desire for unity, which may at first appear contradictory, in fact both express the same need: the desire for a new quality of relationships. The desire for autonomy often stems from a distorted experience of unity as totalitarianism or oppression. In the same way, independence is understood as making an absolute of the particular and excluding diversity. People today require an identity that is not closed in on itself in selfish individualism, but opens itself to communion with other cultural and political realities. They are looking for a unity that will respect differences, not demand mass uniformity. Only in unity can full identity be achieved; and only if people are free can they build unity together. In this harmony of relationship, unity and diversity will be the basic parameters for human growth, the essential dimensions for human living.

All this is evidence of an increasingly vehement, if not always fully conscious, longing among people today to achieve their proper identity as persons created in the image and likeness of the God who is love. They feel called to fulfil their vocation to a unity modelled on that of the triune God. The unity and distinction of the Trinity, expressing one love, is the only possible model.

Our whole century has tended towards unity, in spite of obvious failures. There are many signs of this tenacious pursuit. The welcome given for so many years to Marxism and other forms of socialism was, in its own way, an answer to the clamour for a new balance in society and unity among peoples. New international organizations have been formed in an attempt to create a new order for the world. All the political, economic and social structures of today's world are bound together in an organic and profound interdependence.

The sociologist and historian, N. Elias, compared the moment of history in which we live with the preceding evolution of humanity and noted that

> the development of history has arrived at a point, or better at a phase, in which for the first time human beings are confronted with the task of giving themselves a global organization as humanity. This takes place as the outcome of a long process of development, a development which at the same time provides human beings with the technical means for an organization of the whole of humanity. What I am speaking of is not what is usually called Utopia; the task of developing a social order which will embrace the whole of humanity is a task which is given to human beings as a matter of fact, whether or not they are aware of it.[4]

For three centuries European culture has been dominated by an individualism which has fragmented society. Now, new cultural demands are leading us back to the rediscovery of the person and communion.

Philosophy, sociology and anthropology are seeking to rediscover the relational dimension of human beings. This irrepressible longing for unity challenges us as today's new and great 'sign of the times'. Its witness is everywhere and, in spite of failures and complications, it is undiminishing. On the contrary, it is becoming more pronounced, fostered by the new opportunities of the mass media and by cultural and commercial exchanges, travel, sport, etc.

The longing for unity finds expression not only in political, economic and social fields but also in the Church, through ecumenical dialogue. The relations established between the Churches, through ecumenical gatherings such as the Basle meeting on justice, peace and ecology and the Seoul Assembly, witness to the desire to break down the old barriers which impede full communion. The meetings for prayer of the world religions at Assisi, Kyoto, Warsaw and Bari may be peak moments, but they are also signs of new relations and the will to resist fresh outbreaks of religious intolerance.

The Spirit's Answer to the Desire for Unity

By a divine strategy, the same Spirit who placed the longing for unity in human hearts has also implanted new initiatives for communion in the Church, which enable it to respond to the longings of humanity. In this century particularly, the Spirit is guiding the Church to rediscover and live out with new intensity that mystery of koinonia which is the deepest part of its nature. Thus he enables the Church to respond to the expectations of people today. The efforts of human thought and the human sciences in, for example, the fields of politics or economics are not of themselves sufficient to build that unity which all desire. It has to be given to us. The towering wall of selfishness which sin has established in human beings has to be overcome - and only grace can destroy sin and free the human heart. Therefore the Church, created by the Spirit, rediscovers itself as *the sacrament of the unity of the human race*.

Since the end of the nineteenth century, the Spirit has been creating a new ferment in thinking about the mystery of the Church. Müller, a member of the Tübingen school, gave notable theological expression to this process with his work on the concept of the Church as the Body of Christ animated by the Spirit. Between the two World Wars in this century, theological thought seemed almost exclusively concentrated on ecclesiology: the vital rediscovery of the role of Christ in his Church and the union of all believers with him and, in him, with each other. This rediscovery of the Church as the *Body of Christ* culminated in the encyclical *Mystici Corporis*. It was followed by the definition of the Church as *communion* (see, for example, J. Hamer, *The Church is a Communion*) and then the Church as *sacrament*. Finally, the Second Vatican Council completed this great renewal of ecclesiology by assimilating earlier contributions and giving doctrinal form to what had been discovered through living. The Council penetrated more deeply into the mystery of the unity of the Church and its identity as the People of God.

The Extraordinary Synod of Bishops declared in 1985 that the *ecclesiology of communion* 'is the central and fundamental idea in the documents of the Council'.[5] The Church has always held before it the ideal of the primitive community at Jerusalem; today this ideal has begun to shine with a new light. The Church is experiencing koinonia in a new way, as the first-fruit of redemption. The phenomenon described by the Council seems more vivid today than it did thirty years ago: 'A stream of charism and association runs through all the history of the Church, time after time renewing its communion and its mission in the face of the challenges delivered by the age.' (UR 6) The Council always pleaded for 'a common growth in unity ... to give the Church a greater credibility' in 'a world which is becoming more unified every day' (GS 24); today, this plea speaks directly to all the members of the People of God.

In a survey of the recent past, J. M. R. Tillard writes:

> Our age is troubled by a desire for communication and interpersonal communion which are so characteristic of the life and the quest of the Churches that they are finding them a source of power for their evangelical renewal. New forms of 'Christian communities', arising as a rule not from hierarchical initiatives but from creativity 'at the base' are springing up almost everywhere.[6]

In fact, the history of the consecrated life teaches us that over the centuries the Spirit always has given his Church the charisms it needed to respond to new signs of the times (see LG 12). He brought ancient monasticism into being to meet the demand for evangelical radicalism. He raised up the mendicants to answer the need for evangelical poverty. Every age has had its responses to the signs of the times: Teresa of Avila for prayer; Vincent de Paul for the poor; Camillus de Lellis and John of

God for the sick; John Baptist de la Salle for teaching; John Bosco for the young; Eugène de Mazenod for evangelization ...

Today the Spirit continues to provide his Church with the charisms which will enable it to respond to the signs of the times. One of the most tangible expressions of this activity is the blossoming of new communities and new ecclesial movements. The Focolare Movement, with its characteristic spirituality of unity, is undoubtedly one of the most appropriate responses of the Spirit to that longing for unity which, as we have seen, is so noticeable both in the Church and in the whole of society. Indeed, the specific note of the Movement, as stated in the Statutes approved by the Holy See, is 'unity, which marks its spirit, aims and government'.

In the light of this charism of unity and its accompanying spirituality, I have tried to make a fresh study of the history of the consecrated life, which I see as a progressive development towards the fullness of communion. It is through the various forms of religious community that the whole Church has become aware of its vocation to trinitarian unity. My journey through this history has given me a greater awareness of what is different in today's situation, with its spirituality of unity. This spirituality is concerned with the unity for which Christ asked the Father in his 'Priestly Prayer' (John 17), the unity which was Christ's supreme objective, the summing up of his divine desire and the summit of the Gospel. This spirituality is concerned with the experience of communion in love, of Christ in the midst of those who are united in his name; with the life of mutual love between the divine Persons in the Trinity as a model and plan of action for the spiritual life; with the model of Christ abandoned on the cross as a way of living out that love so that we can be 'one' with each other in the total emptying and gift of self.

Whatever charisms the Spirit gives to the Church are for the whole Church. Today's particular charism of unity can also contribute to the progress of today's religious life, reawakening its sense of communion and developing the potential of its vocation. The charism of unity can enrich the religious life with new sensitivity and values and open it up to the new horizons to which the Holy Spirit is calling the whole Church today - the horizons of ecumenical and inter-faith dialogue and dialogue with all people of good will - in order to fulfil Christ's will 'that they may all be one' (John 17:21).

The document *Mutuae relationes* reminds us (§11) that charisms have to be developed as well as preserved, always growing with the Body of Christ. Precisely because of the charismatic dimension of their life, men and women Religious have a particular duty to listen to what the Spirit is saying to the Church. Their charismatic life has its origin in their founders' unique experiences of the Spirit; this life must continue in unison with the charismatic life of the Church today. They are called, therefore, to respond to the new sensitivity to community; their very life depends upon it. John Paul II said recently that

> all the fecundity of Religious life depends on the quality of fraternal life. Still more, the present renewal of the Church and in Religious life is characterized by a quest for communion and community. Consequently Religious life will be the more meaningful the more it succeeds in building 'fraternal communities in which God is sought and loved above everything' (cf. Canon 619), while on the other hand it will lose its reason for existing whenever the dimension of Christian love is forgotten which is the building up of a little 'family of God' with those who have received the same call.[7]

The Religious Community as a Response to the Signs of the Times

In the present-day context of the demand for relationships informed by mutual respect, love and communion at the human, social, political, ecclesial and inter-ecclesial levels, the religious community can discover a specific mission. If it responds to the breath of the Spirit and finds the deepest riches of communion, it will not only renew itself but also be able to offer its own contribution to the achievement of unity.

A religious community can become a place of communion and reconciliation where every person and interpersonal relationship is fully realized. It can be the sketch and pattern for the completeness of human common life lived according to the values of the Gospel, where 'there is no longer Jew or Greek, slave or freeman, male or female, as all are a single person in Christ Jesus' (Gal. 3:28). The religious community is indeed called to make visible the community life of the Church as a whole, by taking it to its furthest limit. 'A community gathered together as a true family in the Lord's name enjoys his presence, through the love of God which is poured into their hearts by the Holy Spirit.' (PC 15)

Taking time to reflect on the religious community will not, therefore, be a sign of narcissism, introspection, a flight from the responsibilities of social and political involvement, a quest for the protection of a close-knit group or a craving for security. Rather, it will be an expression of the will to rediscover the depths not only of the Christian destiny but also the human destiny at its root, because human beings, by their very nature in relation to others, realize themselves in communion. It will proclaim by deeds that unity is possible, in spite of signs to the contrary, and that the longing for universal brotherhood is not a utopian dream but an experienced and present reality, even though it is accompanied by suffering and needs constant reconstruction. The religious community will be a sign of hope for today's humanity.

The rediscovery of the deepest dimension of community through attentive listening to what the Spirit is saying to the Church provides the religious life itself with a privileged way of renewal. The religious life has already tried, and is still trying, many different ways of renewal in this troubled and exciting post-conciliar age. In particular, there is concern over the serious decline in vocations and the progressive rise in the average age of men and women Religious. The situation is perhaps comparable to that of the Protestant Reformation and the French Revolution and seems to presage the imminent collapse of the religious life, especially in Europe and North America.

Some Religious are seeking renewal by abandoning life in common in order to follow individual apostolic projects. Underlying this choice is a valid need to escape from a common life that humiliates and crushes the person. Others have sought principles for refounding the religious life from the human sciences such as psychology. This too requires an integrated approach to the religious life which will help people to mature with undiminished integrity. Many other Religious seek to rediscover their spiritual inheritance by looking for sources of inspiration for the present in the charismatic history of their community.

I believe, however, that before anything else we need to go back to the evangelical roots which lie beneath every religious community. The specific charism and identity of every community are like the petals of a flower or the fruit of a tree: they draw their vitality from their roots. If the flower is to blossom and the tree bear fruit, we need to work at the roots and, whatever the specific charism of the community, these roots are all sunk deep in a common evangelical earth. This was the first criterion of renewal which the Second Vatican Council offered to Religious: 'Since the final norm of the religious life is the following of Christ as it is put before us in the Gospel, this must be taken by all institutes as the supreme rule' (PC 4).

Perhaps St Stephen Muret (d. 1124), the founder of the Order of Grandmont, best expresses this awareness of the common evangelical root of religious communities in spite of their charismatic diversity. He wrote in his Rule:

> In making our way towards that house of the Father on high where the Son assures us that there are many dwelling places, the chosen ways of travel are different, the direction of the paths well tried, many the ascents of the steps ... These different ways, even if committed to writing by different holy fathers - for which reason we speak of the Rule of St Basil, the Rule of St Augustine, the Rule of St Benedict - are not, however, at the source of the religious life but are its streams; they are not its root but its foliage, they are not its head but its members. Faith is one, in fact the first and principal, rule of the rules which bring salvation, from which all the others derive as streams from a single source: this is the Holy Gospel delivered by our Saviour to the Apostles and by them faithfully proclaimed throughout the world.

Addressing his own monks in particular, St Stephen continues:

> Clinging like branches to Christ the true Vine, endeavour to fulfil the precepts of His Gospel, to the utmost of the power given you. And so, to anyone who asks you to what condition, to what Rule, to what Order you belong, you will be able to say that you belong to the first and principal rule of Christian religious life, the Gospel, which is the source and principle of all Rules.

He goes on to point out that the hallmark of evangelical life and orthodoxy in faith will, of course, only be seen

> if, remaining united, you have one heart and one soul in the Lord upon the model of the apostles. You have tasted, I believe, how sweet the Lord is, and how good it is, how gladsome a thing, to live together as brothers. Let everything, then, be in common amongst you. Let there be a mutual charity, a single current of reciprocal love. Let no one amongst you consider that anything belongs to him as his own, except for loving one another and serving one another.[8]

The renewal of the religious life begins with a return to evangelical radicalism or, rather, to the very heart of the Gospel, the 'new commandment'. In this context, attention to community is not simply deference to a passing fashion. It goes to the essence and core of the Christian message: mutual love expressing and participating in the trinitarian koinonia. In this view, the community is the place and climate in which men and women Religious can rediscover their identity, and the starting point for the new and courageous choices which are demanded of them today. Where there is unity and fraternal communion, everything grows and matures because *'ubi caritas et amor, Deus ibi est'* ('where charity and love are, there God is'). God is in the midst of brothers and sisters who are united in the name of Christ, and he enlightens and guides them all by his Spirit.

Rediscovering community means rediscovering human relationships, human society and the Church. Religious communities that have drawn from the very source of unity can show others how to meet today's challenges: the sense of being a person and the desire for authentic relationships, communion and unity. John Paul II declares that

> Not only the Church but also our society can derive great advantage from fraternal communities, which are called to be beacons of light for all those who have to surmount difficulties arising from difference of interests, generation, race or culture. The Religious community can thus constitute a living witness, amidst a world which desires peace and is seeking to overcome conflicts.[9]

All this requires that men and women Religious, in their turn, allow themselves to be challenged by this sign of the times. The movement is a circular one: the world and the Church's longing for unity leads to a renewed appreciation of the community aspect of the religious vocation; at the same time, community life, restored to authenticity and purity, becomes a hopeful sign for all who seek unity.

Will Christians today, conscious of the Spirit's call to them to live the ecclesial dimension of their vocation in a new way, be able to knock at the doors of religious communities in the hope of finding there people who can communicate their experience to them and show them the way to go? Christians today ought to be able to find in men and women Religious an expertise in ecclesial communion which they have gained through the dynamics of everyday community living in mutual love.

Likewise every person of good will should be able to encounter men and women Religious who, through the exercise of mutual love, have found a way of overcoming the many barriers that separate people from each other. By the very exercise of this communion, such Religious will have become mature and fully realized human beings, open, serene and joyful. They will have grown to the point where they are able to relate effectively to the whole of humanity; they will be people as big, spiritually, as the universe.

It would be absurd, especially today, if those who are called and consecrated to be 'experts in communion'[10] were found wanting in their prophetic mission. It would be absurd, especially today when the demand for unity is so insistent, if men and women Religious failed to live up to the expectations of many and achieve the koinonia to which they are called. They cannot give up working at communion, living and spreading it. To build up living communities of authentic koinonia is one of the most urgent tasks of the religious life. Religious cannot shirk this commitment if they wish to fulfil their role as eschatological signs - a role entrusted to them by the Spirit.

In this book I want to suggest some ways in which religious communities might return to their evangelical roots. By looking in turn at history, theology and spirituality, I hope that we shall find some aspects of the journey made by men and women Religious following Christ in community helpful for our own situation.

In Part One we shall study the community of the Twelve gathered by Christ, and the community which they formed in Jerusalem, as the inspiration for every future form of religious community. Then in Part Two we shall look in detail at the journey of the religious community through history. This will not be a study of the actual history of the religious life but, rather, an attempt to understand the idea of communion that guided some of the principal creators of community. We have space to look at only a limited number of landmarks; many of the medieval communities have been omitted, including those derived from Irish monasticism; the Byzantine, Greek and Russian Orthodox communities; the congregations founded in the seventeenth and eighteenth centuries; and the communities which emerged as a result of the Protestant Reformation. In spite of these omissions, however, this section should provide us with a significant overview. Considerable space is given to the ideas of the founders themselves and their writings are quoted at length, because nothing can take the place of such immediate contact with them.

Part Three discusses the fundamental theology of the religious community and the book ends (in Part Four) with a brief survey of the spirituality of communion and suggestions for a way of building community. My approach is deliberately limited to the theology of spirituality. Other elements that are equally fundamental, such as the psychological, sociological and institutional aspects, have been omitted; there are many excellent studies of these subjects. Even within the narrow area of the theology of spirituality, this work can be no more than an essay, an attempt to study religious community life by looking at its evangelical roots and understanding its history.

I hope that these pages will be of help to men and women Religious and to all who feel called to contribute to the building of communion.

NOTES

1. For a lengthier treatment of these aspects, see my book I *Fondatori, Uomini dello Spirito* (Rome: Città Nuova, 1982); the present book is a development of this work.
2. *Il Fenomeno delle Sette o Nuovi Movimenti Religiosi* (Rome: 1986), 3; EV 10, 402-6.
3. *Reconciliatio et Paenitentia*, 3-4.
4. *Humana Conditio* (Bologna: Il Mulino, 1987), p. 56.
5. *Relatio Finalis*, II, C.1.
6. *Davanti a Dio e per il Mondo* (Rome: Ed. Paoline, 1975), p. 207.
7. Address to those taking part in the plenary assembly of CIVCSVA, *Osservatore Romano*, 21 November 1992.
8. *Regole Monastiche d'Occidente* (Magnano: Qiqajon, 1989), pp. 216-17.
9. Address to CIVCSVA, Osservatore Romano, 21 November 1992.
10. See SCRSI, *Religiosi e Promozione Umana*, 24.

PART ONE

The Evangelical Inspiration

1 Nostalgia for the Beginnings

In the course of its history, the Church has seen the birth of many forms of community life. However great their diversity, all these communities were inspired by evangelical models and rooted in the fertile soil of the Word of God. They may have emphasized different sources of inspiration[1] but the starting point for each of them was the first Christian community formed by Christ and his disciples beside the Sea of Galilee. This community was continued by the Christians in Jerusalem after the disruption caused by the scandal of the cross and the birth of the Church at Pentecost. The written sources of primitive monasticism reveal clearly that the inspiration for their new form of life was the desire to follow Christ unconditionally, like the disciples in the Gospels, and to live according to the *cor unum et anima una* (one heart and one soul) of the first Christian community.[2] In the birth of each new community there was a kind of nostalgia for the beginnings of the Church, an attempt to recreate that unique experience of unity and communion which Christ had taught to his disciples and shared with them, and which had been lived by the first Christians in Jerusalem.

The dream, the Utopia, was to be always with Christ as Peter, Andrew, James and John had been; to be able to follow him always and everywhere; to enter into intimacy with him and, knowing his mystery, centre the whole of life on the mystery of God as the 'one thing necessary'; to recreate the first Christians' experience of unity around the risen Lord. This dream was a living and consuming desire, stirred up by the Spirit in the hearts of believers from the earliest days of the Church. It brought into being the deepest aspirations of the monastic life and religious communities.

When we study the origins of the religious community and its sources, we need to distinguish between the models that provided its inspiration and created community, and the doctrinal justification and explanation by which the community attempted to find its place in the life of the Church. On the level of justification and explanation, the tradition that was most widely known in Christian antiquity and is still the best-known today is that of John Cassian.[3] Analysing Cassian's thought, Adalbert de Vogüé has called this tradition 'the myth of the apostolic origin of cenobitism'.[4] It represented the traditions of Alexandria (expounded in Cassian's Institutes) and Jerusalem (reproduced in Cassian's Conferences).

The first version of the tradition, the Alexandrian, states that Mark, the first bishop of Alexandria, reproduced the life of the apostolic community at Jerusalem but kept his community separate from the life of the city. Thus the life of the first monks was in continuity with that of the first Christians in Jerusalem but at the same time it perfected the apostolic community's rule of life by adding separation and solitude to the sharing of possessions.[5] Monastic life was considered a higher form of Christianity.

The other version of the origin of the monastic community interprets it as a reaction against decadence in the life of the Church. Faced with a decline in evangelical radicalism, those in whom, as Cassian states in his Conferences, 'there was still the zeal of the apostolic days',

> remembered the old perfection and ... went away from their own communities and from the company of those who believed that it was quite lawful for themselves or for the Church of God to display the neglectfulness of a more relaxed way of life. They settled in the neighbourhood of cities and in more remote places and, individually and in their own way, they began to put into practice those rules which, as they remembered, had been laid down by the apostles for the whole body of the Church. And so there came into being that organized life which, as I have said, was characteristic of those disciples who had withdrawn from the contagion of the multitude.[6]

Here, monastic life is regarded as an institution created in Jerusalem by the Apostles themselves; their 'monastic' way of life, weakened by the passage of time, was taken up again by the embryonic monastic community.

However, history itself disproves any continuity between the community of the first Christians in Jerusalem and the later monastic community, and therefore any apostolic origin for cenobitic monasticism. In fact, we shall see that, paradoxically, the monastic life came into being precisely as an *absence* from the community, an unconditional following of Christ and a radical choice of God which demanded solitude and the leaving of all.

If we cannot accept Cassian's proposal of an historical continuity between cenobitism and the primitive Christian community, we must nevertheless recognize the theological value of these traditional accounts. The Jerusalem community was indeed a privileged source of inspiration, and we cannot ignore it in our efforts to understand the nature of the religious community. The appeal to the community at Jerusalem was always present in the Christian consciousness; it became particularly insistent from the third century onwards under the influence of Origen in the East and Cyprian in the West. The whole Church looked to this first community as a model to be reflected and an ideal to be attained.[7]

The religious life was an inspired part of this process in the Church. Explicit references to the Christians in Jerusalem were already present in the first clearly-defined and structured experience of cenobitic life, the Pachomian community. In the preface to his Latin translation of the *Rules* of Pachomius, Cyprian was true to the thought of the founder when he defined monks as 'men who live as in the times of the apostles'.[8] References to the descriptive summaries in Acts were even more explicit in the writings of Basil, and Augustine quoted them at least fifty-three times in his writings as a constant source of inspiration. For Augustine, indeed, community life 'possesses in itself exactly the model and example which are given by Sacred Scripture in the Acts of the Apostles'.[9] Benedict, more soberly, used the model of the first Christians sharing their possessions.

The Augustinian concept made a spectacular return in the eighth and ninth centuries, when various movements to reform the clergy fostered community life and culminated in the rise of the Canons Regular. It also lived on in more specifically monastic circles and can be found, for example, in the writings of St Bernard and the Cistercian Exordium Magnum. The appearance of the Mendicant Orders and other movements that exalted poverty gave prominence to different gospel texts, but the primitive community in Jerusalem continues to inspire the religious life, as the Second Vatican Council recognized: 'Common life, in prayer and the sharing of the same spirit (Acts 2:42), should be constant, after the example of the early Church, in which the company of believers were of one heart and soul. It should be nourished by the teaching of the Gospel and by the sacred liturgy, especially by the Eucharist.' (PC 15).

Explicit reference to the community of the Apostles and disciples around Christ is later in date. It appeared with the movement of evangelical awakening and renewal that pervaded the Church in the twelfth and thirteenth centuries. The life of Christ was re-read with fresh eyes and people were drawn to the mystery of his humanity and the reality of his incarnation and earthly life, his poverty, his journeying and his passion and death. Contemplation of Christ's humanity brought with it the desire to follow and imitate the evangelical model as closely as possible, by recreating the way of life of the Apostles.

Once again, the words that had already brought about the first blossoming of the monastic life, the words used by Christ to invite his disciples to leave everything and follow him, resounded in a new way. They were enriched with new dimensions and a further fundamental evangelical reference: the sending out of the Twelve in poverty as travelling preachers (Matt. 10). The community of the Apostles was seen as wholly at the disposal of the mission of Jesus.

This concept of the apostolic community was taken up again by more modern communities, first by the Clerks Regular, who as priests regarded themselves as the successors of the group of Apostles around Jesus, and then by the congregations and societies of the common life which appeared in the seventeenth and eighteenth centuries and reached their peak in the nineteenth century. Eugene de Mazenod, for example, fixed his gaze on the apostolic community when he founded the Missionary Oblates of Mary Immaculate; he asked: 'What did our Lord Jesus Christ do when he wanted to convert the world? He chose some apostles and disciples, formed them to piety and filled them with his Spirit. Having made them grow in his school, he sent them out to the conquest of the world, which they were soon to subject to his holy laws.' In answer to his question, 'What in their turn are the men to do who desire to walk in the footsteps of Jesus Christ, their divine Master?', de Mazenod set before his Oblates the road travelled by the apostolic community. This is still the dynamic of this missionary community.[10]

The apostolic life has been and will remain the standard for any community which calls itself Christian. This life was experienced at the birth of monasticism because, like the Apostles, the first monks were willing to leave everything in order to follow Christ in radical obedience to his word. It was experienced by the first monastic communities because they took as their model the life of communion and unity instituted by the Apostles in Jerusalem. It was experienced by those communities who, like the Apostles, felt called by Christ to be sent all over the world to proclaim the good news and do every kind of good work.[11]

In the light of this experience, it will be useful to summarize some of the fundamental elements of both the community of the Twelve and the wider community which gathered round them in Jerusalem and, in the newness of the Spirit, prolonged their experience with the Master. This will be the subject of the next chapter. There we shall examine those elements of the apostolic community which inspired the birth and development of the religious community: its origin and nature, the dynamics of its life, and its destination. We shall look particularly at Mark's account of the calling and make-up of the Twelve, and the record of their in the school of the Master. Finally, I will briefly highlight those features of the Jerusalem community which have most influenced religious communities.

It is to these experiences of the apostolic community that any newly-formed community must return. They are the prototype, the icon, the historical model and paradigm for every type of community in the Church.

NOTES

1. There have, of course, been other models of community life such as the prophetic schools of the Old Testament and (particularly influential in the nineteenth century) the Holy Family at Nazareth.
2. For precise historical references to the following of Christ as a source of inspiration for the religious life, see J. M. Lozano, 'De vita apostolica apud Patres et Scriptores Monasticos', *Commentarium pro Religiosis*, 52 (1971), pp. 97-120; 'De vita apostolica apud Canonicos Regulares', ibid., pp. 193-210; 'De vita apostolica apud Ordines Mendicantes', ibid., pp. 300-13; and the same author's *La Sequela di Cristo. Teologia Storico-sistematica della Vita Religiosa* (Milan: Ancora, 1981), pp. 12-16. Also useful are J. M. R. Tillard, *Before God and the World* and, for the Jerusalem community, P. C. Bori, *Chiesa Primitiva: L'immagine della Comunità delle Origini - Atti 2.42-47; 4.32-37 - nella Storia della Chiesa Antica* (Brescia: Paideia, 1974), pp. 145-78.
3. Eusebius, writing as early as the beginning of the fourth century (*Ecclesiastical History*, II. 17), set out to show that the Therapeutae about whom Philo wrote were none other than 'apostolic men' or Christians who preserved the primitive ascetic way of life which was continued by the Christian ascetics of his day. This interpretation was also adopted by Epiphanius, Haer. 61 (PG 41, 1044), Sozomenes, and Jerome (De Viris Illustribus, PL 23, 658.654).
4. 'Monaschisme et Église dans la pensée de Cassien' in *Théologie de la Vie Monastique* (Paris: 1961), pp. 213-40.
5. *De Inst. Coenob.* II, 5.

6. *Confer* 18.5 (Classics of Western Spirituality; London: SPCK, p. 186f.).
7. Cf. Bori, op. cit., pp. 21-83.
8. G. Turbessi, *Regole Monastiche Antiche* (Roma: 1974), p. 105.
9. Rule, 3, 43, in Turbessi, Regole monastiche antiche, p. 164.
10. 'Preface' (1818) to the Constitution and Rules (Rome: 1982), pp. 10-11.
11. In addition to the references given in note 2, M. H. Vicaire OP, *L'imitazione degli Apostoli* (Rome: 1964) discusses the rich evolution of understanding of the apostolic life and its influence on community life.

2 'To Be His Companions'
The Twelve around Jesus

The Birth of the Apostolic Community

Mark's Gospel, in common with the other Synoptics, sees the beginning of the apostolic community in the calling of the first four disciples:

> Jesus was walking by the Sea of Galilee, when he saw Simon and his brother Andrew at work with casting-nets in the lake; for they were fishermen. Jesus said to them, 'Come, follow me, and I will make you fishers of men.' At once they left their nets and followed him. Going a little farther, he saw James son of Zebedee and his brother John in a boat mending their nets. At once he called them; and they left their father Zebedee in the boat with the hired men and followed him. (Mark 1:16-20)

In this passage, Jesus was walking by the lake. It was not a casual appearance. It was a coming and a passing which introduced the eternal into history and brought God to humankind; Jesus upset the normal existence of those he encountered and left an indelible mark on them. His walking recalls Yahweh's interventions for salvation and judgement, but Jesus' intervention was not a striking theophany. Rather, it was hidden and discreet like the incarnation itself, though this did not make it any less effective. 'As of old, the Lord Jesus does not "walk by" in a neutral fashion. His is a passage which draws others into the same journeying.'[1]

Jesus was walking *by the Sea of Galilee*. He meets people in the setting of their daily lives, intent upon their everyday occupations; their calling takes place within each person's particular history. Jesus saw actual people, with names that he knew: Simon, and Andrew, Simon's brother; James, son of Zebedee, and John his brother. Jesus *saw* them - not merely a superficial noticing, but a seeing that penetrated the inmost being of people whom he had always known, loved and chosen; and there he placed the eternal love of God, which can regenerate human beings to the point of radically transforming their existence.

The Evangelical Inspiration   **23**

Like 'knowing', so 'seeing' produces a current of vital participation between the divine subject and the reality that falls within the range of his vision. Afterwards, things do not remain as they were before, and the person is destined to become different. Jesus radiates a look which in anticipation creates something, even before man is aware of it.[2]

A vocation always remains the choice of God, willed from eternity; but for human beings it comes at a definite time and place, in a historical here and now, and as the result of meeting the look of Jesus. This looking at one another establishes the first interpersonal relationship between Jesus and those who are his; later, this will be repeatedly reinforced, purified and renewed by further looks which recall that first indelible meeting of eyes (cf. Mark 8:33; 10:27; Luke 22:4).

Jesus *said to them...* The look became a word. The creative Word which called into existence (Col. 1:16-17: 'All things were created through him and for him...and in him all things hold together') had become an incarnate human word which re-creates by disclosing in time the eternal plan of election. '[Wisdom] renews all things; in every generation she passes into holy souls, and makes them friends of God, and prophets' (Wisd. 7:27).

'Follow me.' The love which elects and the word which recreates were translated into a peremptory and radical invitation which can only be met by an immediate and equally radical acceptance. It was an unconditional invitation which depended upon an act of faith in the person of Christ and a no less unconditional attachment to him and his mission: 'I will make you fishers of men.' *'I will make you':* the word was efficacious and accomplished what it promised. It created the discipleship, the community of people who followed together ('I will make *you*'), and the mission.

Mark emphasizes the immediacy of the response: 'At once'. You cannot respond slowly to Christ's call; Simon and Andrew left their nets, James and John left their father, in order to follow the Master who called them. Leaving and following are two actions in the single event of transferring the self from self-centredness to a new centre in the person of Jesus. Mark seems to describe a progressive renunciation of their own world leading to a progressive belonging to Jesus. The leaving of nets and boat was a departure from all material security; it was even, in a certain sense, a loss of identity, because work provides human beings not only with their living but also with self-realization. Human beings are often defined by what they do, their profession, which determines the way they think, plan and relate to others and to reality. The leaving was made even more specific and radical: it was an abandoning of their father, the loss of the security provided by family ties and affections, the loss of roots. Those who left no longer had economic and emotional security or the protection of the family.

> With the abandoning of their nets and their father, which expresses, so to speak, the personal, socio-cultural and spiritual co-ordinates of the human condition, a point of 'no return' is fixed. Henceforward they are without roots, in past, present or future... Men who appear as if they had never been born, set free in a giddy void.[3]

This complete break with profession and family was certainly not made from any contempt for these things, which determine ordinary existence. The break was made because henceforward the presence of Jesus would determine the existence of the disciples.

Luke, in his vocation narratives, makes the total uprooting brought about by the call even more radical. The disciples at the lake 'left *everything*' (Luke 5:11) and Levi 'leaving *everything*, rose up and followed him' (5:28). Peter summarizes the experience of every disciple: 'We left *all we had* to follow you' (18:28). Responding to the call was a complete exodus from themselves, from everything around them, from everything to which they were bound, in order to follow Jesus and stay with him. They were dispossessed of their own world and made the heirs of a new world defined by the person of Jesus. The demands made by following Jesus indicated the appearance of this new reality, which made all other realities merely relative. The kingdom of God broke in and everything changed. Following Jesus is a lifelong, absolute, unreserved and radical commitment, unlike the usual limited arrangement between a rabbi and his disciples. The place of Jesus in the life of his disciples is above other people and things and all affection for brothers, parents, sons and wife. The emphasis is on 'the unconditional and central character of the commitment to the following of Jesus which surpasses all other values'.[4] In his choosing and calling of his disciples, Jesus showed his exclusive authority; for the disciples, this led to an unlimited sharing or community of life and destiny with their Master and Lord.[5]

Mark brings out further the dynamics of every call in another vocation narrative which, in its negative outcome, serves as a kind of counterpart to the lakeside events.

> As he was setting out on his journey, a man ran up ... And Jesus looking upon him loved him, and said to him, 'You lack one thing; go, sell what you have, and give to the poor, and you will have treasure in heaven; and come, follow me.' At that saying his countenance fell, and he went away sorrowful; for he had great possessions. (Mark 10:17, 21-22)

Once again we have the same look which rested on the fishermen and communicated God's eternal love. Once again love is put into words, more articulate here than by the lake. 'Follow me' is made more explicit and concrete: it means selling and leaving, essential conditions for receiving the gift of the eschatological treasure.

Setting out to follow Jesus, the disciples grew in understanding of what was involved in this following. They perceived that they were following a Master who was going to die in Jerusalem and that following him meant dying with him. Jesus himself explained that anyone who wished to follow him must take up his cross every day (Mark 8:31-35). It is precisely the Passion which is the moment of truth in the following of Jesus. Luke makes the demands of following even more explicit. Attachment to Jesus involves total uprooting, daily insecurity, indifference to family interests, no turning back for useless lamentation (Luke 9:57-62) and a continual leaving of father, mother, wife, children and even life itself (Luke 14:26).

Leaving is understood, however, as the positive choice of something whose value transcends all other values. Jesus offered himself as the object to be followed: 'Follow *me*.' The radical nature of the renunciation shows the radical nature of the choice. Radical following in its turn demands radical renunciation, demonstrated precisely in the 'leaving' and implying a resolute willingness to cut away, at whatever cost, everything which might impede absolute fidelity to Christ. In the parables of the hidden treasure and the pearl of great price, Jesus seems to emphasize the positive aspects of following him and his word unconditionally, and to show the meaning of renunciation. The man sells the field because he has discovered a treasure, and he does it *joyfully*. The trader in pearls also sells everything because he has at last found what he had always looked for (Matt. 13:44-6).

Thus the apostolic community was born from the word of Jesus who called each one of his disciples by name, and from the movement of following which resulted. The vocation was in fact a convocation: the apostles were called two by two to follow Jesus together. The ancient assembly of Israel was the result of a *convocation* by Yahweh; the new Israel, represented by the Twelve, is convoked as an *ecclesia* by the Word, Christ the Word made flesh, who gives fresh utterance in time to the eternal call by which the Father chose us in love (Eph. 1:4). Christ's word called forth a response and a commitment and established a relationship of dialogue. As the disciples left all and unconditionally followed the one who calls them, a progressive communion began between the Master and his disciples and between the disciples themselves, who had been brought together for the same following of the same person.

It was this focus on the person of Jesus which defined the nature of the emerging apostolic community. The destination of the call was clear, whether addressed to one or several ('Follow *me*'); equally clear was the motive for renunciation: it was for the sake of *me* and the *gospel* (Mark 8:35; 10:29). Peter showed how thoroughly he understood this when he exclaimed: 'We have left everything and followed you' (Mark 10:28). It was the presence of Jesus which gave consistency to the apostolic group. The disciples were formed into a community by the relationship of each one of them with Jesus; and this relationship then became the bond between the members of the group themselves.

When Jesus was taken away from them for a short time, the apostolic community disintegrated; this is what happened in the Garden of Gethsemane (Mark 14:51). Jesus had foretold it: 'I will strike the shepherd and the sheep will be scattered' (Mark 14:27). As soon as the following of Jesus and the common bond with him were disrupted, the ties binding them to each other dissolved. This shows the extent to which the community of the disciples depended on the presence of Jesus. At the moment of their call, they had left everything to follow him, and the community had emerged out of that concentric movement of following. Now there was a movement in the opposite direction: forsaking Jesus, all the disciples took to flight and, as a result, the community disintegrated. Peter continued to follow but *at a distance* (Mark 14:54) because physical proximity to the Master would mean sharing his lot. True following of Jesus must involve precisely such a total sharing of his destiny, even to the point of death, so that communion can be established among all those who are making the same journey.

The central place of Christ in the composition of the apostolic community is even more obvious in the account of the appointment of the Twelve:

> Then he went up on the mountain, and called to him those whom he desired; and they came to him. And he appointed twelve to be with him, and to be sent out to preach, and have authority to cast out demons. (Mark 3:13-15)

In verses 16-19, Jesus names the Twelve one by one. The first section of Mark's Gospel had shown three groups around Jesus: the disciples, the crowd and the adversaries. Now Jesus restricts his own range of action, while continuing to announce the Gospel to all. He reserves particular teaching to a privileged small group who will later have to proclaim it to the people when the time is ripe (cf. Mark 4:11, 34; 9:28). He reaches a turning-point in his apostolic method and chooses the Twelve for himself. Jesus is clearly at the centre of this vocation narrative. He goes up into the mountain, which is less a geographical location than a theological point:

> Jesus assumes a particular and authoritative position: from the mountain he is about to act in the same way in which, formerly, Yahweh acted on Sinai (Exod. 19:3ff.; 24:12-17). That is, by going up on to the mountain, Jesus is not imitating Moses... *but assuming the role of God Himself*... Jesus sets himself *on God's side* and acts with His authority.[6]

From his position as God, Jesus issues his call of love. As he did by the lake, he calls personally and by name the very people he has at heart and has loved, chosen and willed from all eternity. He calls them freely and unconditionally, simply because it is his will.[7]

The call of Jesus to the Twelve reveals in history the eternal call of God. The Twelve respond, as they did by the lake, with complete acceptance: 'and they came to him'.[8] This acceptance changes their condition; just as before they had moved away from their nets and their father, now they are no longer part of the crowd. Instead, they are around Jesus. The physical movement away from the crowd and towards Jesus is indicative of a radical transformation of their relations with the Master. Henceforward they derive their identity from *being with him*. Jesus called them precisely so that they could 'be with him' in a stable, permanent and exclusive relationship[9] which was translated into a physical fellowship and way of life. Here we glimpse the deep interior attitude which John's Gospel translates as a mutual 'being', 'dwelling' and 'staying' between Christ and the disciples that introduces them into the ineffable intimacy which unites the Son to the Father.

By the lake, Jesus had promised: 'I *will make* you.' He does this by making the Twelve 'be' with him in this way. It is Jesus who, by his word, forms them into a particular entity, a community. The apostolic community is formed precisely by the act of 'being with Jesus'. The first task of the Twelve, in fact, 'is not to go and preach but *to enter into communion with Jesus!* A fellowship and an intimacy of life, an ineffable experience which tells how Jesus *places himself at the centre* of the new community and wills to set them all in relationship with his person.'[10] The community of the disciples has its centre of gravity in Jesus and this relationship, in turn, forms the centre for the interpersonal relationships among the Twelve. Thus, three interlaced types of intimate relationship exist simultaneously: the relationship with Jesus of each individual called; the relationship between the group as a whole and Jesus; and the relationship of the called among themselves.

The final element in the Marcan pericope is that the community, once formed, does not live for itself, any more than Jesus lives for himself. The Twelve are with Jesus in order to become his envoys and witnesses. He had called them by the lake so that they could follow him and he could make them fishers of men. Now he calls them to be with him in a fellowship which will enable them to acquire his own power to drive out demons, so that their preaching, like his, may be effective. He calls them, in fact, not only to communion with him, but also to go and preach.

From this moment, we find Jesus in the Gospels constantly journeying, followed by the apostles. To the eyes of Israel, this group was a 'living parable'. Who was he, this rabbi whose followers were ready to leave everything behind for his sake? The very existence of the disciples, journeying behind their Master, demonstrated the value of Jesus. If these men were able to leave possessions, profession, family, themselves - in a word, everything - for his sake, then Jesus must be worth more than all these things, even life itself. He will load them with blessings (see Mark 10:29-30); he and the Kingdom are objects of *profession*, that is, the centre of every interest and solicitude, a constant preoccupation; he becomes their family (Mark 3:34-5) and their very life. Jesus is truly able to fill the depths of their life because, as the Lord of existence, he has the words of eternal life. His community has to represent what the new Israel is called to become; in this way it is an effective sign of the Kingdom, a sign that anticipates the perfect communion of the Kingdom which Jesus came to inaugurate.[11]

A Community in the Making

At the moment when he called, Jesus had promised: 'I will make you become ...' This gives us a glimpse of the process of teaching and formation that Jesus had to accomplish in his disciples in order to bring them to full understanding of his identity and bind them together as a group. To become true disciples and form Jesus' authentic community, the Twelve will have to walk behind him, enrol in his school, assimilate his wisdom, and imitate those profound attitudes by which Jesus communicates the divine *agape*. In the Master's school, the community of the Twelve must become what it is meant to be.

It is interesting to note the actual composition of this group of apostles. Jesus seems to have chosen the most diverse people to form this first community, the prototype of the Church and all its communities: the tax-gatherer Levi beside the 'true Israelite' Nathanael; a Zealot like Simon (and perhaps also Judas Iscariot) alongside James and John from the well-to-do family with connections in the High Priest's household. 'One has the impression,' writes Schürmann, 'that Jesus wished to bring together and unify around himself all the divergent tendencies and factions of the Israel of that time.'[12] Jesus makes no distinction between people; there are no barriers for him. He calls to membership of his community publicans and sinners, celibates and married men, Zealots, men of any profession from fishermen to tax-gatherers. Various episodes in the gospels also show how widely the apostles differed in character.

At the end of his life, Jesus prayed to his Father for this diverse group of men: 'May they be perfectly one' (John 17:23). He gave them his commandment: 'As I have loved you, you are to love one another' (John 13:34). Finally, having made them one through the mystery of his death and resurrection and the outpouring of the Spirit, he would be able to send them out into the world to continue the work which the Father had entrusted to him.

But in order to arrive at this climax, Jesus had to provide a patient and progressive education for his disciples, a schooling that began with the calling itself. Being with Jesus and travelling with him, the disciples came to understand his mystery fully (Mark 7:17; 9:28, 33; 10:10). Belief and confession are the fruit of following: 'on the way he asked his disciples' about his identity. The others, 'the people', still had only a limited knowledge of Jesus' mystery. Only the disciples, who followed him closely and were always with him, came to recognize him for who he really was (Mark 8:27-30).

In order to know Jesus truly, however, the disciples will need the strength and courage to follow him to the very end. True profession of faith, the proclamation of Jesus as Messiah and the knowledge of his mystery require a total and unconditional following, a full sharing in his destiny, going all the way to Jerusalem. Peter confesses 'You are the Christ', but immediately afterwards is in fact unable to accept the mystery of Jesus' death. Instead of continuing to follow his Master, for a moment Peter stands in his way to halt his journey - and Jesus says to him 'Out of my sight, Satan!' (Mark 8:33). In the language of following, these words could be translated 'Get behind me; return to your place, which is behind me not in front of me; resume following; and if you follow me to the end, then you will understand, in an authentic and existential way, what my Father has revealed to you.' 'Jesus' identity is not revealed separately from the mystery of the Son of Man and the meaning of the way to be travelled; confession lacks its hallmark if it is not translated into acceptance of that mystery and that way.'[13]

As their relationship with the Master gradually intensifies, so do relations between the disciples themselves. Hitherto, their vocation had been a convocation with Jesus; now following makes them companions on a common journey. Together they follow the Master and discover his mystery. Together they eat with him and rest with him. Communion with the Master becomes communion among themselves; as Jesus discloses his mystery to them, he also guides them towards discovering the consequences of his identity for mutual relationships. Henceforward, these must bear the stamp of the newness of the Kingdom.

In the gospels, teaching on the dynamics of community life often takes place on occasions which show the disagreements and contrasts present in this first community. The sons of Zebedee ask for the chief places in the Kingdom and draw down on themselves the wrath of the others (Mark 10:35-45). They all discuss among themselves which of them is the greatest (Mark 9:34). The question of how often someone should be forgiven reveals glimpses of discord and offence (Matt. 19:21). A certain intolerance surfaces towards those who do not belong to the group (Mark 9.38). Clearly, the community did not create itself. All the disciples had to enrol in the Master's school and, by following him, learn from him. If we pay attention to this formative process, we shall be able to grasp some of the elements which characterized the community of the disciples and enabled it to grow until it reached the point of living the 'new commandment' and continuing the mission of Jesus.

When the disciples discuss among themselves on the way which of them will be the greatest, Jesus teaches them that in his community, 'If any one would be first, he must be last of all and servant of all' (Mark 9:35). When James and John ask to sit on his right and left in the future kingdom, and the others react indignantly, Jesus puts before them a way of acting that contrasts clearly with the methods of the rulers of the Gentiles and the great who exercise authority over them: 'It shall not be so with you; but whoever would be great among you must be the slave of all.' He proposes himself to the community as a model, because he 'has not come to be served but to serve, and to give his life as a ransom for many' (Mark 10:41-5). By washing his disciples' feet, Jesus shows clearly the style of his community: 'I have given you an example, that you also should do as I have done to you ... a servant is not greater than his master' (John 13:15-16). The Gospel of Luke also places this teaching in the context of the Last Supper: 'I am among you as one who serves' (Luke 22:27).

Matthew records a similar teaching. The refusal to exercise any dominion over others springs from the discovery of the one Father, which in turn leads to the discovery of real brotherhood. Therefore the new family gathered around Christ must be governed by a profound equality: 'But you are not be called rabbi, for you have one teacher, and you are all brethren. And call no man your father on earth, for you have one Father, who is in heaven. Neither be called masters, for you have one master, the Christ [Messiah]' (Matt. 23:8-10). The very fact of being disciples of Jesus and sons (or daughters) of the heavenly Father makes the members of the Christian community brothers (and sisters) to each other. The basis of the community is the recognition in faith of a common Father and the same Lord Jesus Christ; all human leadership, which would contradict the fundamental equality of all believers, is thus excluded.

Luke also shows the disciples in the Master's school, discovering the Father, and highlights another characteristic of their community. Following Jesus, they see him pray and in all simplicity ask him 'Lord, teach us to pray.' Then Jesus introduces them into his relationship of love and trust with the Father, to whom they can speak with confidence (Luke 11:1-4). The apostolic community is a community of prayer.

Again, the community of Jesus is built on mutual forgiveness and brotherly correction (Matt. 18:15-17). When Peter asks how many times he should forgive his brother, Jesus proposes a mercy without measure (Matt. 18:21-2). Born of God's merciful love, the community of disciples also owes its continued existence to mutual compassion. It is a community of the reconciled, called to mutual forgiveness. For Luke, they are called to be merciful like their Father (6:36); according to Matthew, they must be perfect like their Father. In this, too, Jesus is their Master, for in him the Father's mercy is literally made visible as he forgives sins and heals infirmities.

The community of apostles is united by brotherly love for each other and a shared relationship with the one Father and the one Master, and safeguarded by mutual service and forgiveness. It therefore cannot close in on itself like some esoteric group. Jesus always keeps it open. When John tries to prevent someone who does not belong to the community from driving out devils, Jesus reminds him that 'he that is not against us is for us' (Mark 9:38-40), and he reacts sharply to the intolerance of James and John towards a Samaritan village that does not welcome him, and rebukes them (Mark 9:51-5).

The last great lesson which the Master gives his community is that of mutual love. The Last Supper is the moment when, through the institution of the Eucharist, the sign of the foot-washing, and his words, Jesus anticipates and communicates to those who belong to him the reality of the imminent paschal event by which he will reunite all people in a single family.

The Eucharist, the outcome of the paschal mystery, brings about the unity of the community. The actions of Jesus already show his resolve to draw his followers closer to himself: he passes his cup round the group and breaks his bread to distribute to them. As always when he sits down to eat with those who belong to him, 'Jesus is the master of the house, gathering his new family around him and pronouncing the prayer of blessing. Later, the disciples will recognize him in the action of breaking bread (Luke 24:30f., 34). Fellowship at table with the earthly Jesus must be indelibly imprinted on their memory.'[14] At this last supper the disciples, fed by the one bread broken and the blood poured out, receive the same life and form the one body of Christ. As the Eucharist is communion with him, it makes possible communion with each other.

At this point, the Fourth Gospel interprets the Synoptics rather than completes them.[15] The action of foot-washing, in the middle of supper, connects up with the teaching of Jesus on service and taking the last place; Luke also (unlike Matthew and Mark) places the teaching in the context of this supper. The washing of feet seems to contain and sum up all the hardest and humblest kinds of service. For Jesus it is the prophetic sign of his assuming the form of a servant (cf. Phil. 2:7) and it reveals not only what he will accomplish on the cross but also what he is: the total gift for others, wholly at the service of humanity, that is signified by the Eucharist. By washing his disciples' feet, Jesus transfers to the community his relationship of loving service towards them. He thus reveals the ultimate meaning of their existence as members of his community: total availability to each other in the mutual exchange of gifts and service that makes the unity of the disciples possible.

Washing one another's feet is translated and explained in the words of the new commandment: 'Love one another as I have loved you' (John 13:14; 15:12). Here Jesus puts himself forward as the model and measure of love. 'The novelty of this foundation will constitute the novelty of the community of the disciples.'[16] This is the self-realization of the Christian community, the culmination of the whole Johannine journey.

The Fourth Gospel, like the Synoptics, always presents following Jesus as a community activity from the moment of the first 'come and see' (John 1:39). Jesus came to gather together the scattered children of God and he seeks to form the new Israel in unity around himself. The image of the shepherd and the flock (John 10) conveys not only the relationship between the shepherd and the individual sheep but also clearly includes the idea of the flock which the Son, according to the Father's wish, gathers together and protects. Just as we cannot imagine the shepherd without his flock, so we cannot conceive the guide to salvation without the community which is saved. In the same way, the image of the vine and its branches, followed by the discourse on the disciples dwelling in Jesus and Jesus dwelling in the disciples, highlights the indissoluble unity between Jesus and his community. He is its foundation and its permanent living centre. 'Christian existence cannot be realized without, or outside, a community.'[17]

Like the Synoptists, John portrays Jesus as placing himself at the centre of his community and communicating the mystery of his identity. This identity is love giving itself, the fruit of that communion of love which he lives within the mystery of the Trinity, where the Son and the Father are one. The unity of the community is modelled on this unity, it shares in it and is formed by it. This is the culmination of Jesus' teaching on the dynamics of community and it discloses the deepest mystery of the disciples' unity: it derives, through the Son, from the very mystery of the unity of the Trinity. Because it is founded on and by God's *perichoresis*, his reciprocal existence of love in the Trinity, the community of disciples can share the same existence. The essential characteristic of this community is the mutual love which generates unity and guarantees the constant presence of the Lord in the future. If he, the Christ, is not present in the community, it *cannot* be Christian. Without him, the group of disciples has no meaning. It is he who draws them to the Father, calls them to himself one by one, and permeates the life of each of them with his own life in order to make them all one: 'I in them and thou in me, that they may become perfectly one' (John 17:23).

A final characteristic of Jesus' community, which is present in all the gospels, is its missionary openness. We have seen how, at the very moment of calling, Jesus gave his disciples a very precise objective: 'I will make you become fishers of men.' In the same way, he formed the Twelve in order 'to send them out to preach'. At the end of the Synoptic Gospels, this objective becomes a specific mandate: 'Go into all the world and preach the gospel to the whole creation' (Mark 16:15; cp. Matt. 28:19; Luke 24:47). For John too, the unity of Jesus' followers has a missionary dimension: 'that they may all be one; even as thou, Father, art in me, and I in thee, that they also may be in us, so that the world may believe that thou hast sent me' (John 17:21). The principle is that of choosing a few with a view to reaching the many. 'Discipleship thus has two essential poles: on the one hand, the relationship of the individual to the following of Jesus, and the radical choice of that following; on the other hand, the "many" or the "all" for whom they are called and chosen.'[18]

Mission is the final act in the formative process which Jesus imposed on his disciples. Having permeated and moulded them in his school, he can now send them out to continue the work that the Father entrusted to him. If the call to follow was addressed to the individual, the mission is now entrusted to the whole group; it is tied to the formation of the group and presupposes it. Being with Jesus is the place of formation and the condition for joining the mission. The mission, in turn, is the mature fruit of following him.

The Characteristic Features of the Apostolic Community

Having studied the process through which Jesus led his followers, we can now identify briefly some of the basic characteristics of the apostolic community. It is these characteristics which have inspired religious communities and which must continually nourish their daily growth.

– The apostolic community is a community of those who have been called. It is formed by the love of God manifested in Christ and translated into a summons to follow. The community does not come into being through the autonomous initiative of its members. Those whom Jesus called to himself, who belonged to his more restricted group of followers, did not put themselves forward; they were chosen: 'You did not choose me, but I chose you' (John 15:16).

– The apostolic community is the community of those who welcome and live the Word, in faith and obedience. To live in community is to answer a call, to recognize and respond to the Father's love manifested in the person of Jesus of Nazareth, and to recognize him as the Son sent by the Father and thus the fullness and meaning of one's own life.

– The apostolic community shares radically and totally in Jesus' way of life: his poverty, renunciation and journeying. Like him, the disciples have nowhere to lay their heads (Matt. 8:20). Their sharing becomes total as they participate in his very destiny (John 11:16: 'Let us also go, that we may die with him') to the extent of drinking his own cup (Mark 10.38-9). They do this in order to become, like him, fully dedicated to the cause of the Kingdom and to have, in him, communion with the Father.

– The apostolic community is the true family of God, gathered around his Son. The disciples are not left without a family just because they have had to leave father, mother, wife and children in order to follow Jesus. Jesus forms a new family of his own, with new titles to kinship: 'Looking around on those who sat about him, he said, "Here are my mother and my brothers! Whoever does the will of God is my brother, and sister, and mother." ' (Mark 3:34-5). Because they have obeyed the call to be with him, the disciples sitting around him are united by a new kinship based on God's will rather than ties of blood (John 1:12-13).

– A profound equality reigns in the new family assembled around the Son of God, because they are all brothers. The apostolic community is a community of brothers, with only one Father, the Father in heaven. The greater the variety and diversity of people called to belong to the community, the more outstanding the fraternity and equality become.

– The apostolic community is a community of service. The members wash one another's feet; the first is called to take the last place; and the one who commands to act as a servant. This community challenges the spirit of domination and bears witness to a new world which recognizes the close interdependence of human beings.

– It is a community of the reconciled and, as such, called to mutual forgiveness. 'If your brother sins, rebuke him, and if he repents, forgive him; and if he sins against you seven times in the day, and turns to you seven times, and says, "I repent," you must forgive him' (Luke 17:3-4). In this community, people have the capacity to see themselves as renewed every day and to make a fresh start, thanks to their trust in one another.

– It is a community of people who pray. Following the example of their Master, the disciples turn confidently to the Father. Jesus himself introduces them into his relationship of love and trust and abandonment towards his Father.

– It is a eucharistic community, united by sharing the one bread and the one cup.

– It is a community with only one rule: mutual love, the love with which Jesus loved, lived out even to the giving of life itself.

– Finally, the apostolic community is a community of those who are sent, wholly dedicated to the Kingdom of God. The very fact that it belongs to Jesus is a witness to the arrival of the new world and the demands this makes on everyone. By its unity, the community witnesses to the great reality of God's unity, the love between the three divine Persons. 'That they may become perfectly one, so that the world may know that thou hast sent me' (John 17:23). For the world, unity is a motive for faith. By its obedience in going and proclaiming the good news through words, the community continues, through the power of the Spirit, the work of Jesus, the one sent by the Father.

NOTES

1. L. Di Pinto, 'Seguitemi, vi farò pescatori di uomini', *Parola Spirito e Vita*, no. 2, July-December 1980, p. 86. For a more extensive study see the following, on the Gospel of Mark: E. Best, *Following Jesus. Discipleship in the Gospel of Mark* (*Journal for the Study of the New Testament*, Supplement Series, 4; Sheffield: 1981); J. M. Castillo, *El seguimiento de Jesús* (Verdad e Imagen, 96; Salamanca: 1986); E. Manicardi, *Il cammino di Gesù nel Vangelo di Marco. Schema narrativo e tema cristologico* (Analecta Biblica, 96; Rome: 1981); K. Stock, 'Vangelo e discepolato in Marco' (*Rassegna di Teologia 19*, 1978), pp. 1-7.

2. Di Pinto, op. cit., p. 88.

3. Ibid., p.101.

4. T. Matura, *Il radicalismo evangelico. Alle origini della vita cristiana* (Rome: 1981), p. 40.

5. While it exhibits some features in common with the rabbinic schools of the period, the relationship between Jesus and his followers appears completely special. For instance, it was Jesus who authoritatively chose and called his disciples, not vice versa. He remained the one and only Master; his disciples could not hope for any career advancement or to become masters in their turn - they would always remain Jesus' disciples and, among themselves, brothers. Above all, Jesus did not offdr an interpretation of the Torah or a doctrine, but simply the radical choice of his own person. Cf. M. Pesce, 'Discepolato gesuano e discepolato rabinico. Problemi e prospettive della comparazione' in *Aufstieg und Niedergang der römischen Welt. Geschichte und Kultur Roms im Spiegel der neueren Forschung* II/1, ed. H. Temporini and W. Haase (Berlin and New York: 1982), pp. 351-89.

6. G. Fattorini, 'Gesù capo della comunità nel vangelo di Marco' (Inter Fratres 32, 1982), p. 106.

7. The use of the imperfect indicates a permanent state of Jesus' will. Moreover, *thelein* corresponds to the Hebrew verb *hapes*, meaning 'to like, to be well disposed towards someone, to wish well', and therefore includes an affective element. Consequently, C. M. Martini notes (in *L'itinerario spirituale dei Dodici nel Vangelo di Marco*, Rome: 1980, p. 42) that this verb does not imply 'as it pleased him' or 'those who came to mind', but rather 'those whom he had at heart'. Jesus therefore calls those he wants, whom he has at heart, for whom he has a predilection. This emphasis is again expressed in *autos*: those whom he wished. Grammatically, *autos* is not necessary, because the sentence is clear without it, but its presence emphasizes that the choice is not because of some quality, beauty or attractiveness in the one called, but because he, Jesus, has them at heart and chooses them. This love is the motive for his actions.

8. The aorist of the verb *aperchomai* indicates separation from the group (ap-) and adherence to a person (*pros auton*, to, near, with him, where *pros* is intended to indicate an intimacy still to be created).

9. The use of the verb 'to be' and the subjunctive mood, *hina osin*, indicate stability: 'that they might be with him steadily, in a settled way'.
10. Fattorini, op. cit., p. 108. We have already seen that, contrary to the customary procedure in the rabbinic and Greek philosophical schools, it was Jesus who chose his disciples, not vice versa. People did not make themselves his disciples; they were made or formed into disciples by him. The verb *matheteuo* is always used in the active sense of 'making disciples', either by Jesus (Matt. 13:52; 27:57) or his emissaries (Matt. 28:19; Acts 14:21).
11. Cf. G. Lohfink, *Gesù come voleva la sua comunità? La Chiesa quale dovrebbe essere* (Cinisello Balsamo: Paoline, 1987).
12. 'Le groupe des disciples de Jésus signe pour Israël et prototype de la vie selon les conseils', *Christus* 13 (1966), p. 205.
13. L. Di Pinto, '"Seguire Gesù" secondo i vangeli sinottici. Studio di teologia biblica', in *Fondamenti biblici della teologia morale. Atti della XXII Settimana Biblica* (Brescia: Paideia, 1973), pp. 234-5.
14. Lohfink, op. cit., pp. 64-5.
15. Cf. R. Schnackenburg, *The Gospel of John*, vol. 3 (London: Burns Oates/ Herder & Herder, 1968, 1980), p. 6.
16 D. Cancian, *Nuovo Comandamento, Nuova Alleanza, Eucaristia nell'interpretazione del capitolo 13 del Vangelo di Giovanni* (Collevalenza: 1978), p. 229.
17. Schnackenburg, op. cit.
18. M. Bordoni, *Gesù di Nazaret, Signore e Cristo. Saggio di cristologia sistematica*, II (Rome: Herder, 1982), p. 327.

3 'One Heart and One Soul'
The first Christian community

Scattered by the betrayal and death of Jesus, the community of the Twelve was re-formed in the power of his resurrection. After passing through the paschal event, a new community was born as a result of a new presence of Jesus and a new call.

Reborn in the Spirit

After his death, Jesus became present as the risen Lord in a new and permanent way among those who belonged to him. Going up to heaven did not separate him from them; rather, his presence multiplied. The post-Easter appearances revealed the new mode of his presence to his disciples. At first they did not immediately recognize him; he no longer had the features of the Jesus who had met them by the lake and lived with them. Neither the apostles, nor the women, nor the disciples on the way to Emmaus recognized him until their eyes were opened in faith. Jesus still bore the marks of his passion (John 20:27); he showed them his hands and feet and ate broiled fish to emphasize the reality of his resurrection (Luke 24:40-3). He was the same Jesus as before, but now he lived in the Spirit, he was the risen Lord.

Gradually, the disciples learnt to meet Jesus everywhere: on the road, walking to Emmaus; at work on the lake; gathered together at home. They could see him everywhere because he was present everywhere.[1] He was no longer physically present with them, as he had been when they walked the roads of Galilee together, but he was really present in a new way: 'The Lord is the Spirit' (2 Cor. 3:17).

The newness of the Lord's presence entailed a new call. Risen, he again called people to follow him. He entrusted to the women the task of giving the disciples his invitation to start following him again in a new way: 'Go, tell his disciples and Peter, that he is going before you to Galilee' (Mark 16:7). The risen Christ again summoned his disciples to Galilee, the place where they had begun their following of him (Mark

1:16-20), in order to start travelling together once more. After Easter, as before, Jesus continued to walk before the disciples - to 'precede' them. Both John and the Synoptics speak of a new call and the start of a new following: turning to Peter by the lake, the risen Jesus said once again 'Follow me' (John 21:19).

Like the earlier apostolic community, the existence of the community after Easter was the result of a call and a decision to follow. But this second call differed from the first. Jesus had passed through the trial of suffering and death and been made perfect by the things he had suffered (Heb. 5:7-9). In the same way, the apostles had all passed through the trial of infidelity and denial. In Matthew's gospel, the invitation to post-Easter following is preceded by the dissolution of the pre-Easter community: 'You will all fall away because of me this night; for it is written, "I will strike the shepherd, and the sheep of the flock will be scattered." But after I am raised up, I will go before you to Galilee' (Matt. 26:31-2). In John's gospel, the second call (of Peter) is preceded by a threefold demand for an affirmation of love that recalls his threefold betrayal (John 21:15-17). The 'yes' given to this second call is a 'yes' purified by trial and made in full awareness of what it means to follow Jesus.

Called together once again by the risen Jesus, the community, like the Lord who goes before it, now lives in the newness of the Spirit. The community is 'new' because the source of its life is the Spirit, which had not been given before (John 7:39) but is now transmitted by the risen Christ. The Spirit which Jesus had poured out on earth like a spring of living water (John 19:30; 7:38) is given to the disciples when the risen Christ breathes on them (John 20:22): or, in Luke's presentation of salvation history, when he comes down upon them at Pentecost (Acts 2:3-4).

But can we in fact speak of a community in the post-Easter period which was created by its common 'following' of Jesus? Can we take as our standard of comparison a way of life which is no longer possible - the physical and literal following of Jesus? Jesus is present, but he is now the risen Lord, no longer tied to space and time. How can he be 'followed'?

The very terminology used shows what a real problem this idea of following was for the first generation of Christians. It is significant, for example, that in the New Testament the verb 'to follow' is found almost exclusively in the gospels, which portray Jesus as constantly travelling the roads of Galilee and Judaea - 'followed' by the crowds, the disciples and the Twelve.[2] In the same way, the term 'disciple', in the sense of 'follower' of Jesus, is used abundantly in the gospels and Acts but disappears completely from the other New Testament writings.[3]

In fact, as generations of Christians have repeatedly stated, Jesus is no longer visibly present among us since his ascension into heaven. It is therefore impossible to 'follow' him, to continue to be his disciples or 'followers'. Yet he, the risen Lord, is still present in some mysterious way through his Spirit. Did he not promise to be with us always, to the end of time (Matt. 28:20)? Did he not promise to be among two or three met together in his name (Matt. 18:20)? After his resurrection he gave the assurance that he would 'go before' the disciples into Galilee, continuing to walk at their head as he had done in the same Galilee when he had called them to follow him. Then why should we not try, in faith and the Spirit, to share the experience of the disciples before Easter?

Care has obviously been taken in the actual text of the Gospels to make the theme of 'following' relevant to the Church of every generation. Mark 10:46-52 is typical when it makes the blind Bartimaeus a model for all future following in the Church. The account follows that of the Twelve: the call; the going after Jesus, having thrown off his cloak; the act of becoming a follower and walking along the way with him after regaining his sight. All human beings, like Bartimaeus, are imprisoned in the darkness of sin by their blindness. The appeal of faith and the call of Jesus can work the miracle of restoring their sight and bringing them into the world of light. In the age of the Church also, people can leave everything, as the blind man left the cloak which might have hindered his journey, and follow Jesus like the apostles.[4]

This process is even more obvious in John's gospel than it is in the Synoptics. John deliberately keeps the number of disciples indefinite: 'the idea of discipleship is transferred to all the faithful'.[5] In fact, in this Gospel the term 'to follow' continues to be used, but it corresponds to what John means by the word 'believing'.

Although he did not know him in the flesh, Paul also experienced the close bond with Christ known by those who followed him before Easter. He did this through communion with the risen Lord. Paul does not, of course, use the concept of following. For him, the Christian walks 'according to the Spirit' rather than behind Christ. Paul's post-Easter experience, like that of other Christians, was different from the experience of the earlier apostles with the historical Christ. To describe it, Paul uses other concepts such as 'being in Christ' or 'having the same sentiments [or mind] as Christ'. The language of following changes to that of imitation.

Imitation becomes the post-Easter reinterpretation of following, now that Christ is no longer physically present on the roads of Palestine. In spite of the complex historical process,(6) the two concepts appear equivalent, as the First Letter of Peter demonstrates: 'Christ also suffered for you, leaving you *an example* [the theme of imitation], that you *should follow in his steps* [the theme of following]' (1 Pet. 2:21). In the post-Easter age, being a disciple can only be achieved according to the teaching of Paul and John.

Following Jesus in the way that those called by the lake followed him is no longer possible. At the same time, the Church recognizes that she still possesses the reality of the graces present in that original experience.

> To follow Jesus 'today' means to rediscover and live a different but real contact with the exalted Jesus still truly present ... Life in common with Jesus is now the common life of the faithful. The Master's directives which guaranteed the communion proper to the Messianic community are reformulated to maintain an evangelical ecclesial community.[7]

To become the servant of all, to be ready to deny self, to love to the point of giving one's live, to put oneself in the last place - these are ideals which can and should continue to animate the Christian community. The Second Vatican Council is faithful to this tradition when it ascribes following to all Christians: 'In different kinds of life and in various duties, a single holiness is cultivated by all who... follow Christ poor, humble and laden with the cross, in order to be worthy to share in his glory.'[8]

The Pentecostal community of Jerusalem in reality prolonged the experience of those who 'followed' Jesus in the period before Easter. Luke, therefore, in his complete work (the Gospel and Acts) continues to use the word *mathetes* (disciple) for the experience of communion with Christ after Easter. The word is no longer used in the Gospel after Jesus' arrest (it last occurs in Luke 22:45), because the passion and death of Jesus were the scandal that interrupted the following and broke up the apostolic community. The risen Christ and the Spirit sent by him brought the community to life again, reassembled the scattered flock, and enabled it to resume following. Consequently, 'disciple' is used again in Acts. 'The homogeneous linguistic usage suggests that the earthly community with Jesus is a prefiguration of the primitive paschal community.'[9] There was an authentic community, even if it was in the newness of the Spirit. The Lord was literally present spiritually, that is, in the *Spirit*, but he was still the same Lord.[10] There was, after all, only one community of Jesus, the community that, begun by the Lake of Galilee, continued in the Jerusalem Church. Only one, even if it used different means of expression.

The Unity of the Community is the Fruit of the Spirit of Pentecost

The presence of the risen Lord gave fresh cohesion to the college of the Twelve, which was now re-formed in all its integrity (cf. Acts 1:15-26). Strong in this new presence, the disciples showed a new determination; now their attitude was one of complete conviction, as they began all over again to experience unity among themselves and with the Lord, in order to be faithful to their Master's directions.[11]

Luke shows how the creation of the Jerusalem community, in its typical aspect of unity, resulted from the outpouring of the Spirit brought about by the risen Christ. Luke's first great 'summary',[12] which gives a snapshot of the first Christians intent on living together with everything in common, is in fact preceded - we might even say caused - by Pentecost. The second 'summary' (Acts 4:32-5), which portrays the community as being of one heart and soul, is likewise preceded and caused by a further descent of the Spirit, known as the 'little Pentecost' (4:31).

Pentecost was the realization in salvation history of the outpouring of the Spirit effected by Jesus in his paschal mystery. The Spirit is the gift of the risen Christ. Koinonia is the gift of the Spirit. The first effect of Christ's work is thus the creation of a community, the beginning of a new people, which lives its unity in mutual love.

It was not by chance that the Christian Pentecost began on the day when the Jewish Pentecost was celebrated and grafted itself on to the older festival. The Jewish Pentecost commemorated the Covenant made at Sinai between God and his people. It was the festival of the giving of the Law which made the tribes of Israel into the people of God.[13] This event now became, in the Christian Pentecost, the foreshadowing of the gift of the new law and the setting up of the new people of God that was brought about in Jerusalem by the descent of the Spirit. The new law brought by Christ, which Jesus himself had summarized in what he called his own new commandment, namely, mutual love, was now promulgated by the descent of the Spirit. It was the law of the Spirit written no longer on tablets of stone but in the hearts of believers. The new Christian community was born with the outpouring of the Spirit.

The Jewish Pentecost was originally the agricultural festival of harvest; only later was it historicized as a commemoration of the Covenant. The Fathers of the Church saw in this also a kind of prophecy of what happened at the Christian Pentecost. The descent of the Spirit was the moment when what Christ had sown in the paschal event was harvested. Like a grain of wheat, Jesus died. And now here was the ripe ear: the multitude of peoples which the Spirit reaped at Pentecost and gathered into the Church.

All the elements of Luke's narrative underline how the descent of the Spirit brought about the unity of the human race and created koinonia. Here we shall only emphasize some of these elements.

The first element - unity - is revealed in the very terminology used to describe the setting for the descent of the Spirit: 'They were all together in one place (*epi to auto*)' (Acts 2:1). It is no coincidence that the expression used here is also used later to describe the community which came into being at Pentecost: 'All who believed were together' (2:44).

The tongues of fire which divided as they came down and rested on each of the disciples are another element which shows unity as the effect of the descent of the Spirit. Together with the speaking in various languages, they recall the voice of God on Sinai; according to an ancient Jewish tradition, as it came down God's voice divided into seventy tongues (the number of the peoples on earth) so that everyone could understand what God said.[14]

The crowd which gathered round the apostles was equally significant. It consisted of 'devout men from *every* nation under heaven' (2:5). Luke's long list of peoples is not just a newspaper report, even though it follows a precise geographical scheme. Luke is concerned to underline that on this day the Spirit re-formed the unity of the human race. All the nations were present and all of them rediscovered, in mutual understanding, their deepest communion. With the descent of the Spirit, the culmination of the paschal experience, God restored the unity of the human race divided by sin. The Fathers saw this as the reversal of what happened at Babel, when pride scattered the peoples. Then, the birth of different languages did not apparently enrich the human spirit; rather, it crippled mutual understanding. At Pentecost, the many languages were able to converse together in harmony and understand each other. As the patristic saying puts it, 'What Babel scattered, Jerusalem reunited.' By sending the Spirit, the risen Christ restored human unity. Unity is the basic sign of redemption.

Pentecost thus marks the beginning of the new humanity, the new people of God characterized by koinonia, which appears as the gift of the Spirit, as grace, and is immediately made visible in the formation of the first community in Jerusalem. Communion is the most obvious fruit of the paschal event, the characteristic feature of the new life brought by the risen Christ. Expressed in the community and experienced through it, this communion was one of those original traits of Christianity that formed the initial paradigm of the new people of God. It has been noted that, even while waiting in the Upper Room, the community

> represents in miniature the new people of God without discrimination or privileges. All belong to it: the disciples from the earliest days, the faithful women, the mother and the relatives. Ties of kinship, social roles and cultural qualifications take second place. A new principle of association unites this group of people: adherence to Jesus, the risen Lord, and his way of life. The dynamism of the Spirit of Pentecost will enable this unifying power to spread beyond the limited sphere of the cenacle of prayer.[15]

As unity around the Master was the characteristic of the disciples before Easter, so the new group of disciples is characterized in its turn by the communion which makes one heart and one soul out of thousands of people. This new presence of the Lord is the fruit of his own gift of the Spirit through his death and resurrection.

It is literally this presence of the Lord Jesus, his body and blood, his suffering, his Spirit, his Gospel, his example and his commandments, which makes it possible for the intense communion amongst the faithful to be called Christian.[16]

The Face of the New Community

The 'summaries' in Acts show us the fruit of Christ's redemptive work, which reached its fulfilment at Jerusalem in the outpouring of the Spirit. Acts 2:42-7 is usually cited as the first 'summary':

> They devoted themselves to the apostles' teaching and fellowship, to the breaking of bread and the prayers. And fear came upon every soul; and many wonders and signs were done through the apostles. And all who believed were together and had all things in common; and they sold their possessions and goods and distributed them to all, as any had need. And day by day, attending the temple together and breaking bread in their homes, they partook of food with glad and generous hearts, praising God and having favour with all the people. And the Lord added to their number day by day those who were being saved.

Set in the context of the Pentecost narrative and Peter's first speech, this summary emphasizes the role of the Holy Spirit in the origin and development of the Christian community. At this point, it must be noted that the whole pericope is characterized by the presence of verbs in the imperfect tense, as participles, or in roundabout periphrastic constructions. This contrasts with the preceding narrative, in which the aorist form predominates. This change in verbal forms is accompanied by a variation in the beginning and end of the passage, expressed in the adverbial formula 'that day' (2:41) and 'one day' (3:1). In the course of vv. 42-8 the narrative moves from describing events which happened once, to the presentation of a stable, continuous, permanent and daily ('day by day', 2:46) way of life. 'There is a passing from "today" to history, from the events of Pentecost (2:4) to a life lived in the spirit of Pentecost.'[17]

One of the first features of the new community to emerge from this summary is that the members 'were together', a characteristic that was already present in the first community as it waited for Pentecost (1:14). Here, 'being together' has the Semitic meaning of interior union rather than a unity in place and time. It could be translated as 'unanimous', 'in agreement'. Unity was not, therefore, simply a question of the physical coming together of several people, but rather of their being in agreement, unanimous. This is a word which recurs several times in the summaries: 'attending the temple together' (2:46); 'when they heard it, they lifted their voices together to God' (4:24); 'they were all together in Solomon's Portico' (5:12). It should also be noted that the term always occurs in a context of prayer. Unanimity imposes itself particularly when the community presents itself before God.[18]

Four more features emerge from this first summary, features which the first believers pursued with tenacity and persistence[19]: the teaching of the apostles, koinonia, the breaking of bread, and prayer.

We need to pause on this word koinonia, which occurs only once in Acts and is therefore difficult to translate.[20] One possible interpretation connects the word with the previous element, the teaching of the apostles, so that it denotes the union of the faithful with the apostles. Another interpretation links koinonia with the following element, the breaking of bread. In that case, it would be a matter of eucharistic communion. The Vulgate takes this view, translating it as 'in communione fractionis panis'. Other interpretations lean towards the sharing of possessions, table fellowship, or the unanimity of spirit which expresses itself in sharing possessions. So it could be understood as brotherly union. More simply, it has been translated as the 'meeting' of Christians.[21]

Although there is no other occurrence of the term koinonia, we do find, in this and in a later summary, a word from the same root, *koina*: 'they had all things in *common*' (2:44); 'they had everything in common' (4:32). This favours an explanation of koinonia as sharing of possessions.[22] The first Christians did in fact put 'everything in common'.

If we take this view, we immediately discover the rich resonances of this kind of sharing in the Greek and the Old Testament. The description of the first Christians' sharing of possessions seems in fact to have been inspired first of all by the Greek theme of friendship, familiar to the recipients of the Lucan writings. According to a widespread maxim, 'Everything is shared between friends', and friendship consists essentially in sharing what one possesses. The Old Testament perspective is equally clear. According to the Greek Septuagint (LXX), in the eschatological community there will no longer be any poor (cf. Deut. 15:4). Christian koinonia thus appears as the effective realization of the noble Greek ideal (even if, in the Christian context, what prompts the sharing is no longer friendship but faith and a common hope), the fulfilment of ancient promises, and the sign of the Church's authenticity.

The koinonia lived by the Christian community is a sharing of possessions. At the same time it expresses a deeper reality of life: the sharing of hearts and souls. The second summary (Acts 4:32-5) brings this out:

> Now the company of those who believed were of one heart and soul, and no one said that any of the things which he possessed was his own, but they had everything in common. And with great power the apostles gave their testimony to the resurrection of the Lord Jesus, and great grace was upon them all. There was not a needy person among them, for as many as were possessors of lands or houses sold them, and brought the proceeds of what was sold and laid it at the apostles' feet; and distribution was made to each as any had need.

This second summary, like the first, is preceded by a descent of the Spirit (4:31), as if to confirm that where there is sharing, there also is the presence and action of the Spirit.

This pericope immediately makes clear, as a characteristic of the primitive Jerusalem community, that all possessed 'one heart and one soul'.

> The binomium 'heart and soul', foreign to Hellenism, is typically biblical; it is to be understood in reference to the love of God and the observance of his commandments 'with all your heart and with all your soul' (cf. e.g. Deut. 4.29; 6.5; 10.12; 11.13; 13.4; 26.16; 30.2, 6, 10; etc.). It indicates the true and proper centre of the human person, the innermost part of a man, the personal self which is expressed in his life. The interior communion of the souls of all the faithful is fundamental for an understanding of the religious meaning of sharing possessions, described in the text under examination.[23]

A second feature which emerges from this summary is that 'they had everything in common'. Like a leitmotiv, the theme of sharing possessions returns, the consequence of an inner sharing given by the Spirit and founded on a common belief in the resurrection (cf. v. 33).

This does not arise from the rejection of property or an ascetic ideal of poverty. Rather, it seems to be motivated by an ideal of brotherhood and a perceived equality based on common sharing of the same values: the fatherhood of God and Christ's death for all. These two fundamental equalities make all other differences irrelevant. The believers

> share their possessions not because they find themselves (locally) together, but because they know they are united in a single reality, a

single body. Thus the expression seems to translate the believers' sense of community: they have become aware of their unity. Sharing their possessions is only a consequence of their awareness of forming a community together, a community in which everyone knows themselves to be in agreement with all.[24]

Contrary to what usually happens in society, property was no longer a reality which divided but a means of creating brotherhood; it did not separate the community into rich and poor but was a means of constructing the type of social equality that leads to the disappearance of poverty (v. 34a). The members of this new community were in fact inspired by a profound conviction that, even without renouncing the right to property, among brothers in the faith everything should be shared, which meant property and all other material possessions as well.

At the end of his study, Dupont concludes that the motive which prompted the Christians to share their possessions is to be sought above all in the unity of hearts and souls; at the same time, however,

> it must be added that this sharing of possessions makes possible the full and authentic realization of the sharing of souls. The union of souls is thus both the cause and the effect of an attitude which leads each person to consider his own possessions as belonging to all ... The ideal aimed at is not exactly an ascetic renunciation, nor detachment from earthly goods in accordance with eschatological expectation, or even the generous practice of almsgiving. It is an ideal of charity which realizes, on new foundations, the Greek ideal of friendship.[25]

We can now summarise the koinonia which inspired the first Christians at Jerusalem. It had three dimensions.[26] First of all, their unity was founded on their common faith (Acts 2:44; 4:32; 5:14) which was inseparable from their common hope (2:47); this enabled them to understand that, together, they formed a community. Secondly, this unity had to be lived out. It was translated, above all, into a unity of spirit: 'the company of those who believed were of one heart and soul' (4:32). This unanimity was particularly strong when the Christians stood before God, either meeting in the Temple (2:46; 5:12) or praying together (1:14; 4:24). It was, moreover, bound up with the teaching of the apostles and the breaking of bread. It is impossible to isolate the more material koinonia from the other expressions of the Christians' community life, without distorting it. Thirdly, koinonia (especially spiritual koinonia) needed to be 'incarnated' and transposed on to the tangible level of this world's goods. It would not have been authentic if it had not become, in some way, a sharing of possessions. From the point of view of the summaries in Acts, this is not exactly detachment towards possessions, nor is it an ideal of poverty. Those who share what they have with others do so not in order to be poor themselves, but so that no one in the community may be poor. A community is not worthy of the name if some of its members live in abundance while others are left without necessities. For this reason, koinonia assumes the concrete aspect of sharing one's possessions to ensure that everyone has what they need.

Thus the summaries in Acts portray Christians as closely united among themselves in a rich and coherent fraternal sharing. This unity is brought about and nourished by the word of God, received in the teaching of the apostles. In this way the community is built up as it listens to the Word. United in the breaking of bread, it is founded upon, and nourished by, the Eucharist, and expresses itself in prayer. Acts offers us a picture of Christians united to the point where they form one heart and soul and can express this unity in the most concrete sharing of possessions, so that none among them is in need. The emerging Church shows that it has grasped the heart of the gospel message.

Jerusalem: A Paradigm of the Ideal

It is evident from Luke's description that he idealized the primitive Church, but precisely because of this it became even more of a paradigm than it would have been in any case. This is the Church: living in a profound sharing which eliminated divisions of race, nationality and social class. At Jerusalem, the fruit of Pentecost was the recovery of that primordial unity of humanity which, as the result of sin, had been shattered at Babel. Jerusalem was the realization in history of the work accomplished by Christ in his paschal mystery: the recapitulation of all things in himself. It was the historical fulfilment of his prayer to the Father, already granted: 'that they may all be one' (John 17:21). Luke wanted to emphasize that the mystery of sharing, an original and characteristic feature of Christianity, had already been realized. The Church itself is this mystery of communion, the One Church.

Henceforward, this image of the original community will be, for the Church throughout the ages, the ideal to be aimed at. Koinonia and Jerusalem will be synonymous. Origen wrote: 'When the heart and soul of the faithful are one (Acts 4.32) and the members have the same care for each another (1 Cor. 12.25), then they are Jerusalem.'[27]

By the third century, writers had already begun to lament departures from the primitive ideal. Cyprian, for example, wrote:

> Yes, the sons of God must be... agreed in love, faithfully united amongst themselves by the bonds of agreement. This is the unanimity which existed once, under the apostles: this is how the new people of the believers maintained charity, keeping the commandments of God. Scripture proves this, when it says 'The company of those who believed were of one heart and soul' (Acts 4.32); and again: 'All these with one accord devoted themselves to prayer, together with the women and Mary the mother of Jesus, and with his brothers' (Acts 1.14). Amongst us, on the other hand, such agreement is compromised (*diminuta est*); this is proved by the fact that generosity in works has also declined.[28]

Cyprian does not here emphasize disagreement on questions of belief. From the lack of sharing material possessions, he establishes that sharing hearts and souls is also lacking.

Through a combination of ecclesial, social and cultural factors - which this is not the place to analyse - the Church seemed, in the eyes of many Christians, to lose something of the authenticity and freshness of its beginnings. Consequently, some men and women were convinced that there was nothing for it but to leave everything and go and seek God in solitude, beginning again the experience of the disciples and apostles around Jesus and reliving in a radical way the experience of the first Christians of Jerusalem. Anachoresis was born and the religious community set out on its journey through history.

NOTES

1. '[Jesus] uses [the apparitions] to show that he will always be with them. The fact that he suddenly appears in the midst of his disciples is not to prove that "he can pass through closed doors". It is a sign that he is always present, even when they do not see him. The risen Lord is the new creation in our midst. The apparitions are implicit indications of his permanent presence.' (*A New Catechism*, London: Burns Oates/Herder & Herder, 1967, p. 183).

2. *Akoloutheo*, 'to follow', 'to travel with someone', is found fifty-nine times in the Synoptics and eighteen times in John. *Erchomai*, 'to go', is also found in all the Synoptics.

3. *Mathetes* occurs forty-five times in Mark, seventy-one times in Matthew, thirty-eight times in Luke, seventy-eight times in John and twenty-eight times in Acts. In the post-Pentecostal community 'disciple' is already synonymous with 'believer'. For an introduction to the terminology of following, see biblical dictionaries such as *A Theological Dictionary of the New Testament* Vol. 4, edited by Gerhard Kittle (ET 1967), pp. 415-60.

4. See J. Dupont, 'Il cieco di Gerico riacquista la vista e segue Gesù (Mc 10,46-52)', *Parola, Spirito e Vita* 2 (July-December 1980), pp. 105-23.

5. Schnackenburg, *The Gospel of John*, p. 331.

6. The idea of imitation has at times been linked with a more static type of spirituality, and following with the more dynamic type. The theme of imitation has also acquired ethical, ascetic and moral connotations, while following has a more ontological and mystical sense. In its reaction against medieval piety, the Protestant Reformation opposed imitation, seeing it as an endeavour of human pride and the following of Christ as a response to his call. According to Lossky, the Eastern Church defines spirituality more as life in Christ and has never practised the way of imitation in its spiritual life, regarding it in fact as somehow incomplete, a merely external attitude towards Christ. A book which, more than any other, brings out the difference between life in Christ and imitation of Christ is Nicholas Cabasilas' *Life in Christ*. Cabasilas states quite simply that there is no opposition between imitation and following but a real identity: 'To imitate Christ and to live according to him is to live in Christ, and it is the work of free will, when it subjects itself to the divine will' (see T. Spidlík, *The Spirituality of the Christian East: A Systematic Handbook*; Cistercian Studies CS79, Kalamazoo: Cistercian Publications, 1986, p. 37).

7. Di Pinto, 'Seguire Gesù', p. 222.

8. LG 41a. Following tends towards imitation, not in a moral sense but in its full and unconditional attachment to Jesus and his word. Di Pinto's article 'Seguire Gesù' is a very useful introduction to the complex question of the relation between following and imitation. For the strictly biblical approach, see G. Turbessi, 'Il significato neotestamentario di "sequela" e di "imitazione" di Cristo' (*Benedictina* 19, 1972, pp. 162-225) and E. Cothenet,

'Imitation du Christ' in *Dictionnaire de Spiritualité*, VII/2 (1971, 1536-62). For the historical side, see E. Ledeur (ibid., 1562-87).

9. Di Pinto, 'Seguire Gesù', p. 231.

10. In connection with the inspiration of religious communities, it is significant that the first great monastic text, the *Vita Antonii*, portrays the origin of Antony's vocation as simultaneously the invitation of Jesus, calling him to follow, and the example of the first Christians in Jerusalem, who sold everything to give to the poor. The religious life takes as its ideal the community at Jerusalem described in the summaries in Acts, the post-Easter interpretation of following Christ, as well as the evangelical model of the group who followed Jesus during his earthly life.

11. Acts 1.14 describes the *perseverance* of the disciples. As in the other summaries, the text here uses the verb *proskartereo*, with the meaning of 'to persist, persevere, remain firm, even obstinate, in something or some decision, unyielding in spite of all difficulties, etc.'. Luke 'expresses another important attitude of the Christian life of individuals and the community: perseverance, patience, and a readiness to start again, enduring unexciting, even extremely prosaic situations' (A. Weiser, 'Il Domenica di Pasqua, At 2,42-27 - VII Domenica di Pasqua, At 1,12-14' in H. Kahlefeld and O. Knoch, *Esegesi e Annunzio. Commento delle epistole domenicali e festive. Anno A* (1974), p. 240). The periphrastic construction of participle and imperfect in this verse indicates continuity and unyielding constancy.

12. In the summaries, Luke interrupts his narrative to give a résumé description of the community's way of life. The main summaries are Acts 2:42-7; 4:32-5; and 5:11-16. Their structure and vocabulary suggest that Luke used a document or account which came directly from the first group of Christians living in Jerusalem; cf. L. Cerfeaux, 'La première communauté chrétienne de Jérusalem', in *Recueil Lucien Cerfeaux*, II (Gembloux: 1984), pp. 125-54; M. Del Verme, 'La comunione dei beni nella comunità primitiva di Gerusalemme', *Rivista Biblica* 23 (1975), pp. 363-82; J. Dupont, 'La comunità dei beni nei primi tempi della Chiesa ...', in *Studi sugli Atti degli Apostoli*, (Rome: Paoline, 1971), pp. 861-89; *idem.*, 'L'unione tra i primi cristiani', in *Nuovi studi sugli Atti degli Apostoli* (Cinisello Balsamo: Paoline, 1985), pp. 277-97; C. Ghidelli, 'I tratti riassuntivi degli Atti degli Apostoli', in *Il Messaggio della salvezza*, V (Torino-Leumann: LDC, 1968) pp. 137-50.

13. Cf. J. Dupont, 'La prima Pentecoste cristiana (Atti 2,1-11)', in *Studi sugli Atti degli Apostoli*, pp. 823-60

14. Cf. L. Cerfeaux, 'Le symbolisme attaché au miracle des langues', in *Recueil Lucien Cerfeaux*, II, pp. 183-7.

15. R. Fabris, *Atti degli Apostoli* (Rome: Borla, 1987²), pp. 79-80.

16. Cf. P. C. Bori, *Koinonia. L'idea della communione nell'ecclesiologia recente e nel Nuovo Testamento* (Brescia: Paideia, 1972), p. 114; G. Panikulam, *Koinonia in the New Testament; A Dynamic Expression of Christian Life* (Rome: Pontifical Bible Institute, 1979).

17. B. Papa, *Gli Atti degli Apostoli. Commento pastorale*, vol. I (EDB, Bologna 1981), p. 88.

18. There is an echo here of Jesus' teaching: 'If two of you agree on earth about anything they ask ...' (Matt. 18:19); it is impossible to come before the Father without agreement. Hence the need for brotherly reconciliation before presenting an offering (cf. Matt. 5:23-24). Paul takes up this teaching in his turn when he writes that Christians must 'live in such harmony with one another, in accord with Christ Jesus' in order to glorify God 'together ... with one voice' (Rom. 15:5-6).

19. Like the disciples waiting for Pentecost in the upper room, the first Christians are presented here as 'persevering' and 'assiduous', terms which could be translated as 'strongly welded together, in a spirit of fidelity and perseverance' (Papa, *Atti degli Apostoli*, p. 104).

20. Cf. Dupont, *La comunità dei beni nei primi tempi della Chiesa*, pp. 860-89.

21. Dupont, *L'unione tra i primi cristiani*, p. 279.

22. 'While the term *koinonia* has a very extensive semantic value, in the immediate context (cf. [Acts] 2,44-45) and for the general content of the following passages (cf. 4, 32-35; 4,36-37 and 5,1-11) it seems to refer to the practice of holding possessions in common as an external sign of that inner sharing of hearts which reigned in the community at Jerusalem' (Del Verme, La comunione dei beni, p. 361).

23. Del Verme, *La comunione dei beni*, p. 367.

24. Dupont, *L'unione tra i primi cristiani*, p. 289.

25. *La comunità dei beni*, pp. 887, 889.

26. Dupont, *L'unione tra i primi cristiani*, pp. 289-90.

27. Origen, *Selecta in Psalmos 121*, 3 (PG 12, 1633).

28. *L'unità della Chiesa*, 24-6, in St Cyprian, *A Donato. L'unità della Chiesa. La preghiera del Signore*, ed. C. Failla (Rome, 1967), pp. 109-10.

PART TWO

Historical Understanding

1 Above All, The Choice of God
Solitude and communion in primitive eremitism

The community of the Twelve and that of Jerusalem inspired the birth and development of the distinctive way of life which we know today as the monastic or religious life.[1] Beyond the complex task of reconstructing the origins of monasticism,[2] one fact is immediately evident and may appear disconcerting: at the beginning we find not community but solitude. The monastic life without community! Today we are so sensitive to the communal dimension of the consecrated life that the realization that this new form of discipleship, which was to occupy an ever-increasing space in the life of the Church, was born in solitude may seem strange, perhaps even scandalous. At the very least, it may prompt a question. Why, scarcely two centuries after the outpouring of the Spirit at Pentecost and the birth of a Christian community which was immediately characterized by a deep and visible koinonia, did this new form of life arise, almost unforeseen and unforeseeable and apparently contradicting the Christian beginnings?

Perhaps, beyond the multiplicity of sociological and cultural factors which brought it into being, the solitude that we find at the beginning of the monastic life contains one of the most profound secrets for the cenobitic and communal life of the future, which will increasingly characterize the way of consecration in the Church: community itself necessarily presupposes a dimension of *solitude* that roots the person in the deepest and most intimate communion with God. Only through this unique personal relationship with God can human beings achieve inner wholeness and consistency, that full identity which allows them to enter into a relationship of communion with each other that is not challenged by egotism, self-seeking or the desire for support and consolation.

The Quest for Solitude

Saint Athanasius, in his famous work, the *Vita Antonii* (*Life of St Antony*) makes monasticism begin with the call of Antony, who chose to live in progressively radical solitude.[3] St Jerome, in his turn, claims that another hermit, Paul, was the father of monasticism and, to emphasize his seniority and greater authority with respect to Antony, makes his solitude even more austere and prolonged.[4] In any case, the setting for the birth of eremitism was the desert, a place with almost mythical connotations which, departing from its original geographical meaning of an uninhabited or normally unfrequented land, increasingly acquired a moral significance as flight from worldliness, a break with everything that impeded the way to God, the radical choice of celibacy, an exclusive dedication to the praise of God and communion with him, listening to his word with attention and perseverance, uninterrupted prayer. More simply, the birthplace of monasticism was physical solitude, the symbol of a deeper interior solitude which leads to *hesychia*, peace, calm, the absence of everything that can disturb the soul and distract it from its relationship with God, the necessary prelude to full communion with him.

Antony's call and spiritual journey were typical. In fact, when Athanasius wrote his *Life*, he offered Antony as a model for those, by then numerous, who had embraced this new way of life. As a pastor who felt responsible for guiding the usually simple and illiterate faithful who became the first hermits, Athanasius chose the literary genre of hagiography and in so doing drew up an authentic rule of life. And so Antony, aged about twenty (the date is roughly 270), is driven into the desert by the desire to imitate the apostles who left all to follow the Saviour; at the same time, he is attracted by the example of the believers described in Acts, who sold their possessions and brought the proceeds to the feet of the apostles for distribution to the poor.

The first stage of Antony's progress into the desert brings him to a hut just outside the village. After some years, he settles further away, in a cemetery, where he takes up residence in an abandoned tomb and stays until he is thirty-five. Afterwards, he moves further into the desert and settles in a small half-ruined fort at Pispir, where he remains enclosed for twenty years. The final stage takes him towards the Dead Sea, into an even more perfect and isolated solitude on a mountain near Sinai which still bears the name of Mount St Antony.

The geographical distances which Athanasius makes Antony travel suggest a comparable spiritual journey. On the same principle, we see Simon Stylites distancing himself further and further from the earth. The first column on which he established himself was ten feet high. Subsequently, it was replaced by increasingly higher columns, until the last one reached a height of sixty feet.[5] The spiritual life is seen as something dynamic, wholly aimed at a progressive closeness to God through a continual renunciation of everything that might hinder the quest. Antony, 'day by day, as if making a beginning of his asceticism, increased his exertion for advance, saying continually to himself Paul's word about *forgetting what lies behind and straining forward to what lies ahead ...* not counting the time passed, but as one always establishing a beginning, he endeavoured each day to present himself as the sort of person ready to appear before God - that is, pure of heart and prepared to obey his will, and no other.'[6] For this reason the hermit (from the Greek *eremos*, desert) takes the name of ascetic (from the Greek *askein*, to exercise), one who trains himself in this way to develop the energy of the spiritual life until union with God is achieved.

Solitude was a fundamental element in this ascetic process. Perfection seemed to grow in proportion to the growth of solitude.

It seemed natural at that time that the monk (from the Greek *monos*: alone and single) should be called an anchorite (from the Greek *anachorein*: to go away, withdraw, retire). The monk, as required by a law of Theodosius promulgated in 390, ought to live in 'desert places', in 'vast solitudes'.[7] St Jerome reminded Heliodorus: 'Translate the word "monachos", that is to say, the name you bear: what are you doing in the midst of crowds, you who are alone?'[8] Ammonas, a disciple of Antony, represents the purest tradition of the Egyptian solitaries when he writes: 'First, solitude; solitude begets asceticism and tears; tears engender fear; fear brings forth humility and [the gift of] foresight; foresight engenders charity. Charity makes the soul free of disease, dispassionate; after all these things, man then understands that he is not far from God.'[9]

Certainly, physical solitude is not everything. 'He who wishes to live in solitude in the desert,' explains Antony, 'is delivered from three conflicts: hearing, speech, and sight; there is only one conflict for him and that is with fornication.'[10] In the desert there are in fact three ways of living in solitude: the material solitude of the man who lives in a place which does not allow him to meet other people; the solitude of silence which precludes conversation; and the solitude of the heart, when every preoccupation, every anxiety and every bad thought are completely eliminated. Without doubt, this last is the most perfect solitude. When it has been achieved, the heart is open and free to aim only at union with God. Nevertheless, physical solitude continued to be considered indispensable for access to the mystery of God. Cassian sings its praises: 'Free to wander through immense solitudes, immersed in a vast silence, it was easy for us to be often rapt in ecstasy... With all the ardour of my soul I embraced the secrets of tranquil solitude, a life like the beatitude of the angels.'[11]

The origins of the monastic life, then, were characterized by solitude and the absence of a communal dimension, at least in such exemplars as Antony, Paul and Simon Stylites. The first hermits made solitude the primary expression of their consecration to the service of God, the very condition of their religious life. The apostle Paul, when he urged celibacy, intended a liberation from all the preoccupations which might in any way divide the heart and divert it from the Lord's service (1 Cor. 7:32-34). Eremitism radicalized this celibate solitude by renouncing not only wife and children but also relations with anyone else, in order to dedicate itself exclusively to recollection of God with an undivided heart and free from all other preoccupations. It is significant that before the word *monachos* came to signify the Christian who retired into the desert, it had been used to denote the Christian who had decided to live in virginity and continence.[12] Already in the second century, Symmachus used it in his translation of Gen. 2:18 to designate the solitude of Adam before the creation of Eve and indicate that the first man lived alone, without wife or companion.[13] Solitude was thus interpreted, in the monastic context, as a radical celibacy, the negation not just of one form of society, marriage, but of every form of society. Not even the later gradual evolution into cenobitic life or mitigated eremitism ever wholly supplanted strict eremitism.

The Cultural Motivation of Solitude

The absence of the communal dimension found expression on two distinct levels. First of all, there was the renunciation - in fact, if not in doctrine - of the mediation of the ecclesial community and the sacraments. There was a lively awareness of belonging to the Church as a communion of saints (an inner sharing which presupposed unity in the faith); but there does not appear to have been - at least in the initial, model phase - a similar need felt for the liturgy and the sacraments.[14]

Secondly, there was the rejection of all human relationships and hence the renunciation of the enrichment to be gained from advice, dialogue and even conflict. The following apophthegmata (sayings or maxims) of Arsenius, often quoted in monastic tradition, are significant:

> While still living in the palace, Abba Arsenius prayed to God in these words, 'Lord, lead me in the way of salvation.' And a voice came saying to him, 'Arsenius, flee from men and you will be saved.'[15]

Abba Mark said to Abba Arsenius, 'Why do you avoid us?' The old man said to him, 'God knows that I love you, but I cannot live with God and with men ... I cannot leave God to be with men.'[16] Note, in this last answer, the interior struggle undergone by the *Abba* (father) Arsenius and many other hermits like him. The *fuga hominis* which made the *fuga mundi* more radical was not dictated by a lack of love for humanity but by the conviction that it was impossible to be with both God and human beings at the same time. Hence it was not a refusal of love but an expression of brotherly love towards others.

The hermit was, in fact, strongly conditioned by a particular outlook on the world and humanity which derived from extra-biblical cultural factors. If the quest and motivation of the first hermits were evangelical, the manner of their response and realization was indebted to the history and culture in which they lived, a context characterized by the oriental dualism which had penetrated the area of Mediterranean cultural. The hermit's own vision of the world was dominated not by the biblical idea of the divine transcendence, but by an antithesis between God and the material world, between God and human society, between this life and the other, led by the angels. It is in this context that the *fuga mundi* takes on its full significance as a passage from this world to the 'angelic'. The idea of man, in its turn, is characterized by some equally dualistic basic concepts which produce tension and division within him. Man appears as a soul in conflict with his own body and called to a progressive flight from it. Inevitably, this conflict with the body led to the hermit rejecting human sociability, that is, to the *fuga hominis*. In reality, our *body is* our fundamental language and the means of communion. The corporeal and the social are closely connected.[17]

There were also plenty of social factors which favoured withdrawal to the desert, such as fleeing from persecution or trying to evade military conscription, payment of taxes, judicial inquiries, and so on.[18]

Solitude as the Prelude to Communion with God and the Brethren

Of course, the deepest motives, the evangelical ones, were different. Above all there was the constant inspiration of the biblical tradition which describes the desert as a privileged place for knowing God and entering into relationship with him. It was here that the most significant experiences of the people of Israel and their greatest prophets, from Moses to Elijah to John the Baptist, took place.[19]

Like Jesus (cf. Matt. 4.1), the monk also went into the desert to be tempted by the devil, to seek him out and do battle with him, to defeat him and, in this victory over evil, find the way to the only good, which is God.[20] For, when all is said and done, this is the ultimate object of going into the desert: the search for God. The monks were driven by the love of Christ to leave everything and go to meet the Lord who comes.[21]

To find the theological reasons for solitude, we must go to where flight from the world and ascesis were most rigorous: the monasticism of Syria. It was here that the principles of renunciation, ascesis, solitude and detachment from things, people and one's self were carried to their extreme limits. Theodoret of Cyrus (c. 393-460) provides us with a sketch of about thirty of these ascetics. Some chained themselves to rocks, either in caves or in the open air; others remained standing, motionless (the 'Stationaries'); others spent long years in a tree (the 'Dendrites') or on a column (the 'Stylites'), and so on. Syrian monasticism reached to the limits of human possibility.

Precisely because of these extremes of solitude and ascesis, Theodoret felt the need to question the motivation behind the incipient monasticism. 'Now one has to speculate, investigate and understand properly why they embraced that way of life, and the principles behind their attainment of the heights of ascesis.'[22] At the end of his description of the heroic feats of his athletes, therefore, Theodoret writes a short treatise on charity. It is worth stopping for a moment to read some extracts from this attempt at doctrinal interpretation of the ascetic fact. If at the beginning of his work Theodoret had explained that the monks withdrew from the world to fight demons, to destroy the effects of passion in themselves and achieve an inner equilibrium, by the end he is looking for another, deeper, motivation to avoid the risk of confusing the monks with 'philosophers', who are also capable of submitting themselves to a rigid discipline. Above all, Theodoret did not want to attribute their exceptional willpower and personalities to a human origin, instead of to the work of God.

The motive which draws the monk into solitude is clearly the love of God:

Only love for God has enabled the ascetics to exceed the limits of human nature. Enflamed by the divine fire, they willingly endure the assaults of cold and, sprinkled with heavenly dew, alleviate the burning heat of the sun. The divine love nourishes them, warms them, clothes them, gives them wings and teaches them to fly, prepares them to scale the heavens and enables them to see, as far as possible, the Beloved Being. It kindles in them the desire for contemplation and makes their zeal more ardent. Just as the sight of the beloved attracts those in love and makes its goads more terrible, so those who have received the goads of divine love and constantly picture to themselves the pure beauty of God make the darts of that love more sharp, and the more they long to enjoy it, the more they drive away its gratification. This is because earthly love can be satisfied, but love for God knows no limits to its satisfaction ... So he who welcomes the love of God at the same time despises all earthly things and tramples on all sensual pleasures; he disdains riches, glory and human fame, makes no distinction between the purple of a king and a cobweb, and compares precious stones to pebbles on the beach. He does not regard good health as the greatest asset, illness as a misfortune or poverty a calamity; he does not make happiness consist in riches and pleasures, but rather treats them like streams, which water the trees planted along their banks without stopping at any of them ... Only an ardent lover of God can perfectly understand philosophy, that is to say, 'love of wisdom', because wisdom is God himself ... The true 'philosopher' that is 'lover of wisdom', should correctly be called 'philotheus', 'lover of God'. And this person, the lover of God, scorns all things because he sees only the Beloved, puts his service before everything, says, does and thinks only what pleases the Beloved and rejects everything that he forbids ...

So the new athletes have learnt from Holy Scripture that Christ is beautiful, possesses untold wealth, is the source of wisdom, can do what he wills, and that for man he has infinite goodness and flowing streams of gentleness and wills only good towards all men everywhere.

From men inspired by God they have learnt the incalculable variety of his favours and, pierced by the sweet arrows of his love, they make their own the words of the Bride: 'I am sick with love'

(Song of Songs 5.8) . . . The athletes of virtue find these and similar expressions in those who have put themselves at the service of God; they receive the arrows of divine love from every side and, despising all things, I direct their minds to the Beloved and, while awaiting their hoped-for incorruption, have made their bodies spiritual.[23]

While wholly centred on the love of God - the one true and profound reason for solitude - the *Treatise on Charity* equally makes room for love of the brethren. Paraphrasing John 21:15-19, Theodoret shows how love for God has to be shown in dedicated care of the brethren: 'Even if I have no need of anything,' says the Lord to Peter, 'I regard the care of my sheep as the greatest service, and care for them is care given to me. You must give your brethren the same caring service which you enjoy, feed them as I feed you, govern them as I govern you, and thus, through them, you will repay the gratitude you owe me.'[24]

After all, even if the first, eremitic, phase of monasticism lacked community life, it did not positively exclude that communion in faith and love which unites the solitary with the Church as a whole and with his own brothers in the desert. Rather it underlined the primordial and fundamental reality which constitutes the very being of humanity: relationship with God. Attracted by the love of God, it highlighted in a radical way the first great commandment: 'You shall love the Lord your God with all your heart, and with all your soul, and with all your mind, and with all your strength' (Mark 12.30). The eremitic life is thus the existential proclamation, the icon, of what God is: his greatness, his transcendence, his glory - God as the fullness of life. God is all, and everything must be abandoned for him. Before him everything loses value and becomes relative: God is all, and you must give yourself wholly and unreservedly to him.

Solitude serves communion with God; it is a prelude to the harmony of paradise. Gregory of Nazianzus wrote, recalling his own monastic experience:

Nothing seems greater to me than this, to impose silence on your own senses, leave the flesh of the world, recollect yourself, no longer occupy yourself with human things unless absolutely necessary; to speak to yourself and God and lead a life which transcends visible things; to carry in your soul divine images which are always pure, unmixed with earthly and mistaken forms; to be truly a spotless mirror of God and divine things, and to become so more and more, catching light from light and using the darkest to draw from the most splendid; to enjoy future good in present hope, and converse with the angels; to have already left the earth, transported on high by the spirit.[25]

You cannot approach life in common unless you have first been struck by the thunderbolt of God's love, unless - at the invitation of Jesus and after the example of the Twelve - you have left everything for the one thing necessary.

It is precisely this union with God, attained in the total stripping away of every attachment and the maximum human openness to the will of God, which will give the hermit the wisdom he needs to enlighten his brethren, the magnanimity to console them, the peace that accepts everyone, and the love, completely purified of selfishness, that can go out to all.

'Communion' in the Eremitic Life

By such means the solitude of the hermit is open to communion with the Church and with other human beings. The monk, declares Evagrius Ponticus in a celebrated definition, 'is he .who, separated from everyone, is united to all'.[26] Origen expressed the same principle: 'The saints are united to God and among themselves through contemplation.'[27] Antony did not hesitate to leave the solitude of the desert and hasten to Antioch to support the martyrs claimed by the persecutions of Diocletian and Maximian. Even from his final refuge, his deepest and most definitive solitude in the mountain opposite Sinai, he returned to the great city of Alexandria to defend the orthodoxy of the faith in the war declared by Athanasius on the Arians. Here again Antony is the prototype of every monk who is called to live in a communion of faith and love with the whole Church.

Typical of the fruitfulness which solitude can take on in this direction is spiritual fatherhood, the charism which a hermit acquires in order to enlighten and counsel, and to heal both soul and body.'[28] Solitude is transformed into hospitality; the hermits open the doors of their cells to rich and passers-by, to pilgrims both humble and powerful, to saints and sinners. This is how Athanasius describes the fruitfulness of Antony's solitude:

Nearly twenty years he spent in this manner pursuing the ascetic life by himself, not venturing out and only occasionally being seen by anyone. After this... many possessed the desire and will to emulate his asceticism, and some of his friends came and tore down and forcefully removed the fortress door... Through him the Lord healed many of those present who suffered from bodily ailments; others he purged of demons, and to Antony he gave grace in speech. Thus he consoled many who mourned, and others hostile to each other he reconciled in friendship, urging everyone to prefer nothing in the world above the love of Christ. And when he spoke and urged them to keep in mind the future goods and the affection in which we are held by God, *who did not spare his own Son, but gave him up for us all*, he persuaded many to take up the solitary life. And so, from then on, there were monasteries in the mountains and the desert was made a city by monks, who left their own people and registered themselves for the citizenship in the heavens.[29]

These hermits did not lack mutual contact or regular meetings. In fact, eremitism, though it did not have stable community, recognized a 'temperate and humane solitude'.[30] Reasons for meeting were provided by the celebration of prayer, the need for advice, work, instruction, and mutual help. The phenomenon of 'spiritual fatherhood' and the 'novitiate school' brought the monks into communion with each other in a common search for the will of God and to learn the way of perfection. Once again, the evidence comes from Athanasius: 'their cells in the hills were like tents filled with divine choirs - people chanting, studying, fasting, praying, rejoicing in the hope of future boons, working for the distribution of alms, and maintaining both love and harmony among themselves.'[31]

The monk, writes Bouyer on this subject, is a monk because he separates himself from the world. Nevertheless, what impels him towards solitude 'is not in fact a desire for an idle, aesthetic and self-centred contemplation; it is the most realistic Christian charity'.[32]

In eremitism itself, therefore, with its practice (albeit more or less intermittent) of such attention and mutual charity, we can glimpse the elements which will form community. Some of the sayings of the Fathers clearly confirm the necessity of love for one's brother. 'Our life and our death,' said Antony, 'is with our neighbour. If we gain our brother, we have gained God, but if we scandalize our brother, we have sinned against Christ.'[33] And Agathon: 'I have never gone to sleep with a grievance against anyone, and, as far as I could, I have never let anyone go to sleep with a grievance against me.'[34]

Although the *Apophthegmata* and the first histories of the monks do not theorize about fraternal charity and communion among the hermits, as was done later in 'learned monasticism', they are full of simple episodes which make us realize the depth of relationship which united the monks who peopled the desert, even in their solitary life. It was a matter of sharing trials, covering the faults of the brethren, overcoming resentment, and going out to meet the sinner. 'The elders said: Each one must make his own what happens to his neighbour, suffer with him on every occasion, weep with him, feel as if he had his very body and as if he himself were troubled when a trial comes upon the brother, as it is written: We are one body in Christ (Rom. 12:5) and: The multitude of believers were of one heart and one soul (Acts 4:32).'[35]

Sometimes we come across little acts of charity and attention which are unexpected in men as rough and solitary as the hermits:

A solitary had under him another solitary who lived in a cell about ten miles away. The thought came to him: 'I will summon the brother to come and get his bread.' But then he thought: 'Why should I force him to toil for ten miles for bread? I will go and take it to him myself.' He took the bread and headed for the brother's cell. On the way, he tripped over a stone and hurt his foot, which bled a lot. He began to cry out because of the pain and at once an angel appeared to him and said 'Why are you crying?' Showing him the wound, he replied 'This is what I am crying about.' The angel said to him, 'Don't cry for that; every step you have taken for love of the Lord has been counted and will earn you a great reward before God.' Then the ascetic thanked God and resumed his journey full of joy; arriving at the brother's with the bread, he told him about God's goodness towards himself, then gave him the bread and went back again. The next day, he took bread again and set off towards another monk. But as it happened, this monk was on his way to see him and they met on the road. The one who was going said to the one who was coming, 'I had a treasure and you have tried to take it away from me.' The other said to him, 'Are only you allowed through the narrow gate? Let me come with you!' Suddenly, while they stood talking, an angel of the Lord appeared to them and said, 'Your contest has gone up to God like a sweet-smelling fragrance.'[36]

Another scene of simple and profound communion, in the following lively picture:

Seven very experienced monks were living in the desert which borders on the Saracens, each one by himself in his own cell but united to one other by bonds of love . . . These blessed ones, living in solitude, used to meet together for None on Saturdays, and each would provide a little something to eat, one nuts, another figs, another dates, another herbs and another parsnips, and thus they showed charity to one another.'[37]

This emphasis on the diaconal and charitable dimension is obvious evidence of the influence of the cenobitism which arose almost at the same time as eremitism. Thus a rich doctrine of brotherly love and communion gradually developed in the setting of ancient monasticism. What we read in the *Spiritual teachings* of Dorotheos of Gaza is typical of this development. Here we see the convergence, in a magnificent synthesis, of the eremitic monastic stream of the Nitrian deserts and the cenobitic stream of Pachomius and Basil. Dorotheos begins his instruction on love by recalling one of the sayings of Abba Ammonas:

What did the blessed Ammon do when those brothers, greatly disturbed, came to him and said, 'Come and see, Father. There is a young woman in brother X's cell!' What tenderness he showed to the erring brother. What great love there was in that great soul. Knowing that the brother had hidden the woman in a large barrel, he went in, sat down on it, and told the others to search the whole place. And when they found nothing he said to them, 'May God forgive you!' And so dismissing them in disgrace, he called out to them that they should not readily believe anything against their neighbour. By his consideration for his brother he not only protected him after God but corrected him when the right moment came. For when they were alone he laid on him the hand with which he had thrown the others out, and said, 'Have a care for yourself, brother'. Immediately the other's conscience pricked him and he was stricken with remorse, so swiftly did the mercy and sympathy of the old man work upon his soul.

Taking this teaching as his starting point, Dorotheos turns to his own monks:

Let us, therefore, strive to gain this love for ourselves, let us acquire this tenderness towards our neighbour so that we may guard ourselves from wickedly speaking evil of our neighbour, and from judging and despising him. Let us help one another, as we are members one of another . . . In this way we ought to bear one another's burdens, to help one another and be helped by others who are stronger than ourselves, to think of everything and so everything that can help ourselves and others, for 'we are members one of another,' as the Apostle says. *If we are one body each is a member of the other.* If one member suffers, all the others suffer with it. What does our 'cenobia', our community life mean to you? Do you not reckon that we are one body, and all members of one another? . . . Let each one give assistance to the body according to his ability and take care to help one another, whether it is a matter of teaching and putting the word of God into the heart of a brother, or of consoling him in time of trouble or of giving a hand with work and helping him. In a word, as I was saying, each one according to his means should take care to be at one with everyone else, for the more one is united to his neighbour the more he is united to God.[38]

Finally, there is a detailed explanation of a vivid and effective image which resolves the contradiction between the search for God and brotherly relationships which had also troubled both Abba Arsenius ('I cannot live with God and with men') and the earliest eremitic monasticism:

And now I give you an example from the Fathers. Suppose we were to take a compass and insert the point and draw the outline of a circle. The centre point is the same distance from any point on the circumference. Now concentrate your minds on what is to be said! Let us suppose that this circle is the world and that God himself is the centre; the straight lines drawn from the circumference to the centre are the lives of men. To the degree that the saints enter into the things of the spirit, they desire to come near to God; and in proportion to their progress in the things of the spirit, they do in fact come close to God and to their neighbour. The closer they are to God, the closer they become to one another; and the closer they are to one another, the closer they become to God. Now consider in the same context the question of separation; for when they stand away from God and turn to external things, it is clear that the more they recede and become distant from God, the more they become distant from one another. See! This is the very nature of love. The more we are turned away from and do not love God, the greater the distance that separates us from our neighbour. If we were to love God more, we should be closer to God, and through love of him we should be more united in love to our neighbour; and the more we are united to our neighbour the more we are united to God.[39]

This agrees entirely with the teaching of Basil. Henceforth the hermit and the cenobite live in a fruitful state of mutual influence. 'The abbot of a community asked our holy father Cyril, bishop of Alexandria, "Who are the greater in their way of life: we who have brothers under us and guide each one of them to salvation in a different way, or those who, in solitude, save only themselves selves?" The bishop replied, "There is no need to distinguish between Moses and Elijah; both of them, in fact, pleased God.'[40]

Beyond the ascetic practices which were due to a particular culture, the compelling motive of the hermits appears profoundly evangelical. 'For the first monks, ascesis became the essential instrument for achieving the perfect love of God . . . Monks leave the world in order to be able to love God better and more deeply.'[41] This, and only this, is the fundamental objective which inspires and guides them. 'He is a monk,' wrote Theodore of Studios, 'who has eyes only for God, desires only for God, zeal only for God; who wants to serve only God and is therefore at peace with God and becomes a source of peace for others.'[42] Their solitude graphically illustrates the radical demands of the choice of God: to please him, you must leave everything and everyone, that is, root out every sort of attachment. Once solitude with God has purified the heart, it floods it with the very love of God and makes it capable of an authentic love and communion.

Christ himself - and the hermits wished to imitate him - withdrew into solitude with the Father before he went to the crowds. Before he began his messianic activity, he withdrew to the desert (cf. Mark 1:12-13). Before he faced the day in Capernaum, with its proclamation of the Kingdom, its healings and its immersion in the crowd, 'he went out to a lonely place' (Mark 1:35). It was the same before choosing the Twelve (Luke 6:12). Habitually, 'he would withdraw to solitary places' (Luke 5:16), alone on the mountain (cf. Mark 6:46; Matt. 14:23).

The fact that monasticism was first born in solitude and only subsequently enriched by the cenobitic dimension provides a permanent lesson for all types of Christian community. True love of the brethren requires a pure heart, presupposes having been flooded with the very love of God, demands being rooted in God himself and, having left everything, loving him with all one's heart and soul and strength.

NOTES

1. At its birth, the religious life had a variety of designations, such as 'angelic life', 'apostolic life', 'evangelical life' and so on. For an introduction to this rich terminology, see Jean Leclercq's valuable study, *The Perfect Life* (Liturgical Press, 1961).

2. The problem of the origins of monasticism turns fundamentally on two questions: the originality of the phenomenon, i.e. whether and to what extent it depended on similar phenomena in the Greek world (such as the recluses of the temple of Serapis) and the Hebrew world (the Essenes and similar groups); and, secondly, its motivation, whether evangelical, Christian, or connected with other cultural and sociological factors. See M. Augé, *Lineamenti di storia dell'antico monachesimo* (Rome: 1981), pp. 7-15. For a fuller survey, see G. Turbessi, *Ascetismo e monachesimo prebenedettino* (Rome: 1961); A. Vogüé, *Monachisme et Église dans la pensée de Cassien*, in *Théologie de la vie monastique* (Paris: 1961), pp. 213-240; article, *Monachesimo*, in *Dizionario degli Istituti di Perfezione* (DIP), VI (Rome: 1973), cols. 1672-1742.

3. St Antony the Great (c. 250-356) gained his experience of eremitism in Egypt, where this new form of Christian life originated, even if the monastic movement also appeared almost contemporaneously in Syria and, soon after, in Palestine. Antony is regarded as the initiator of the monastic movement and is therefore called 'the father of monks'. Through his 'sayings', the letters attributed to him, the place accorded to him in early monastic literature and, especially, the biography of him written by St Athanasius (ET *Athanasius: The Life of Antony and the Letter to Marcellinus*, trans. Robert C. Gregg; London: SPCK, 1980), Antony's influence has been of the utmost importance in both East and West. A critical edition of Athanasius' work, with an ample introduction, thorough commentary and comprehensive bibliography, can be found in *Vita di Antonio* (Verona: 1974), with Introduction by Chr. Mohrmann and critical text and commentary by G. J. M. Bartelink; see also F. Giardini, 'La dottrina spirituale di S. Antonio Abate (t 356) nelle sue sette lettere autentiche', in *Rivista di Ascetica e Mistica* 2 (1957), pp.124-39; *idem.*, 'Doctrina espiritual en la "Vita Antonii" de San Atanasio', in *Teologia Espiritual* 4 (1960), pp. 377-412. For the theme of solitude and flight from the world in the Desert Fathers, see G. M. Colombás, *El monocado primitivo*, I: *La espiritualidad* (Madrid: 1975), pp. 109-41; T. Spidlík, *The Spirituality of the Christian East: A Systematic Handbook* Cistercian Studies CS79, (Kalamazoo: Cistercian Publications, 1986), pp. 205-17.

4. Cf. San Girolamo, *Vita di Paolo, Ilarione e Malco*, prepared by G. Lanata, Milan: 1975.

5. Teodoreto, *Storia dei monaci della Siria*. Introduction, translation and commentary prepared by S. Di Meglio, Padova: 1986, pp. 196-212.

6. Athanasius: *The Life of Antony and the Letter to Marcellinus* (trans. Robert C. Gregg; London: SPCK, 1980) p. 36f.

7. *Codex Theodosianus*, 16, 3.1.
8. *Epistles*, 14, 6.
9. *Apophthegmata*, quoted in Spidlík, op. cit. p. 212.
10. *The Sayings of the Desert Fathers: The Alphabetical Collection*, trans. Benedicta Ward SLG (London: Mowbray, 1975), p. 3.
11. *Conferenze Spirituali*, XIX, ed. O. Lari (1965), Vol. III, p. 94.
12. Cf. Eusebius, *Commentaria in Ps.*, PG 23; 689.
13. Cf. J. Alvarez Gomez, *Historia de la vida religiosa*, vol. I (Madrid: 1987), pp. 183-4. 'What was denoted, first of all, by the word *monachos*, Syriac *ihidaya* - as is now clear - was celibate ascesis, the believer who lives "alone" not, it is agreed, in the solitude of the desert, but without women. Historically but also, it may be said, phenomenologically, that is what the monk is, above all: no celibacy, no monk! (A. Guillaumont, *Aux origines du monachisme chrétien. Pour une phenomenologie du monaachisme* (Abbaye de Bellefontaine, 1979), p. 229).
14. The rigorous solitude of Antony, Paul and the young Benedict shows clearly the absence of the Eucharist and the liturgico-sacramental dimension. Cf. E. Dikkers, 'Les anciens moines cultivaient-ils la liturgie?' *La Maison Dieu* 51 (1957), pp. 31-54; G. Penco, 'La partecipazione alla vita eucaristica presso il monachesimo antico', *Rivista Liturgica* 48 (1961), pp.183-192.
15. *Sayings of the Desert Fathers*, p. 9.
16. Ibid. p. 11.
17. Cf. A. Guillaumont, 'Le dépaysement comme forme d'ascese dans le monanachisme ancien', *Annuaire de l'École des Hautes Études* 76 (1968-9), pp. 31-58; J. M. Lozano, *La sequela di Cristo* (Milan: 1980), pp. 223- 5; B. Bauer, *Alle origini dell'ascetismo cristiano* (Brescia: 1983), pp. 11-47; much more positive is the interpretation of L. Bouyer in *The Spirituality of the New Testament and Fathers* (London: 1960), pp. 302-21.
18. 'The third century, which prepared for monasticism, was a time of recession which brought about the collapse of the Empire beneath the pressure of the barbarians. Progress in scientific research and philosophy ended; general impoverishment and continual military expeditions reduced the lower classses to slavery. A society which no longer produces enough and where the worker is exploited tends to give up consumption and production; to give up all efforts to amass wealth or create a fami ly, even the scrap of land burdened with taxes, is a form of strike which was given the name of *anachoresis* and often ended in banditry' ('Monachesimo', col. 1962). Under this same entry in the *Dizionario degli Istituti di Perfezione* can also be found references to other, psychological, components in the origins of monasticism.
19. For the biblical spirituality which inspired monasticism, see M. Todd, 'Tipologia dell'Esodo e del deserto nella tradizione patristica', *Servitium* 9 (1975), pp. 383-97; fr. Daniel-Ange, *Les Feux du Desert. 1: La solitude* (Andennes: 1973). Cf. also the article 'Profetismo' in *DIP*, VII, 972-3.
20. The desert was considered the favourite domain of devils and therefore represented, for the ascetics, the privileged place where they could hunt

them out and combat them. Cf. A. Guillaumont, 'La conception du desert chez les moines d'Égypte', in *Aux origines*, pp. 69-87; Colombás, *El monacado Primitivo*, pp. 234-41.

21. 'Because of its birth in the desert, eastern monasticism appeared to the consciousness of the Church as a nation of "searchers after God" who made no concessions to the "established" world: "Monks are the new Israel" (Cassian). The resulting implication for ecclesiology is clear enough: the Church, itself a pilgrim community bearing "truthful witness" to the *eschaton* of Christ, must not form an alliance with any established historical structure' (*Monachesimo*, col. 1717).

22. Theodoret, *Storia dei monaci*, 226. On the works of Theodoret and Syriac monasticism, see P. Canivet, 'Théodoret et le monachisme syrien avant le Concile de Chalcédoine', in *Theologie de la vie monastique*, pp. 241-82; idem., Le Monachisme syrien selon Theodoret de Cyr (Paris: 1977). For the treatise on charity, see particularly pp. 87-102.

23. Theodoret, op. cit., 229; 238-239; 243-4.

24. Ibid., p. 235.

25. *Orationes* II, 7; PG 35, 413.

26. *De Oratione* 124; PL 97, 1192.

27. *In Proverbia* XVI, PG 17, 196D. More correctly, this is a commentary by a pseudo-Origen.

28. Cf. E. Ghini, 'Il "Padre spirituale" secondo i monaci del Deserto', in *Mistagogia e direzione spirituale*, . E. Ancilli (Rome: 1985), pp. 55-71. A fundamental work is I. Hausherr, *La direction spirituelle en Orient autrefois* (Rome: 1955).

29. *Life of Antony*, p. 42f.

30. Cf. L. Leloir, *Deserto e comunione. I Padri del deserto e il loro messaggio oggi* (Turin: 1982), pp. 56-91.

31. *Life of Antony*, p. 64.

32. Bouyer, op. cit., p. 309. L.-A. Lassus has formulated a conjectural pun: Solitaires, solidaires' ('solitaries, solidarity'); *La Vie Spirituelle* 58 (1976), pp. 584-99.

33. *Sayings of the Desert Fathers*, p. 3. The necessity of love for one's brother is a recurrent theme in the *Apophthegmata*: 'Abba John the Dwarf said, "A house is not built by beginning at the top and working down. You must begin with the foundations in order to reach the top." They said to him, "What does this saying mean?" He said, "The foundation is our neighbour, whom we must win, and that is the place to begin. For all the commandments of Christ depend on this one" (ibid., p. 93). The following parable of the three friends is also significant, showing as it does the superiority of fraternal charity over ascesis: 'A secular man of devout life came to see Abba Poemen. Now it happened that there were other brethren with the old man, asking to hear a word from him. The old man said to the faithful secular, "Say a word to the brothers." When he insisted, the secular said, "Please excuse me, abba; I myself have come to learn. " But he was urged on by the old man and so he said, "I am a secular, I sell vegetables and do

business; I take bundles to pieces, and make smaller ones; I buy cheap and sell dear. What is more I do not know how to speak of the Scriptures; so I will tell you a parable. A man said to his friends, 'I want to go to see the emperor; come with me. ' One friend said to him, 'I will go with you half the way.' Then he said to another friend, 'Come and go with me to the emperor,' and he said to him, 'I will take you as far as the emperor's palace.' He said to a third friend, 'Come with me to the emperor.' He said, 'I will come and take you to the palace and I will stay and speak and help you to have access to the emperor."' They asked what was the point of the parable. He answered them, "The first friend is asceticism, which leads the way; the second is chastity, which takes us to heaven; and the third is almsgiving which with confidence presents us to God our King." The brethren withdrew edified' (ibid. p. 182f.).

The ultimate expression of this evangelical vision is the following saying of Apollo on the subject of hospitality: 'One should bow before the brethren who come, because it is not before them, but before God that we prostrate ourselves. "When you see your brother," he said, "you see the Lord your God"' (ibid., p. 37).

34. *Sayinngs of the Desert Fathers*, p. 20.
35. *Detti inediti dei Padri del deserto*, trans. and ed. with an Introduction and notes by L. Cremaschi (Bose: 1986), p. 160f.
36. Ibid., p. 176f.
37. Quoted by Turbessi, *Ascetismo*, p. 160.
38. *Dorotheos of Gaza: Discourses and Sayings* (Cistercian Studies Series CS33; Kalamazoo: Cistercian Publications, 1977) p. 137f.
39. Ibid. p. 138f.
40. *Detti inediti*, p. 142.
41. M. Augé, *Ritorno alle origini. Lineamenti di spiritualità dell'antico monachesimo* (Rome: 1984), pp. 32-3. Chiara Lubich has summed up their message as follows: 'There's no question about it. We can love the world, because everything in the world is made by God, directly or indirectly. But if it's true that eternity exists, and that Heaven exists, then this life which is so short must be viewed in its proper perspecptive and given its true meaning...

'Yes, we can be people of our times. We can satisfy modern tastes. But if we want to avoid making a serious mistake, let's first be *eternal* people, who do not die and who follow in the footsteps of those who were truly wise - the saints!

'Their life, their austerity, the flight- at least spiritually - from the world, their mortifications, may disturb us, but they are reasonable and sound. The rest is madness.' (*Knowing How to Lose*, London: New City, 1981, p48f.)
42. *Parva Catechesis*, 39, quoted by L. Leloir, op. cit., p. 59.

2 Holy Koinonia Appears
The dawn of the monastic community

Notwithstanding its profound understanding of the communal dimension of the Christian vocation, the life of solitude proper to the eremitic life could engender a certain forgetfulness of others, as if they were the antithesis of God. This is what happened to the young Pachomius.[1] The account of his vocation relates that the angel who appeared to him found him preoccupied. When the angel asked him the reason, Pachomius replied: 'I am searching for the will of God.' 'The will of God,' the angel answered, 'is that you serve other people.' 'I am seeking how to do the will of God,' Pachomius retorted, still wholly absorbed in the early stages of his experience as a hermit, 'and do you come and tell me to serve people?' He had not yet discovered the service of God in the service of others. The angel had to repeat the invitation three times. Obeying, Pachomius built a house to receive brethren.[2] It is the beginning of the cenobitic life, the birth of religious communities.

The new reality appeared immediately as an extraordinary gift from above. 'It is by a favour from God ... that there appeared upon earth the holy koinonia.'[3] That was how Theodore, the disciple and successor of Pachomius, regarded the birth of the monastic community within the Church. Like him, Horsiesios, another disciple and successor of Pachomius, summed up and justified community life by recourse to the model of the primitive Church. Let us, he said, carry out everything 'in conformity with the law of the holy koinonia ... as one man, as it is written: "All who believed formed but one heart and one soul" (Acts 4:32).'[4] Yet even before it was an object of doctrinal reflection, the Pachomian community was the outcome of an experience of life.

The Community is Born Out of Experience

Pachomius became a Christian because he was struck by the practical love shown to him by the unknown people of a village, while he was being taken by force and in chains to be enrolled in the Roman army. The Coptic *Life* tells what happened:

> In the evening, some citizens of that city brought bread and victuals to the prison, and they compelled the recruits to eat, because they saw them sunk in great affliction. When young Pachomius saw them, he asked the men who were with him, 'Why are these people so good to us when they do not know us?' They answered, 'They are Christians, and they treat us with love for the sake of the God of heaven.' He withdrew to one side and spent the whole night praying before God saying, 'My Lord Jesus the Christ, God of all the saints, may your goodness quickly come upon me, deliver me from this affliction and I will serve humankind all the days of my life.'[5]

Consequently, from the beginning Pachomius' life was marked by love. At the root of Antony's vocation was the text of Matt. 19:21, the invitation to abandon everything to follow Christ, and so the emphasis was on renunciation. At the root of Pachomius' vocation there was a concrete act of charity. Antony had listened to the words of the Gospel in church, in a liturgical context. Pachomius encountered the Word of God made flesh in some Christians who came to visit him in prison. 'The model, the rule of Pachomian koinonia must be found in this concrete act of love and fraternal service.'[6]

Pachomius' conversion coincided with a specific vocation: to place himself at the service of humanity. The traditional ascetic practices of the hermit life were replaced by commitment to helping the brethren and teaching them the way to God.

A further experience helped the idea of a life lived in community with brethren to mature, and marked a further growth in awareness of the value of human relationships. After seven years of experience as a hermit, Pachomius should have been mature in the interior life. Yet when he met his brother John and with him began to enlarge his own dwelling in order to receive other monks and so respond to the angel's invitation, Pachomius started to quarrel acrimoniously with him over a trifle. He realized then how far he still was from a perfect life and that God and his neighbour were inseparable realities on the spiritual journey. 'He who is at enmity with his brother,' he could write later, 'is an enemy of God; and he who is at peace with his brother is at peace with God.'[7] From this came another lesson: 'One single heart with your brother.'[8] The experience had made Pachomius aware that the hermit has few opportunities to practise some of the virtues and discover his own limitations, and that relationships with others are often the occasion of purification and growth in virtue.

One more significant experience: the failure of the first attempt at community life. The grave dissensions within the first group of disciples who gathered round Pachomius - which was actually more like a colony of semi-hermits than anything resembling the later community - forced him to send them all away. The first community, like the first partnership with his brother John, was a failure and brought home to him the need for a certain communal order. He had to give life together clear and demanding rules. Obedience, he had discovered, is a decisive element in community life.

Finally, we can say that the birth of the first explicit form of community life, in both its more spiritual implications (such as understanding the value of charity and unity) and its more institutional elements, was the fruit of experience. As we are dealing with the first experience of community life, it would be interesting to study all aspects of the structure and articulation of the Pachomian community. But, faithful to our purpose, we shall here dwell only on its more doctrinal and spiritual aspects.[9]

The Foundation of Charity

We have seen that Pachomius' first image of Christianity was of a religion wholly orientated towards the service of humanity for the love of God. This experience contained the seed from which the spirituality of Pachomius and his successors would develop. The Coptic author of the Life of Pachomius is so conscious of the value of communion and unity that he anticipates the experience of charity as already present in the eremitic period. In fact, he writes that after Pachomius' monastic profession, his relationship with his master Palamon was such that the two of them 'lived together as one man'.[10]

The Pachomian institution remained closely connected with the Egyptian monasticism from which it derived. Consequently the central figure of the elder, around whom a stable group of disciples gathered and eventually formed a community, remained pre-eminent. Given this traditional structure, the organization of the cenobium showed signs of a remarkably hierarchical arrangement. At the same time, an innovation came in: the powerful vision of fraternity, the discovery of the brother and the importance of mutual relationships based on charity. When a newcomer entered a monastery, he no longer, as in the eremitic life, looked for a spiritual father to initiate him into the solitary life; instead, he sought a community of brothers, a koinonia, with whom he could live in mutual love. From now on, the sources constantly use the word 'brother' to describe the cenobitic monk.[11] The word 'monk' was used for the solitaries; the disciples of Pachomius were known as men who lived in brotherhood and made fraternal relationships the framework of their life.

The central role of fraternal unity is already clear in the oldest legislative code, the *Praecepta atque Iudicia*. It is not by chance that it begins with the words of Paul: 'Love is the fulfilling of the law' (Rom. 13:10).[12] The majority of the failings mentioned in the code are offences against charity. Recognizing their particular gravity, it punishes them energetically.

Brotherly love is one of the principal themes of the only *Instruction* of Pachomius preserved in Coptic. This is addressed to a brother who has been nourishing hard feelings; Pachomius invites him to have or, better, to be 'one heart with your brother'.[13] Then he begs him,

> Do not be at enmity with anyone, because he who is at enmity with his brother is an enemy of God; and he who is at peace with his brother is at peace with God. Have you not learned by now that nothing is preferable to peace, which makes each person love his brother? Even if you are free of all sin, [yet] being your brother's enemy you are a stranger to God ... What danger we are in then, when we hate one another, when we hate our co-members, one with us, sons of God, branches of the true vine, sheep of the spiritual flock gathered by the true shepherd, the Only-Begotten son of God who offered himself in sacrifice for us! ... What defence will you present before Christ? He will say to you, 'Inasmuch as you hate your brother I am he whom you hate.'[14]

The monk who dies in hatred and hostility towards his brother will be judged without mercy, because in this world he gave no proof of mercy. Lack of mercy is a mortal sin which will come to light when his sins are uncovered, sins which could, according to 1 Pet. 4:8, could have been covered with the cloak of love. All appeals to penance or personal austerity will be useless, because the Lord will say, 'If you have hated your brother, you are an alien in my kingdom.'[15] Peace with the brethren is the guarantee of peace with God.

The love taught by Pachomius is always a concrete love which shows itself in a thousand ways. It is compassion: 'This is God's love, to take pains for each other.'[16] It is mutual help in the fight for salvation and perfection. It is brotherly correction in order to achieve the fulfilment of the law, that is, charity. It is a place of mutual edification: 'Let everyone be profitable to you, so that you may be good to everyone.'[17]

The Coptic *Life*, restating Pachomius' message in symbolic form, relates that shortly before he died, the father of the koinonia saw Gehenna, gloomy and dark, and also saw

> some of those who were in the darkness, as if circling a pillar and thinking they were going forward and drawing near the light, not realizing that they were only turning around a pillar. He looked again and saw in that place the whole community of the Koinonia walking one after the other, holding fast to each other for fear of getting lost by reason of that deep darkness. Those who were in front had a small light like that of a lamp to light their way; only four of the brothers saw that light, while all the rest saw no light whatever. Our father Pachomius watched their way of progressing; if one let go his hold on the man in front of him, he would lose his way in the darkness, along with all those who came after him.[18]

Then Pachomius called the brothers by name, one by one, before they could separate from the others: 'Hold to the man in front for fear of going astray!' As the *Apophthegmata* attest, achieving salvation had been the great quest of all the hermits. 'What must I do to be saved?' was the ritual question put by the novice to the elder. All the elder's wisdom was condensed into his reply to this demand. Pachomius discovered that salvation is achieved together, helping and supporting one another in positive mutual care. Pachomius laid down a new way of going to God. 'We were all as one man', he could say at the end of his own life.[19]

Doctrinal Development

The theme of brotherhood was energetically resumed by Pachomius' disciples, Theodore and Horsiesios. Indeed, it was precisely they who translated their master's experience and the reality of his institution into theological and spiritual terms. Even the use of the term 'koinonia' to describe the new community was coined by them.

The same progression that we noted in the discovery of community life is met again in the doctrinal reflection. There is, in fact, no reference to the primitive community in Jerusalem in the writings attributed to Pachomius. Not until Horsiesios is the experience of koinonia reinterpreted in the light of explicit references to the Jerusalem community, in order to justify and interpret community life and find new starting points for it. From Theodore onwards, there is a discovery of the Johannine texts of the Lord's commandments (cf. John 13:34) and the distinguishing mark of his disciples (cf. John 17:21). Then other scriptural references emerge, such as Paul's exhortation to practise the works of mercy and unity as a sacrifice pleasing to God. The exclamation in Psalm 133, 'How good and pleasant it is when brothers dwell in unity!', is also applied to community.

In his *Instructions*, Theodore expounds the motives for holy koinonia:

> It is by a favour from God ... that there appeared upon earth the holy *Koinonia* by which he made known the life of the Apostles to those who desire to follow their model forever before the Lord of all. Indeed, the Apostles *left everything* and, with all their heart, *followed* Christ; they *stood steadfast with him in his trials*, and shared with him in the death of the cross.[20]

The apostolic life is described here simply as a life of poverty and imitation of Jesus even to sharing in his cross. This is the 'apostolic life' as it had been discovered by primitive eremitism. For a doctrinal development of community modelled on the way of life of the apostolic community, separation from the world and sharing of possessions, we have to wait for Horsiesios who, as already mentioned, was the first, in his *Regulations*, to establish a connection between koinonia and the explicit ideal of community which emerges from the summaries in Acts.

Although Theodore does not refer to Acts, for him imitation of the apostles leads to community life. Awareness of being together in following the Master is enough for Theodore to know how they should love each other: 'We are disciples of Christ, so as to love one another without hypocrisy.'[21] Everything, even the family, is left behind, in order to enter into another family. In fact, holy koinonia can only be realized when the bonds of purely natural love, 'according to the flesh', are broken and all the brethren are wrapped round in spiritual love. Hence the repeated rules prescribing separation from the family and regulating contact with relatives. To the father who wants to come and see his own son, for example, the answer will be, 'There is neither affection according to the flesh nor authority according to the flesh in our vocation, but we are all brothers, in accordance with the Saviour's saying, *you are all brothers* (Matt. 23:8).'[22]

For Theodore, as for Pachomius, charity remains at the centre of koinonia and gives it its deepest meaning: 'Let us choose the part of the vocation of the holy koinonia and mutual love with everyone.'[23] 'The precept "Love your neighbour as yourself" surpasses all the commandments, and we owe it to the Lord to fulfil it.'[24] 'We see as well the fervour of the love of each of us by the calm speech, the manner in which each justifies his neighbour more than himself.'[25] 'Let us guard the grace fallen to our lot far beyond the desert of our works. Let us keep the law, each being a subject of edification to his neighbour and a way [for him] to enter into the joy of the kingdom of heaven.'[26]

For Theodore there is no more heinous crime than to become a cause of suffering or scandal to a brother; it is a far more serious offence than impurity. The following sentence applies to brothers who offend in this way: 'They have tried to turn back, giving scandal to those who had come to them and to those who through them had come near to God.'[27] 'Our duty is to confirm the brethren who have loved the institutions of Koinonia with all their heart.' Hence the insistent recommendation to all: 'Let us keep it in mind to stir up one another, so that we may bring forth all our fruits into things pleasing to God.'[28]

Theodore found himself succeeding Pachomius at a moment when the community was torn by schisms and divisions, and he invited them to return to the roots of their vocation. Returning to the roots meant above all returning to brotherly love. Hence the urgent prayer to God that he may 'cause each one of us to go back to the beginnings of his vocation, that is, to the expectation of the promises of God made to our father Apa, to him whose commandments we have promised [to observe], walking truly in fulfilment of the law, that is to say, *being all of one heart, toiling for one another, practising brotherly love, compassion and humility...*'[29]

Love for God's law and holy koinonia are in fact a duty for monks, obliging them to live the life of heaven here on earth. So when people see their good works, they can praise God and recognize the monks as authentic disciples of Christ who, in accordance with their vocation, truly love one another. A vocation to holy koinonia is a destiny indissolubly tied to 'mutual love with everyone'.[30] Theodore was deeply convinced that this commandment of love was both obligatory and important: '[The] commandments "Love your neighbour as yourself" and "Hold your tongue" (Jas. 1:26; 1 Pet. 3:10) will march with honour at the head of your people until [your people] reach the kingdom of God, monks as well as seculars.'[31]

The doctrinal teaching of Horsiesios enriched the understanding of community with new references to Scripture. He was the first to make an explicit connection between the experience of the Pachomian community and the model of the Jerusalem community, as he wrote in his *Testament*:

> The Apostle taught us that our community, the communion by which we are joined to one another, springs from God ... We read the same thing in the Acts of the Apostles: *For the multitude of believers had one heart and soul, and no one called anything his own. They held everything in common* ... The psalmist is in agreement with these words when he says, *Behold, how good and how delightful it is for brothers to live together*. And let us who live together in the Koinonia, and who are united to one another in mutual charity, so apply ourselves that, just as we deserved fellowship with the holy fathers in this life, we may also be their companions in the life to come.[32]

Horsiesios also taught that the modern expression of this model of the first Christians is an everyday communion which permeates actual experience. The koinonia of charity is lived simply in the ordinary circumstances of everyday life, imbuing everything with itself. We read in the *Regulations*: 'And every other duty which we must perform in conformity with the law of the holy *Koinonia*, let us all perform with the prudence of piety, as one man, as it is written: *All who believed formed but one heart and one soul* (Acts 4:32); so that God may bless our bread, that we may eat it with joy and pleasure in the Holy Spirit ...'[33]

The concept of community was further enriched by being seen as the place where people gather together in the name of the Lord, and therefore the place where the Lord himself is present. We continually read in the *Regulations*: 'Let us fear mightily lest we be in any way a scandal in the place where *two or three are assembled in the name* of Jesus, for he is with them and in their midst, as he has said (cf. Matt. 18:20).'[34] This shows a deep grasp of the theological value and mystical meaning of a community appointed by the Lord himself present in the midst of monks united in his name.

The precept of mutual love is always on the horizon: 'Our Lord and Saviour gave his apostles this precept, *I give you a new commandment: Love one another, as I have loved you. By this you shall truly be known as my disciples.* We should, therefore, love one another and show that we are truly the servants of our Lord Jesus Christ and sons of Pachomius and disciples of the *Koinonia.*'[35] This is a love which, picking up again the teaching of Pachomius, knows no distinction of persons: 'I will say it again and again and will repeat it: Take care not to love some and hate others, to sustain this one and to neglect that one ...'[36]

Like Theodore, Horsiesios, reproves those in community have lost this attitude of practical and attentive love for their brethren:

'There are some who consider themselves as living by God's law, and say to themselves, 'What have I to do with other people? I seek to serve God and fulfil his commandments. What others do does not concern me.'[37] Instead, Horsiesios knows and teaches that 'when we have rendered the account of our life, we shall also have to render an account for the others, those who were entrusted to us.' This, he continues, is not just a matter for superiors; rather, it is the task of 'each brother in the community, because all of them must bear one another's burdens in order to fulfil the law of Christ (Gal. 6:2)'. And after recalling Paul's words to Timothy, 'Guard what has been entrusted to you', he concludes: 'After we have rendered an account of our own life, we shall likewise render an account for those who were entrusted to us.'[38] Thus Horsiesios completely excludes any individual search for salvation.

Good works and koinonia are the sacrifice that pleases God. Being of one heart and mind like the believers of the first community at Jerusalem in fact demands absolute submission to the brethren, a 'not-belonging' to oneself. It has been well written that in the Pachomian koinonia there was no room

for seeking a personal perfection or pursuing one's own plan of sanctity. The frequency and, if you like, the severity with which the *Precepts* root out all individualism and seeking for privilege, even in their most everyday and mundane expressions - from demands for food to regarding anything whatsoever as personal property - must be read from this point of view. Henceforth the monk not only has nothing of his own but no longer belongs to himself because he has freely handed over his life to his brothers. From the start, everything is offered and given.[39]

Some Fundamental Principles Take Shape

After this survey of the birth of the Pachomian community and the way it was understood, we can now conclude that, in spite of a certain rigidity in its laws which was typical of this beginning of cenobitic life, koinonia was a state inspired by and lived under the law of love, or rather the law of mutual love.

The models and scriptural references which would from now on illuminate the monastic and religious community were clearly identified: Psalm 133, the Johannine texts on mutual love and the unity of believers, the summaries in Acts, the Pauline passages on charity.

The Pachomian community retained strong ascetic elements inherited from eremitism; nevertheless, a new sensitivity had taken over. 'To the ascetic practices of the anchorites - long prayers, fasts, a sometimes bizarre asceticism - Pachomius opposed the way of service, a privileged way for the little and weak.'[40] As he taught, the least of the brethren in the cenobium 'do not give themselves to great exercises and an exaggerated asceticism, but behave simply, in obedience and the spirit of service, purity and observance of the rules: in the eyes of the hermits, they do not live a perfect life and are considered very inferior.' On the contrary, however, 'they are greatly superior to the hermits, because they act in that spirit of service in which the Apostle walked, as it is written: "For love of the Spirit, serve one another in a spirit of kindness and unfailing forbearance".'[41]

Asceticism in the koinonia expressed itself principally in renunciation for the sake of the community, thus enabling it to become a unity in obedience, compassion, help, edification, care and vigilance towards each other. Even radical poverty was for the sake of sharing possessions.

Community had found its theological foundations: the supernatural origin of koinonia, as a result of the divine call, and thus its nature as gift and charism; charity as the basis of koinonia; and the ecclesial dimension which allowed the use of the same images for both koinonia and the Church: body, vine, flock, family of God, people of God...

The Pachomians thus opened the way for a fertile doctrinal reflection, based on an intense experience of life, which would allow the monastic community to set out on its way in the Church, in a rich multiplicity of expressions.

NOTES

1. Pachomius was born at Esneth in the Upper Thebaid in 288. Forcibly enrolled in Maximian's army in 312, he was discharged after Constantine's victory. He probably received baptism during the Easter night of 313. Three years later he embraced the monastic life under the direction of Palamon. After seven years, he moved to Tabennisi in Upper Egypt, where he was joined by his older brother John. Together they built accommodation for other monks. After an initial failure in community life, new disciples gathered round Pachomius. The flow increased steadily, but Pachomius' wisdom and organizing abilities enabled him to cope with the ever-increasing numbers of disciples. He built a second monastery in the desert nearby at a place called Phbow and further foundations followed. Soon a monastery for women came into being in the shadow of the monastery for men. In fact, when his sister Mary visited him Pachomius invited her to imitate his way of life. Mary established herself near him and founded a cenobium for women which adopted the Rule for monks. We know of at least one other monastery for women in the Pachomian sphere of influence. In his *Lausiac History* Palladius writes of the Pachomians: 'They also have a monastery of about four hundred women which observes the same rules and follows the same pattern of life, except for the goatskin [garments].' Eventually the federation consisted of nine monasteries of men and two of women. Pachomius died at Phbow on 9 May 346. A complete English translation of the writings of Pachomius and his disciples Theodore and Horsiesios, with introduction and copious notes, can be found in Armand Veilleux, *Pachomian Koinonia*, 3 vols. (Cistercian Studies CS45-47, Kalamazoo: 198-82). References below are to this translation.
2. Cf. J. M. Lozano, 'La comunità pacomiana dalla comunione all'istituzione', *Claretianum* 15 (1975), pp. 237-67. For a careful analysis of the different versions of the call of Pachomius, cf. H. van Cranenburgh, 'Étude comparative des récits anciens de la vocation de Saint Pachôme', *Revue Bénédictine* 82 (1972), pp. 280-308.
3. *Second Instruction* 1 (*Pachomian Koinonia* vol. 3, p. 91).
4. Regulations 51 (vol. 2, p. 216).
5. *Bohairic Life (Vita Copta)* (vol. 1, p. 27)
6. L. Cremaschi, *Pacomio e i suoi discepoli* (Bose: Edizioni Qiqajon, 1988), p. 15. For an introduction to the communal dimension of Pachomius' spirituality, cf. H. Bacht, 'Pachôme et ses disciples', in *Théologie de la vie monastique*,

p. 69; *idem.*, 'Monachesimo e Chiesa. Studio sulla spiritualità di s. Pacomio' in J. Daniélou and H. Vorgrimmler, eds, *Sentire Ecclesiam* ... (Rome: 1964) pp. 193-224; P. Desaille, *L'esprit du monachisme pachômien* (Bellefontaine: 1968); E. Bianchi, 'La vita di comunione in S. Pacomio e i suoi discepoli', *Parola Spirito e Vita* 11 (1985), pp. 265-78. A recent study in English is Philip Rousseau, *Pachomius: The Making of a Community in Fourth-century Egypt* (Berkeley: University of California Press, 1985).

7. *Instruction* 36-7 (vol. 3, p. 29).
8. *Instruction* 8 (vol. 3, p. 14).
9. Looking at the Pachomian community, the features which immediately stand out are the efficient organization, the strong hierarchical structure, a certain rigidity and a sustained asceticism. We cannot trace here the complex development of either the legislation or the Pachomian institution in itself. We simply note that in the transition from Pachomius to Theodore, the community seems to have been gradually institutionalized. The successors of Pachomius seem in fact to have been preoccupied with the discipline and organization of a group which had become a people. The members of the community had multiplied within a few decades. When the legislation was codified, between 1200 and 1600 monks lived in each monastery. Each monastery was a true and proper village.
10. *Bohairic Life* (vol. 1, p. 32).
11. 'In the Pachomian tradition ... the term "monk" is carefully avoided and the technical term used to designate a Pachomian is "brother" ' (Lozano, 'La comunità pachomiana', p. 250). The centrality of community and its superiority with respect to eremitism emerge in the teachings of the Coptic lives. Cf. *Bohairic Life* (vol. 1, pp. 147ff.).
12. *Precepts and Judgements* Proemium (vol. 2, p. 175).
13. *Instruction* 8 (vol. 3, p. 14).
14. *Instruction* 36-7 (vol. 3, p. 29f.).
15. *Instruction* 41 (vol. 3, p. 32).
16. *Bohairic Life* 42 (vol. 1, p. 66).
17. *Instruction* 14 (vol. 3, p. 17).
18. *Bohairic Life* (vol. 1, p. 143).
19. *Third Sahidic Life,* quoted in L. Cremaschi, op. cit. p. 31).
20. *Second Instruction* 1 (vol. 3, p. 91).
21. *Third Instruction* 27 (vol. 3, p. 109).
22. *Third Instruction* 17 (vol. 3, p. 103).
23. *Third Instruction* 36 (vol. 3, p. 114).
24. *Theodore, Fragments* 4 (vol. 3, p. 134).
25. *Third Instruction* 26 (vol. 3, p. 108).
26. *Third Instruction* 4 (vol. 3, p. 94).
27. *Third Instruction* 20 (vol. 3, p. 105).
28. *Third Instruction* 41 (vol. 3, p. 116).
29. *Third Instruction* 23 (vol. 3, p. 107).
30. *Third Instruction* 36 (vol. 3, p. 114).
31. *Fragments* 4 (vol. 3, p. 134).

32. Horsiesios, *Testament* 50 (vol. 3, pp. 208f.).
33. *Regulations* 51 (vol. 2, p. 216).
34. *Regulations* 2 (vol. 2, p. 197).
35. Horsiesios, *Testament* 23 (vol. 3, p. 188).
36. Ibid. 16 (p. 181).
37. Ibid. 8 (p. 175).
38. Ibid. 11 (p. 178).
39. L. Cremaschi, op. cit., pp. 31f.
40. Ibid., p. 32.
41. *Bohairic Life* (vol. 1, p. 149).

3 The Excellence of the Common Life
The evangelical brotherhood of Basil

The most significant community after the Pachomian koinonia was undoubtedly the Basilian brotherhood. This community differed in many respects from the Pachomian community. To begin with, its geographical position was different: no longer in the desert but close to the city. The Basilian community, unlike the Pachomian, was not protected by an enclosure wall. It was no longer a large village but a small community. Its superior was regarded not as the head of the community so much as its attentive, watchful, discreet and caring 'eye'. The new community was in fact governed by a system of fraternal interpersonal relationships rather than a complex Pachomian system of rules. It did not arise from common submission to a rule or a charismatic father. Instead, 'horizontal' relationships predominated among its members, based on love, edification and correction. For this reason the community was called a 'brotherhood' and its members 'brothers'.[1]

Besides being the creator of an original form of community, Basil, who unlike Pachomius was an educated person, was to be above all the *theologian* of the monastic life.[2]

The Beginning of Monastic Experience: Solitude and Ascesis

Like Pachomius, Basil's monastic outlook and the identity of the community he brought into being were profoundly affected by his own experiences.

A first decisive factor was his conversion to the Gospel, which would stamp a deeply evangelical character on his community. He himself relates the 'awakening' which took place in him:

> I wasted much time in the service of vanity and spent all my youth in useless labours, since I consecrated it to the acquisition of the doctrines of a wisdom which God had condemned as folly (cf. 1

Cor. 1:20). Suddenly, one day, as if coming out of a deep sleep I raised my eyes to the wonderful light of gospel truth, I realized the futility of the wisdom of the princes of this world who are engrossed in futility (cf. 1 Cor. 2:6). I mourned bitterly over my wretched life and I prayed that a guide might be granted me who would direct me to the principles of sound religion.[3]

His 'pilgrimage' to the 'sources' of monasticism - Egypt, Palestine, Syria, Mesopotamia - with the aim of meeting the most famous ascetics, was another determining factor in Basil's experience. He was attracted by the ascetic elements which would have such a large place, especially in the first phase, in his own monastic experience. Recalling his meetings with the monks, he wrote:

> I admired the strictness of their lives, their firmness in toil; I was amazed by their application to prayer, by the way they mastered sleep and did not give in to any natural need. They always kept their mental feelings elevated and free, through hunger and thirst, cold and nakedness, without giving in to the body or consenting to waste their attention on it. As if they were living in an alien body, they showed by their actions what it means to live as a pilgrim here below and to be citizens of heaven. All this attracted my admiration, and I esteemed the life of these men as blessed since they showed by their actions that they carried in their bodies the death of Jesus. And I prayed as much as I could to obtain the grace of imitating them.[4]

On his return from pilgrimage, Basil distributed his goods to the poor and retired into solitude on the Iris. At the beginning, his monastic ideal did not include community life. Struck by precisely those ascetic elements that inspired eremitism, he abandoned everything in the belief that solitude and ascesis would bring him to God.[5] He had a single ideal: 'total separation from the world', as he wrote to his friend Gregory from his own place of retreat - a place he wanted to be 'free from contact with people' so that the continuity of his ascesis would not be 'interrupted by any outsiders'. He thought that this was the only way to 'follow in the footsteps of him who was our guide to salvation - as it is written: "If anyone would come after me, let him deny himself, take up his cross and follow me".'[6] We shall see what a great change took place in Basil as he moved from the eulogy of the solitary life described in this letter to explaining the reasons why life in community is superior to life in solitude.

However, it is these ascetic elements which will give its distinctive character to what Basil considered his true rule, the *Moralia*. This is a collection of biblical texts (about 1500 verses from the New Testament) arranged according to theme. It is the fruit of his 'journey' to the sources of faith: the New Testament which, as we have seen, began his conversion. At the same time it was also the fruit of his journey to the sources of monasticism. It is a book composed entirely of sentences from Scripture lined up one after another according to a criterion of reading derived from the ascetic milieu. Basil in fact bases the whole thing on the concept of penitence. Detachment from secular tasks and from the family follow, and in third place are rules on the two commandments of love of God and neighbour.

The work appears quite modest: at first sight, it is merely an anthology of biblical texts. However, Basil always considered it his fundamental work, precisely because it provided him with the evangelical inspiration for all his ministry and literary activity. It was the only one he called a 'rule'.[7] There are thus two features which stand out in the young Basil: the centrality of evangelical inspiration; and renunciation as the basis of life according to the Gospel.

The Discovery of the Precept of Charity

Basil's next work, the *Asceticon*, resulted from dialogue with his disciples. In it we can discern a new arrangement: the point of departure for thinking about the monastic life is now different. Basil reads Scripture afresh, no longer beginning with penitence and detachment but with the two greatest commandments. As has been rightly noted, if in the *Moralia* 'the starting point is still the invitation to repentance', 'in the *Asceticon* this theme is reduced to the corollary of the love of God'.[8]

The transition was due to Basil's personal experience and that of the community which had formed around him. His continual return to the primary source, the Gospel, led him to understand that the heart of the evangelical life does not lie in renunciation but in the twofold commandment of charity. This, therefore, must be the foundation of the monastic life and community. Even if Christ began, according to the Synoptics, by preaching repentance, this was really no more than preparation. When the Lord wanted to sum up the essentials of the law and the prophets, he did so by recalling the two commandments.

The structure of the *Asceticon* is thus the opposite of the *Moralia*. It deals initially with the love of God, then with charity towards the neighbour (Questions 1-3). Only afterwards, at the eighth question, does it confront the theme of renunciation as a consequence of the love of God. Thus it was that in the Basilian community the twofold commandment gradually acquired its central position.

In his reply to Question 3, Basil explains how the two commandments of love harmonize with each other: love of God demands love of neighbour and through love of neighbour we come to love of God. Love of neighbour is second to the commandment to love God, but must be regarded as its complement and dependent upon it. 'It is therefore by means of the first commandment that the second is realized as well and, by means of the second, one goes back again to the first. He who loves the Lord consequently loves his neighbour as well ... In turn, then, he who loves his neighbour fulfils the love of God, since God receives this goodwill as directed towards himself.'[9]

It is all about one love. In fact, love of God and love of neighbour exhibit the same characteristics which speak of an identical nature. Both are the gift and fruit of the Spirit[10], the distinctive mark of the Christian.[11] The one love is mother of the commandments[12], the first and greatest good,[13] a combination which summarizes the law.[14] Moreover, Basil defines love of neighbour as 'the first and greatest commandment, the same as is said about love of God'.[15]

In his reflection, Basil develops a whole series of philosophical considerations which explain man's 'agape dimension'. The first philosophical premise, which explains humanity's innate propensity to fulfil the first commandment, is that human beings are by nature attracted to good and therefore to God. There is in fact a 'natural propensity', an 'innate desire', a 'loving desire for God'. He explains how 'the love of God cannot be taught ... It is not possible to learn from outside the loving desire for God.' The Lord himself has put into human nature, 'as a seed', as 'powers', the capacity to love.[16] Still in Question 3, we read that 'As then the Lord himself has given the seeds in advance, obviously he also looks for the fruits, saying: "I give you a new commandment, that you love one another".'[17] Nevertheless, this capacity to love, inherent in human nature, can only be awakened by the action of the Spirit, through whom nature and grace interpenetrate each other.[18]

The second philosophical premise, which enables human beings to welcome the second commandment, is borrowed from Aristotle and asserts that humanity is made to live in society. The law of human sociability lies at the root of the natural love of people for people. Humanity appears as being in relationship, made for community. Basil in fact discovered that there are two presuppositions about natural love for the neighbour: having a sociable nature inclined towards living together in community, together with the faculty to communicate our own thinking and love; and having a need for one another which obliges us to communicate between ourselves. Basil explains:

As we have been commanded to love our neighbour as ourselves, let us seek to understand whether we have also received from God the power to fulfil this commandment. Who, therefore, does not know that man is a tame and sociable animal, not solitary and savage? Nothing, in fact, is as proper to our nature as communicating with one another, needing one another, and loving those of our race.'[19]

There is, therefore, an element of contingency which drives us to mutual relationships: human beings are not self-sufficient, they need others. And there is a yet deeper aspect, connected with humanity's very nature: their very being is open to dialogue and communion. People can therefore realize themselves only to the extent that they open themselves to others, where openness to others must be understood precisely as love.

The discovery of the philosophical roots of humanity's sociability came later, however, as confirmation of Basil's deduction made directly from Scripture and his experience of life. In effect, although love of the brethren is based on human sociability, it transcends it and finds its most profound motivation on a theological plane. Evangelical fraternal charity has many motivations. We need to love our neighbour because the Lord considers and rewards the good done to our neighbour as done to himself; in order to obey the Lord; to please the Lord; to imitate the charity of God the Father and Jesus; to make ourselves like Christ by loving one another as Jesus loves us.

The Excellence of the Common Life

The progressive discovery of the centrality of love both determined the evolution of the Basilian community and was at the same time the fruit of its experience. The love of God would actually seem to require radical renunciation of a world that scorned the precepts of the Gospel, and it was in this direction that Basil took his first steps. Nevertheless, brotherly love does not permit separation from the brethren. Hence the necessity for a community life which expressed itself in the creation of brotherhood.[20]

The community was born out of the evangelical command of brotherly love. In Question 7, which works out a comparison between eremitism and cenobitism, Basil develops the arguments that form the basis of his community. In view of the richness of the themes involved and the vast influence this text was to have on the future of the religious community, it will be appropriate to stop and read at least the main points of Basil's reply to those who wondered whether it was better to live alone or 'to live together with like-minded brethren'. Basil explained:

> First of all, none of us is self-sufficient, not even for our bodily needs ... In the same way, in the solitary life ... we cannot obtain what we need, because God the creator has decreed that we must be useful to each other ... But apart from this, on the grounds of the love of Christ as well, it is not right that everyone should be occupied only with their own concerns. It is said: Love does not seek its own ... Moreover, in such a separation it will not be easy for a man to know his own sins, because he will have no one to accuse or correct him ... Again, it is easier to keep a greater number of the commandments when many have gathered together, whereas this does not happen for the man on his own, because while he is carrying out one he is inevitably prevented from performing the others.
>
> All of us who are engaged in the one hope of our calling, are one body with Christ as its head, and we are all members one of another: if then we fail to be joined harmoniously in the unity of a single body in the Holy Spirit, but individually choose isolation ... how shall we, divided and separate, be able to maintain mutual relationships and service of the members or submission to our head, who is Christ? It will not be possible either to rejoice with those who are exalted or suffer with those who suffer, if we live

separately, unable to understand in a normal way what is happening to our neighbour.

Moreover, since no-one is able to receive all the spiritual gifts... in community life each person's particular gift becomes common to all those who live with him ... Of necessity, therefore, in community life the energy of the Spirit in one person passes to everyone at the same time. So someone who lives for himself may perhaps have a spiritual gift, but he renders it useless by leaving it unused... and all of you who have read the Gospel will know how dangerous that is. On the contrary, someone who shares his life with others not only enjoys his own gift, but multiplies it by sharing it and enjoys the fruit of the gifts of others as if it were his own ...

To be woken up by someone vigilant offers the best guarantee of safety from the external snares of the Enemy, because then one will not doze off into that sleep which leads to death ... It is much easier for the sinner to renounce sin when he has to blush in the face of unanimous condemnation ...

The solitary life, on the other hand, is full of dangers ... The first and greatest is self-complacency ... [The solitary] does not know his own defects, nor does he notice his progress in good works, because he has eliminated the very means of fulfilling the commandments. How, in fact, can he show humility when he has no one to surpass in humility? How can he show depths of compassion if he is cut off from communion with others? And how can he exercise patience if there is no one to oppose his will? ... Whose feet will he wash? Who will you care for? How will you find fulfilment in the solitary life of that goodness and sweetness that comes from brethren living together, which the Holy Spirit compares to the ointment exhaling fragrance from the head of the High Priest?

Living together as brethren is thus an arena for struggle, a sure road to progress, and a continual practice of and meditation on the Lord's commands. And its aim is the glory of God, according to the commandment of our Lord Jesus Christ, who said: 'Let your light so shine before men, that they may see your good works and glorify your Father who is in heaven.'[21]

The wealth of the themes set out in such a few densely-written pages is obvious. To list just the main ones:

– It is not possible to live in self-sufficiency. The philosophical motivation for human sociability reappears.

– Christian charity does not seek its own interest but that of others. Community makes it possible to avoid the risk of each person living for himself.

– Being one body in the unity of the Church is translated into a communal way of life, as a natural expression of the ecclesial community. The Pauline analogy of the body and its members is carried to its maximum extent on both the theological and practical levels.

– Community life allows for fraternal correction.

-- Community makes possible the sharing of personal gifts and the making use of the gifts of others, as an immediate consequence of the circulation of the *energeia* of the Holy Spirit and trinitarian life which is realized in the setting of a community.

– The common life makes possible the concrete exercise of mutual charity. Without brothers to love, it is impossible to attain the perfection which expresses itself in the fullness of charity.

– The community seems to be the place for mutual evangelization, where the practice of the commandments becomes easier and the risk of neglecting some commandments is avoided.

– Community guards against the dangers which come from lack of landmarks in one's own spiritual way, with the attendant possibility of self-deception and illusion.

– Community keeps eschatological vigilance awake.

– Community is able to provide a witness so that people glorify God.

– Community is organized to the glory of God.

Finally, we can say that 'the preference which Basil gives to the cenobitic type of monastic life is based substantially on the presupposition that in it one can live more fully and constantly the ideal of Christian *charitas*, and on the conviction that the cenobium (not the individual monk) is endowed with the fullness of the gifts of the Holy Spirit'.[22]

Question 7 ends with its gaze turned to the model of community: the first Christians in Jerusalem. The life of the community 'keeps alive the distinctive characteristics of the saints of whom Acts speaks and of whom it is written: "All who believed were together and had all things in common"; and again: "The company of those who believed were of one heart and soul and no one said that any of the things which he possessed was his own, but they had everything in common".'[23]

This is a theme dear to Basil. 'Let us take the example of the three thousand (cf. Acts 2:41),' he writes elsewhere, 'let us imitate the first Christian community! They held everything in common: life, soul, concord, table, indivisible brotherhood, the unfeigned love which makes one body out of many bodies, harmonizing different souls in a single thought.'[24]

An Open Community

With its gaze turned on the first community at Jerusalem, the Basilian community presents a distinctive dimension of ecclesiality.[25] The way of life begun by Basil was not intended to be of itself a 'monastic' ideal. He had intended to create a way of life which was simply 'Christian', even if later, inevitably, it assumed typically monastic forms, creating a particular evangelical community in the Church. The main objective was to achieve the most perfect Christian brotherhood possible, according to the gospel models. Basil's greatest friend, Gregory of Nazianzus, evaluating his work when he delivered his funeral oration, considered the Basilian brotherhood an original synthesis of Christian life open to the world and monastic practice.[26]

Dom Jean Gribomont, one of the greatest authorities on Basil, notes that the roots of his monasticism are to be found not in Egypt, like those of Pachomius, but in Syria. Consequently, unlike Pachomius, Basil 'does not conceive monastic brotherhood as a particular institution existing within the Church, an addition to the schemes foreseen by the New Testament, based on observance of the counsels, but simply as the most perfect possible realization of Christian brotherhood'. In his eyes, the life of the monastic community is simply a 'favourable condition for the attainment of the Christian ideal', with nothing specific to distinguish it from the morality of the Gospel. 'Christians who live in the same evangelical spirit outside the community are considered brothers in the fullest sense. And Basil energetically rejects the custom of using a specifically monastic title; his friends and disciples are simply called "Christians", who have chosen to "live devoutly" ...'[27]

The Basilian communities wanted to be 'the very cells of the Church which rediscover the vigour of gospel discipline'[28], almost a leaven within the wider ecclesial community to enable it to conform increasingly to the purity of its origins. They intended to live a typical

Christian life, with the aim of restoring to the Church its primitive aspect.

The community, finally, wanted to be the Church. For this reason the relationship between this community and the wider ecclesial community was translated into actual structures for living which, for example, brought the community close to the bishop's city and entrusted it with the task of welfare and charity. Love of neighbour extended beyond the community of brethren and poured itself out on all people through the preaching of the Word and the service of charity to the poor. We catch a glimpse of new ways for the monasticism of the future, which was destined to open itself increasingly to a dimension of ministry and evangelism.

NOTES

1. With the passing of the years, even in the Basilian community there was a strengthening of the norms regarding obedience to the superior and a progressive institutionalization of community life.

2. Basil was born at Caesarea in Cappadocia in 330 into a deeply Christian family. His mother, paternal grandmother, sister and two brothers are venerated as saints. His maternal grandfather had died a martyr. He received his classical training at Caesarea, then at Constantinople and Athens. On his return to his own country Basil was baptized in 357. After making a journey through the monastic East, he settled near Neocaesarea, in the Pontus on the banks of the River Iris, where he began a kind of monastic experiment, which was also to be shared by women. Small communities of women grew up around him, about which, however, we know very little. There are only occasional references in the Little and Great *Asceticon* to the experience of women, for example, a question put to him by a sister about her wool work, one of the main employments of the nuns. Even if the account is secondary, it is of considerable interest to note that Basil, in composing his Rule, was surrounded by a mixed group and also questioned by women. They therefore played an active part in the development of the Basilian 'brotherhood'. In 370 Basil was appointed Bishop of Caesarea. He died on 1 January 379. There is a good English translation of his monastic writings (with introduction and notes) by W. K. L. Clarke, *The Ascetic Works of St Basil* (London: 1925). The notes below refer to this edition, although the translations are those of the author/translator of this present work.

3. Letter 223, 2 in Roy J. Deferrari, *Saint Basil: The Letters, with an English Translation* (4 vols, Loeb Classical Library, London: 1926), vol. 3, pp. 291ff. References to *Letters* in the notes below are to this work.

4. Ibid., pp. 293-5.
5. A further element which will enable us to understand the ascetic components of the community founded by Basil is the influence exercised by Eustathius of Sebaste on his monastic formation and, previously, on other members of his family. Even if later Basil was to distance himself from Eustathius' doctrinal deviations, he would always remember how much he was indebted to him (*Letters* 223).
6. Cf. *Letters* 2, vol. 1, p. 9.
7. Scripture is regarded as the foundation of the monastic life, the one 'rule' for both the Christian and the monastic life. Unlike later tradition, Basil never called either the Little or the Great *Asceticon* a 'Rule'.
8. M. Augé, 'La fraternità evangelica di Basilio', in *Storia della vita religiosa* (Brescia: 1988), p. 67.
9. *Question 3*, Clarke p. 158.
10. *Letters* 65, vol. 2, p. 25; *Letters* 172, vol. 2, p. 447; *Letters* 133, vol. 2, p. 303.
11. *Question 3*, p. 157.
12. *Hom. dicta tempore famis*, 8 (PG 31, 324B).
13. *Letters* 9, vol. 1, p. 93.
14. *Letters* 204, vol. 3, p. 155; *Letters* 237.
15. *Letters* 204, vol. 3, p. 155. Cf. the analysis of Basil's texts in G. M. Cossù, *La dottrina della carità nel pensiero di San Basilio* (Cuglieri: Magno, n.d.), pp. 29-30.
16. *Question 2*, pp. 153-4.
17. Ibid., p. 157.
18. Cf. *Question 2*, p. 153.
19. *Question 3*, p. 157.
20. Cf. A. Bona, 'L'idea di "vita comunitaria" nelle opere ascetiche di Basilio', *Studia Patavina* 35 (1988), pp. 15-35.
21. *Question 7*, pp. 163-6.
22. Turbessi, *Regole monastiche*, p. 134.
23. *Question 7*, p. 166.
24. *Hom. dicta tempore famis*, 8 (PG 31, 325A-B).
25. Cf. P. Scazzoso, *Introduzione alla ecclesiologia di s. Basilio* (Milan: Vita e Pensiero, 1975).
26. Cf. J. Gribomont, 'Saint Basile', in *Théologie de la vie monastique*, p. 103.
27. Gribomont, *Basilio*, 1106-7.
28. Augé, 'La fraternità evangelica', p. 68.

4 The Centrality of Love
The trinitarian unity of the Augustinian community

Augustine, the 'doctor of charity', brings to the vision of religious community all his weight as a spiritual giant and the wealth of his profound theological inquiry, as well as his indefatigable work for the unity of the Church.[1] With him, the design of the monastic community integrates the values of the earlier experiments but at the same time transcends them in a new synthesis. Augustine surpasses the eremitic vision of Antony and the communal asceticism of Pachomius, as well as the moderate asceticism lived in common which Basil taught.

Charity, fraternal communion, and unity were to become the central, component and characteristic factors of Augustine's community. They no longer appeared simply as three elements, however important, among others. Rather, they constituted the very identity of the community, the point around which all the other aspects of the religious life harmonized and received their form. In its very first line, the Rule states the purpose of the monastery immediately and unequivocally: 'The essential reason for which you have come together is that you may live of one mind in the house and may have one soul and one heart in God [on the way to God].'[2]

Basil had begun his *Asceticon* with the twofold commandment of charity. Augustine puts unity at the beginning of his Rule, the unity for which the life of the first Christian community provided the model.

Attracted by the Sweet Melody: 'Brethren Living Together'

The beginning of the Rule provides a statement of Augustine's experience which is already complete. In fact, the history of the birth of his community confirms the motivation provided at the opening of the Rule.[3]

Augustine, like his disciples, was attracted by the image of the first Christians who had one heart and one soul amongst themselves. His first biographer wrote that 'he began to live with the servants of God according to the custom and rule in force at the time of the apostles'.[4] He himself, speaking of his own experience to his faithful flock, said:

> All, or nearly all, of you know by now that those of us who are here in what is called the bishop's house, try to imitate in our life, as far as we can, the model of those saints of whom, according to the book of the Acts of the Apostles, 'No one claimed as his own property anything which belonged to him. but everything was held in common amongst them' ... I began, then, to bring together brothers of good will who might wish to be my companions in poverty, who like me would have no possessions of their own, who would be disposed to imitate me ... We would all live on the common possessions. We would all share a large and very fertile land, God Himself. And that is how we live. Ever since we have been in community, no one has been allowed to possess anything of his own..[5]

Augustine, like his companions, seemed to be spellbound by the 'sweet sound' of Psalm 133 (132): 'Behold, how good and pleasant it is when brothers dwell in unity!' He went on to explain to his flock:

> These words of the Psalter, this sweet harmony, this melody as delightful to sing as to turn over in the mind, have effectively given birth to monasteries. This is the harmony which aroused those brothers who fostered the desire to live in unity. This verse was like a trumpet to them: it rang throughout the world and behold, people previously scattered were reunited. The divine cry, the cry of the Holy Spirit, the cry of prophecy, not heard in Judea, was heard throughout the world.

It was, of course, the first Christians of Jerusalem on whom the Spirit came down at Pentecost and who, continues Augustine, 'began the life of unity'. 'They were therefore the first to listen to the words "Behold how good and joyful it is for brothers to dwell in unity!" They were the first to listen to them, but they did not remain alone. In fact, this love and brotherly unity did not just extend to them: both the joyful fruit of charity and the vow made to God also spread among those who came after them.'[6] Thus he declares, once again, his wish to place himself in continuity with the experience of the primitive Church: 'The model to which we refer and the practice we already achieve, with the help of God, are indicated in the passages from the Acts of the Apostles.'(7) The basic ideas of the Rule would all be built around the fundamental idea of the Jerusalem community.

The emphasis had decisively shifted from asceticism, so strongly present in Augustine's earlier experiments, to life in community, which finds, in the practice of mutual love, the way to achieve its proper objective: unity among the brethren and fullness of life in God. Mutual love is the result of the one heart and one soul which characterize the life of the members of the community: 'Through the fire of love, they are one heart and one soul.'[8]

Mutual love and the common life are expressed primarily in the sharing of possessions, as in the first community in Jerusalem. The exhortation to be one heart and one soul is followed immediately in the Rule by the exhortation to poverty and the sharing of possessions as the first expression and realization of mutual love. Unity is expressed and tested in the sharing of material possessions, which makes possible the sharing of values and each person's interior riches. Poverty is therefore simultaneously both renunciation and sharing. Commenting again on Psalm 132(133) and applying it to the life experience of his own community, Augustine writes: 'Whoever intends to prepare a dwelling for the Lord must rejoice not in what is private but in what is shared. That is what these people did with their private possessions. They shared them.'[9] Without this sharing, unity is shattered.

Augustine's new approach is already clear.

Compared to other earlier monastic institutions, the shape of St Augustine's ideal has a clearly independent character. The Saint sought to establish a monastery entirely founded on the common life through the union of minds and hearts in God and permeated with the primitive spirit of Christian faith. The simple gathering together of monks for mutual edification was transformed into an authentic community in God by means of the essence of the monastic life itself. To be a community of love and so to achieve the highest ideal of life is the central point of the Augustinian monastic heritage. St Augustine's foundation ... was simply a community which, holding everything in common and united interiorly by a brotherhood of spiritual love, formed a little church of chosen members, full of God's vitality. The enterprise was the work of charity;

it was not based on the simple love which is natural goodwill, but on the unity which has its immediate roots in God. God is the centre and Christ the soul of the community.[10]

He set the same ideal of unity before the nuns. When he thinks of their monastery, he wants to see it always consistent with its purpose. The nuns have in fact received the grace 'not only to renounce earthly nuptials, but to prefer living perfectly at one in the community of God's house, in order to be entirely one heart and one soul on the way to God.'[11] Augustine did not regard the community of women as in any way different to that of the men. He gave the same Rule, written for men, to the community presided over by his own sister.

Alluding to the rebellion which broke out in the nuns' monastery when there was a change of superior, Augustine deplored the discords and rivalries in the community, exhorting them firmly 'not to fall back into quarrels, jealousies, antipathies, discords, backbiting, rebellion and murmuring'. So grave is disunity that the punishment for those who provoke it must be equally grave: 'If those who have caused the trouble do so again, without correcting themselves, they will be condemned, whoever they are.'[12]

The Nature of Community: Love and Unity

In Augustine's thought, charity and community are interdependent: charity leads to unity, unity preserves and perfects charity. Unity and charity therefore stand at the beginning and the end of community. 'Charity produces agreement, agreement generates unity, unity maintains charity, charity leads to glory': Augustine's expression is both terse and to the point.[13]

> The charity that creates brotherly concord finds practical expression in life together, the basis of unity of thought and affection ... It is this which creates mutual and brotherly concord, which brings Christ into the midst of the community and enables everyone to communicate with him ... This charity leads to full unity in Christ and with Christ.[14]

Life together, as it is described in the Acts of the Apostles, to which Augustine constantly refers, is not based on natural sympathy or common interests. It springs precisely from charity, favours its maximum expression and leads back to it again. For this reason Augustine, in his reflection, habitually unites concord and unity with charity. His commentary on Psalm 132(133) which, as we have seen, is explicitly applied to the monastic life, is very clear on this point:

> Only those who perfectly possess the charity of Christ can live the common life. In fact, once they live together, those who do not possess the perfection of charity in Christ will inevitably hate each other, make trouble for themselves, behave turbulently, spread their own restlessness to others, and be concerned only with picking up gossip about others. They will be like an unbroken mule harnessed to a cart. Not only will it refuse to draw the cart but it will kick out and break the cart to pieces. If, on the other hand, a brother possesses the dew of Hermon ... he will be a peaceful person, calm, humble, able to tolerate [evil] and responding to murmuring with prayer.[15]

Murmurers are like a creaking cartwheel, so that 'these brethren only live in physical unity. Who, on the other hand, are the brothers who really live in unity? Those of whom it is written: "They had one heart and one soul in their quest for God."' The Lord's blessing descends among these 'brothers who live in unity'.[16]

On the basis of the connection between unity and the monastic life, Augustine offers his original explanation of the term 'monk': 'In reality,' he writes, ' monos means one, but not in the ordinary sense of the word. One can also be used of someone immersed in a crowd, or who finds himself in the company of many other people; but you cannot say of him that he is monos, that is, alone. Monos in fact means one alone.' He then draws the attention of the faithful to the members of his own community, viewed as people who relive the experience of the Jerusalem Christians: 'Now here are people who live in unity as a sign of being one man, people who truly have, as it is written, one soul and one heart. Their bodies are many, but not their souls; their bodies are many, but not their hearts. Of these it is justly affirmed that they are monos, that is, one only.'[17]

Unity of soul and heart is achieved in Deum, that is, by aiming for God. 'The essential motive for your coming together,' we read at the beginning of the Rule, 'is that you may live with one mind in the house and have one soul and one heart in God.'[18] They are together in order to go together to God, helping one another. In the Soliloquies Augustine had written: 'Why do you want those dear to you to live with you? So that we can work together in harmony, in the quest for what concerns our souls and God. In this way, he who arrives first will be able to lead the others without difficulty to the same result.'[19]

If charity leads to unity, unity leads to God. The purpose of the community's unity is to set out towards God. Entering the community signifies being caught up in a movement towards God, having the same goal. Thus unity acquires a religious significance and, at the same time, an eschatological perspective.

This journey towards God - which characterizes the community - is made together: it is mediated by the brethren. Love of God and love of neighbour are therefore inseparable and express a single love:

> Love cannot be divided ... If you love Christ's members, you love Christ, and when you love Christ, you love the Son of God; and so you love the Father as well ... You may say, I love only the Son. Yes, you say, I love God the Father and God the Son and that is enough ... You are wrong! If you love the Head you love the members too, and if you do not love the members you do not love the Head either.[20]

> Love of God is the first to be commanded, love of neighbour the first to be practised. When he sets out the two precepts of love, the Lord does not command you first to love your neighbour and then to love God. He puts God first, and then the neighbour. But since you do not yet see God, you will earn the sight of him by loving your neighbour. Loving your neighbour will make your eye pure so that you can see God.'[21]

Other people are indeed the surest and shortest way to attain to God: 'There is no more secure step for reaching the love of God than the charity of man for man.'[22]

At the same time, the soundest criterion for testing love of God remains love of the brethren. This is why, in chapter 5 of his Rule, Augustine makes care for others the test of the community's spiritual progress.

The love of God is the first to be commanded, but love of neighbour is the first to be practised. Love of neighbour in its turn flows from love of God, it is certain and concrete proof of love of God and must be referred to God:

In reality, he truly loves his friend who loves God in his friend, either because God is already in him, or so that he may be there. This is true love; loving in any other way is not love but hatred.[23]

Although there are two precepts on which depend all the Law and the Prophets, love of God and love of neighbour, it is not without reason that Scripture usually mentions one for both. Sometimes it speaks only of the love of God ... Sometimes Scripture mentions only love of neighbour ... And we meet many other passages in sacred Scripture in which only love of neighbour seems to be ordained for perfection, while nothing is said about love of God ... The real reason for this silence is that he who loves his neighbour must of necessity love, first of all, love itself. Now, God is love.[24]

Since God is love, one goes to him by loving, he is loved simply by loving. Augustine continues:

No one should say: 'I do not know what to love'. Let him love his brother and he will love love itself. In fact, he knows the love with which he loves better than the brother he loves. And that is why God is better known to him than his brother; much better known, because more present; better known because more interior; better known and so more certain. He embraces God who is love and embraces God with love. And what is he full of, this man full of love, if not of God? This brotherly love - the brotherly love that actually enables us to love one another - does not just come from God, but ... is God himself. Consequently, when we love our brother according to love [de dilectione], we are loving him according to God [de eo].[25]

This strong theological stamp does not prevent the life of brotherly communion from preserving the characteristic freshness of Augustinian friendship.

Conversation; shared laughter; the exchange of affectionate courtesies; shared readings; enjoyable books; common pastimes, sometimes frivolous, sometimes serious; occasional disagreements without rancour, like those a man has with himself; the more frequent agreements, seasoned by those same very rare dissensions; the fact that everyone is now master, now disciple of someone else; the impatient longing for those who are away and the festive welcomes for those who return. These and similar signs of hearts that love each other, expressed with the mouth, tongue, eyes, and in a thousand most agreeable actions, are the tinder, so to speak, behind the flame which fuses souls together and makes many one.[26]

The Rule is careful, however, to specify that love must always elevate this friendship: 'The love between you must not be carnal but spiritual.'[27] Every type of community relationship must therefore spring from theological charity.

This is possible if 'brother' is taken in its true theological sense: 'Live, all of you, in unity and concord, and honour God, whose temple you are, in one another', we read in the Rule.[28] Your brother becomes a kind of sacrament of meeting with God: the service of God - the monks are *servos Dei*, according to the title of the Rule - is realized in brotherly harmony. To honour God through a brother, the temple of God, is to make the whole community a temple of God. Augustine actually says of the first Christians that 'they had truly become temples of God, not simply as individuals but all together. They had become, in other words, a place sacred to the Lord; and you know that from all of them there had come one single place for the Lord.'[29] To show the importance of this statement, he declares that 'he who violates unity, desecrates the temple of God'.[30]

The house of God is not so much the material church as the brothers who live in unity: 'This church building is our house of prayer, but we ourselves are the true temple of God. Moreover, we also together form the house of the Lord, but only if we are united with one another in love.'[31] 'We are all a temple, both collectively and individually. He wants to dwell in all of us as a unity, and in each person.'[32]

As a temple of the Lord, the community offers its praise to God in the loving relationships between the brethren, even before it does so in common prayer, which only appears in the second chapter of the Rule. This is its primary form of worship. Commenting again on Psalm 132(133), Augustine actually writes: 'Among brethren who live in unity. That is where blessing has been ordained and that in fact is where the Lord is blessed by those who live in harmony.'[33] The essence of divine worship is love and love is the fulfilment of the law.

In its aiming for God, its communion and the mediation of the brethren, the community becomes one heart and one soul: there is true koinonia in Christ. 'Your soul,' writes Augustine again, in his terse and concise style, 'is no longer yours. It belongs to all the brethren and their souls belong to you, or better, their souls together with yours are now but one soul, the unique soul of Christ.'[34]

Unanimity and concord become God's favourite place, the place of his presence. The Lord

> blesses only one, since he has made one man out of the many, because it is a good and joyful thing for brethren to dwell together in unity. 'Brethren' is in the plural, but in unity they are singular ... But of whom do you think it is said: 'May the Lord bless you from Zion'? He blesses the unity. Share in the unity and the blessing will extend to you.[35]

The result is a new way of thinking about the divine indwelling, no longer seen as being in the individual but in the whole community:

> When you think of the indwelling of God, think of the unity and communion of the Saints, especially in heaven, where God is particularly said to dwell because it is where his will is perfectly fulfilled ... and in the second place, on the earth, where God dwells in his house while he is building it, the house which will be dedicated at the end of the world.[36]

God in the individual and God in the community become inseparable realities: 'You yourself will be a dwelling for the Lord and form a unity with all who have become the Lord's dwelling.'[37]

After analysing Augustine's usage in the texts relating to charity and unity, Manrique concludes:

> Love in the community is founded on two evangelical principles: 'Where two or three are gathered together in my name, there I am, in the midst of them' (Matt. 18:20); 'He who loves his own soul, will lose it' (John 12:25). The Lord is in the midst of the community. Those who live in the monastery possess God ... And all those who are able to live in the intimacy of this mystical body feel God near, enjoy a great peace and can live in true freedom. The nearer they are to the community and to what is common, the nearer they are to God. To love the community is to love Christ, who is its soul.[38]

The Trinitarian Model

So far, we have seen that Augustine constantly kept the model of the Jerusalem community before him and understood the dynamics of communal unity in its light. However, his point of reference reaches beyond the community of the first Christians to the very source of unity. He actually looks for the ultimate foundation of the community's unity in the life of the Trinity and participation in its charity and koinonia. From the primitive community he ascends to the trinitarian 'community', pushing forward doctrinal reflection on the earlier elaborations of monastic theology.[39]

It is precisely from reflection on the unity practised by primitive Christianity that Augustine sets out to enter into the mystery of the Trinity. If so many men can have one heart and one soul, it is all the more possible for the three divine Persons to be one. The Spirit, *pax unitatis* (the peace of unity), descending on the Jerusalem Christians, 'from many souls and many hearts ... made one soul and one heart, seeking God, inspired by religious feelings.' If *pax unitatis* did this in some human beings, he continues,

> we believe that, even more, in the peace of God which passes all understanding, the Father, the Son and the Holy Spirit are not three gods but only one God; this unity is as superior to that which formed one soul and one heart in the first Christians as the peace which passes all understanding [the Holy Spirit] is superior to the peace possessed by all those first faithful, who were one soul and one heart seeking God.[40]

Augustine can penetrate the mystery of the Trinity by starting from the community because the former is related to the latter as cause is to effect.

In another passage, he posits a line of continuity between Christ's prayer for unity, the community at Jerusalem, and his own monastic community:

> The Lord, addressing the Father, says of his disciples: 'May they be one, as we also are one'. Furthermore, in the Acts of the Apostles it is said: 'The community of believers was one soul and one heart' ... Since only one thing is necessary, the heavenly unity by which the Father, the Son and the Holy Spirit are one ... But we shall not be able to attain this unity unless, as well as being many, we have one heart.[41]

Jesus did not desire unity of heart and soul just for the first Christians. He prayed for all, that they might be one. Here it is a question, of course, of a unity that transcends us. It is a unity to which the members of the community are called to aspire in a constant upward movement, a conversion to God in the literal sense of the term, a going towards God: *anima una et cor unum in Deum* (one soul and one heart towards God). This upward movement is, however, impossible without the downward movement of the Trinity, descending to transmit and achieve this work of sanctification and unification.

Continuing his reflection, Augustine points to Christ as the mediator of the movement from the trinitarian koinonia to the koinonia of the Church. The trinitarian unity is bestowed on us by Christ, who sends the Holy Spirit into the hearts of the faithful. As head, he creates unity. The one soul of which Acts speaks finds its deepest explanation in the fact that all have become the *anima unica Christi* (the one soul of Christ). The soul of the community is the very soul of Christ.

The Spirit, because he is the Spirit of Christ, poured out by him, creates the unity of the brethren and becomes a principle of unity in and among them, just as he is within the Trinity. The unity which makes one God out of the three Persons is transmitted by him to the community, since he is the *communio* of the Trinity, the *communitas* of the Father and the Son. If the first Christians in Jerusalem were one heart and one soul, it was because the Spirit of unity had come down upon them.

The monastic community is called to relive the dynamics of the first Christian community and therefore to have the same unitive principle that inspired that first community. If Basil saw his community as inserted into the Church, Augustine sees his as inserted directly into the mystery of the Trinity. The *anima una* and the *cor unum*, fruit of the community's mutual love, are a participation in the God who is love. Fraternal charity thus appears as the most expressive image and closest analogy of the Trinity.

NOTES

1. Born at Thagaste in Numidia in 354, Augustine moved to Milan to teach rhetoric, after studying at Carthage and Rome. Here he underwent a spiritual conversion which coincided with a monastic vocation and, together with his son Adeodatus, he received baptism. Returning to Rome, he became acquainted with Roman monasticism. At Thagaste he began to experience the monastic life with a group of friends in his own home. After three years, in 391, he went to Hippo where he was ordained priest. Here he founded a true and authentic monastery for laymen. In 395 Augustine was consecrated bishop. He founded a new monastery, which was soon made up of clerics, in his episcopal residence. Having fostered poverty, the common life, and *vita apostolica* among the clergy, he was the inspiration for the Canons Regular in the Middle Ages. He also developed and organised the monastic life for women, giving the nuns the same Rule he had written for monks. He died in his episcopal city on 28 August 430.

   There is a critical edition of the Rule by L Verheijen (Paris: 1967). In English there is *The Rule of St Augustine, Masculine and Feminine Versions*, with an Introduction and Commentary by Tarsisius J. van Bavel OSA, translated by Raymond Canning OSA (London: 1984). For an introduction in English to St Augustine's thought on the religious life, see *Augustine of Hippo and his Monastic Rule* by George Lawless OSA (Oxford: 1987). The best biography in English is Peter Brown's *Augustine of Hippo. A Biography* (London: 1967); *St Augustine of Hippo, Life and Controversies* by Gerald Bonner (Norwich: 1963, revised 1986) is also very good. The largest single translation in English to date is in the *Select Library of the Nicene and Post Nicene Fathers of the Christian Church* (Buffalo: 1886). New City Press, New York, is currently publishing the first complete collection in the English language. Translations of various parts of the works have been and are being published, and reference is made to them in these notes. The translations in the text of this chapter are the work of the author/translator.

2. *Rule* I, p. 11 in R. Canning's translation.
3. Cf. J. García Alvarez, 'La communauté augustinienne', *Vie Consacrée* 59 (1987), pp. 85-99, 160-73.
4. Possidius, *Vita Augustini*, 5.1.
5. *Sermon* 355.2.
6. *Enarrationes in Psalmos* 132.2; in English, *Nicene and Post Nicene Fathers*, vol. 6, p. 111.
7. *Sermon* 356.1.
8. *Contra Faustum* 5.6.
9. *Enar. in Ps.* 131 (op. cit. vol. 6, p. 93).
10. A. Manrique, *Teologia agostiniana della vita religiosa* (Milan: 1968), pp. 103-4.
11. *Letter* 211.2.
12. *Letter* 211.3.

13. *Enar. in Ps.* 30.1 (op. cit. vol. 1, p. 217).
14. J. Morán, *Agostino Aurelio*, DIP, I, 434, 432.
15. *Enar. in Ps.* 132.12 (op. cit. vol. 6, pp. 120-1)
16. *Ibid.*
17. *Enar. in Ps.* 132.6 (ibid. p. 116)
18. *Rule* I (Canning, p. 11)
19. *Soliloquy* I, 12, 20. There is an English translation of the *Soliloquies* by John Burleigh in *Augustine: Earlier Writings* (The Library of Christian Classics, 1953, p. 35).
20. *In Johannis* 10.3.
21. *In Jo.* 17.8.
22. *De moribus Ecclesiae Catholicae* I.26.8.
23. *Sermon* 336.2.2.
24. *De Trinitatis* 8.7.10-11 (p. 253 in the English translation by Edmund Hill OP in the series *The Works of Saint Augustine. A Translation for the 21st Century*).
25. Ibid.
26. *Confessions*, book 4, ch. 13. Several translations are available in English, such as the Orchard Books edition (Sir Tobie Matthew's translation, revised by Dom Roger Huddlestone, London: 1954) and the Penguin Classics translation by R. S. Pine-Coffin (1961).
27. *Rule* 6.3 (Canning, p. 22f.).
28. **Ibid.** 1.8 (p. 13).
29. *Enar. in Ps.* 131.5 (op. cit. vol. 6, p. 93).
30. *Enar. in Ps.* 10.7 (op. cit. vol. 1, p. 99).
31. *Sermon* 336.1.1.
32. *The City of God* 10.3.2 (p. 375 in the Penguin Classics translation by Henry Bettenson).
33. *Enar. in Ps.* 132.13 (op. cit. vol. 6, p. 121).
34. *Letter* 243.4.
35. *Enar. in Ps.* 133.3 (op. cit. vol. 6, p. 124).
36. *Letter* 187.13.41.
37. *Enar. in Ps.* 131.5 (op. cit. vol. 6, p. 93).
38. Manrique, op. cit. p. 154.
39. Cf. M. Verheijen, 'Saint Augustin', in *Théologie de la Vie Monastique*, pp. 205-9).
40. *Letter* 238.2.16.
41. *Sermon* 103.4.5 (*The Works of Saint Augustine. A Translation for* the 21st Century: *Sermons* III/4 (New York: 1992), p. 78).

5 A School For the Divine Service

The Benedictine monastery

Together with Pachomius, Basil and Augustine, Benedict puts in place the last great pillar to support the entire edifice of monastic life.[1] He stands at the confluence of the great streams that preceded him. In fact, he writes at the end of his Rule: 'There are for him who would hasten to the perfection of the monastic way the doctrines of the holy Fathers, which, if a man keeps them, will lead him to the height of perfection.' After referring to Scripture as 'a most direct rule for our human life', he sets out explicitly the two great sources which inspired his own teaching: 'the *Conferences*, and *Institutes*, and the *Lives of the Fathers*, and the *Rule* of our holy Father Basil'.[2]

The Benedictine monastic community has its roots in both the model of the more individual life, which came to it from Egypt through Cassian and the *Rule of the Master*, and the more communal life derived from Basil and, especially, Augustine.[3] Thus we see a synthesis of these two great orientations which had been present from the beginnings of mo-, nasticism. The eremitic ideal, made up of ascesis, solitude, prayer - the expression of an eager quest for God - had never been lost from the Christian consciousness. It constantly returned as a profound nostalgia, not least to Benedict. The ideal of communion and unity, in its turn, had come to occupy an increasingly large place in monastic experience, creating communities whose aim was to attain one heart and one soul, in a desire to imitate the primitive Church. This second dimension also enters gradually but decisively into the Benedictine Rule.

The Monastery, School of the Divine Service

As a result of this synthesis of the various earlier experiences of monasticism, the image of the Benedictine community, compared with those already analysed, shows one particular characteristic. 'The *coenobium* is, of course, fundamentally an attempt to organize on a community scale the spiritual fatherhood of the desert.'[4] The experience of the Desert Fathers, as it had been transmitted by Cassian, was in fact the primary determining influence on Benedict. We must not forget that he began his own monastic experience in solitude.

We know that the relationship between spiritual father and disciple was one of the traditional elements that made up monastic life in the desert. This same relationship makes its appearance at the beginning of the Benedictine Rule, when cenobites - that is, the members of the community established by Benedict - are described as 'the "monastery" kind, who do battle under a Rule and an Abbot'.[5] Basil's Rule began with the twofold commandment of charity, Augustine's with the one heart and one soul turned towards God; Benedict's begins with obedience to a rule of life and an abbot.

The Benedictine community is portrayed as a cenobitic society, understood as a place of formation for the journey towards God rather than as a community of brotherly life with value in and for itself. It appears as an educational institution centred on relationship with the master, while the relationships of the disciples among themselves seem less obvious and blurred. Its objective is to lead each person to eternal life, rather than to be a house in which to experience, already here below, 'how good and joyful it is to live together'. The texts quoted are no longer from Acts, Psalm 132(133) or Psalm 67. The *Prologue* of the Benedictine Rule begins by addressing an individual in order to show him the way that will lead him to salvation: 'Listen my son to the instructions of your Master, turn the ear of your heart to the advice of a loving father; accept it willingly and carry it out vigorously.'[6] Clearly here we are in continuity with the eremitic tradition, where the end of the monastic life is the quest for salvation and the absolute, and the radicality of following Christ in order to arrive at dwelling in his house (Psalm 33).

To achieve these objectives, Benedict establishes a 'school'. The word 'school' has to be understood in the twofold meaning of 'a place for learning' Christ's teaching, where monks come together to submit to Christ's teaching mediated by a master, the abbot, who stands in his place; and 'a place reserved for a particular association', where monks come together to carry out a particular public function in the midst of the people of God.[7] Enrolled in the service of God and freed from every other occupation, the monks attend only to serving God, doing the will of the king, Christ the Lord.

Like every other school, of course, this one has its master, the abbot, and is established under his teaching and guidance. Like every other school, the *schola Dominici servitii* also has its textbook, the Rule. The Benedictine community is formed by obedience to the abbot and the Rule.

There are many motives which keep the monks united: they are animated by the same *propositum*; they are wholly dedicated to the same task, the divine service expressed in the *opus Dei*, liturgical prayer, and the *opus manuum* or work; together they pursue the quest of Christian perfection. They make up a common army,[8] and form an *acies* or line of battle.[9] Nevertheless, it can be said that submission to a Rule and an abbot constitutes the formal element of the monastic community, what makes it effectively a community. As de Vogüé stresses,

> In our view, no one can insist too much on the importance of the vertical relation which unites disciples to master in the *coenobium*; it is the constitutive axis of cenobitism ... it would be wrong to think first of the monastery and then of the abbot. The abbot, the man of God invested with the charismatic mission of teaching and governing souls, comes first. The *coenobium* is nothing more than the assemblage of his disciples.[10]

Cenobitism is therefore essentially constituted by the relationship that unites each of its members to a man who represents Christ. From this basic relationship spring the ties that unite the disciples of the same master among themselves. The cenobitic society exists firstly between the monk and his abbot, between the monk and the God whom he seeks.[11]

The importance of the role of the abbot resides in the fact that he is seen as the very presence of Christ in the midst of his disciples. The abbot occupies the place of Christ, as the Rule says explicitly in its second chapter: 'For he is believed to act in the place of Christ in the monastery, since he is called by his title, as the Apostle says, "You have received the Spirit of adoption as sons, through whom we cry, Abba! Father!"'[12] At the end of the Rule this vision of faith is reaffirmed in the same way: 'The Abbot, ... as he is believed to act in the place of Christ, should be called Lord and Abbot, not because he demands these titles, but for the honour and love of Christ.'[13] Thus once again we find the prototype of the group of the Twelve around Jesus.

The abbot, the representative of Christ in the midst of his own, continues to perform some of the functions of Christ. His first task, in line with the concept of the monastery as *'schola Dominici servitii'*, is to teach. The abbot's role is typically magisterial. Recalling that he must keep to the law of the Lord, the Rule prescribes that

> his commands and his teaching should mingle like the leaven of divine justice in the minds of his disciples. The Abbot must always remember that at the fearful judgement of God two things will be discussed: his own teaching and the obedience of his disciples.[14]

In relation to the abbot-master, the Rule often gives the monks the name of 'disciples'.

The structure of the community appears hierarchical. Unity between all is guaranteed by the vertical relationship of obedience to the abbot. It is around his person, as around Christ, the Father, the Master, that all converge and form a community.

The inspiration for this concept of community and the prominent role of the abbot is now even clearer. The Benedictine monastery reproduces the structure of primitive eremiticism, in which the 'novices' gathered round the charismatic 'abba' to learn how to save their souls.

Unity and Charity

The centrality of the abbot and the hierarchical arrangement of the monastery do not exclude horizontal relationships between the monks. Rather, they set them in order. The word *'communitas'* never appears in the Rule, but the word *'congregatio'* occurs twenty-five times. The monks are people who want to go on a journey together and for this they have gathered round an abbot. Benedict wrote his Rule for cenobites, for 'the "monastery" kind', those who live together.[15] With them he wants to organize a school, a society of 'brothers' - the word appears about a hundred times, against thirty-six instances of the term 'monk'.

First, however, it must be noted that the Rule seems to envisage an evolution in the concept of community. In the first series of chapters (1-7), the inspiration of the *Rule of the Master* is evident and therefore, as we have already emphasized, the link with the eremitic origins of monasticism. In line with the inheritance of the desert experience, the function of the community is seen rather as the formation of individuals.

The Rule itself, describing the life of the hermits, seems to reflect this idea when it says that the purpose of practising the common life with the brethren is in order to be able to 'do battle against the devil' and undertake 'the solitary combat of the devil'.[16] Chapters 4-7,

> which contain Benedictine spirituality ... are like a summary of individual perfection, in which the community serves only as the setting in which to strive for virtue, the workshop in which "we make use of all these tools" (RB 4.78). The final goal of this spirituality, described in RB 7.67-70, corresponds to the characteristics of the eremitic life.[17]

Chapters 67-72, no longer depending on the *Rule of the Master*, testify to an encounter with Basil and therefore with a different concept of community, one with more horizontal characteristics. We can therefore assume an evolution in Benedictine experience which led little by little to a discovery of the intrinsic value of community.

An evolution in Benedict's thought can also be observed in his portrayal of the figure of the abbot, undoubtedly the fruit of his experience. Chapter 64 breathes a different atmosphere to chapter 2. In fact, we read that '[The Abbot] ought to be of profit to his brethren rather than just preside over them.'[18] 'It should be his aim to be loved rather than feared.'[19] 'It is rightly said that St Benedict corrected himself, as the fruit of his personal experience; the tone is more affectionate and paternal, with an emphasis on discretion, prudence and charity. The Augustinian inspiration is clear.'[20]

Leaving aside the rich, complex and wise organization of the monastery, with its perfect ordering of roles, we will pause only to highlight the quality of relationships in order to grasp the underlying theological vision. What catches the attention immediately is that every kind of relationship must be marked by fraternal charity.

Even in the hierarchical arrangement of responsibilities, we can still note the profound consciousness of equality between all the members of the monastery. As the Rule says on this subject,

> The Abbot must not show personal preferences in his monastery. He must not be more loving to one than to another ... A free-born man must not be put before one entering the monastery from slavery ... But if it seems to the Abbot that there is good reason for it, let him do so, and let him do the same about the rank of anyone.

Otherwise let them keep their normal order. For whether we are slaves or freemen, we are all one in Christ ... 'for God has no favourites' (Rom. 2:11) ... Therefore the Abbot should show himself equally loving to all.[21]

Because of this fundamental equality, obedience - which at the beginning of the Rule was inculcated exclusively towards the abbot - is transformed into 'mutual obedience', the fruit and expression of mutual love: 'The goodness of obedience is not to be shown only through obedience to the Abbot, but the brethren should also obey each other.'[22] If the obedience owed to the abbot expresses the search for God's will, mutual obedience springs from the awareness that our brother is a way to reach God. The Rule expresses the conviction that only 'by this path of obedience will [the monks] draw nearer God'.[23] In this case, obedience becomes synonymous with a relationship of mutual submission.

Another aspect which guides community relations, besides universal equality, is the place reserved in the monk's spiritual journey for the twofold command of charity. It heads the long list which occupies the whole of chapter 4 of the Rule, describing the tools of good works. This chapter depends entirely on Cassian for the form of the list. However, Benedict shows his originality over against his source by putting the twofold command of charity (not even mentioned by Cassian) above all the other means of sanctification.

The Master and Benedict are not ignorant of Cassian's structure. Indeed, their chapter on humility reproduces it. But even if they put charity at the top of that ladder, they show no reluctance in speaking of the love of God and neighbour at the beginning of their list of good works ... Putting love at the beginning of their catalogue, they offer an image which completes and balances that of De humilitate [chapter 7]. Charity is not only the end of a long climb, the sublime state in which the whole divine will is kept 'effortlessly and naturally', but it is also and above all the 'first' commandment, which every Christian puts into practice as soon as he resolves to work for God. Thus even in its first steps the monastic life is completely enveloped in the love of God and neighbour.[24]

In Benedict there is no shortage of allusions to the primitive community at Jerusalem. The monks must have nothing of their own, chapter 33 of the Rule cautions, 'for they are not allowed to retain at their own disposition their own bodies or wills',[25] and it quotes in support the words of Acts: 'Everything should be common to all, as it is written, and no one should call anything his own.'[26] Acts is quoted again in the following chapter, to explain why not everyone should receive an equal share of what is needed: 'Distribution was made to each as he had need'.[27]

In the last part of the Rule, charity becomes increasingly prominent, until it shapes the whole 'order of the community'. The Rule, which had begun with the figure of the abbot and emphasized his central importance, here recovers the element of interpersonal relationships inspired by charity. What gives meaning to the whole chapter on the order of the community is, in fact, Paul's dictum: 'Forestall one another in paying honour.'[28] The same love must guide not only relations between those with different roles, but also between different age groups: 'Juniors ... must show respect for their seniors, and seniors must love their juniors.'[29] And so we come to chapter 72 of the Rule. It has been maintained that this chapter should be the starting point for re-reading the whole Rule from the point of view of communion and charity.[30] At its end, in fact, the Rule reaches the deepest point of its progressive discovery of charity as the norm of community relationships between the monks.

> They should forestall one another in paying honour. They should with the greatest patience make allowance for one another's weaknesses, whether physical or moral. They should rival one another in practising obedience. No one should pursue what he thinks advantageous for himself, but rather what seems best for another. They should labour with chaste love at the charity of the brotherhood. They should fear God. They should love their Abbot with sincere and humble charity. They should prefer nothing whatever to Christ. May he bring us all alike to life everlasting.[31]

'All alike', _ariter_: the monks walk united in communion among themselves and in the love of Christ who guides them all and brings them to eternal life. We are back with the experience of Basil and Augustine.

Thanks also to this profound balance between the different elements of community, the Benedictine Rule was to inspire later centuries and, together with those of Basil and Augustine, yield new forms of monastic community throughout the Middle Ages. Even if their experience varied, the doctrinal and spiritual principles which were to guide the different communities in the seventh to twelfth centuries retained substantially the characteristics derived from these fundamental forms. As the first millennium progressed, two distinctive types of community emerged, with differing life styles: the *professio canonica* which looked to the Augustinian Rule, and the *professio monastica*, which looked to the Benedictine Rule, with Bernard of Clairvaux and the Cistercian school making a notable contribution to its renewal. Finally, after the Reform of Gregory VII (1070-85), many reforms flourished that tended to restore the traditional values of the eremitic life and ascesis, such as the experiments at Camaldoli, Fonte Avellana, Chartreuse, Cîteaux and Vallombrosa.[32] At this point we have nearly reached a form of community which will take the experimental route of the mendicant movement.

NOTES

1. Benedict of Nursia (c. 480-547), after his first schooling, was sent to Rome for higher education. Confronted with the dissipated life of the city, he abandoned Rome for the service of God while still young, withdrawing into a solitary life in the valley of the Aniene. After directing the community at Vicovaro, he again retired into a life of solitude and asceticism near Subiaco. Here he was joined by his first disciples, whom he divided between twelve monasteries in the surrounding region. As a result of opposition from a priest in the nearby church, Benedict left Subiaco and moved to Monte Cassino. There he built a new monastery in 529; a monastery for women was also established nearby under the direction of his sister Scholastica. His Rule became famous and spread widely, until it had imposed itself almost throughout the West.

    There are innumerable editions of and commentaries on the Rule. For a thorough study, you should refer to the edition prepared by Dom Adalbert de Vogüé and J. Neufville (vols 181-6 of *Sources Chrétiennes*, Éditions du Cerf, Paris: 1971-2). The second book of the *Dialogues* of Gregory the Great tells the story of Benedict's life.

    Several translations of the Rule are available in English. A convenient edition is that of Abbot Justin McCann (Orchard Books, London: Burns and Oates, 1952), with introduction, notes, and Latin text. *Benedictine Monachism* by Abbot Cuthbert Butler (London, 1919) is a valuable historical study of the Rule. This extensive book provides a systematic exposition of what may be called the philosophy and theory of the Benedictine Rule and life, its inner spirit and traditions and their outward manifestations.

Quotations from the Rule in this chapter have been taken from Dom David Parry's translation (London: DLT, 1984); references to this work are given in the following notes.

2. *Rule*, ch. 73, 2-5 (Parry, p. 117).
3. Cf. de Vogüé, *La Règle de Saint Benôit*, I, p. 39.
4. De Vogüé, *Community and Abbot in the Rule of Saint Benedict* (Kalamazoo, MI: Cistercian Publications, 1979), p. 477. On the Benedictine community, cf. I M. Gomez, 'La vida comunitaria en la Regula Benedicti', *Yermo* 14 (1976), pp. 305-45.
5. *Rule*, ch. 1, 2 (Parry, p. 7).
6. *Rule*, Prologue, 1 (Parry, p. 1).
7. In general this term denoted professional or military associations.
8. *Rule*, Prologue.
9. *Rule*, Prologue.
10. *Community and Abbot*, p. 102.
11. Cf. ibid., p. 112.
12. *Rule*, ch. 2, 3 (Parry, p. 11).
13. *Rule*, ch. 63, 13 (Parry, p. 99f.).
14. *Rule*, ch. 2, 4-6 (Parry, p. 11).
15. Cf. *Rule*, ch. 1, 2 (Parry, p. 7).
16. *Rule*, ch. 1, 4-5 (Parry, p. 7).
17. A. Metzinger, 'La comunidad y los ideales comunitarios en la Regla de San Benito', *Cuadernos Monásticos*, 8 (1969), pp. 58-9.
18. *Rule*, ch. 64, 8 (Parry, p. 101).
19. *Rule*, ch. 64, 15 (Parry, p. 102).
20. L. Sena, *Fondamenti e prospettive della vita comune secondo la Regola benedettina* (Parma: 1984), p. 10.
21. *Rule*, ch. 2, 16, 22 (Parry, p. 12).
22. *Rule*, ch. 71, 1 (Parry p. 113).
23. Ibid.
24. De Vogüé, *La regola di S. Benedetto. Commento dottrinale e spirituale* (Padua: Messaggero, 1984), pp. 129-30.
25. *Rule*, ch. 33, 4 (Parry p. 58).
26. *Rule*, ch. 33, 6 (Parry p. 58).
27. *Rule*, ch. 34, 1 (Parry p. 59).
28. *Rule*, ch. 63, 17 (Parry p. 100).
29. *Rule*, ch. 63, 10 (Parry p. 99).
30. E. Manning, 'L'importance du chapitre 72 de la Règle de S. Benôit', *Regulae Benedicti Studia*, 5 (1977), pp. 285-8.

31. *Rule*, ch. 72, 4-11 (Parry, p. 114).
32. For a first look at the development of the community in this period, see J. Leclercq, 'Monasticism and Asceticism in Western Christianity', in *Christian Spirituality, Origins to the Twelfth Century*, eds Bernard McGinn and John Meyendorff (London: 1986), 5, II.

6 The Spacious Cloister of the Whole World
Franciscan brotherhood

In some ways, the beginnings of the thirteenth century recall the situation of the Church in the fourth century. Then, the end of persecution and the slackening of eschatological tension had stirred up a desire to return to the beginnings, which gave rise to monasticism. Now, new ecclesial needs gave life to a number of movements which, though varied in form, demanded the same return to the *Ecclesiae primitivae forma* (the form of the primitive Church).

On the one hand, a large proportion of the clergy, in spite of the Gregorian reform, were trapped in feudal privileges and embroiled in simony and nicolaism. On the other hand, countless lay movements of an evangelical character had flourished since the twelfth century, aiming at the reform of the Church through a return to the simple, poor and evangelical life of the early days. Like a current of spiritual awakening, a profound and widespread yearning had emerged for the authenticity of an evangelical life directed towards radical poverty and opposition to all formalism and legalism. These new spiritual directions were expressed in groups such as the Humiliati, the Poor Men of Lombardy, the Cathars and the Waldensians, which always hovered between heresy and orthodoxy.

This was a context full of contradictions. On the one hand, there was an unrestrained desire for luxury and well-being, fostered by sociological factors such as the birth of free communities with the resultant new political orders, together with the development of commerce with its new economic structures. On the other hand, there was the longing for a pure and poor Church, as it had been in the beginning. The Crusader movement, even if it favoured the race for wealth, also opened the way for the rediscovery of Christ's humanity and the birth of a lively interest in radical evangelism.

During this time of distress we witness the rise of the Mendicant Orders, which were able to interpret and channel the widespread yearning for an 'apostolic' life, or a way of life that would closely reproduce the model of the life of Christ and his disciples, above all its real poverty and itinerant preaching. We are confronted by a new model of the consecrated life, which also expressed itself in a new model of community - the mendicant - as it was lived in the different Orders which sprang up at this time: the Franciscans, the Dominicans, the Carmelites, the Trinitarians, the Servites, the Augustinians ...[1] We can consider the experience of the Franciscan community as typical of this shift in the religious life, a community which perhaps expressed its theological and spiritual characteristics in a more original way.[2] With it 'a new order sprang up in the world, an extraordinary new life'.[3]

A New Form of Community

The evangelical inspiration behind this new form of community was no longer the Christians of Jerusalem. There is never any mention of the first Christian community in the writings of Francis and Clare. The model was the apostolic life, understood as life in the footsteps of Christ, in imitation of the apostles who shared totally the life of their Master and Lord. Francis was to be a man spellbound by Christ, whose whole desire would be literally to travel again in the footsteps of Christ. 'He did not want anyone to surpass him in Christ's way,' wrote Giordano da Giano, 'but rather he wanted to go ahead of everyone.'[4] The primitive First Rule which he was to give to his friars would be only 'the life of the Gospel of Jesus Christ'.[5] The *Second Rule* would also begin with a similar statement: 'The Rule and life of the Friars Minor is this, namely, to observe the holy Gospel of our Lord Jesus Christ ...'[6] In fact the Most High himself had revealed to him that he was to live 'the life of the Gospel'.[7]

Primitive monasticism had also sprung from the desire to leave everything in order to follow Christ. Now, however, discipleship no longer led, as it had then, to withdrawal into the desert. Following Christ, Francis would feel impelled to imitate the apostles by taking the Gospel he lived to everyone and sharing with all, by witness and word, the experience of life with Christ. It was a new way of carrying out 'the imitation of the apostles'. To his contemporaries Francis would appear as 'a new evangelist'[8], one who had 'filled the whole earth with the Gospel of Christ'.[9]

The new models of inspiration for the community were no longer those that had created the monastic or canonical communities. The gospel quotations were no longer Acts 2 and 4 but the 'apostolic discourse' of Matthew 10 and Luke 10, as it had been for all the *pauperes Christi* (poor ones of Christ) who travelled Europe from the second half of the twelfth century. The idea of *vita apostolica* was enriched with a new meaning: going to preach conversion and the Word of God in poverty, as the apostles had done. The *vita apostolica* also involved a particular life style: going 'apostolically', that is, 'without purse or bag ...' Starting with this gospel text, we can thus grasp the fundamental features of the mendicant community: itinerant preaching, not being bound to any place or house, poverty, and an insecurity that exalted abandonment to the Father's love.[10]

Even if Francis, in his biblical inspiration, went beyond the Jerusalem community, bypassing it, so to speak, in order to reach the Gospel directly, it is interesting to note that the outcome was the same as that which flourished in Jerusalem. In the Gospel Francis found the archetype of brotherhood. In fact, the Franciscan brotherhood seemed to its contemporaries to be the perfect realization of the primitive Church as it appears in Acts 4:32.[11]

The novelty of the evangelical inspiration, which translated itself into wandering for the Gospel, involved a change in the understanding of community, so that the features adopted by the Franciscan brotherhood (which were substantially shared by the other Mendicants) showed their originality.[12]

In contrast to the Benedictine monastery, the new community presented itself instead as a small brotherhood made up of a few members. Jesus actually sent them out 'two by two'. This encouraged the intensification of interpersonal relationships. Consequently, the members of the new community were no longer called *monaci* (monks) but *frati* (brothers or friars), because it was precisely fraternity which characterized their way of life.[13]

The houses of the community were no longer called 'monasteries' but 'convents'; the community was the result of a convergence of people rather than external structures. It was no longer the place that formed the community but the 'coming together' (*convenire*) itself and the assembling of the friars. The community of the preceding centuries had found the most adequate idiom for translating the values of mutual love and unity in the *vita communis* or common life: the cloisters, the refectory, common food and dress, the choir. In the Premonstratensian *Constitutions* the term 'common life' also designated the uniformity of observance which 'fosters and represents outwardly the unity of hearts which should exist inwardly'.[14] Now, instead, the life of the community was no longer conditioned by place but by ministry, which was precisely that of itinerant preaching. The new type of community lived in the wide expanse of the 'spacious cloister which is the whole world'.[15] The mutual relations between the friars and their meeting together constitute the community's first house. Francis refused a monastery both for himself and his followers. Not possessing monasteries became one of the characteristics of the Friars Minor.[16]

A further consequence of wandering, of being 'pilgrims and strangers in this world',[17] was the disappearance of the vow of stability. Commerce and the Crusades were opening the way for a new energy throughout Europe. To keep up with the times, the community had to start moving with the people, in order to be near them. Recurrent changes of residence demanded a new flexibility, unknown in previous communities. Before, when someone entered a monastery, he bound himself to those particular people for the whole of his life. Now what was required was the ability to create new relationships all the time, because of frequent changes of community, and therefore a constant readiness to meet new members of the community.

Since, as we shall see, the ideal was no longer to establish a particular brotherhood but to spread the evangelical ideal of brotherhood to all people, the community went back into the city, into the working-class neighbourhoods. It left the secluded and desert places in order to mix with people and make possible a continuing relationship with them. Hence, amongst other things, the popularity of the Franciscan movement, the deep impression it made on people, and the involvement of laypeople in it through the Third Order movement.

All this enables us to understand the need for centralized direction of the Order and its consequences for the idea of community. Because a new type of community was being set up, no longer bound to a place and a house, a sudden change in the quality of relationships was required, a new openness to a wider community. A process was set in motion which would reach its full development in the Society of Jesus and modern Congregations, with their emphasis on the whole apostolic body as one great community, rather than on the individual local community.

A movement of friars with no fixed abode, sent out two by two like the disciples, demanded one central superior whom all could obey. 'The personal bond and relationship of obedience with the superior constituted the true "convent" of the first Friars Minor.'[18] Henceforward a centralized government was imperative for the sake of serving the Church through evangelism.

Consequently, the result was other innovative tools for guaranteeing the unity of the Order, such as the participation of all the friars in the General Chapters, the division into provinces, the Chapters at regular intervals, the visits by superiors, and the possibility of appeal in case of difficulty.

As we did with the previous experiences of community life, let us now try to discern in outline the theological and spiritual vision which underlay the new type of community, rather than immerse ourselves in the institutional structures and interesting sociological implications raised by the Franciscan brotherhood.

Brotherhood, The Constituent Element of Cohesion

Franciscan brotherhood, like that of earlier forms of community, was born out of the experience of its founder, the experience that Francis had of the fatherhood of God, beginning with the reality of the Son's incarnation. In his *Testament* Francis points to his meeting with the lepers as the beginning of his conversion: 'God himself led me into their company, and I had pity on them.' From that moment his change of life began: 'After that I did not wait long before leaving the world.'[19] If he discovered brothers in the lowest of men, the lepers, it was because Christ had carried his incarnation to the very extreme of love, even to identifying himself with the lowest. If Francis, following in the footsteps of the poor and crucified Christ - whose full depths he did not yet know - could discover a brother in a leper, he would be able, from now on, to recognize brothers and sisters in everyone.

The other profound experience which marked him, and which would be at the base of the new brotherhood, was awareness of the love of God the Father, in which he felt himself enveloped from the first moment of his conversion. He proved his faith in this love by painfully renouncing of the affection of his father, Pietro di Bernardone: 'Until now I called you my father, but from now on I can say without reserve, "Our Father who art in heaven". He is all my wealth and I place all my confidence in him.'[20]

Recognizing the incarnate Christ as his brother and welcoming the fatherhood of God, Francis discovered universal brotherhood. All creatures are sisters and brothers, because they all bear the 'meaning' of God's fatherhood, as he exclaims in the *Canticle of the Creatures*. Yet amongst all the creatures he focused his attention particularly on human beings, who bear the image and likeness of God. Having discovered God as Father, he discovered human beings as brothers and sisters. In all of them, as in the leper, he saw the Son of the Father who for love of us took flesh and identified himself with everyone, making himself our brother. 'Before brotherhood as the ideal of evangelical life, Francis encountered his *brother*.'[21] Francis' desire would be to pass on to everyone his awareness of the fatherhood of God, and to make everyone brothers in Christ. He aimed at the creation of a universal brotherhood, to which all people are called, rather than the creation of a particular community. In every man he saw a brother, in every woman a sister. Indeed all creatures, because they come from the hand of the Father, appear as brothers or sisters in his eyes: 'brother wind, brother fire, sister water ...' Poverty, so typical of the Franciscan experience, is the concrete instrument for reordering everyone's relationships from the point of view of brotherhood instead of domination, in order to emphasize their gratuitousness.

The brotherhood to which Francis gave life was only the start of that universal brotherhood in which he wanted to get everyone involved. It was a kind of provocation to share brotherly attitudes. Brotherhood was a witness to the Father's love; it became a witness to love between the children of the one Father. He would call his companions 'Friars Minor' precisely in order to point them out as the smallest brothers in the great family which has God as its Father.

> At the spiritual level, the Franciscan brotherhood can be described as a message of witness, offered to the world, of a the universal fatherhood of God and the universal brotherhood of humanity ... As the word of God became 'humanity' to restore the gift of the divine life to all human beings, so St Francis becomes 'fraternity' in order to restore to every creature the love of God's fatherhood and the joy of many brothers and sisters.[22]

The brotherhood, as Francis understood it, did not derive from human will, precisely because it was the fruit of being God's children. It was made up of members of the same family given to one another by God. Francis was the first to experience this, as he bears witness in the *Testament*: 'The Lord gave me brothers'.[23] Celano tells of Francis' joy when he received God's gift of his first companion, Bernard: 'The Lord was seen to have a care for him by giving him a needed companion and a faithful friend.'[24]

The living centre of the brotherhood was Christ himself. If God is discovered and experienced as Father, Christ is immediately understood as the Son, the firstborn among many brethren. Chapter 22 of the *First Rule* offers perhaps the deepest theological key to an understanding of the mystic nature of the community, uniting as it does perception of the divine fatherhood with the brotherhood and presence of the risen Lord in a single experience.[25] This text was probably dictated as a spiritual testament before Francis went to Egypt in 1219 in the hope of suffering martyrdom there. It lists a long series of New Testament quotations, which culminate in the prayer that Jesus addressed to the Father at the end of the Last Supper. First come the verses of Matt. 23:1-12: 'You are all brethren ... call no man your father on earth ... Neither be called masters ...' The Franciscan idea of brotherhood is, once again, clearly inspired by God's fatherhood and the divine sonship of Christ, our brother. Then follow the words of Matt. 18.20: 'Where two or three are gathered in my name, there am I in the midst of them' and Matt. 28:20: 'I am with you always, to the close of the age', which denote 'a living faith in this vital presence of the Risen Christ in the midst of brethren brought together in his name',[26] as of him who constitutes the bond of brotherhood. The words of Jesus' sacerdotal prayer lead the brotherhood into the very mystery of trinitarian unity.[27]

The Franciscan brotherhood is thus represented as a new family united by the bonds of charity, even if Francis did not intend to create a new community but, rather, simply to put into practice Christian community according to the teaching of the Gospel.[28] Innocent IV, approving the Rule of St Clare in 1253, wrote something which could be said of the whole Franciscan brotherhood: 'You have chosen to live in communities in unity of spirits and pledged to the utmost poverty.'[29]

The wanderings of the friars did not prevent them from living in the bond of unity. Francis wanted to preserve this bond 'so that those whom the same spirit drew together and the same father brought forth might be nurtured peacefully in the bosom of one mother'.[30] They were in fact brought together by the love of Christ, having responded to the invitation to be with Christ in order to be sent out to preach. They seemed to be united by sharing in the one reality of being God's children and their common following of Christ.

Celano saw them as united among themselves like living stones which, cemented by charity, build up the holy temple of the Spirit.[31] He found the same unity in the Poor Clares: 'For above everything else there flourishes among them that excelling virtue of mutual and continual charity, which so binds their wills into one that, though forty or fifty of them dwell together in one place, agreement in likes and dislikes moulds one spirit in them out of many.'[32] Like the friars - though now it is St Clare herself who writes - they have come together to live in 'holy unity'.(33) They must have everything in common in order to maintain 'the unity of mutual charity and peace'.[34]

Finally, since the friar was without house or country and in the most absolute poverty, all that Francis could offer him was brotherhood, the fruit of charity, understood as perfect sharing of life, a place where every one of his friars could and should find refuge and support.[35]

The Expressions of Fraternal Charity

Unity and charity within the brotherhood were expressed in concrete actions. Exhortation to a love shown in deeds and the avoidance of everything that might do harm recurs insistently in Francis' writings: 'The friars are bound to love one another because our Lord says: "This is my commandment, that you love one another as I have loved you." And they must prove their love by deeds, as St John says: "Let us not love in word, neither with the tongue, but in deed and in truth".'[36] 'We must love our neighbours as ourselves. Anyone who will not or cannot love his neighbour as himself should at least do him good and not do him any harm.'[37] St Clare in her turn propounds the same teaching: 'Love one another in the love of Christ; and the love that you have in your hearts, show outwardly by your deeds.'[38]

The brotherhood is nourished by this charity, which is clearly theological in character. 'Out of respect for my memory, my blessing and my testament,' we read in the *Little Testament*, 'let [my friars] always love one another as I have loved and do love them.'[39] This is echoed by St Clare: 'Love one another in the love of Christ ... so that the Sisters, stimulated by this example, may grow in the love of God and mutual charity.'[40]

The love that binds the members of the community appears in these texts to have a deep christological motivation (Christ's own love circulating among the members). It shows the same theological nature when Francis describes it in his writings as 'spiritual': 'Wherever the friars meet one another, they should show that they are members of the same family', we read in the Rule. 'And they should have no hesitation in making known their needs to one another. For if a mother loves and cares for her child in the flesh, a friar should certainly love and care for his spiritual brother all the more tenderly.'[41] The opposition between 'in the flesh' and 'spiritual' brings out the novelty of the religious community with respect to the family community. The term 'spiritual' is to be understood in its strict sense. The brethren are spiritual because they are given by the Spirit ('The Lord gave me friars'[42]) and have to be loved with the power of the Spirit, or more than a mother can who loves and feeds with the power of nature.[43]

This theological dimension, which is entirely spiritual, does not prevent the relationship between the friars from being permeated with a love which finds authentically human expression. Relations between the friars, then, took on a characteristic style, made up of spontaneity, telling the truth, and family warmth, creating a friendly and peaceful atmosphere between them all. The divine permeated the human and carried it to its maximum strength. Consequently, the example of maternal love recurs several times in the sources, as an expression of the most genuine and purest way of loving. Thus in the Rule: 'They are bound to love and care for one another as brothers, according to the means God gives them, just as a mother loves and cares for her son.'[44] And the *Legend of the Three Companions* relates that each of the friars 'deeply loved the other and cared for him as a mother cares for a cherished only child. Charity burned so ardently in their hearts ...'[45]

Celano's testimony remains a classic description of the life of Francis' first disciples:

> O with what ardour of charity the new disciples of Christ burned! How great was the love that flourished in the members of this pious

society! For whenever they came together anywhere, or met one another along the way, as the custom is, there a shoot of spiritual love sprang up, sprinkling over all love the seed of true affection. What more shall I say? Chaste embraces, gentle feelings, a holy kiss, pleasing conversation, modest laughter, joyous looks, a *single eye*, a submissive spirit, a *peaceable tongue, a mild answer*, oneness of purpose, ready obedience, unwearied hand, all these were found in them.

And indeed, since they despised all earthly things and did not love themselves with a selfish love, pouring out their whole affection on all the brothers, they strove to give themselves as the price of helping one another in their needs. They came together with great desire; they remained together with joy; but separation from one another was sad on both sides, a bitter divorce, a cruel estrangement. [46]

The idealization of these earlier times emphasizes the character of this description as a paradigm, almost a norm.

The Chapters were privileged meetings where the same joy was expressed. As the Lord used to invite his disciples to go apart with him, to rest from their apostolic labours and exchange their experiences (cf. Matt. 6:31), so the friars would meet in Chapter to have the joy of being together again and to speak of the things of God and the happenings in their lives. The friars, Giacomo da Vitry testifies, used to come together 'once a year at a predetermined place to rejoice in the Lord and eat together, deriving notable benefits from these meetings'.[47] In this way, the Chapters appear as times of communion and an opportunity for reinforcing the bonds of brotherhood, before they were places for discernment or the elaboration of legislation.

The Rule afforded many explicit and concrete opportunities for practising fraternal charity. It finds expression, for example, in voluntary submission to one another: 'Far from doing or speaking evil to one another, the friars should be glad to serve and obey one another in a spirit of charity.'[48] Again, there is joyful mutual welcome:

And all the friars, no matter where they are or in whatever situation they find themselves, should, like spiritually minded men, diligently show reverence and honour to one another *without murmuring* (1 Pet. 4:9). They should let it be seen that they are happy in God, cheerful and courteous, as is expected of them, and be careful not to appear gloomy or depressed like hypocrites.'[49]

Love was also expressed in taking care never to offend against charity,[50] in care and availability to the sick,[51] and in the capacity to forgive.[52] Francis warned against pride, vainglory, envy, avarice, care for and preoccupation with this world, detraction, and murmuring.[53] St Clare also exhorted her nuns to guard against 'discord and division'.[54]

These innovative fraternal relationships were also focused, in a way all their own, on the vision of an obedience wholly marked by charity and the spirit of service. The very terminology used to denote superiors revealed a new outlook. They were called minister, custodian, guardian - all titles of biblical origin which precisely convey the desire to serve. 'Those who are put in charge of others,' writes Francis, 'should be no prouder of their office than if they had been appointed to wash the feet of their confrères.'[55]

The first task of all those in positions of responsibility was the spiritual care of the friars. They should in fact attend to 'the service and common good of the friars'.[56] They were to visit them, admonishing and correcting them 'with humility and charity';[57] (they were to welcome them 'charitably and with goodwill' when they found themselves in difficulties, and to impose penance on them 'with mercy'[58]. Those in positions of responsibility must preside more by holiness of life than by giving orders, so that they are obeyed more through love than through fear. Francis himself, although he could have made himself feared with all the force of his authority as founder, preferred to adapt himself to all, as the smallest of all the friars of the Order.[59]

One of the most obvious fruits of this new system of community was the equality established among all its members. 'No one is to be called "Prior",' we read in the Rule. 'They are all to be known as "Friars Minor" without distinction, and they should be prepared to wash one another's feet.'[60] This was something which struck their contemporaries, together with the other elements typical of the brotherhood: poverty, the powerlessness of 'minority', simplicity, and brotherhood open to everyone and everything. They saw that

> the friars, clergy and laity, formed a single community and the whole Order agreed together to the point where nobles and commoners, learned and illiterate were united in it under the same motto and in the same way of life; all, near or far, were bound by habits of affection like members of the same family and enjoyed equal rights within the Order.[61]

Francis' ideal of universal brotherhood began to take concrete form. He actually wanted 'the greater to be joined to the lesser, the wise to be united with the simple by brotherly affection, the distant to be bound to the distant by the binding force of love'.[62]

At the same time, because of Francis' own spirit of interior freedom, his brotherhood, characterized by unity as it was, did not lead to a levelling out of people. 'Love them as they are',[63] he wrote to a Minister about the friars under him. Francis was more interested in each person's spiritual physiognomy, as we read in an exquisite passage from the *Mirror of Perfection*, where he could find in each friar some aspect which characterized him in a positive way: faith and love of poverty in Bernard; simplicity and purity in Leo; courtesy in Angelo; attractive appearance, good sense, and fine and devout speaking in Masseo; contemplation in Giles; prayer in Rufino; patience in Juniper; physical and spiritual robustness in John of Lodi; charity in Roger; and holy restlessness in Lucido.[64]

With the Mendicants, the religious community has reached a turning point which will mark every subsequent form of community in the second Christian millennium. The community had resolutely opened itself to the Church and the whole world in order to help build from within it the great family of the children of God.

NOTES

1. 'Mendicanti', in *Dizionario degli Instituti di Perfezione*, V, 1163-1212.
2. The sources for early Franciscan life are available in a complete edition, *Fonti Francescane* (Assisi: 1977). In English there is *St Francis of Assisi: Writings and Early Biographies. English Omnibus of the Sources for the Life of St Francis* (ed. Marion Habig; 3rd edn (revised), London: 1979). The page references in brackets after the notes below refer to this translation. For a scholarly study of the texts, see John R. H. Moorman, *The Sources for the Life of St Francis of Assisi* (Manchester: 1940). For an introduction to the Franciscan community, cf. K. Esser, *Origini e inizi del movimento e dell'ordine francescano* (Milan: 1975); L. Iriarte, *Vocazione francescana. Sintesi degli ideali di san Francesco e di santa Chiara* (Rome: 1987); *Temi di vita francescana: la fraternità* (Rome: Antonianum, 1983); F. de Beer, 'La genesi della fraternità francescana secondo alcune fonti primitive', *Studi Francescani* 65 (1968), pp. 66-92; P. Iozelli, 'La vita fraterna nell'Ordine francescano primitivo', *Studi Francescani* 65 (1986), pp. 66-92; P. Iozelli, 'La vita fraterna nell'Ordine francescano primitivo', Studi Francescani 74 (1977), pp. 259-313.

3. Sequence for the feast of St Francis, attributed to Tommaso da Celano.
4. *Chronicle*, 10.
5. *First Rule* (of 1221; *Regula non Bullata*), Title (*Omnibus*, p. 31).
6. *Second Rule* (of 1223; *Regula Bullata*), 1, 2 (*Omnibus*, p. 57).
7. *Testament*, 17 (*Omnibus*, p. 68).
8. Celano, First Life, 84 (Omnibus, p. 299).
9. Ibid. 97 (*Omnibus*, p. 311).
10. Cf. *First Rule*, 14 (*Omnibus*, p. 42).
11. Cf. Jacques de Vitry, Letter written in October 1216, from Genoa, 9.
12. The novel features of this community have been well described by Esser, *Origini e inizi*; and by A. G. Matanic, '*Novitas franciscana*'. *Francesco d'Assisi nel suo rapporto con le preesistenti forme e dottrine di vita religiosa, in Lettura biblico-teologica delle Fonti Francescane* (Rome: Antonianum, 1979), pp. 165-82.
13. In the writings of St Francis the word '*frater*' occurs most frequently (306 times, second only to the 410 occurrences of '*Dominus*'); '*fraternitas*' occurs only ten times, referring not to the local community but to the whole Franciscan family (equivalent to 'religio'). The word '*sorella*', 'sister', appears sixty times in the *Rule* of St Clare, seventeen times in her *Testament* and eighteen times in her other writings. Already in the use of vocabulary it is clear that the brother and sister are the basic elements in the construction of the community.
14. F. Petit, *La spiritualité des Prémontrés aux XII et XIII siècles* (Paris: 1947).
15. Jacques de Vitry, *Historia Occidentalis*.
16. 'They do not possess monasteries,' Jacques de Vitry notes, 'churches, fields, vineyards or animals, houses or other sorts of property, not even somewhere to lay their heads' (ibid.). In this respect the Rule prescribes: 'The friars are to appropriate nothing for themselves, neither a house, nor a place, nor anything else' (*Second Rule*, 6, 2 [Omnibus, p. 61]).
17. *Second Rule*, 6, 3 (*Omnibus*, p. 61).
18. Esser, op. cit. p. 83.
19. *Testament*, 1 (*Omnibus*, p. 67).
20. *Major Legend*, 2, 4 (*Omnibus*, p. 643).
21. Iriarte, *Vocazione francescana*, p. 158.
22. A. Boni, 'Fraternità', in *Dizionario Francescano* (Padua: 1984), pp. 613, 615.
23. *Testament*, 16 (*Omnibus*, p. 68; here, translator's own version).
24. Celano, *First Life*, 24 (*Omnibus*, p. 249).
25. Cf. *First Rule*, 22, 29, 35-7, 39-40 (*Omnibus*, pp. 47-50).
26. Iriarte, op. cit. p. 161.
27. Cf. W. Viviani, *L'ermeneutica di Francesco d'Assisi. Indagine alla luce di Gv 13-17 nei suoi scritti* (Rome: Antonianum, 1983).
28. Jacques de Vitry writes: 'However, if we observe the way of life of the primitive Church attentively, we must conclude that [Francis] did not so much add a new Rule as renew religion, which was almost dead' (*Historia Occidentalis*).

29. *Rule*, Bull of Pope Innocent IV, 5.
30. Celano, *Second Life*, 191 (*Omnibus*, p. 515).
31. Cf. Celano, *First Life*, 38 (*Omnibus*, p. 260).
32. Ibid., 19 (*Omnibus*, p. 244f.).
33. *Rule*, Prologue.
34. Cf. *Rule*, 4, 22; 10, 7; 4, 13-14.
35. Cf. O. Schmucki, 'Linee fondamentali della "forma vitae" nell'esperienza di san Francesco', in *Lettura biblico-teologica*, pp. 183-231.
36. *First Rule*, 11, 4-5 (*Omnibus*, p. 41).
37. *Letter to all the faithful*, IV, 25-7 (*Omnibus*, p. 94); *First Rule*, 4, 3-4; 5, 16-17; 11, 6; 6, 2; 11, 1-3; 7, 16 (*Omnibus*, pp. 35, 36, 41, 37, 41, 38).
38. *Testament*, 59
39. *Little Testament*.
40. *Testament*, 59-60.
41. *Second Rule*, 6, 8-10 (*Omnibus*, p. 61).
42. *Testament*, 16 (*Omnibus*, p. 68).
43. Cf. M. Steiner, 'El Espíritu Santo y la fraternidad según los escritos de san Francisco', *Selecciones de Francescanismo* 11 (1982), pp. 75-88.
44. *First Rule*, 9, 14 (*Omnibus*, p. 40).
45. *Legend of the Three Companions*, 41 (*Omnibus*, p. 930).
46. Celano, *First Life*, 38-9 (*Omnibus*, p. 260f.).
47. Letter written in October 1216, from Genoa.
48. *First Rule*, 5, 16-17 (*Omnibus*, p. 36).
49. Ibid. 7, 14-17 (*Omnibus*, p. 38).
50. Cf. ibid. 11 (*Omnibus*, p. 41).
51. Cf. ibid. 10 (*Omnibus*, p. 40).
52. Cf. *Letter to a Minister*, 7-10 (*Omnibus*, p. 110).
53. *Second Rule*, 10, 8 (*Omnibus*, p. 63). One day when he heard a friar speaking ill of his brother, Francis said, turning to his vicar, Pietro Cattaneo: 'Serious dangers threaten the Order, if a remedy is not found for detractors. Very soon the fine fragrance of many will be changed into a disgusting stench if the mouths of these fetid persons are not closed. Courage, bestir yourself, examine diligently and if you find that a brother who has been accused is innocent, punish the accuser with a severe and exemplary chastisement ... My wish is, he said, that with the greatest care you and all the Ministers ensure that this pestiferous disease does not spread further' (Celano, *Second Life*, 182 [*Omnibus*, p. 507; here, translator's own version]). Rather, 'happy the servant who can love and fear his brother as much when he is far away as if he were close at hand, and says nothing behind his back that he cannot say charitably to his face' (*Admonition* 25, 2 [*Omnibus*, p. 86; here, translator's own version]).
54. *Rule*, 10.
55. *Admonition* 4, 2 (*Omnibus*, p. 80).
56. *Second Rule*, 8, 5 (*Omnibus*, p. 62).
57. Ibid. 10, 2 (*Omnibus*, p. 63).

58. Ibid. 10, 6 (*Omnibus*, p. 63).
59. Cf. *Legend of Perugia*, 106 (*Omnibus*, p. 1081f.); *Mirror of Perfection*, 46 (*Omnibus*, p. 1171).
60. *First Rule*, 6, 3 (*Omnibus*, p. 37).
61. Quoted by Esser, op. cit. p. 243.
62. Celano, *Second Life*, 191 (*Omnibus*, p. 515).
63. Cf. *Letter to a Minister*, 5 (*Omnibus*, p. 110).
64. Cf. *Mirror of Perfection*, 85 (*Omnibus*, p. 1218).

7 United In Order to be Scattered
The Society of Jesus

To find a new and significant turning point in the idea of religious community, comparable to that which came with the Mendicants, we have to wait for the Clerks Regular.[1] The fourteenth and fifteenth centuries, together with aspects of decadence in the life of the Church which culminated in the Western Schism, had seen a growing desire for reform. If the watchword of the preceding periods had been 'return to the purity of the primitive Church', the word which spread throughout Europe was 'general reform of the Church', *'in capite et in membris'* ('head and members'). This deep desire had already borne fruit, taking concrete form in the self-reform of the older Orders. There was, for example, the rise of the Benedictine Congregation of Santa Justina and the establishing of 'reformed and observant' branches of the Franciscans, Dominicans and Augustinians. New foundations were also born, such as the Olivetans, Jesuits and Brethren of the Common Life.

Yet the reform of the Church proceeded slowly, until the two great events which dominate the history of the Church in the sixteenth century: the Protestant Reformation and the Council of Trent. This was the context into which the origin and work of the Jesuits slotted, a typical example of those Clerks Regular who were to make a new contribution to the vision of community, causing it to go beyond the monastic and conventual forms and so adapting it to modern times. It was to be characterized above all by its apostolic aim.

We can certainly find antecedents for the ministerial and apostolic activities of the community. The association between religious life and charitable ministry goes back to the earliest days in the history of the monastic life, and was evidenced by the receiving and care of the poor and wayfarers already practised in the desert, the hospital established by Basil, and all the extraordinary social works performed by the Benedictine abbeys. At the beginning of the second millennium, Orders arose which had the exercise of charity as their very *raison d'être*, such as, for example, the Hospitallers, the Military Orders, the Mercedatians and the Trinitarians.

The association between religious life and pastoral ministry was also by then an established fact, beginning with Eusebius of Vercelli, Ambrose and Augustine, and continuing with the rise of the Canons Regular and the progressive clericalization of monasticism. With the Mendicants the *apostolic* purpose became more obvious and central. Yet conventual observances of the monastic type remained or came in, with the consequent tensions between the occupations of the common life such as choral prayer, and apostolic occupations such as preaching, the care of souls, and teaching. For the Dominicans, a typical example of the 'mixed life', divided between conventual observances and exterior ministry, the bridge between these two realities was formed by the juridical instrument of *dispensatio*: the friar called to a ministry could be dispensed by his Prior from assisting at community exercises. The community continued its tranquil cloistered rhythm, while some of its members worked in the Lord's vineyard.

The rise of the Clerks Regular marked the start of a new type of community. Originally they continued the medieval tradition of the Canons Regular: priests in search of community. It was the same with the first group, the Theatines, and with the Barnabites. Originally they retained the choir office, the penitential practices, and other conventual observances. The Theatines had papal enclosure. Yet by a number of elements they distanced themselves from earlier forms of religious life. They were priests united by bonds of charity with the aim of living an authentic priestly life and also making their ministry more effective in an institutionalized form: schools, education, catechesis, helping in hospitals ... Consequently, their habit was ordinary priestly dress. The choir office, when it was retained, was simplified and followed the Roman rite and calendar. Their dwelling took on the look of an ordinary house. It was no longer a monastery or even a friary, but precisely a religious 'house'. Even the word 'Rule' gave way to the milder 'Constitutions' (already in use for many centuries, but always dependent on the Rule). These were all factors, small and great, that denoted a move away from earlier monastic or conventual models in order to create a new type of community.

To understand the shape of this community better, especially its charismatic features, we shall concentrate on the experience of Ignatius and the Society of Jesus which he founded. In fact, as a distinguished Theatine scholar has written, it is the personal achievement of St Ignatius of Loyola to have definitively freed the Clerks Regular from all the monastic observances - including the office in choir - to which most of the kindred Institutes of his time remained faithful. This was due to his broader vision of the Catholic, and in particular the priestly, apostolate, as well as the missionary and apostolic spirit which has always inspired his Institute. Loyola is the true inspiration of modern Clerks Regular. The majority of the religious Congregations which came into being after the sixteenth century found their model and inspiration in the Jesuit way of life.[2]

He was, in fact, able to adapt the religious life of the older Orders to the apostolic needs of Christianity.

A New Apostolic Community is Born

The Jesuit community, like the earlier types of community, was born out of the charismatic experience of its founder.[3] At the beginning we find his conversion, occasioned by his reading the lives of Christ and the saints, and the mystical experience of light undergone at Manresa. From these experiences sprang a passionate desire to follow Christ as intensely and closely as possible, in imitation of the apostles. In the *Exercises* Ignatius allows us to glimpse this deep yearning of his when he sets before the retreatant the Christ who, as king, calls men to follow him as 'the supreme and true captain under whose banner he longs to fight'.[4] Again, in the 'third form of humility' he emphasizes the desire to 'imitate and resemble Christ our Lord more effectively'.[5]

The whole of his life was marked by this authentic seeking to follow Christ and be assimilated to him, to 'be with Christ' and to love him 'more'. His own pilgrimage to the Holy Land, which he embarked on once he had left Manresa, was tangible evidence of his desire to live with Christ and like Christ, to know his historical dimension as well, as the apostles had done. In his autobiography he deliberately recounts several episodes which illustrate this persistent eagerness, as when, following his own method of *compositio loci* (composition of place), he found at the University of Paris

spiritual comfort in setting before himself the following considerations: he imagined that the master was Christ; to one fellow disciple he gave the name of Peter, to another that of John, and so on with the names of all the apostles. He reflected: When a master gives me an order I shall think that Christ commands me; if someone else asks me something I shall think that it is St Peter who demands it of me.[6]

His experience at La Storta marked the culminating moment of this quest. He himself relates that

> one day, when he was within a few miles of Rome, while praying in a church, he felt a profound change in his mind and saw so clearly that God the Father was putting him with Christ his Son that he could no longer in any way doubt that in fact God the Father was putting him with his Son'.[7]

In this event, which would profoundly mark Ignatius' life and the future direction of the Society, 'the Father closely united Ignatius to Jesus burdened with the cross, and stated his will that he should dedicate himself to his service. Ignatius was thus called to the mysticism of union, to being "put with Christ", and to the mysticism of service, or to the consecration of his life to the divine service.'[8]

The experience of Christ which Ignatius had was in fact that of the Son sent by the Father for the salvation of the world. His discipleship therefore became a participation in the same mission of Christ. Ignatius felt himself called to relive the mystery of Christ in his obedience to the Father who sent him into the world for the salvation of humankind, to relive Christ who 'humbled himself and became obedient unto death, even death on a cross'. Made one with Christ, he worked as he did, continuing his mission in obedience to the Father.

This obedience was not ascetic but theological and 'missionary', as we can see throughout the book of the *Exercises* which inspired the very nature of the Society. In the meditations on the Kingdom and the Two Standards, we see clearly the outlook which later brought the Society into being. In the meditation on the Kingdom, the king speaks to all his subjects and says: 'It is my will to conquer the whole world and all the territory of the infidels.' Therefore he calls them to him and says: 'It is my will to conquer the whole world and all my enemies, and so to enter into the glory of my Father; accordingly, anyone who wishes to come with me must work with me...'[9] The meditation on the Two Standards leads to the consideration that 'the Lord of the whole world chooses many people, disciples, etc., and sends them out all over the world to spread his sacred doctrine among people of every class and condition'.[10]

The starting point and very beginning of the mission is Christ who calls to himself those whom he will and sends them out to extend throughout the world his mission as the one sent by the Father for the salvation of all people. For the Society, this mission, which starts from the love of Christ who calls and sends all his members together for a universal work of salvation, is the basic and most concrete element of the charism which constitutes it as a priestly body in the service of the Church and humanity. It relates to the *magis* (more) of the constant search for God's will and full conformity with Christ, which later, because of the mission, came to occupy a central position even in the Order's apostolic experience. In fact, his mystical experiences at the Cardoner and Manresa had aroused in Ignatius a longing to share his own experience and the new life which had been born in him; it had transformed the convert into an apostle. With the vision at La Storta, the bond, dependence and continuity between this apostolate and that of Christ finally became clear.

Sharing the experience of Ignatius, the aim of the Society was seen as clearly apostolic: 'The aim of the Society,' we read at the beginning of the Constitutions, 'is not only to attend, with God's grace, to the salvation and perfecting of our own souls but, by this same grace, to make sure that with all our strength we help the souls of our neighbours towards salvation and perfection.'[11]

The aim of the new Order was plainly and directly apostolic, in the modern sense of the word. It set itself the tasks of the defence and propagation of the faith, the good of souls, and the practice of spiritual and corporal works of mercy. What came into being, as we read in the Formulae of the Institute, was 'a Society established for the primary purpose of occupying itself particularly with the defence and propagation of the faith and the progress of souls in Christian life and doctrine', with a variety of works ranging from preaching to teaching, from administering the sacraments to charitable work on behalf of prisoners, the sick, and the needy of all kinds.[12]

Henceforward, the Jesuit community was characterized by its apostolic dimension and its call to mission. '*Vita apostolica*' no longer evoked the memory of the Jerusalem community united around the apostles, as in earlier forms of the religious life, but rather the dispersal throughout the world which came about when Peter sent the apostles to spread the Gospel in the name of the Lord. The Jesuit community is an 'apostolic community' in this sense, even if the phrase itself is entirely absent from the Constitutions.[13]

The Value and Meaning of Obedience to the Pope

In the context of mission, or the apostolic mandate, the tie with and dependence on the Pope takes on a very special character. When Ignatius, with his companions, presented himself to Paul III, to be entirely at his disposal to do whatever he asked, he knew with complete clarity the kind of service to which he and his Society had been called and the way in which they should serve Christ. As Christ had sent out his apostles, so now the Vicar of Christ would send out Ignatius and his companions to evangelize. The 'obedience of mission' was translated into obedience to the Pope, sealed with a special vow, and a vision of trust in the superior, in whom the members of the Society 'must recognize Christ, as if he were present'.[14]

At its very beginning, the *Formula Instituti* declares that the Society wants to fight for God and serve only Christ and his Church and that therefore it is 'at the disposal of the Roman Pontiff, the Vicar of Christ on earth'.[15] Further on, it reminds all who enter it that 'the Society as a whole and the individual members who make profession in it fight for God, faithfully obedient to our Most Holy Lord Pope Paul III and the other Roman Pontiffs his successors'. By virtue of the special vow, the Pope could dispose of each one as he thought best, so that the apostolic mission could have 'a more assured direction from the Holy Spirit'.[16]

The vow of obedience to the Pope became, in Ignatius' own words, 'our starting-point and our main foundation'.[17] It made real and specific the Society's particular service, that being 'placed with Christ' for which Ignatius asked so insistently and which gave the Society its distinctive features. It was a question, wrote Nadal (one of Ignatius' companions who was best able to translate the new charism into doctrinal terms), of 'a special grace which God Our Lord gave to the Society'.[18]

Summing up their particular vocation in the Church, today's Jesuits can write: 'Impelled by the love of Christ we embrace obedience as a charism given to the Society by God through its Founder ... In fact the Society of Jesus is a group of men who live in close union with Christ and share in his mission of salvation, which he brings to completion through obedience unto death.'[19]

The Features of the New Community

What constituted the Society in the unity of one body was the love of Christ who called and sent for a mission that was fundamentally communal. The mission was, in effect, given to the whole body, or to the body as such and then, through it, to each of its members. The apostolate, understood as a help to souls, was not exercised primarily and of itself by the individual but by the Society. Ignatius was at pains to point out that the individual 'should be deeply persuaded that he belongs to a Society established for a chief aim ...'[20] Consequently the Jesuit feels responsible, jointly with his own companions, for the fulfilment of their common vocation and must live out his own mission as the mission of the whole body.

What constituted the *proprium* of the Jesuit community, therefore, was not the Acts ideal of 'concord and unanimity', nor the 'behold how good and joyful' of Psalm 132(132). Community life was not to be sought as an end in itself. It occurred in order to achieve a common mission entrusted to it by Christ who has called and sent his members to work together for a particular apostolic purpose. The carrying out of a common apostolic plan is usually the main point of reference for the life of a community and the 'making of community' by all its members. The community is a place of discernment, where the apostolic design is drawn up, the ways and means of carrying out the mission.

Before considering the results of this outlook for the community, it must be appreciated that although the Ignatian community was in a certain sense functional, or dependent on the mission, it did have a loving nature, like every other type of community. The Constitutions clearly affirm that 'the most effective help towards attaining this end comes, more than from any external constitution, from the inner law of charity and love that the Holy Spirit writes and imprints on hearts'.[21] 'The principal bond which, on both sides, contributes to the unity of the members among themselves and with their head, is the love of God our Lord ... Thus both sides will be helped by union, charity and, in general, every goodness and virtue which enables them to proceed in faithfulness to the Spirit.'[22] The *Exercises* show well the value of love for mutual relationships and so for the building up of community. 'Love,' Ignatius wrote in them, 'consists in communication between the two parties, that is, in the fact that the lover gives and communicates to the beloved all or part of what he has or may have, and the beloved does the same to the lover'.[23] In a letter to Claude le Jay he wrote, in a very concrete way, 'As for your person and affairs, believe and rest assured that all of us are as your own soul.'[24] The Society was not only a single body, it was a single soul!

Even if the characteristic elements of the Jesuit community are particularly the apostolate and obedience (with the resulting coherent organizational structures), it remains true that once again we also find in this sort of community the centrality of supernatural love as a theological element fundamental to everything.

Having affirmed this fundamental reality, it must at once be noted that the element which immediately catches the attention when looking at the Jesuit community, is that of a group of men who have come together not so much to be together as to part. It would be enough, on this topic, to reread the steps by which the Society was constituted, in a long and profound process of discernment carried out by Ignatius and his companions at Rome in 1539. It had to be decided whether each would work alone, following his own path, or whether they would stay united as one body. As we read in the account written at the time,

> In the end, we decided ... that since the Lord in his generous kindness had chosen to bring us together and unite us ... we ought not to break this union and community willed by God; rather, we should keep it strong and reinforce it, binding ourselves into a single body, attentive to and concerned for one another, with a view to the greater good of souls. The value of many united together is certainly greater vigour and consistency for obtaining any difficult result than if they were dispersed in several directions.'[25]

The first group united in order to go out and was held together by the same mission plan. Thus the Society was one body united in one mission. This one body was obviously the Society as a whole, rather than individual local communities. There was in fact one large community, to which every Jesuit belonged even when he was on his own, because even when alone he was bound by the same orders and the same plan.

The Society's unity was that of a living being, not a federation of communities; it started from the centre, not the periphery. Its mission was seen as an extension and reproduction of the mission of the apostolic college, which in its turn prolonged the mission of Christ, the one sent by the Father. Indeed, Ignatius wrote: 'Regarding our intentions, what concerns the universal body of the Society is of primary and greatest importance, for which we seek principally unity, good government and preservation in fullness of life.'[26] For this reason Father Arrupe could say: 'The Society is essentially one and pre-exists the Provinces. It is precisely true to say that the Society "is divided into Provinces. Vice-Provinces and Missions", but not that it is "formed out of Provinces".'[27]

For this reason, the local communities are given only a relative role, in favour of the one great community which is the Society. Availability, universality and mobility are the characteristics of this community, precisely in order to achieve its mission. Talk of unity, communion or community primarily refers to the Society as such. Wherever a Jesuit may be, he is there as a member of the one great community, sent by it and embodying it.

The real superior is the General, rather than the local superior, because the whole Society has to pursue a single apostolic plan. The superior is no longer an 'abba' or a prior, *primus inter pares* (first among equals), nor a minister, but a 'chief', the 'head' of a body. Consequently, the members of the Society regard themselves more as comrades than as brothers.

A community thus scattered for mission, a 'koinonia in diaspora', needs strong ties of unity. We have already seen that its foundation was theological love. Nevertheless, Ignatius provided a whole series of tools for safeguarding the tie between the members of the Society, above all the centralization of government and the strict bond of obedience.

For Ignatius the most effective means of unity seemed to be obedience, which ensured a direct and fundamental relationship with the superior. 'The more that inferiors depend on their superiors,' we read in the Constitutions, 'the better will love, obedience and unity be preserved between the same.'[28] In fact, 'the more difficult the union of the members of this congregation with their head and each other, because they are so scattered across the different parts of the world among faithful and infidels, the more we must seek what fosters it. The Society cannot, in fact, be preserved, governed, or even achieve its purpose for the greater glory of God if its members are not united among themselves and with their head.'[29]

Unity in agape and unity in obedience do not, however, conflict with each other. One is expressed in and proved by the other. 'Rest assured, dearest brother,' Polanco wrote to a member of the Society on behalf of Ignatius, 'that although separated from the body, you are closely united by the bond of charity on our part and also, I think, on yours. You may be sure that you are united by not only this tie but also by that of holy obedience, which binds all the members of the Society into one spiritual body, to which you belong wherever you may be.'[30]

Accordingly, like the founders we have already studied, Ignatius too issued a warning against those who disturb the community, with a more direct emphasis on offences against obedience: 'The person responsible for division among those who live together, or between them and their head, must be sent away from that community as quickly as possible, like a plague that can infect many if the remedy is not applied at once.'[31]

To live the obedience 'of mission' in all its theological nature, requires the virtue of obedience itself. Here too Ignatius gives a masterly description of its smallest details and recommends it forcefully. 'Let everyone form a single unity in our Lord Jesus Christ,' he wrote to his students at Coimbra, indicating immediately that obedience is the way to attain this union: 'Since such a union between many cannot be maintained without order, nor order without the necessary bond of obedience between inferiors and superiors ... I very strongly commend this holy obedience to you, which everyone must observe with his superiors at whatever level.' Specifying further the kind of obedience needed to achieve this aim in the Society, he wrote again: 'If this obedience is to be the cause and guarantee of union, it must not be simply external but internal as well, that is, of the will.'[32] On internal obedience as an essential factor in the unity of the Society, Ignatius wrote on another occasion:

> As for the union which forms the basis of the life of every Institute, St Paul exhorts vehemently 'that all should think and say the same' in order to support one another by their union of judgement and will. And if there must be one attitude between head and members, it is easy to see whether it should be a matter of the head thinking like the members, or the members like their head. That said, the need for intellectual obedience is obvious.[33]

The relationship with the Superior General will also find expression in personal correspondence and regular meetings.[34] What we see here is a new tool for unity in the community, the result of the immediate and wide diffusion experienced by the Society both in Asia and the new American territories. The Constitutions also emphasize the importance of circulating news among the members.[35]

The unity of the apostolic body demands additional tools, such as strong formation. Because they have to be ready to go anywhere, even without the support of a local community, Jesuits must be particularly strong and well-prepared people, in order to carry out the mission entrusted to them within the framework of the Society, that great community. Compared to earlier religious systems, the Constitutions provided new arrangements for training. They prescribed that admission to the Society should be granted 'only to selected people ... In fact, the presence of a large number of people who have not mortified their vices would be a great obstacle to the Order and to that unity in Christ our Lord which is essential for maintaining the full vitality and good functioning of this Society.'[36]

The preparation of suitable men to carry out this new kind of apostolate also involved a new sort of formative process, structured in accordance with the apostolic aim. The length of the noviciate was increased from one to two years. 'Exercises' were introduced to train the candidates for every kind of ministry and way of life. Further innovations were the taking of simple but not perpetual vows which bound the individual to the Order but not vice versa; the making of solemn vows after a 'third year of probation'; and the division of the members of the Society into three different classes.

Ignatius indicates that uniformity of life is another element which guarantees the unit of the community: 'Uniformity can also be a great help, both inner uniformity of doctrine, judgement and will, as far as possible, and outer uniformity of dress, ceremonial at Mass, and so on, as far as the different conditions of people, places, etc., allow...'[37]

Finally, we can mention several other characteristic features of this community, the product of its specific apostolic charism. The office in choir was suppressed and, in order to safeguard apostolic freedom, was not replaced by a series of devotional community prayers. The typical Jesuit prayer would be mental prayer and examination of conscience of a kind which allowed a man wholly dedicated to the external ministry to interiorize.

In addition, poverty was modelled on that demanded by Christ from his apostles when he sent them out on mission, and motivated by the freedom needed by an apostle. Chastity too was always seen from an apostolic point of view, as a condition for the building up of positive relationships. 'And let them often be exhorted to seek God our Lord in all things,' Ignatius wrote on this subject to the novices, 'banishing from themselves, as far as possible, love for all creatures in order to give it to their Creator instead, by loving him in all things and all things in him, in conformity with his most holy and divine will.'[38]

The clear apostolic aim, the extreme mobility of the Society, its adaptability to different settings and situations, its strong centralization and type of government which gave the General a remarkable breadth of movement, the fourth vow of obedience to the Pope, and its freedom from aspects of the life previously considered essential to the religious state - all these led to a new kind of structure and formation appropriate to the modern society which had come into being along with Humanism and the Renaissance. This type of community would, from now on, increasingly be the pattern for new religious institutions.

NOTES

1. As we shall have occasion to observe later on, an earlier creation of a new form of religious community can be seen in the foundation of the Brothers and Sisters of the Common Life by Gerard Groote (1340-84). This was perhaps the most mature expression, at least as regards life-experience, of the *Devotio Moderna*.

2. F. Andreu, 'Chierici regolari', DIP, II, 908.

3. Born in 1491, Ignatius of Loyola spent his youth in a military setting. He was seriously wounded in one leg in the defence of the citadel of Pamplona against the French. During his long convalescence he made the acquaintance of Ludwig of Saxony's *Life of Christ* and a collection of Lives of the Saints, which led to his first spiritual experience and conversion. At Montserrat he took the habit of a pilgrim but then settled at Manresa where, after mystical experiences, he began to write his *Exercises*. After a journey to the Holy Land, Ignatius studied in Paris where he gathered around him his first group of companions with whom he began the Society of Jesus at Rome in May 1538. While the Order spread rapidly all over the world, Ignatius worked out the Constitutions, which were to be definitively approved two years after his death, which occurred on 31 July 1556. The great collection of source material for Ignatius and the first Jesuits is

the *Monumenta Historica Societatis Jesu*, 100 volumes (Madrid and Rome: 1894-1969), with an important subdivision entitled *Monumenta Ignatiana*, containing the writings, correspondence, early Lives, etc., of St Ignatius. The *Monumenta Ignatiana* is divided into four series: the correspondence, the Spiritual Exercises, the Constitutions of the Society of Jesus, and early writings about Ignatius. The latter series has been replaced by the *Fontes Narrativi de S Ignatio de Loyola* (4 vols, Rome: 1943-65), and the second series by a new critical edition of the Spiritual Exercises, volume 100 of the MHSJ (Rome: 1969). There are many English translations of the Spiritual Exercises, for example that of Fr Thomas Corbishley SJ, *The Spiritual Exercises* (London: Burns and Oates, 1963). The Constitutions of the Society have been translated by George Ganss (St Louis, MO: The Institute of Jesuit Sources, 1970).

For the Jesuits as a religious community, cf. *La communauté dans la Compagnie de Jésus* (Rome: CIS, 1979); D. Bertrand, *Un corps pour l'Esprit. Essaie sur l'expérience communautaire selon les Constitutions de la Compagnie de Jésus* (DBB, Paris: 1974); J. Osuna, *Amigos en el Señor. Estudio sobre la génesis de la comunidad en la Compania de Jesús* (Bogotá: 1975); G. Wilkens, *Compagnons de Jésus. La genèse de l'Ordre des Jésuites* (Rome: CIS, 1978); P. Arrupe, *L'ispirazione trinitaria del carisma ignaziano* (Supplement to no. 6 of the 1980 Notizie of the Jesuits of Italy, Rome: 1980); M. Ledrus, 'L'amicizia nella Compagnia di Gesù', in *Scienze umane et religiose*, ESUR vol. 2, ed. A. Spadaro (Messina: 1989), pp. 23-4; Peter Hans Kolvenbach, *Men of God: Men for Others. The Jesuits an obedient avant-garde confronting the challenges of the modern world* (an interview with Renzo Giacomelli, translated by Alan Neam; Slough: 1990).

Works in English on this chapter as a whole include James Brodrick SJ, The Origin of the Jesuits (London: Longman, Green: 1940); *The Progress of the Jesuits* (London: Longman, Green, 1947); *Saint Ignatius Loyola: The Pilgrim Years* (London: Burns and Oates, 1956).

4. *Spiritual Exercises*, 143.
5. Ibid., 167.
6. *Autobiography*, 75. The English text is available in J. O'Callaghan, *The Autobiography of St Ignatius Loyola* (London: Harper & Row, 1974).
7. Ibid., 96.
8. C. de Dalmases, *El Padre Maestro Ignacio* (Madrid: 1979), p. 131.
9. *Spiritual Exercises*, 91-98
10. Ibid., 136-47.
11. *Constitutions*, General Examination, I, 2.
12. Cf. *Formula Instituti*, 1.
13. The word 'community' occurs four times (but never referring to the Society), and 'apostolic' occurs twenty-two times (always with reference to the Apostolic See).
14. *Formula Instituti*, 6.
15. Ibid., 1.
16. Ibid., 3.

17. *Constitutiones de Missionibus* (1544-1545), in *Constitutiones Societatis Jesu* (Rome: 1934), p. 162.
18. *Exhortationes anni 1554 in Hispania*, in *Commentarii de Instituto Societatis Jesu* (Rome: 1962), p. 38.
19. *31st General Congregation*, d. 17, n. 2.
20. *Formula Instituti*, 1.
21. *Constitutions, Proemium*, 1.
23. *Spiritual Exercises*, 231.
24. *Monumenta Ignatiana*, Letters, I. 343-4.
25. *Gli scritti di Ignazio di Loyola*, ed. M. Gioia (Turin: 1977), pp. 207-8.
26. *Constitutions*, Proemium, 2.
27. Quoted by M. Costa, 'Notes sur la communauté apostolique dans la Compagnie de Jésus', in *La communauté dans la Compagnie de Jésus* (Rome: 1979), p. 26.
28. *Constitutions*, VIII, I, 6.
29. Ibid., 1. In one of Ignatius' letters, addressed to Melchior Carneiro (*Letters*, VIII, 489-90), we read: 'I am sure that, on your part, you will as far as possible maintain full union with our men, while on our part you may be certain that we shall always have you in our hearts wherever you may be: the interior union will be all the closer the further you are, through obedience, from our physical presence.'
30. To Francesco Mancini (*Letters*, VI, 585-7). In another of Polanco's letters (to Giovanni Battista Viola, *Letters*, VI, 447-50) we read: 'You protest that you are not separated from the Society in spirit but only temporarily in the body. N. P. [Our Father] says this is quite obvious: even if you wanted to separate yourself, we should hold you with cords. Neither should you consider yourself separated even in the body, because one who is sent by obedience to one place or another, though alone, is not really separated from his Institute either in soul or body as long as the union of obedience persists.'
31. *Constitutions*, VIII, I, 5.
32. To the Jesuit students at Coimbra, 15 January 1548.
33. To the Jesuits of Portugal, 26 March 1553.
34. *Constitutions*, VIII, I, L. M. N.
35. Ibid., VIII, I, 9.
36. Ibid., VIII, I, 2.
37. Ibid., VIII, I, 8.
38. Ibid., III, 26.

8 'Among Yourselves, Love, and Outside, Zeal for Souls.'
The experience of the Congregations

The seventeenth to nineteenth centuries witnessed the rise of an extraordinary variety of new religious communities. In the wealth and diversity of their works they demonstrated the great fruitfulness of life which was released in the Church immediately following the Council of Trent. Yet the Congregations did not apparently make any particularly important or new contributions to the doctrine and spirituality of community life.[1] The Jesuit community continued to give a decisive imprint to the new communities which appeared during this period. Beginning with the Council of Trent, which exhorted faithful observance 'in what concerns the maintenance of the common life, food and clothing',[2] the guidelines for the common life offered by the Magisterium tended increasingly to insist on observance and uniformity.

After the great climax of the seventeenth and eighteenth centuries, one of the most prominent events was undoubtedly the French Revolution, which marked on the one hand a collapse of the religious life and on the other the providential circumstances for its renewal. Membership of men's Institutes, for example, dropped from 300,000 to 70,000 between 1775 and 1850. The Revolution was not, in fact, a local occurrence. It crossed the frontiers of France and swept on into Belgium, Holland, Germany, Austria, Switzerland, Italy, Spain and Portugal. Everywhere, the religious life was hit by French legislation or that of countries influenced by it, which followed the French pattern: confiscation of monasteries, secularization of Religious, suppression of the Orders. At the same time the Revolution brought about an extraordinary blossoming of the religious life, with the rise of large numbers of new Congregations which from exactly that moment gained increasing ground in the Church as a new form of the religious life.[3]

These new Congregations exhibited common features. The first was the ability to identify local needs and respond to a variety of social and ecclesial emergencies. Nursery schools came to the aid of parents working in the fields or factories; professional training enabled boys and girls to face life with a good preparation; charitable and welfare work was particularly necessary in the suburbs of the cities to which the work forces of the new industrial plants flocked, or in the national ghettos of the New World. Initiatives positively teemed, starting with the basic needs. Besides the brilliant development of the Congregations,

> we must not underestimate the global importance of the small-scale activities of lesser institutions in all fields of the apostolate: teaching, especially the instruction of children; care for the sick; help for the socially weak, which became increasingly specialized (orphans, the aged, domestic servants, young women workers, prisoners, the blind, the deaf and dumb), and not least, catachesis, the press, missions, etc...[4]

A second characteristic of the new Congregations was a renewed dedication to mission. Some Congregations (such as the Oblates of Mary Immaculate, the White Fathers, the Society of the Divine Word, the Combonians or Verona Fathers...) came into being with this express aim.

Another typical feature of the religious life in this period was its international character, which called for greater centralization.

As far as community was concerned, especially with the blossoming of the nineteenth-century Congregations, there was nothing particularly new to note. While there was a bubbling creativity in the field of the apostolate, there was a corresponding paucity in the development of original forms of community. Indeed, there was a persistent repetition of earlier schemes in which rigid asceticism and uniformity, devotional spiritual practices and regular observance predominated. There was in fact a conviction that the collapse of the religious life at the end of the seventeenth century had been largely caused by the poor observance prevailing in the monasteries of the time.

Yet there is no lack of examples of a search for a synthesis between a model of community based on communion and one based on mission. In this respect the community of the Missionary Oblates of Mary Immaculate, founded by Blessed Eugène de Mazenod, can be considered typical. We shall focus our analysis on the theological and spiritual elements of this community because, like Hostie, we regard it as typical of the period.[5]

A Community for Mission

Once again, in order to enter into the living reality of a religious community, we need to turn to the experience of its founder. The climax in the conversion of Eugène de Mazenod[6] was his meeting with Christ one Good Friday. Contemplating the unveiling of the cross, he experienced God's merciful love in the crucified Christ, his Saviour. Redeemed by him, de Mazenod felt called to become, in him and with him, an instrument of redemption for all people, his brothers and sisters, a co-operator with the Saviour Christ. In the light of this mystery and with new eyes of faith - the very eyes of the Saviour with whom he was identified - he gazed on the Church and recognized it as the Bride of Christ, the fruit of his martyrdom. He saw the state of abandonment in which it lay after the storm of the French Revolution, he heard 'the cry of her who calls loudly to her children', as he himself wrote, and he declared himself ready to answer. He was moved to compassion at the sight of the poor, the people whom the ordinary pastoral care of the Church reached least. In them he saw children of God, people for whom Christ gave his blood, and he decided to dedicate his whole life in the priesthood to them and enable them, through the ministry of evangelization, to know who Christ is, and so help them to become aware of their dignity as sons and daughters of God. Although de Mazenod's first years in the ministry were intense and devoted to an innovative pastorate, he realized that he could not offer an adequate and lasting answer on his own. He then formed an association with some other priests, and later brothers, with whom he chose to live the evangelical counsels and the common life, after the example of the apostles. The aim of this way of life was to realize radically and completely the Christian vocation to holiness, and to embark together on the ministry of evangelizing the whole person, all people, especially the poorest and most forsaken. Gradually he discovered the presence of Mary in his life and in the ministry of his religious family. He recognized that he was an instrument of her compassionate love for humanity and felt called to bring the scattered children of God to her, the Mother of Mercy. So, with his brethren, he began to go to those whom the Church's ordinary pastoral ministry found it most difficult to reach, and where others were unwilling or unable to go. They went with a bold, avant-garde style of evangelism that could open up new ways and leave nothing untried, and in which they could devote themselves to the uttermost. It was the story of many other founders of that time and the birth of many other nineteenth-century Congregations.

The purpose for which this new family came into being in the Church was clear: evangelization, aimed at realizing the mystery of the Christ who proclaimed Good News and the apostles who, like him, proclaimed the Word.

When the first community got under way on 25 January 1818, with the name of Missionaries of Provence from the region where it had been formed, it had no clearly defined structure. Was it to be a community of priests bound only by mutual love, or a religious community? Life would decide. For the moment, two things were clear: the value of community life, and the ideal of the apostle who could realize such a community and direct it in a precise programme of evangelization.

The importance of community life was asserted right from the start, though without explicit reference to the structure of the religious life. Sharing his plan with Tempier, who was to become his first companion, de Mazenod wrote:

> We shall live in a house which I have acquired, under a Rule which we shall adopt by common consent ... Happiness awaits us in this holy society which will have one heart and one soul ... We shall not bind ourselves by vows; but I hope that it will be for us as it was for the disciples of St Philip [Neri] who, free as we shall remain, would have died before thinking of leaving a Congregation they loved as a mother.[7]

The ideal apostolic person, or the 'truly apostolic person' as de Mazenod used to say in order to clear the ground of false images of soulless preachers, must be 'an extraordinary person'[8] able to combine in himself the life of holiness and the life of evangelical proclamation.

By extraordinary people Blessed Eugene did not mean people with uncommon gifts, renowned preachers who would even be able to win souls. To his first companion, prevented from joining him to start the community, he wrote:

> If it was just a question of going to preach the Word of God well or badly, together with a lot of human chatter, or going all over the countryside with the aim, if you like, of gaining souls for God without bothering to be interior men, truly apostolic men, then there would not, I think, be any difficulty in finding someone to replace

you; but do you think I want that kind of rubbish? We have to be saints.[9]

When, therefore, he launched his project of a missionary community and had to explain why he had only succeeded in bringing together a small number of people, he further clarified what he meant by 'apostolic men': 'The fact is that we want to choose people who will have the will and courage to walk in the footsteps of the apostles.'[10]

What was needed, in a word, was not good preachers but, to use the equivalent words in de Mazenod's writings, interior people, truly apostolic people - in short, saints. 'We ourselves must truly be saints. This word sums up all we can say.'[11] Being truly apostolic people, that is, interior and at the same time full of zeal, and walking in the footsteps of the apostles, began to be the key words that typified the missionary called to form the community of Oblates.

Numbers did not matter. What did matter was quality. Even while still at the start of his foundation, de Mazenod said this very clearly to his friend Forbin-Janson as well. The latter, who was to found the 'Missionaries of France', was advertizing grandiose schemes and enrolling large numbers of priests for the evangelization of the whole of France. Blessed Eugene, on the other hand, was less preoccupied with numbers and intended to build a community of men who could live out brotherly charity with a particular intensity. With great outspokenness he remarked to his friend that the greatest difference between the two projects, apparently so similar and both drawn up in response to Pius VII's invitation to re-evangelize France by missions to the people, lay in their very concepts of mission and community:

In your place, I would be less concerned with appearances and more with substance. What use are fine speeches if people are proud? Humility, the spirit of abnegation, obedience, etc., the most intimate charity, are necessary both for good order and the happiness of society, and not all your people have understood this properly. I ascribe this mistake to the sort of need you have created for yourselves to accept people for preaching. Here we do not think about what has to be done. There are six of us ... Our community is truly fervent; nowhere in the diocese are there better priests.[12]

The apostolic man takes the pursuit of sanctity seriously. Mission demands, as de Mazenod was later to write in the Rule, 'apostolic people who, fully aware of the need to reform themselves, will labour with all their strength to convert others'. Again, in the Rule, he proposed an austere and exacting programme that left no room for compromise:

> They must renounce themselves completely; aim solely for the glory of God, the good of the Church, the edification and salvation of souls; renew themselves constantly in the spirit of their vocation; live in a habitual state of abnegation and a constant desire to attain perfection, working non-stop to become humble, meek, obedient, lovers of poverty, penitent, mortified, detached from the world and their relatives, full of zeal, ready to sacrifice all their possessions, talents, rest, themselves and life itself for love of Jesus Christ, the service of the Church and the sanctification of their neighbour.[13]

'The aim of this society,' wrote de Mazenod as far back as his first prospectus, 'is not only to work for the salvation of our neighbour by dedicating ourselves to the ministry of preaching. Its principal purpose is also to offer its members the means of living the religious virtues.'[14]

Just as not every sort of preaching would suffice, neither would all individual apostolic people. In order to be 'truly apostolic people', it was necessary to be in deep communion with one another. Walking in the footsteps of the apostles meant living in unity as they had around Jesus, according to the model they taught the first Christians at Jerusalem. A 'common sanctification' is needed, de Mazenod wrote to Tempier, suggesting a first meeting of all the future members of the community: 'At the first meeting ... we shall reach agreement on how we are to do good, we shall help one another with advice and everything that God inspires in each of us for our common sanctification.'[15]

A Community United Like a Family

When de Mazenod wrote again to Tempier, telling him about his plans for the foundation, he said that the house in Aix-en-Provence, where the first community of the Missionaries of Provence was to be born, must, 'according to my thought and hopes, reproduce the perfection of the first disciples of the apostles', that is, the first Christians at Jerusalem, because, he continues, 'I place my hopes more on this than on eloquent sermons. They have never converted anyone!' There is a clear allusion here to the witness given by the first Christian community through its life of mutual love.

The conditions for making a good start on the work were in fact demanding. It was a question of having perfect unanimity of outlook, the same good will, the same detachment from everything that might impede the work of evangelization. Everything, even the pursuit of holiness, had to be shared.[16] This required perfect unity, in a consensus that achieved the same attitudes. The community had to be characterized by the possession of one heart and one soul, just like the first Christians, so that they could taste together the same spiritual joy: 'How sweet are the bonds of perfect charity!'[17] The common life appeared an essential element for 'apostolic man', both for the effectiveness of his own missionary activity and for his sanctification. Even as a seminarian de Mazenod had written that strength does not consist in numbers but in unity, and that only if they were united by the bonds of the same charity and inspired by the same spirit would they be able to conquer the world for God.[18]

Right from the start, the first community showed signs of the intense communion dreamed about by its founder. One of the first members has left a description which in certain respects recalls the first Franciscan brotherhood as described by Celano:

> The community at Aix was truly a family. All lived the same life, and all hearts opened beneath the rays of one and the same sun. It was as if they were unceasingly warmed by the affection of a father whose kindness to all of them was the best that could be imagined ... The 'cor unum et anima una' which the Founder recommends in the Rules as one of the characteristics of his Congregation, was truly the distinguishing mark of this little community which was trying, amidst a thousand external difficulties, to put down its first roots in order to grow up later to the point to which God wanted to raise it ... The members of this little family, clustering round their Superior like chicks beneath the wings of a hen, were a moving sight on account of the bonds of love which united them both to their Superior and to each other. They were truly the image of the first Christians portrayed in the Acts of the Apostles. There was no rivalry, no self-seeking, no prejudice against others, but joy, almost pride, at the successes of a brother ... It was, in miniature, the most perfect communion of saints.[19]

At first sight, this text seems to idealize the early days. However, the truth of this description is confirmed when we read the letters that de

Mazenod wrote to the community during a prolonged stay in Paris two years after the foundation. For the first time he was obliged to live at a distance from his comrades and, as he wrote to the community at Aix:

> Far away from you, I am bored and want only to be back with you; nothing can be a substitute for the pleasure of dwelling in our holy house with good brethren like you. Never have I experienced so well the significance of the expression *'quam dulce et quam jucundum habitare fratres in unum'*. And I say this with all the more conviction because I see with my own eyes that it is not granted to all communities to have such joy, which is rare here below, rarer than is thought. Let us beg the Lord to preserve this precious blessing for us; it will be our own fault if men are able to rob us of it...[20]

In Paris, far from his own people, de Mazenod became even more aware of the value of community. 'We are on earth, and especially in our house, to become saints, helping one another by our example, our words and our prayer.'[21] The year before, when he had to be away from the community for a period of rest, he had already declared that he felt like a fish out of water, far from 'my dear brethren whom I love tenderly in the Lord, our common love'.[22]

De Mazenod considered that the strong ties of charity, the family spirit, the sharing of one heart and one soul, were distinctive and inalienable characteristics of his community. Even when he was drawing up his plan to form a group of missionaries, he had written that 'happiness awaits us in this holy society, which will have one heart and one soul'.[23] Towards the end of his life he tried to sum up and describe his religious family; he wrote: 'This has always been our distinctive feature, as it was for the first Christians ... the spirit which I wanted to establish in our Congregation.'[24] Again, in answer to a letter from a young man who had recently entered the Congregation, he wrote: 'You have already understood that we form a family whose members wish to have one heart and one soul.'[25]

'United by Bonds of the Most Fervent Charity'

The family spirit and unity of heart and soul so emphasized by the founder of the Oblates were the fruit of the charity that circulated among all the members of the Congregation. Charity, according to de Mazenod, was in fact the distinctive mark of the Oblates. He wrote, in a text which can be considered a manifesto for charity:

> We need to be imbued with our spirit and live by it alone. This is so obvious that no explanations are needed. Just as a society has a common dress and rules, so too we need to have a common spirit giving life to this particular body. The spirit of a son of St Bernard is not that of a Jesuit. Ours, likewise, is proper to us. Those among us who have not understood this because they did not make the best of their noviciate are like dislocated limbs: they make the whole body suffer and they themselves are uncomfortable. It is essential that they find their proper place.

Then, when it was a matter of defining this spirit, he did not hesitate to set it within a threefold dimension of charity: charity towards God, which produces consecration; charity towards the members of the religious family, which produces community; and charity towards all people, which produces mission. He continued:

> Charity is the pivot on which the whole of our existence turns. The charity we owe to God has made us renounce the world ... Charity to our neighbour forms an essential part of our spirit. We practise it first of all between ourselves by loving one another as brothers, regarding our society as the most united family on earth; rejoicing in the virtues, talents and other qualities of our brethren as if they were our own, patiently bearing the small defects which this or that one has not yet overcome and covering them with the cloak of sincerest charity, and so on. Towards others, we practise charity by considering ourselves as merely servants of the Father of the family, responsible for aiding, helping, reuniting and bringing back his children through unremitting work, in the midst of suffering and persecution of every kind, not expecting any other reward for ourselves than that promised by the Lord to faithful servants who worthily carry out their mission.[26]

Unity in the community is the result of living at the highest level of perfect mutual charity, since charity at its highest level becomes unity. Mutual love and unity permeate each other so deeply in de Mazenod's language that he uses them impartially to define the distinctive character of the Congregation.

Charity and unity are theological and christological concepts and so that is what the deep nature of the community looks like. Explicitly,

'Let us love one another in God and for God';[27] let us love one another 'tenderly in the Lord'.[28] Mutual love and unity are possible because God is Love and communicates his love. At the root of the community is the very love of the Father. 'O my dear sons, how I love you!' de Mazenod wrote to the Oblates. 'And you truly deserve all the love I have for you, because you are one among yourselves and one with me. God commands this of us, because he is the source of our unity and its good.'[29]

De Mazenod was always very conscious of his spiritual fatherhood, as a sharing in the divine fatherhood of God.[30] God, he wrote, 'has predestined me to be the father of a numerous family in the Church'.[31] He felt that his fatherhood was founded on that of God and derived 'from one of his finest attributes, and I am given to believe, with good reason, that he does not grant it to everyone in the measure he has given it to me'.[32] This theological love, coming from the Father and mediated through the founder, flows through all the members of the community, making them one among themselves. Here the community finds its first and surest foundation. 'I have seen many Religious Orders', de Mazenod wrote, reflecting on this topic,

> I have a close relationship with those most faithful to their Rule. I have recognized in them, quite apart from their virtues, a great *ésprit de corps*. But nowhere else have I found that more than fatherly love of the head for the members of his family and that warm mutual affection of the members for their head which establishes relationships between them which come from the heart and form family ties among you, of father to son and son to father. I have always thanked God for it, as a particular gift that he has deigned to grant me.

After reaffirming the particular kind of love he had for his sons, he continued: 'It is this feeling, which I know comes from him who is the source of all charity, that has stirred up in the hearts of my sons that mutual love which constitutes the distinctive character of our beloved family.'[33]

Invigorated by the love of the Father, the community found itself united around Christ, showing its christological nature. The unity which de Mazenod recommended to the Oblates was in fact 'inspired by the supernatural dimension of the charity of Christ'.[34] Christ was regarded as the real founder of the Congregation. The Saviour calls all the members of the community to follow him, to be fully conformed to him, to be his fellow-workers in the task of redeeming humanity. In the Rule we read: 'The missionaries must, as far as human frailty allows, imitate the example of Our Lord Jesus Christ in everything ... they will seek to become other Christs.' This identification with the one Christ meant that the missionaries would be one among themselves: 'They will be united by the bonds of the closest charity and in perfect submission to their Superiors.'[35] Commenting on this passage, de Mazenod himself noted that in the Rule,

> Jesus Christ constantly recurs as a model. Closely united to Jesus Christ, their head, they will be one among themselves, his sons, firmly united by the bonds of the most fervent charity, living in the most perfect obedience ... *arctissimis caritatis vinculis connexi*. They must not, therefore, become irritated or distress themselves with signs of indifference or coldness.[36]

Apostolic man' must aim at fully reliving Christ. But there are not as many Christs as there are members of the apostolic community. There is but one Christ. The members of the community all together are called to become the one Christ. 'Let us be united in the love of Jesus Christ, in our common perfection; let us always love one another as we have done hitherto: in a word, let us be one.'[37]

The Shape of the Community and the Marks of Unity

In addition to the theological and christological dimensions of charity, de Mazenod identified other ties between the members of his religious community which guaranteed its unity.

Above all, there was faithfulness to the Rule and a certain uniformity of life style. In this de Mazenod adopted an attitude that we find constantly from the Council of Trent onwards. The call to observance as a guarantee of unity occurs very frequently in his letters. If the Rule is interiorized and observed, it cannot fail to yield the fruit of unity. It is necessary 'to be permeated with the spirit of the holy book which the Church has placed in our hands as a rule of conduct. Each of you should make it a habitual object of study and meditation, and then peace, union and charity will constitute the charms of our life.'[38]

The more the Congregation spread to every corner of the earth - America, Asia, Africa - the more the need for the Rule was appreciated, as a tool for the maintenance of unity. To the Oblates in Canada, for example, de Mazenod wrote:

All I recommend is that you do not neglect the holy Rule. However far you may be from the centre of the Congregation, you must know that you have to live the life of the family to which you belong. It is consoling to think that at the furthest ends of the earth, where you are, you are living the same life in intimate communion with your brethren scattered over the face of the earth.'[39]

Along with the Rule, and dependent on it, there was obedience, the other factor in the group's solidarity; de Mazenod quoted the Rule again: 'They will all be united by the bonds of the most intimate charity and in perfect submission to their Superiors, living in dependence on them in the exact practice of holy obedience.'[40] The role of the superiors, therefore, seems extremely important. 'Encourage one another and edify one another,' he wrote to the Oblates leaving for Canada, and continued:

> Be united in the same spirit, collaborating in the spread of the Gospel. Those of you especially whom we place at the head of your brethren, be great through your merits and virtues rather than through your position. Take care to win the hearts of your brethren by charity and gentleness rather than ruling them with power. Endeavour, through observance of the Rule and the practice of piety towards God, to behave in such a way that they will be spurred on to walk in your footsteps and vie with one another in imitating you.[41]

Finally, de Mazenod attached the utmost importance to silent prayer before the Blessed Sacrament, which he regarded as the common meeting-place for all the Oblates scattered throughout the world, the daily appointment in which they could all be united.[42]

As a consequence, the community appears - and these are images of the Church - as a building 'that we have to build together';[43] as a body: 'We are all members of one and the same body, let each one co-operate with all his strength and sacrifices if need be, for the well-being of the body and the development of all its faculties';[44] and as a tree in which the same sap flows.[45]

Because the community is a single body, its mission belongs to all its members, leaving on one side the task that each individual is called to perform. Each one shares the fruits of everyone's work, and the good of one is to the advantage of all. They are 'in close relationship, in communion of action and merits' with one another.[46] De Mazenod exhorts them to 'Share everything for the benefit of all. All of you must be members of one and the same body and make good use of your individual talents, so that the body will lack nothing.'[47] 'Rejoice with one another over all the good which is being done by our members in the four corners of the world. We do everything in solidarity. Everyone works for all and all for everyone. How splendid, how moving, is the communion of saints!'[48]

On the basis of this theological dimension and the precisely structured life, the dynamics of unity found expression in a very real mutual love. De Mazenod constantly pointed out new possibilities and nuances for this love, ranging from bearing with a brother to cloaking his defects with compassion, from caring for his health to brotherly correction, from rejoicing in one another to making time for recreation and rest together, from cultivating a sincere and deep friendship to practising those little attentions that are part of being together. Everything contributes to creating the sense of family. In this way everything becomes common property: 'You know that we must say, in the fullest sense, *omnia mea tua sunt* [everything of mine is yours] because we form one heart and one soul, all of us, both in heaven and on earth; that is our strength and our consolation.'[49] One reaches the stage of living heaven on earth: 'Live constantly in that intimate union which makes your house a true earthly paradise.'[50]

The Call to Unity

Rereading de Mazenod's writings, it is striking how constantly the members of the community are exhorted to preserve charity and unity. In fact, these are areas requiring continual reconquest, in order to live according to one's vocation.

Unity always has first place in his advice: unity 'before everything', 'always' unity, 'perfect' unity. 'Let us be united, let us aim only for God, and so we shall be truly steadfast',[51] we read in his exhortations. And again: 'Be together often and live in perfect union. When I speak of union it is not because I am afraid you are at loggerheads with each other. I do not even think that! Rather, I want to speak about that warmth, what I would call that fusion, which should exist between all the members of our society, who should have one heart and one soul.'[52] 'I do not say to you: Love one another. Such a recommendation would be ridiculous. Rather, I say: care for one another and each be attentive to the well-being of all.'[53] 'Grow in grace, my dear friends, and virtue in the love of Jesus

Christ, and the unity of the deepest charity.'[54] 'Have a single spirit and bear with one another. Even if something goes against your liking, beware of grumbling. Share gently with one another, without arguments or sourness, what seem to you useful comments. If they are not accepted, remain at peace and do not depart from obedience. No personal attacks or hurt feelings but straightforwardness, frankness, simplicity, gentleness and, above all, charity. *Omnia vestra in caritate fiant* [let everything be done with charity].'[55]

In his first circular letter - though we are now almost at the end of his life - de Mazenod could write:

> I sum up all my advice and good wishes in these words of the apostle St Paul to the Corinthians: 'Finally, brethren, farewell. Mend your ways, heed my appeal, agree with one another, live in peace, and the God of love and peace will be with you. Greet one another with a holy kiss ... The grace of the Lord Jesus Christ and the love of God and the fellowship of the Holy Spirit be with you all. Amen' [2 Cor. 13:11-14].[56]

De Mazenod also often urged Superiors to preserve unity, fostering and cementing union between all the members of the community. This is how he wrote to the Superior at Oregon, for example: 'Strictly maintain the utmost union among the brethren and let charity always reign among you.'[57] And to the missionaries of Lac-la-Biche in Canada: 'What I ask of you above all is that charity should reign among you. *Ubi caritas ibi pax* [Where charity is, there is peace].'[58]

His last words before his death provide a spiritual testament in keeping with all his teaching: 'Really practise charity among yourselves, charity, charity - and, outside, zeal for the salvation of souls.'[59]

The Missionary Character

It is precisely this 'spiritual testament' which shows the missionary character of the community and its close connection with the interior life of unity. This testament was like that of other founders (we have read Francis of Assisi's), modelled on the words of Jesus, who had linked proclamation with mutual love: 'By this all men will know that you are my disciples, if you have love for one another' (John 13:35), words that recall those spoken a little later: 'May they all be one ... that the world may believe that thou hast sent me' (John 17:21). Unity within the community was essential for preaching the Gospel. During the first public mission preached as soon as the community was formed, de Mazenod could already say 'How difficult the apostolic ministry is if spirits and hearts are not indissolubly united'.[60] During the same mission he wrote: 'We missionaries are as we should be. That is to say, we have one heart, one soul, and one thought. It is wonderful!'[61]

It was a question of a truly 'apostolic' community. A community that, like the apostles, lived around Jesus and found there a deep bond of unity among all its members. A community that, like the apostles, was sent to proclaim the good news. A community that was inspired by love within ('charity among yourselves, charity, charity') and burnt with apostolic zeal without ('outside, zeal for souls'). Strong in the unity of the Oblates, and in accordance with the Rule, they threw themselves 'into the struggle' to 'fight to the death for the greater glory of his infinitely holy and adorable name'. They felt driven to 'do everything to extend the Kingdom of the Saviour and destroy that of Satan'.[62]

'Apostolic man', guided by love, has the ability to read deeply the signs of the times. He knows how to listen to humanity's groanings and identify its needs. Guided by love, he makes every effort to look for adequate answers and devise ways to spread the saving Word, since 'Charity embraces everything; and for new needs it invents, when necessary, new means.'[63] 'Apostolic man' does not spare himself. He does not rest on his laurels. He is never content with what he has achieved, because he sees more and more distant goals, more and more new needs. An inner fire consumes him, the fire that Christ brought on the earth, which, like Christ, he wants to see burn everywhere - and soon. He is guided by the Spirit who, by nature, is always creative.

NOTES

1.   Two types of association arose during this period: those for clerics with a common life but without vows, such as the Oratory of St Philip Neri, the Congregation of the Mission of St Vincent de Paul, the Doctrinarians of Rome and France, etc.; and those with a common life and simple vows. There were also attempts at new forms of consecrated life, such as St Angela Merici's Company of St Ursula, the Piarists of St Joseph Calasanctius, the Sisters of Charity of St Vincent de Paul, and John Baptist

de la Salle's Brothers of the Christian Schools. But these new forms of life did not always succeed in remaining faithful to their original inspiration. In general, they developed into Congregations with simple vows, or secular societies.

2. Session XXV, *Decree on Religious Men and Nuns*, ch. 1.
3. During the nineteenth century the number with pontifical jurisdiction reached 625. A chronological list of them can be found in Lopez Amat, *La vita consecrata* (Rome: Città Nuova, 1991), pp. 443-58. Much larger, though uncertain, was the number of diocesan Institutes.
4. R. Auber, in Jedin, *History of the Church*, vol. VIII (ET, London: 1981), p. 212.
5. Cf. *Vie et mort des ordres réligieux* (Paris: 1972), pp. 241-2. I admit to being influenced in this choice by personal motives, which the reader will kindly allow me.
6. While still a child, Charles-Joseph Eugene de Mazenod (1781-1861) was forced to leave France by the French Revolution and spent his early years in Italy. When he returned to France in 1802 he was struck by the state of religious neglect among the people, especially in the countryside. He decided to put himself at the service of the Church and became a priest. In his native city, Aix-en-Provence, after a brief period of intense pastoral work on behalf of the young and the less well-to-do, he gathered some other priests around him and with them founded the Missionaries of Provence. In 1826 he received pontifical approval of his Institute, with the name of Missionary Oblates of Mary Immaculate. He became Bishop of Marseilles but continued to direct the Congregation, which in a few years spread to all the continents. On the Oblate community, see the following works by F. Ciardi: 'Oblati di Maria Immacolata', DIP, IV, 624-34; 'Fisionomia e natura della comunità oblata nel periodo di fondazione (1815-1818)', *Claretianum* 16 (1976), pp. 173-275; 'Quelques traits de la communauté à la lumière de la vie apostolique', *Vie Oblate Life* 36 (1977), pp. 203-24. See also 'La mission oblate par la communauté apostolique, Actes du Premier Congrès de l'Association d'Études et de Recherches Oblates, Ottawa 7-11 août 1989', *Vie Oblate Life* 49 (1990), pp. 109-377. In English there are the four volumes of *Eugène de Mazenod* by Jean Leflon (ET, New York: 1961).
7. To the Abbé Tempier, 9 October 1815; *Lettres*, VI, pp. 6-7. References are to the edition of the writings by Y. Beaudoin. So far fifteen volumes have appeared (Rome: 1977-91).
8. To Forbin-Janson, 9 October 1816; *Lettres*, VI, pp. 26-7.
9. To the Abbé Tempier, 13 December 1815; *Lettres*, VI, p. 13.
10. To the Abbé Tempier, 9 October 1815; *Lettres*, VI, p. 6. Tempier, who was in complete agreement with Eugene's thought, saw immediately what kind of man was needed to accomplish the work that he had in mind: 'I see clearly that you are looking for something more in your choice of collaborators. You do not want preachers who will follow humdrum routine ... but who will be prepared to walk in the footsteps of the apostles and work

for the salvation of souls without expecting any other reward here on earth, but much suffering and labour.' (Letter to de Mazenod, 27 October 1815; *Lettres*, VI, p. 12.

11. To the Abbé Tempier, 13 December 1815; *Lettres*, VI, p. 13.
12. 9 October 1816; *Lettres*, VI, p. 26.
13. Preface (1818) to the *Constitutions and Rules* (Rome: 1986), p. 11.
14. 'Petition addressed to the Capitular Vicars General of Aix', 25 January 1816, in Écrits du Fondateur, fasc. 4 (Rome: 1952), pp. 269-70. However, three centuries after Ignatius, from whom de Mazenod did draw inspiration, the emphases of the Jesuit community have been reversed. Ignatius in fact wrote, as we have seen, that 'the end of the Society is not only to attend, with God's grace, to the salvation and perfection of our own souls, but by the same grace to try with all our strength to help in the salvation and perfection of the souls of our neighbours' (*Constitutions*, General Examinations, I, 2; *Writings*, p. 391). For Eugène, the direct aim is found in the area of personal sanctification which then opens out into the apostolic dimension. For Ignatius, the primary emphasis is on the apostolic dimension, which is, however, supported by the religious life which then forms an essential part of the overall purpose.
15. 13 December 1815; *Lettres*, VI, p. 14.
16. Cf. letter to the Abbé Tempier, 13 December 1815; *Lettres*, VI, pp. 13-15.
17. 15 November 1815; *Lettres*, VI, p. 12.
18. Conference for the day of ordination to the subdiaconate, 23 December 1809, OMI Postulation Archives.
19. J. Jeancard, *Mélanges historiques sur la Congrégation des OMI* (Tours: 1872), pp. 26-9.
20. To Fr Tempier, 12 August 1817; *Lettres*, VI, pp. 33-4.
21. To Fr Tempier, 22 August 1817; *Lettres*, VI, p. 38.
22. To Fr Tempier, July 1816; *Lettres*, VI, p. 22.
23. To Fr Tempier, 9 October 1815; *Lettres*, VI, p. 7.
24. To Fr Durochewr, 17 January 1851; *Lettres*, II, p. 8.
25. To Fr Guibert, 20 January 1823; *Lettres*, VI, p. 108.
26. To Fr Guibert, 29 July 1830; *Lettres*, VII, pp. 206-7.
27. 19 July 1917; *Lettres*, VI, p. 30.
28. July 1816; *Lettres*, VI, p. 22.
29. To Fr Semeria, 15 December 1843; *Lettres*, X, p. 45. In another exhortation addressed to the Oblates at St Boniface in Canada, unity is once again related to the love of God: 'Be truly united, *cor unum et anima una* ... You know well that *Deus caritas est*' (26 May 1854; Lettres, II, p. 80).
30. Cf. F. Ciardi, I *fondatori uomini dello Spirito. Per una teologia del carisma di fondatore* (Rome: Città Nuova, 1982), pp. 346-50.
31. To Fr Aubert, 4 January 1856; *Lettres*, II, p. 15.
32. To Fr Mouchette, 17 July 1854; *Lettres*, XI, p. 217.
33. To Fr Mouchette, 2 December 1854; *Lettres*, XI, p. 253-4.
34. To Fr Honorat, 31 May 1843; *Lettres*, I, p. 50.

35. *Constitutions et Règles de la Société des Missionaires de Provence*, in *Écrits du Fondateur*, fasc. 4 (Rome: 1951), pp. 54-5.
36. *Nos saintes Règles*, p. 22.
37. To Fr Courtès, 3 March 1822; *Lettres*, VI, p. 95.
38. To the Fathers at the Red River, 28 June 1855; *Lettres*, II, p. 108.
39. To Frs Maisonneuve and Tissot, 24 November 1858; *Lettres*, II, p. 210.
40. Constitutions, p. 55.
41. To Fr Honorat, 29 September 1841; *Lettres*, I, pp. 14-15.
42. Cf. F. Ciardi, 'L'Eucaristia nella vita e nel pensiero di Eugenio de Mazenod', *Claretianum* 19 (1979), pp. 259-89.
43. To Fr Tempier, 1 August 1830; *Lettres*, VII, pp. 208-9.
44. To Fr Honorat, 9 October 1841; *Lettres*, I, p. 17.
45. To Fr Aubert, 20 April 1858; *Lettres*, II, p. 189.
46. To Fr Grandin, 4 December 1955; *Lettres*, XI, p. 297.
47. To Fr Honorat, 17 January 1843; *Lettres*, I, p. 34.
48. To Fr Baudrand, 11 January 1850; *Lettres*, I, p. 242.
49. To Fr Faraud, 10 May 1848, OMI Postulation Archives.
50. To Fr Sumien and the Oblates of Aix, 18 March 1823; *Lettres*, VI, p. 111.
51. 22 October 1817; *Lettres*, VI, p. 44.
52. To Fr Courtès, 8 November 1821; *Lettres*, VI, pp. 90-1.
53. To Fr Mye, 19 June 1825; *Lettres*, VI, p. 184.
54. To the Oblate students, 29 November 1820; *Lettres*, VI, p. 75.
55. To Fr Honorat, 9 October 1841; *Lettres*, I, p. 17.
56. Circular letter no. 1, 2 August 1853; *Lettres*, XII, p. 186.
57. To Fr Aubert, 4 March 1849; *Lettres*, IV, p. 220.
58. To Frs Maisonneuve and Tissot, 13 December 1859; Lettres, II, p. 232.
59. J. Fabre, 'Circulaire no. 9', 26 May 1861, *Circulaires administratives*, I, (Paris: 1887), p. 63.
60. A. Rey, *Histoire de Mgr. Charles-Joseph-Eugène de Mazenod*, vol. I (Rome: 1928), p. 195.
61. 24 February 1816; *Lettres*, VI, p. 20.
62. Preface (1818) to *the Constitutions and Rules* (Rome: 1982), pp. 11-12.
63. Pastoral Letter, 7 February 1847, OMI Postulation Archives.

9 'The Attraction of Modern Times'

New communities for today's Church

And so we have arrived at our own times, the period of history in which we have to play a part. Have new and significant forms of community life arisen in our times, in the context of the religious life, and are they still arising? The subject becomes complex, particularly because we do not yet possess that historical distancing which would allow us to interpret the moment in which we live with the greatest objectivity. The discernment of history has not yet been exercised on contemporary events to show the transient and episodic nature of certain phenomena which can only be objectified, classified and examined with difficulty.

We are in fact living through a particularly rich and creative phase in the Church's career, in which the Spirit is powerfully at work. In an effective image, people have spoken of 'multiple sparks' being struck, under the impact of the Spirit, from the hard rock of our historical paths.[1] Marta Robin, who was to bring the Foyers de Charité into being and also play a decisive role in founding the Saint-Jean and Lion of Judah communities, was already in the Thirties announcing the appearance in the Church of 'a new Pentecost of love' with laypeople in the forefront, organized in 'groups and centres of light, charity and love'.[2] Pius XII glimpsed the coming of a new spring in the Church, just as John XXIII spoke at the Second Vatican Council of a 'new Pentecost'. Theologians and important figures in the Church see in the blossoming of today's new church movements a response to the promise of the Council and the process of renewal embarked on by the Church. 'The future of the Church,' declared Cardinal Suenens, 'signifies a renewal of what happened at Pentecost.'[3] And Cardinal von Balthasar has said: 'Perhaps we had to wait for our century to witness a similar blossoming and multiplication of lay movements in the Church, some of which do indeed keep to the great traditional charisms, while the majority have emerged as a result of new thrusts of the Holy Spirit.'[4]

New charisms of the Holy Spirit are at work which seem to be directed more towards the laity than the traditional religious life, and which find different expressions from those we have been used to seeing up to now. The awakening of the Church in the consciousness of the faithful, prophesied by Romano Guardini, has in fact resolved itself into an awakening of all the laity. The results already discernible are nevertheless designed to involve fully the whole ecclesial team. New types of relationship are emerging between presbyters, laypeople and Religious, and the latter are also benefiting from the new charismatic breath which is leading the Church to rediscover itself as the one People of God.

Our brief excursion in these pages in search of the spiritual journey of the religious community ends by flowing into the ocean of the wider ecclesial koinonia, its natural destination.

Conscious of the new ecclesiological horizons opened up by today's emphasis on association, let us try to make a preliminary assessment of the appearance of new forms of community and, at the same time, briefly recall and underline some of the factors which contributed most to their creation.

The Secular Community

Typical of the twentieth century is, above all, its new sensitivity to secular realities and a new kind of Christian presence in their midst. There is a marked attraction exerted by a Christian life that does not refuse to become involved in the social and political spheres, but rather penetrates these fields, the city of humanity, and divinizes them. We need only mention, as typical examples, Teilhard de Chardin, the YCW, the experience of worker priests, and the theologies of history and earthly realities which stress all the positive aspects of creation and incarnation. There is a desire for a consecration which, unlike earlier patterns of the religious life, will not hold aloof from the world but rather make the secular realities of the world the proper setting of life and action. This tendency seeks to break the 'salt-cellars' of convents, where the 'salt' of holiness has usually been kept, so that it can spill out into the world and the salt can dissolve and give its flavour to all the everyday realities of ordinary people. The universal vocation to holiness has been rediscovered in a way at once both doctrinal and existential, and this liberates the laity from the position of 'proletariat' in the Church. The barrier between the so-called 'consecrated' and those who appear, by contrast, more or less 'unconsecrated' is being broken down. This century of ours has restored their full dignity to the laity as sons and daughters of God, People of God, called to the perfection of charity in the world.

We can look at two texts written by laypeople - women - which are typical of this new sensitivity. Madeleine Delbrêl writes:

> There are people whom God takes and reserves for himself. There are others whom he leaves in the crowd and does not 'withdraw from the world'. There are people who do ordinary work, have an ordinary family, or who are ordinary single people. People who have ordinary illnesses, ordinary bereavements and sufferings. People with an ordinary home and ordinary clothes. They are the people of ordinary life. The people you meet in any street. They love their door that opens on to the street just as much as their invisible brothers love the door that finally closes behind them. We, the people of the street, believe with all our strength that this street, this world, in which God has set us, is for us the place of our holiness. We believe that we lack nothing essential, because if we did lack what is needed, God would already have given it to us.[5]

Another woman, Chiara Lubich, continually discerns the attraction for today of the divine made everyday and ordinary:

This is the great attraction
of modern times:
to penetrate the highest contemplation
whilst mingling with everyone,
as one person next to others.

I would say even more:
to lose oneself in the crowd
in order to fill it with the divine,
like a piece of bread
dipped in wine.

I would say even more:
made sharers in God's plans
for humanity,
to embroider patterns of light on the crowd,
and at the same time to share
shame, hunger, troubles
and brief joys with our neighbours.

For the attraction
of our times, as of all times,
is Jesus and Mary;
the highest conceivable expression
of the human and the divine:
the Word of God, carpenter's son;
the Seat of Wisdom, a mother at home.[6]

One of the first responses to this contemporary sensitivity, especially the demand for a holiness diffused in the world and able to permeate secular structures with the divine, has been made by the Secular Institutes.[7]

The document *Primo Feliciter* was drawn up scarcely a year after the Holy See first recognized this reality that had appeared in the Church. It describes the novelty of the vocation in terms of the following exhortation:

> Let them be the salt that does not lose its savour for this insipid and darkened world to which they do not belong but in which, nevertheless, they have to remain by divine arrangement; let them be the light that shines and is not put out amidst the darkness of this world, let them be the small but effective leaven which works always and everywhere and, mixed with every level of the population from the humblest to the most exalted, tries to reach and permeate each and every person by word, example and every other means, until the whole is permeated and totally leavened in Christ.

Consecration and secularity: the apparent contradiction between the two terms, so distinct and almost in opposition during a long history of monastic and religious life, is overcome. 'Secular consecration' or 'consecrated secularity' is at last a possible reality. Consecration is not, in fact, to be understood as a separation but as a vocation, the result of a call and a response to that call. In the case of members of Secular Institutes, God calls them to live where they are already, to remain as seculars. Secular consecration is therefore the radical response to God, who calls people to live in secularity, and confirms them in their secular state so that they will remain in the environment entrusted to them in order to transform it from within. We are in line with the incarnation: Christ assumed humanity without destroying it in order to transform it and bring it to its full realization.

Is there still a place for the community in this new form of conse-crated life? There are Secular Institutes which have within them groups living a common life. Apparently, however, this is not what determines the typical vocation of these Institutes. They almost seem to have gone back to the beginning of the road travelled by the consecrated life - and found opposite answers. It is a question of completely diversified solu-tions: then, the hermits were laypeople who wanted to live the Gospel radically by withdrawing into the desert; today, members of Secular Institutes are laypeople who not only want to live a consecration in the world but also maintain a positive attitude towards the mundane reali-ties among which they feel called to live and work. Yet in both experi-ences, the value emphasized is 'communion' rather than 'life in com-mon'.

So to understand this new form of community, we shall have to clear the ground of references to religious community. We are not faced with a form of 'common life'. Yet we have a true and real 'community' inas-much as consecration involves incorporation into the Institute.

> The community of the lay Secular Institute has a peculiar dimension of its own, inasmuch as it is not just the concern of the individual but has a dimension which qualifies as ecclesial and communal. This is not, however, to be understood as 'common life' in the tradi-tional and canonical sense, but as 'communion' realized in unity of the same spirit, in sharing in the apostolate which is their specific mission, in a shared vocation, in sharing in the same charism of a secular consecrated life recognized by the Church, in the fraternity of the relationships between the members of the Institute themselves.[8]

Community in the Secular Institute also displays typical forms of ex-pression, such as active collaboration in the life of the Institute, forming groups or small associations of its members, holding training meetings together, and so on. The character of this secular 'community' is, there-fore, one of *spiritual* communion and community in diaspora.

'The members of any one Institute', the new Code of Canon Law prescribes, 'should maintain communion amongst themselves, paying very careful attention to unity of spirit and true fraternity.'[9] And again, recalling their varied existential situations, 'The members of Secular Institutes should lead their lives in the ordinary situations of the world, alone or each with their own family, or in groups of fraternal life, in accordance with the constitutions.'[10]

New Communities

Besides Secular Institutes, our time has witnessed the blossoming of a different style of consecrated life, expressed in the growth of a multiplicity of associations of believers in small, more or less informal groups. Though the experiences of these groups are extremely varied, they share a similar aim. They are the so-called 'new communities' which reached their culmination in the Sixties, Seventies and Eighties. There have been many fragmented experiments, some little more than episodes, others having a happy outcome. Some have remained on the fringes of the Church or separated themselves from it altogether in persistent and bitter protest. Others have given rise to lively and influential communities. Compared with the Secular Institutes, all the 'new communities' have been marked by a powerful recovery of the common life.[11]

For all the fragmentary and sometimes episodic nature of the phenomena, the experience of these communities revealed new needs that we shall meet again later channelled into more lasting foundations. As a rule, they came into being as an alternative to large religious communities and the monopoly of evangelical perfection by Religious. Their intention was to inaugurate a new experience of evangelical life outside existing institutions, sometimes placing themselves on the fringes of the Church itself. They greatly emphasized the shared life, as the announcement of a new sort of egalitarian and fraternal society. They meant to be provocative within a divided and classified society. Unprotected by strong institutional structures and remaining relatively small in their membership, the relationships within them were very close and demanded constant scrutiny, without protective screens. As one of the leaders of these communities has written:

> Religious men and women have become too accustomed to living in systems of 'conventual life' and too little used to meeting one another as brothers and sisters. The new communities have perceptibly different needs, which are more direct than in religious Institutes.[12]

They were sensitive to the earthly values of friendship: the joy of being together, pleasure in the presence of others, welcome, humour, children's games, decorating the home, the strength and enrichment that comes from the presence of men and women, married and single, young and old, the celebration of anniversaries. Furthermore, the presence in almost all new communities of men and women living side by side demanded a well-balanced affective maturity. This too was set in deliberate contrast to religious Institutes, which were regarded as places where love, friendship and tenderness were stifled. The members of the new communities 'have thus rediscovered that life together and sharing in faith, love and a sometimes foolish hope, are at the very centre of Jesus' insight as it was understood and put into practice by the first Christian communities.'[13]

On this foundation we see fresh communities emerging which have assimilated the demands of the 'new communities' while purifying them of negative elements such as challenging and distancing themselves from ecclesial institutions, which might have contaminated the experiment.

Some of these communities present themselves as a new realization of the monastic ideal. Others place themselves more within the renewal of the traditional religious life. A list of such groups in chronological order would read: the monastic Fraternity of Bethlehem; the Milan Centre Group; the Community of Monteveglio (Little Family of the Annunziata); the Bose community; Memores Domini (Mindful of the Lord); Seguimi (Follow Me); Sant'Egidio (St Giles); Redemptor Hominis (Redeemer of Man); monastic Fraternities of Jerusalem and Montecroce; the Ecumenical Little Brothers, etc. Many groups living a common life have come out of the charismatic renewal, such as Emmanuel; Theophany; Leone di Giuda (Lion of Judah); dell'Agnello (of the Lamb); and Fondazione (Foundation). Other groups have arisen in the context of service, such as the Abele Group; the Capodarco Community; and the Community of John XXIII. Yet others have a more 'secular' character, such as Tenda del Magnificat (Tent of the Magnificat); L'Arche; and the Church-World Mission. In this category we also find forms of consecrated life that carry on the tradition of 'consecrated virgins', as proposed in the new rite for the *Consecration of Virgins*. The prelature of Opus Dei, like the Fraternity of Communion and Liberation or the Teresian Institute, exhibit different features in their turn, together with other forms of law.

Finally there are the experiments such as the Little Brothers and Sisters of Jesus that are closer to the religious Congregations, even though they have new characteristics. Indeed, it must not be forgotten that every year the Congregation for Religious and Secular Institutes approves new

Institutes of a traditional type. In spite of everything, the era of the Congregations continues on its way.

In spite of their enormous variety, these communities have common elements such as the strong emphasis on community life lived in a deeply personal way with sharing of prayer, ideas and feelings; hospitality and a welcome for all who want to share the joy of the common life, prayer and service; ecumenism understood as openness to the great Christian tradition as it is expressed by different Churches; and a mixed membership of men and women which often includes married couples with their entire families.

A profound authority on monastic history such as Dom Jean Gribomont writes about these communities: 'A good historical training shows that these foundations often exhibit a kinship with the most fundamental and traditional forms of monastic life in their initial stage, that is, before they became established after centuries of history and ecclesiastical control.'[14] Finally, while taking into account the new sensitivity they express, particularly with respect to communion, it has been observed that

> these 'new' foundations are, in reality, structured after the old pattern of religious Congregations; that is, they can be considered as a continuation, to a lesser extent, of the great Congregationist movement which had characterized the nineteenth century and the first decades of the twentieth. They are not a novelty.[15]

Sometimes the novelty is explicitly denied by the initiators of the new communities themselves. Referring to the Bose community of which he is the initiator and moving spirit, Enzo Bianchi has written:

> None of us is called to do anything new, to build up monasticism *ex novo* [from scratch]: each one of us is called simply to be a product of monasticism. If a new Rule has been written and adopted, that was also because we did not feel mature enough to live the monastic life as Basil or Benedict conceived it ... Our intention at the moment when we drew up a Rule for our common life was not to invent an absolute *novum* [something entirely new], still less to break with tradition: on the contrary, we wanted to make it live again in us, as far as we could.[16]

Our Brothers' Keeper

Precisely because he is a typical representative of a new and always old monasticism, we can ask Enzo Bianchi to sketch his community's spiritual features for us, with regard to its brotherly relationships.[17] It will be enough to read some lines from the commentary on the community Rule, which declares: 'Henceforward, you are no longer alone! You must count on your brethren in everything.'

> Who is my brother, who is my sister? The one who does the will of the Father is a brother and sister to me: blood relationships do not count, but neither does belonging formally to a community if it is not constantly renewed by the Lord, purified by obedience to the Word of God, and founded afresh every day by the power of the Holy Spirit ... To spoil community life, you do not need to go to the extreme of falling in love with your brothers or sisters. It is enough to make human sympathy the criterion of communion, instead of adherence to the will of the Lord. The community that the Lord wills is formed by those who are doing the will of the Father.[18]

He goes on:

> The Gospel speaks to us through the Church, the community, actual brothers and sisters. The immediate face of Jesus is the people to whom we are bound in the name of Christ himself ... The statement in our Rule ('Henceforward you are no longer alone') does not mean the end of emotional or psychic solitude, it does not mean that when someone comes into the community he leaves behind the solitude which may have been his lot in his previous state. Exactly the opposite is true: a certain type of solitude can only be discovered on arrival in the community, because it is a condition tied up with chaste celibacy. The statement ... is meant, instead, to indicate that once a brother has been received into the community, he begins a process of self-denial in obedience to a very real neighbour, in daily service, in the common way with which he may sometimes disagree, in a life which no longer makes its own rules. This 'neighbour' is not simply people with whom he lives but brothers and sisters whom the Lord has willed to be our keepers ... No longer being alone means that from the moment someone makes a definitive commitment to the community, he cannot think things through without the community; without the help of others, without mutual submission, he cannot even know himself in any depth. No longer being alone also

means the end of every personal plan, however good or holy it may be; there is only participation in community plans, and adapting to them may sometimes be at the cost of suffering. No longer being alone also means - and this is hard to admit, but we all know it in our hearts through experience - that from the moment of profession every sin, every infidelity to the two vows of celibacy and the common life defiles the whole body of the community. The sin of an individual involves all the brethren as well, it becomes a community sin in God's eyes ... All are together in sin and in grace, since the community is a communion of saints and sinners. Without this solidarity in sin and grace, the monastic community remains simply a peaceful living together, a being together side by side under the authority of a guide. But if this is so, it is only an *appearance*, part of the 'stage scenery' of this world but without any real existence; the community is only when brotherhood and mutual keeping exist among its members, when every brother and sister becomes a Word of God to be considered together with the whole Bible. With only an elementary knowledge of the Christian faith, you can regard the brother living at your side as a *logos* come forth from the mouth of God; either a person feels he is a son of God and recognizes a son of God in the other as well, or his confession of Jesus as Son of God remains gnosis, a purely intellectual knowledge...

Sometimes people think that the monastic life is austere or hard because of the intensity of its prayer or the burden of celibacy. This can be true, but the greatest difficulty in our way of life is precisely being together as the Lord's community ... The article in our Rule, 'You are no longer alone', is not, therefore, a consolation. The joy of solidarity, brotherly love, *habitare in unum* [dwelling together] is a grace made possible by the common life, but at a high price. In community, there are joyful moments, shared happiness in the Lord, but there are also difficult situations, unhappy moments or moments of trial. The common life is not idealistic but evangelical, and the Gospel does not suggest a peace that is easy to attain ... Community is not based on human affinities or horizontal convergences. It is a gift of the Lord to each one of us; consequently, its definitive character transcends the tensions and divergences which constantly arise to disturb its way.[19]

Ecclesial Movements

Besides the Secular Institutes and the new communities which, for all their enormous variety of forms, faithfully follow the way of the religious life, the second half of the twentieth century has also presented us with the unhoped-for innovation of the movements. In the words of John Paul II, 'the great blossoming of these movements and the display of ecclesial energy and vitality that characterizes them should certainly be considered one of the finest fruits of the vast and deep spiritual renewal promoted by the recent Council'.[20] We speak of them here, as an epilogue to our journey, both because the phenomenon involves (as we have noted) the religious life itself,[21] and because individual communities have sprung up or are springing up within a large number of the movements, and these can be regarded as, in a certain sense, sharing the experience of evangelical deepening of communion that is effected by religious communities.

What confronts us are 'associative phenomena having new characteristics in comparison with those recognized by the Church during the most recent periods of its history'. The ecclesial nature of such movements does not, in fact, result simply from their pursuit of the Church's aims, but also from the fact that they are 'known to be open to participation by all the different members of the People of God, with not only laypeople but also priests and Religious involved in their life and action'.[22]

This is not the place to analyse the phenomenon of the movements.[23] As we trace the development of the idea of community, we need only identify the communal elements in the phenomenon and omit other aspects. When thinking of the movements one naturally tends to notice the trait of 'spiritual experience lived together', 'standing united' before God, an 'experience of intimate charitable communication among the members as an expression of their common faith', a 'spiritual way travelled among and with others', a 'remembrance of the solidarity of the spiritual collective', a 'joyful initiation into social and community life among members who share problems and programmes', and 'mutual caring friendship'.[24]

The component of sharing was already strongly present in the socio-cultural genesis of the movements. As the [late] President of the German Bishops' Conference has shown, the ecclesial movements are 'an answer to the challenges of an epoch', in particular the need to combine simultaneously subjectivity and 'rediscovery of the communality and solidarity of life and sharing in faith.'[25] K. Hemmerle also places the birth of the movements in the context of the longings of today's world for personal freedom and the need for fellowship: 'the quest for a new and universal unity which will include the freedom of the individual'.[26]

Among the religious motivations of the movements we again find the element of sharing. A powerful rediscovery of koinonia as characteristic of the life of the Christian and the Church is the basis of the birth and development of the ecclesial movements.[27] J. Beyer has emphasized that

> the very notion of communion, which is a distinctive note of the Church ... is not comprehensible unless it makes itself visible in the living Church itself. These new forms of communion transcend the present structures of the Church, inasmuch as they contain all kinds of people, ministries and apostolic activities, and elevate them into a witness to the mystery of the divine charity, from which the Church is dignified as a communion, a people brought together in the unity of the Father, Son and Holy Spirit. These new forms of sharing seem to have come into being precisely in order to enable such communion to be understood and experienced ... What the Holy Spirit illumined in the Council, he has expressed by this new gift in the life of the Church.[28]

The banding together of laypeople is 'a sign of the communion and unity of the Church in Christ'. (AA 18)

If the movement as a whole is the expression of sharing and aims to realize a communion that involves the whole person and people between themselves in the multiplicity of their conditions and vocations, particular communities, bound by vows or promises, are often formed within the movement itself. We are going to make a closer study of one of them, the focolare, a typical expression within the *Opera di Maria*, which is the official name for the Focolare Movement.

The Focolare

As with earlier forms of community, we do not intend to examine here the aims of the Focolare Movement, the complex ramifications of its branches and manifestations, or even its rich and articulate spirituality,[29] even though we are aware that once again this would enable us to understand how the Spirit intends to respond through it to the longing for unity felt by the Church and humanity today. Everything in it speaks of a tendency towards unity: unity between Catholics, between the Churches, between the members of various religions, between all men and women of good will. 'Unity', Chiara Lubich, the foundress, writes, 'is our specific vocation. Unity is what characterizes the Focolare Movement ... Unity is the word that sums up our spirituality. Unity, which for us includes every other supernatural reality, every other practice or commandment, every other religious attitude.'[30]

Here we want simply to capture the novelty of the movement's unique form of community, the element which, as it were, carries it: the focolare.

Again, at the root of this new type of community there is the particular experience of its foundress. She herself has related how she received the vocation to a life which was quite different from earlier forms such as marriage, the religious life, or a Secular Institute.

It was then 1939 and I had gone to Loreto for a meeting of Catholic Women Students. It was my first long journey. I still did not know what the Lord wanted from me and was not worrying about it. The first time I went into the little house at Loreto, protected by the fortress-like church, I was seized by a great emotion. I certainly had no time to wonder whether or not it was historically certain that this was the house that had sheltered the Holy Family. I was alone, immersed in that great mystery and, in almost continual tears (something quite unusual for me), I began to meditate on everything that might have happened there: the Angel's annunciation to Mary, and the life of those three, Jesus, Mary and Joseph. Reverently I touched those stones and boards, seeing again in my imagination the house built by Joseph. I seemed to hear the voice of the child Jesus, I saw him crossing the room, I looked at those walls privileged to have echoed Mary's voice and her singing ... While my companions remained in the college where we were staying, I took part in the meeting but did not let a day go by without running to the little house. And there, always, was more or less the same impression, the same very deep emotion, as if a particular grace of God was completely enfolding me, the 'divine' almost crushing me. It was contemplation, it was prayer, it was, in a certain way, a living together with the three of them. I shall never forget it. Then the course ended, in that very church, full of people in white veils, especially girls. I joined in with all my heart. Suddenly I realized: I had found my way, and many, many people would follow it.

I returned to Trent happy. Nothing else remarkable had happened, apart from what I have described. However, when a priest asked me how I had fared at Loreto, I replied, 'I have found my way.' 'And what is it?' he asked. 'Marriage?' 'No', I replied. 'Virginity in the world?' 'No.' 'A convent?' 'No.' The little house of Loreto had revealed something mysterious but certain to my heart: a fourth way, whose details were still completely unknown to me.

The concrete realization of this 'fourth way' was the focolare, which is, as Chiara again explains, 'the fundamental unit of our movement and its first-born'.[31]

> The intuition gradually took shape in the focolare, defined thus: The focolare is a modern community of a few people living in the world, camouflaged to resemble the world, dressing like everyone else in the world, working like other people. However, unlike others, they are people who have left the world; they have left their country, their own families and work, in order to give themselves to the cause of unity in the world.[32]

> And there is another element that makes the focolare an innovation. It is not made up just of virgins, but has married people belonging to it as well, with equal rights and duties - married people who feel called to be wholly God's spiritually, even if, obviously, their family duties limit their participation in the life of the focolare. This was made possible by the fact that the ideal of both the focolare and the Movement is supernatural love, charity, which all can practise. With the passing of the years it has also become obvious that it is possible for married couples, as well as the focolarini who live the common life, to make vows, or rather promises, of poverty, obedience and chastity (in accordance with conciliar and pontifical directives) according to their state, as supports for charity.[33]

The life of the focolare is regulated by its own Statutes; however,

> the norm of norms, what underlies all rules and is the basis of its whole life, is the unbroken charity that must never flag among the members of the Movement, and which ensures that - as far as is humanly possible for us - Christ is always present among the members. This is the focolare. Without Jesus among its members it is no longer a focolare.[34]

It was precisely 'Jesus in the midst' that would characterize the focolares and the life of their members. So Chiara compares the focolare to the house at Nazareth: 'The focolare is a house which shelters members of the Mystical Body who, united by charity, have Jesus mystically present in their midst. The focolare must be like the little house at Nazareth where Jesus was physically present with Mary and Joseph.'[35] Now, in the focolare, he must still be present, mystically not physically, a real presence. Jesus in the midst is not is not an idea or a feeling: 'Jesus in the midst is a person! The most holy and glorious person of Jesus.'[36] He is 'a brother among brothers, master, guide, comforter, light. We have no reason to envy those who had him as their neighbour in Palestine.'[37]

'If we ask ourselves what a focolare is in a few words, we can and must define it straight away as "a little community with Jesus in its midst"'.[38]

What is highlighted here is a new evangelical dimension. In the course of the history of the religious community, we have already met the text of Matt. 18:20: 'Where two or three are gathered in my name, there am I in the midst of them.' Yet it had never been taken as a theme or given rise to a particular form of community life. Here, on the other hand, it became the source of inspiration for the community, to the extent of determining its nature. All the different aspects of the life of its members are actually governed by this presence:

> The focolare is a house whose life is ordered according to very particular points of view ... ranging from complete sharing of possessions to a specific apostolate, particular prayers, levels of training for its members ... a precise way of looking at physical health, a particular arrangement of the various rooms in the house; from sacred and profane study to using every means to maintain unity among all the members scattered throughout the world. These are aspects which in turn clothe and facilitate the presence of Jesus in our midst.[39]

From this sprang a 'new' asceticism and a 'new' mysticism. The life of mutual love, which attracts and gives life to the presence of Jesus among the members of the focolare, proved in fact to be

> a powerful asceticism, because people always have to be ready to die for one another, and bear one another's burdens and preoccupations, as well as share one another's joys. And the focolare also

produces a modern communal mysticism, because it brings the presence of Christ who enlightens its members about what they must do, with the result that focolare life is action-contemplation. The focolare, in a word, is a little bit of living Church. The focolare, if it is true to itself, is heaven on earth.[40]

Life within the focolare, the way of holiness, and outside it, the spreading of communion, proves to be entirely the fruit of this mystical presence. 'In the focolare we are between two fires: God in us and God in our midst. There, in that divine furnace, we develop and train ourselves to listen to and follow Jesus.'[41] In fact, the presence of Jesus in the focolare acts as a 'loudspeaker' for the voice of God, which speaks to the heart of every one of its members, amplifying it and enabling it to be heard with greater clarity. Outside the focolare, life is still guided by the presence of Jesus in our midst:

> Focolarini have just one task: to offer Christ to the world ... not so much through works of charity as through charity itself, which is then mutual, and offers the presence of Christ in the midst ... For the rest, what other idea can God have, after sending his Son for the salvation of humanity, but to stir up his presence again in some way among human beings and continue it?[42]

NOTES

1. B. Secondin, *I nuovi protagonisti. Movimenti, associazioni, gruppi nella Chiesa* (Cinisello Balasamo: Paoline, 1991), p. 8.
2. Cf. F. Lenoir, *Les communautés nouvelles. Interviews des fondateurs* (Paris: Fayard, 1988), p. 75.
3. 'Il mistero della Chiesa', in *I movimenti nella Chiesa*, Atti del II Colloquio Internazionale (Milan: Jaca Book, 1987), p. 30.
4. Quoted by P. J. Cordes, *Dentro il nostro mondo. Le forze di rinnovamento spirituale* (Casale Monferrato: Piemme, 1989), p. 14.
5. *Nous autres, gens des rues* (Paris: Éd. du Seuil, 1966), p. 67.
6. Meditations (London: New City, 1989), pp. 14-5.
7. Cf. *Gli Istituti secolari. Documenti* (Rome: CMIS, 1986); M. Albertini, *Istituti secolari* (DIP, V, 106-21); A. Oberti, *Per una teologia degli Istituti secolari* (Milan: O.R., 1983); G. Sommaruga, 'L'Institut séculier, une communauté?' *Vie Consacrée* 57 (1985), 340-6.
8. SCRIS, 'Riflessioni sugli Istituti secolari', 22 April 1976, in *Gli Istituti secolari. Documenti*, p. 72.
9. *Code of Canon Law*, 716.2.

10. *Code of Canon Law*, 714.
11. The Centre Communautaire Internationale in Brussels, closed in 1976, offered during its lifetime a rich and exhaustive documentation on the development of community in the world, to which reference should be made for information on the different groups. See also M.-A. Trapet, *Pour l'avenir des nouvelles communautés dans l'Église* (Paris: DDB, 1987); M. Hébrard, *Les nouvelles communautés, dix ans après* (Paris: Le Centurion, 1987); *Religieux et moines de notre temps* (Paris: Cerf, 1980); 'Nuove comunità' (DIP, VI), 279-87.
12. M. van Tente, in 'Nuove comunità' (DIP, VI) 282.
13. Ibid., 280.
14. 'Nuove comunità', 486.
15. G. Rocca, 'Le nuove comunità', *Vita Consacrata* 24 (1988), 125.
16. E. Bianchi, *Il mantello di Elia. Itinerario spirituale per la vita religiosa* (Bose: 1985), pp. 47, 49.
17. For an introduction to the experience of Enzo Bianchi and the Bose community, see G. Rocca, 'Bose', *DIP*, I, 1533-7.
18. *Il mantello di Elia*, pp. 63, 76.
19. Ibid., pp. 64-9.
20. In *I movimenti nella Chiesa*, pp. 23-6.
21. I have expressed my thoughts regarding the relationship between Movements and Religious in *L'Unità un segno dei tempi. I giovani religiosi si interrogano* (Rome: 1990). The canonical aspect has been treated by L. D'Angelo, 'La partecipazione dei religiosi ai movimenti ecclesiali', *Commentarium pro Religiosis et Missionariis* 71 (1990), pp. 67-117. Some attempts have already been made to compare individual Institutes and the ecclesial Movements, e.g., T. Janssen, 'Il carisma francescano-cappuccino e i movimenti ecclesiali oggi', *L'Italia Francescana* 66 (1991), 219-32.
22. G. Feliciani, *I diritti fondamentali del cristiano nella Chiesa e nella società*. Atti del IV Congresso Internazionale di Diritto Canonico (Milan: 1981), pp. 239-40.
23. Cf. *I movimenti nella chiesa negli anni '80* (Milan: Jaca Book, 1982); *Movimenti ecclesiali contemporanei. Dimensioni storiche teologico-spirituali ed apostoliche*, ed. A. Favale (Rome: LAS, 1982); B. Secondin, *Segni di profezia nella Chiesa. Comunità, gruppi, movimenti* Milan: O.R., 1987); J. Castellano, 'I movimenti ecclesiali. Una presenza carismatica nella Chiesa di oggi', *Rivista di Vita Spirituale* 49 (1987), 494-618; L. Gerosa, *Carisma e diritto nella Chiesa. Riflessioni canonistiche sul 'carisma originario' dei nuovi movimenti ecclesiali* (Milan: Jaca Book, 1989).
24. T. Goffi, *La spiritualità contemporanea* (Bologna: EDB, 1987), pp. 291-321.
25. K. Lehmann, 'I nuovi movimenti - perché?' *Gen's* 17 (1987), pp. 2-8.
26. 'Lo Spirito Santo e la sua azione nel mondo di oggi', *Gen's* 20 (1990), n. 5, pp. 169-72.
27. Cf. P. Coda, 'I Movimenti ecclesiali. Una lettura ecclesiologica', *Lateranum* n.s. 57 (1991), pp. 109-44.
28. 'I movimenti ecclesiali', Vita Consacrata 23 (1987), p. 156.

29. Cf. A. Favale, 'I Focolarini', in *Movimenti ecclesiali contemporanei*, pp. 203-34; G. Boselli, 'Focolari (Movimento dei)', *DIP*, IV, pp. 87-92; M. Cerini, 'Il Movimento dei Focolari', in *Movimenti nella Chiesa negli anni '80*, pp. 84-92; J. Castellano, 'Focolari (Movimento dei)', in *Dizionario Enciclopedico di Spiritualità*, II (Rome: Città Nuova, 1990), pp. 1014-16.

30. *L'unità e Gesù Abbandonato*, pp. 26-7.

31. *Intervista al Movimento dei Focolare*, ed. G. Lubich (Rome: Città Nuova, 1975), pp. 10-11.

32. 'Cos'è il focolare?', *Città Nuova* n. 14 (1977), p. 41.

33. *Intervista al Movimento dei Focolari*, p. 17.

34. 'Cos'è il focolare?', p. 41.

35. Quoted by J. Povilus, *'Gesù in mezzo' nel pensiero di Chiara Lubich'* (Rome: Città Nuova, 1981), p. 134.

36. *Scritti spirituali*, 3 (Rome: 1979), p. 161.

37. Ibid., p. 169.

38. Ibid., p. 180.

39. Ibid., p. 181.

40. 'Cos'è il focolare?', p. 41.

41. *Scritti spirituali*, 4, p. 245.

42. Povilus, *Gesù in mezzo*, pp. 134-5.

10 Love is Greater
The feminine accent in the experience of community life

Following the spiritual journey of the religious community through history, we have several times mentioned the presence of women alongside men. Beside the desert *fathers*, the history of monasticism recognizes the desert *mothers*. They too, with no less courage and heroism, faced ascesis and the search for God. In the cenobitic life, at the side of Pachomius, then of Basil, Augustine, Benedict and Francis, we have always found women who shared their ideals.

Hitherto, however, we have not stopped to consider any female community explicitly, because it has in fact been men who particularly marked the stages in the evolution of the consecrated life. We could ask the reason for this phenomenon. Given the scant social and even ecclesial importance given to women, it will doubtless have to be ascribed particularly to cultural or sociological factors. Here it should be borne in mind that whereas today the consecrated life shows a preponderance of females, in the past - at least until the seventeenth century - men living some form of the consecrated life far outnumbered women. In fact it was always men - Pachomius, Basil, Augustine, Benedict, Martin of Tours, Columban, Francis, Dominic, Ignatius - who were the great creators of the different forms of community which succeeded each other in the course of the Church's history. Similarly, the theologians of the monastic life and its propagators were men: Origen, Athanasius, Gregory of Nazianzus, Cassian, Bernard...

We must, however, ask ourselves whether women have not had their own way of living out community, and made their own contribution to theological reflection and spiritual experience in this field. There is no easy answer because, while female monasticism and religious life have been the object of historical and sociological research, there has not yet been any adequate study of their more intimate spiritual and theological dimensions.[1] Nevertheless, we can try to take our usual quick look at the path travelled by the female religious community.

The Difficult Path of the Female Community

From the beginning, the cenobitic life, in Egypt as in Italy, Gaul and Spain, saw communities of women who wanted to share together the experience of the monks. In his *Lausiac History*, for example, Palladius tells us of numerous female communities in Egypt and Palestine. Seventy virgins lived together at Alexandria, three hundred at Athribe, four hundred and forty at Tabennisi, and so on. The account of a visit he paid to one of these monasteries enables us to appreciate the atmosphere of fraternity and liberty in which they lived:

> In this city of Antinoe there are twelve monasteries for women. In one of them I also met Talis, who was called *amma* - an old nun who had spent eighty years in ascesis, as she and her neighbours told me. Sixty young women live with her, who love her so much that, unlike the usual practice in other monasteries, the outer gate of their monastery had no lock on it. *They were governed by the love they had for Talis.* The old woman had reached such a degree of detachment from ordinary passions that when I entered and sat down she came and sat down beside me and put her hands on my shoulders in an extraordinary impulse of openness.[2]

A letter from Ambrose to the Bishop of Verona in 380 reveals the existence of a monastery of virgins in his city, founded by St Zeno. In his *De Virginibus* Ambrose praises a community of twenty virgins living in Bologna. Echoes of female monastic communities in Spain can be found in Egre's *Diary*. In France Martin of Tours was entrusted with the care of a female monastery. The Latin monasteries in Palestine in the fourth century, directed by Melon and Paula with the help of Jerome, gained such prestige that they gave birth to similar monastic communities of men.

In Italy, again, there are brief mentions of the founding of a monastery for women by Eusebius of Vermicelli in the fourth century, the group of virgins in the sixth century who gathered together in a house belonging to Bishop Venantius in Luni, and the house near Cassino where Scholastica lived with a few companions. We have to wait until the arrival of the Lombards to see female monastic foundations springing up more or less everywhere, alongside those for men, then increasing in number during the period of the Franks. Following the Cluniac reform, female monasteries also acquired new prestige.

In spite of the large numbers of monasteries, it is difficult to learn much from within about the life of the communities, their lifestyle, spirituality, and the theological vision that sustained them. Their experience, unlike that of the men, was not recorded by history, except occasionally. Literary testimony is scanty, at least compared with that for men. There are few apophthegmata of the *ammas*, the desert 'mothers', for example. The alphabetical collection includes only Theodora, Serra and Syncletica. In the early days of female monastic life there was nothing corresponding to Athanasius' *Vita Antonii*, except perhaps Gregory of Nyssa's *Vita Macrinae*.

What is immediately apparent is how greatly the communities depended on the masculine model for their inspiration, founding and legislation. The case of the brother who arouses or directs the vocation of his own sister and the community formed around her recurs throughout the history of monasticism. Antony entrusted his sister to a community of virgins. The sisters of Pachomius, Isidore, Augustine, Cassian, Benedict, Leander of Seville and Caesarius of Arles were each in charge of a cenobitic community. And every one of these women was prompted by the desire to imitate her brother, who introduced her to her experience of community and sustained her in it.

More rarely it was the sister who exercised an ascendancy over the brother. Thus Marcellina, Ambrose's sister, had preceded him in experience of the divine service by twenty years. Basil's sister Macrina not only preceded her brother but directed the whole family along the monastic way.

At other times, the relationship was constituted not by kinship but by a profound spiritual affinity through which, in a different way, the man exercised his influence on the female foundation. This was the relationship between Jerome, Paula and Melania, and later between Francis and Clare and right up to Francis de Sales and Jeanne de Chantal, Vincent de Paul and Louise de Marillac, John Bosco and Maria Domenica Mazzarello, Giacomo Alberione and Tecla Merlo.

Like the inspiration and creation of the community, the legislation was almost always of masculine origin. The Rule followed by the women was a Rule written for men and then transposed into the feminine, often without even being adapted. This was the case with the Rules of Pachomius, Augustine and Benedict.

An exception was the Rule of Caesarius of Arles. This was the first Rule written expressly for women. Indeed, contrary to the usual tendency, Caesarius himself translated it into the masculine for the men's monastery. Yet even this Rule drew its fundamental inspiration from earlier Rules and was the fruit of male experience. Furthermore, it was - again - written by a man. Nevertheless, throughout the Middle Ages women generally followed the Benedictine Rule, while the Rule of Caesarius of Arles spread very little, even in France. Variations in the observance of the Rule, if they existed at all, were very limited and determined by the stereotype of feminine weakness. Gregory the Great had shown in his *Regula Pastoralis* that women needed to be treated differently from men. Whereas graver obligations could fittingly be imposed on men, women could justly be expected to fulfil other, lighter, obligations because of their frailty, both spiritual and physical. We have to wait until Clare of Assisi to see a Rule written by a woman for women. But it remains a rare occurrence.

The new cultural sensitivity of the second millennium questioned the adoption by a female monastery of a Rule originally written for men. Héloïse asked Abelard what model they, as women, should look to in their consecrated life and what should be its foundation. In the same way, she asked him to compile a Rule for the community of the Paraclete, in which she was living, that 'will be given to us women and comprehensively formulate the community's obligations'. She pointed out that it was impossible for women to observe many of the prescriptions of the Benedictine Rule, to the extent that she was convinced that 'those who composed the rules for monks ... deliberately said nothing about women', indeed, they 'established norms that they knew perfectly well women would never be able to attain'. She explained to Abelard various principles to be taken into account in drawing up a Rule for women. Yet it has been rightly observed that 'the fact remains, and should be underlined, that although Héloïse saw the problems of female monasticism very clearly, she asked Abelard for a Rule without suggesting a norm of life and behaviour herself'.[3] Together with a whole series of practical pronouncements, Abelard offered a typically evangelical model for female monasteries: imitation of the women mentioned in St Luke's Gospel (cf. 8:2-3) who left everything to follow Jesus. To his mind, 'those holy women can be considered true and proper nuns'. In his exegesis of the gospel texts, imitation of the women changed into imitation of Christ the servant. 'The Gospel,' Abelard wrote, tells us only of women who served the Lord, consecrating all their possessions to his daily maintenance and obtaining all he needed. Christ himself, on the other hand, behaved with great humility towards his disciples. He served them at table and washed their feet, though we are not told that, for example, he ever received a similar service from them or anyone else ... only women helped him with these and all his other material needs.

Women are re-evaluated here on the basis of the very principle by which they were relegated to second place: they were given the privilege of serving the Lord.[4]

The eleventh and twelfth centuries witnessed flourishing female branches (or Second Orders) of the new male monastic institutions such as the Camaldolese, the Vallombrosians, the Cistercians, the Carthusians, the Premonstratensians, etc. These envisaged differentiated Constitutions and therefore legislation for the common life that was more in keeping with the nuns' position as women. Yet rigid enclosure and the prevention of any spread of life to the outside were common to all institutions, however varied, and constituted a considerable hindrance to the expression of the new spiritual and religious requirements of women. Significantly, Dom Jean Leclercq gave the final chapter of his essay on female monasticism in the twelfth and thirteenth centuries the title 'The misfortune of being a woman'.[5]

However, the relationship of communion with the 'First Order' opened up new spiritual possibilities for nuns. While the monks took their place at the forefront of the Church's advance - in the struggle against heresy, the preaching of the Crusades, the Christianization of society and the evangelization of new peoples - the nuns prayed for these apostolic activities, interceded with their Bridegroom, and so supported the progress and consolidation of the Kingdom of God. Their prayer became effective and reliable action.

The institution of enclosure, periodically reinforced by Councils, prevented any noteworthy developments in female communities.[6] However, there were some new experiments in community such as the Brothers and Sisters of the Common Life, set up by Gerard Groote (1340-84). These women took no vows or promises, they were free to leave the community at any time, they wore no common habit, and they elected their superior annually. Theirs was an intermediate state between life in the world and the regular life. According to Thomas à Kempis, this new type of community was organized 'according to the form of the primitive Church and the praiseworthy custom of the holy fathers introduced by the apostles ... "They had one heart and one soul in the Lord"'.[7] This kind of life seemed so new and revolutionary compared to the usual monastic pattern that the matter was immediately brought before the Council of Constance. Its accusers asserted, amongst other things, that 'it is not possible to practise the evangelical counsels of poverty, chastity and obedience outside the approved Orders [extra veras religiones]'.[8] It was difficult for such a community to be recognized as a 'vera religio'.

The attempt, in a more secular form, was made again by Angela Merici (1470/74-1540); Antonio Maria Zaccaria who, with Ludovica Torelli, founded the Angelicals of St Paul in 1530; Mary Ward (1585-1645); Louise de Marillac (1626?-60), and in other similar experiments. With the arrival of the modern age, there was a universally observed need to establish new forms of community and presence in the world. These sought to break the rigid patterns of enclosure which prevented many forms of apostolate. But every time, the women who started new forms of community found themselves blocked by prejudice and hindrances designed to impede a life style open to the world, without enclosure.

Within a few years Angela Merici's foundation was set back on the classic track, and went from a free form in the world to the imposition of a common habit and, eventually, papal enclosure. Even the Angelicals ended up with enclosure, after they had been taken before the tribunal of the Inquisition in Venice. In the same way, Jeanne de Chantal had given her Institute the name 'Visitation', to signify her and her Sisters' aim of 'visiting' the sick, but she found herself unable to 'visit' because they were shut in by enclosure. If the Daughters of Charity remained free in their vocation it was because they were able to camouflage themselves, always denying that they were Religious. Mary Ward's Institute was able to go on its way through history as a pious association without vows, on condition that it did not regard Mary Ward as its foundress. She had been too daring!

However, slowly the way was prepared for the Congregations of the nineteenth century, which succeeded in gaining recognition as religious communities in the true sense.

Profiles of Some Female Communities

It will not be easy to move from the external kind of interpretation we have done so far to a more internal one. This is because, in the first place, there is a scarcity of historical documentation and, secondly, the sources for both monasticism and female communities were for the most part written by men. The doctrinal interpretation of community, for example, is almost always the work of men. The theological interpretation of female community offered us by St Peter Damian remains a rare pearl. It is contained in a letter to the Countess Bianca, a widow who had resolved not to remarry but to enter a monastery. Peter Damian praises this intention, which will take her *'in angulo monasterii cum pauperibus Spiritus Sancti mulieribus humiliter residere'* ('to dwell humbly in a corner of a monastery with the poor women of the Holy Spirit').[9] He regarded the female monastery as the place where people lived in a relationship characterized by a particular presence of the Holy Spirit. But this was still a matter of masculine interpretation.

I believe that what F. Raurell has written about Clare of Assisi and the Poor Clares, in his introduction to a series of studies on 'Clare and the female form of Franciscan life', can be applied to the history of the female community in general. Speaking of the Franciscan Sources, he notes that

> for too long the materials have been investigated by historians who, consciously or unconsciously, look at them from a masculine point of view ... The authors and editors of hagiography or legends about devout Franciscan women have been men, they are the ones who have reflected on women, on Clare and her first *sorores* (sisters) ... The texts of the sources do not reflect the complete reality of the primitive Franciscan movement, in which woman - in this case St Clare - appears not just as object but as subject ... It is possible, perhaps probable, that part of female Franciscan history was lost from the moment that the editors of the texts selected traditional material and references on the basis of their own outlook. So we can surmise that they transmit only a fraction of the possible very rich tradition on the role of women in the primitive Franciscan communities.[10]

In spite of these obvious difficulties, we shall try to take at least a look at some features of community as they have been described for us by women themselves, beginning appropriately with Clare of Assisi.

Even for such an outstanding figure as Clare, what we have said in general about dependence on a male foundation still holds good. It was the masculine foundation of the Friars Minor that, as the fruit of Francis' particular experience, showed signs of originality compared to earlier communities. Francis' fatherhood towards Clare, and therefore the female community's derivation from the male community, are constantly asserted by the sources. 'On rereading,' writes a woman who has studied Clare, 'it does not seem to us that Clare gave to her relationship with Francis any idea of parity.'[11] In this kind of dependence we certainly need to distinguish between the reality of the relationship and the cultural stereotype that conveys and interprets it, which led Clare to define herself as 'a humble little seedling planted by the most blessed Father Francis'.[12] Nevertheless, it remains true that there was a real dependence.

The same scholar still, however, poses the question: 'Did Clare always continuously depend on Francis because she was a woman or because it was Francis who had brought about the way of life she followed faithfully and completely?' Beyond the metaphor of 'little seedling', the relationship with Francis was not just one of dependence and being a daughter. On Clare's side there was also a positive influence on the relationship; it was interactive. In her own account of her life experience, the meeting with Francis actually marks the beginning of her own 'doing penance'. She recognized, in the experience of Francis, what she had already felt called to live. She saw the same expectation already working and active in him, her own profound and secret longing to translate the demands for a new evangelical life into a form not completely recognized until that time. So it is that 'towards Francis, Clare appears in the character of a follower'. He conveyed the Word of God to her, he was the source of wisdom for her, he showed her how to incarnate that yearning to follow the poor Christ which God himself had put into her heart.[13]

Clare's feminine sensitivity reinterpreted the elements of community. She defined herself as a 'sister', and her associates are 'sisters' throughout the *Rule* and the *Testament*. It was this term which sustained the entire organization of the community. Those who asked for admission to the community were sisters, those who received them were sisters; the nuns were sisters, and the abbess was a sister. It is a term which opens up vistas of shared life, service and common ideals, as well as the mutual recognition of all who are bound together by the same choice of life. 'Sister' is a title of equality, freedom, and being on the same level; it springs from having one Father, and Christ as common brother. The structure of the community, as well as the system for electing and removing the abbess, were aimed at maintaining the relationship of sister, 'for the purpose of preserving the unity of mutual charity and peace'.[14]

The way in which this ideal of sharing was put into practice with a meticulous series of prescriptions takes more account of little things, perhaps, than did the Friars' community. It is indeed the task of the abbess 'to maintain the common life in everything, especially in the church, the dormitory, the refectory, the infirmary, and clothing'.[15] This style of prescription provides for a rigid distinction of roles, and for ascetic tools such as silence, segregation, enclosure, prayer, fasting, penance, work with their own hands, not possessing anything, and always under the sign of charity, as the Rule again reminds them: 'I admonish the sisters, then, and exhort them in the Lord Jesus Christ to keep themselves from all pride, vainglory, envy, avarice, care and solicitude for this world, detraction and murmuring, discord and division. On the contrary, let them always be careful to preserve mutual charity among themselves, the bond of perfection.'[16]

Besides the external structure, we can deduce the quality of the sharing from a whole series of adjectives which outline the model provided by Clare for the whole community. In the *Bull of Canonization* she appears as vigilant, considerate, prudent, charitable, moderate, temperate, admirable, discreet, sensible and shrewd. And again: 'vessel of humility, ark of chastity, fire of charity, sweetness of goodness, strength of patience...'[17] We would need to analyse every one of these traits in order to imagine the mark that Clare must have left on the shared way of life. Feminine stereotypes are then typified by looking at their opposites: she shows herself strong in the weakness and frailty of her sex; sweetness and gentleness are combined with firmness and robustness; obedience and compliance with resoluteness and tenacity; mildness and compassion with determination and rigour.[18]

The Company of St Ursula founded by Angela Merici was fresh and wholly feminine.[19] Even the Prologue to her *Rule* introduces us to an understanding of the Company: 'To you, my beloved daughters and sisters, God has granted the grace to separate yourselves from the darkness of this miserable world and join together in the service of his divine

Majesty.'[20] In this 'together' lay the strength of an institution which, by its very nature, seemed scattered. The members of the Company did not actually take vows - only the vow of chastity was recommended. They did not wear a distinctive habit. They continued to live with their families. They went to Mass in the parish church. And yet, even in this freedom Angela Merici showed a lively sense of unity and communion. She wanted the members of the Company to be 'all with the same will'[21] and to this end she composed rules for them and designed particular structures to ensure unity. They had regular meetings for prayer, supported one another economically, helped each other in sickness, welcomed one another when they had to be on their own.

But it was particularly in her *Memories* and her *Testament* that Angela Merici revealed her most profound idea of the life of unity that ought to bind the virgins of the Company to each other. She addressed the 'governesses', the women to whom she entrusted her virgins, asking them, as their first commitment, to maintain her concrete ideal of communion among the virgins. 'Especially,' she wrote to them, 'take care that they are united and of one will, as we read of the apostles and other Christians in the primitive Church.'[22] She further recommended them to organize frequent meetings for the virgins, 'in order that, together thus, they may look on you as dear sisters and, reflecting spiritually in this way, have cause to congratulate themselves and console one another, which will be of no little help to them.'[23] She recommended the governesses themselves to live the same unity they have to maintain among the virgins: 'You also must endeavour to be so with all your daughters, because the more you are united, the more Jesus Christ will be among you as father and good shepherd.'[24] 'My last word that I say to you, and beg even with my blood, is to be in agreement, all united together in one heart and one will. Be joined to one another by the bond of charity, esteeming one another, helping one another, bearing with one another in Jesus Christ. Because if you endeavour to be so, the Lord God will undoubtedly be in your midst.'[25]

Like every other foundress, Angela Merici warned against dissension, the exact opposite of the vocation to unity to which they were all called: 'And on no account let such a seed [dissension] grow in the Company, because that would also create a plague of bad example for the city, as well as elsewhere.'[26] Here unity showed its intrinsic apostolic value. It is, moreover, the sign for measuring love for God:

There can be no other sign that you are in the grace of the Lord but loving one another and being together, united ... Yes, loving one another and agreeing together are a certain sign that you are walking in the right way, the way pleasing to God. And so, O my Sisters and Mothers, be vigilant about this, because here especially the devil will entrap you under the appearance of good.[27]

A further guarantee of unity is obedience. To those in charge Angela recommended: 'Be submissive to the principal mothers, whom I leave in my place, as is right ... For by obeying them you will obey me; and by obeying me, you will obey Jesus Christ.'[28] And it was precisely he, Jesus Christ, who was the definitive bond between them all, he who 'without doubt will be in your midst'.[29]

With Mary Ward we go on to another type of community, influenced by the Jesuit model. Attracted by the idea of having to work for the spiritual regeneration of England, Mary Ward envisaged a way of life whose most striking outward features were the absence of enclosure and the wearing of secular dress. As she wrote to Pope Paul V when she presented him with her plan for the Institute's way of life, in view of the 'sad condition of England ... it seems that women too, in their own way, can and therefore ought to do something out of the ordinary in this time of common spiritual tribulation'. She therefore resolved to devote herself 'according to our weak strength, to the practice of those works of charity which cannot be undertaken inside a convent'.[30]

The most relentless opposition was again aroused against her and her Institute. It is worth considering some of the accusations brought against this new form of life, because in themselves they show us the beauty and reality of the projected community as it came into being. The English ladies were accused of wanting 'to work for the conversion of England just like men'. And the novelty of their style of community was that 'they go around here and there, change places and dress as they please, adopt the behaviour and condition of seculars ... In a word, there is nothing they will not do, always on the plea of charity towards their neighbour, and thus they undoubtedly expose themselves to much criticism.' 'They go around freely even with men, and have dealings with them - often in private - on problems of life and morals.' 'They dare to speak before serious men, sometimes even in the presence of priests, about spiritual matters, and to give exhortations at meetings of Catholics.'

'They are accustomed to travelling through the cities and provinces of the kingdom, they enter the houses of Catholic noblemen and often change their dress. Sometimes they pass as women of the highest nobility, in a carriage with a considerable retinue; at other times they dress like servants from the lower classes or tradespeople.' The most serious charge was that, in spite of this life style, they claimed to be Religious: 'If they were content to stay in their cells like other religious families, they would perhaps deserve high praise, but because they demand to be counted as a religious family and insist that they are', they ran counter to canonical legislation.[31] These accusations are the highest possible commendation for an institution that provided a glimpse of a new type of community which, while drawing inspiration from the Society of Jesus, displayed a unique freshness and modernity of its own.

The Daughters of Charity, founded by Vincent de Paul together with Louise de Marillac, had a similar character.[32] This too was a company of women in secular dress without cloister or enclosure. A new kind of open community, bursting into the streets and the homes of the poor. Naturally, in order to serve the poor and sick in their homes they had to renounce any claim to be Religious. 'The Daughters of Charity will never be able to be Religious,' Vincent de Paul stated categorically, 'and woe to anyone who talks of making them into Religious.'[33] For 'to say "Religious" is to say "enclosure" and the Daughters of Charity must go everywhere'.[34] Nothing in their house, dress or way of speaking must recall the cloister. 'For your monastery you have only the homes of the sick and the house where the Superior lives, for your cell only a rented room, for your chapel the parish church, for cloister the roads of the city, for enclosure obedience, for grille the fear of God, for veil holy modesty.'[35] Vincent de Paul did not want them to end up enclosed like the Sisters of the Visitation.

Precisely because they were immersed in the realities of everyday life, the original community of the Daughters of Charity demanded a profound unity between all its members. We can read some of the pages written by Louise de Marillac to her daughters.

What emerges from them above all is that the trinitarian model of fraternal union must be referred to in organizing life in communion.

> True Daughters of Charity, in order to do the good that God commands them, must be one among themselves, and since corrupt nature has robbed us of this perfection of heart by separating us from

the source of our unity, which is God, we must all be of one heart and work in the same spirit, like the three divine Persons, in order to draw nearer to the Most Holy Trinity.[36]

Louise bore witness to this unity between her daughters: 'I experience a great joy when I think of you, and of the unity, concord and cordiality which reign amongst you.'[37]

With a sensitivity which takes account of the psychology appropriate to women, she goes on to describe the actual forms of communion:

To carry out his design of love on which your salvation depends, you must have a great unity among you, so that you will make allowances for one another and have no answer when you are reproved for your shortcomings and told what you have to do. Moreover, when you notice some defect in this sister or that, excuse her promptly. Doesn't this seem very reasonable, seeing that we so often fall into similar faults and therefore ask to be excused? If your sister is lively, or a bit sharp, or too quick or too slow, what do you want? That is her nature, and however often she tries to master herself, she cannot prevent her natural tendencies from showing themselves now and then. And should a sister who ought to love her as she does herself, lose her temper, behave badly, or sulk? O my sisters, keep yourselves from that, I beg you! Pretend not to notice what she does or says, and bear in mind that you too could fall into some defect and then it will be you who need her to behave charitably ... The great unity which should exist among you will be maintained by the patience with which you bear with one another's little defects and by your thoughtfulness in telling one another where you are going and letting each other know what you have done during the day ... I am so pleased to think that you are living in greatly unity and warmth, since it is certainly divine Providence which has put you together! If there is some difference in your characters, in the name of God, Sisters, make sure that, outwardly at least, only his holy love appears to reign in your hearts.[38]

The writings of Louise de Marillac are also full of advice for maintaining friendship and unity by small attentions such as caring for one another's health, taking recreation together, sharing a sister's grief, rejoicing with the joyful in a complete sharing of feelings, providing mutual support in everyday life, practising forgiveness, and sisterly correction. At the same time she puts them on their guard against envy, suspiciousness, rash judgement, intolerance, opposition between young and old, and all obstacles to the life of communion.[39]

The female Congregations of the nineteenth century, like those of the men, do not exhibit any very novel elements, apart from the fact that the specific purpose for which they came into being now made it possible for them to work among the people in a wide variety of ministries. What they have done for the poor, the sick, children, the aged and the young remains one of the finest pages in the history of the religious life.[40]

Nevertheless, as far as community life was concerned, the picture that emerges seems rather poor, both doctrinally and in the experience of everyday life. Most attention was paid to 'regularity', understood as the exact observance of timetables and regulations, which became extremely minute and concerned with even the smallest details. Being together was constantly muffled by silence, interrupted by scant moments of recreation, the demands of the tasks entrusted to individual sisters, and prayer in common. Outside work and contacts were strictly controlled in accordance with the provisions of the Rule and customaries. The horarium was punctuated by the sound of the bell, which in some cases rang every half-hour to signal the change from one duty to another. Relations between the sisters were somewhat formal, because spontaneity and the most innocent expressions of sisterly friendship were repressed. The style of relationship with Superiors was reminiscent of the veneration, affectionate devotion and respect shown by servants to their mistress.[41] From 1600 onwards a whole series of customs was progressively accumulated, passing from social custom into the religious life, to burden it and help make it rather formal. Patterns of behaviour that in the seventeenth and eighteenth centuries had ensured a harmonious common life in the setting of the family and society, and therefore also within the religious life, became anachronistic when perpetuated in the nineteenth and twentieth centuries. Even in male religious communities we find a whole corpus of detailed regulation, though they did not cover as many aspects of life as those of the female communities. Moreover, the men's way of life seemed freer with regard to rules and regulations, which were often treated with a certain liberty and interpreted more elastically. The female community, on the other hand, gives the impression of having been partially stifled by observance and regularity.

The Charism of Love

At the end of this rapid survey of the path taken by the female community, we can identify some constants and some queries.

A first constant is a certain dependence by women on men to initiate and organize community life. Even the most feminine models often had a man behind them, as happened with the Sisters of the Common Life, the Daughters of Charity, and the Sisters of the Visitation. The majority of the female Congregations from the eighteenth century onwards were founded by men; if women were the founders, they often had a man at their side directing them on how to write the Constitutions - always inspired by men's Rules - and organize community life.

An opposite process can also be noted, though less often: the way in which female communities influenced those of men. This second phenomenon is to be found in 'double monasteries', in relations between Second and First Orders, in the personal communion established between man and woman. Paula exercised a powerful influence on Jerome, Clare on Francis, Jeanne de Chantal on Francis de Sales, and so on.

There were also original communities created by women which, because of a complex of social factors, remained fairly limited and ineffectual. Catherine of Siena's 'merry brigade', to which people of every class and vocation belonged, remained very confined in both time and space. Others, like those of Angela Merici and Mary Ward, were immediately checked and unable to express themselves in complete freedom and fruitfulness. Moreover, even when there was an original and novel understanding of community, it is difficult to find any trace of it because the written accounts, like the preservation, evaluation and interpretation of the sources, are mostly the work of men.

There are therefore times when we are confronted with a real dependence of women on men, without any originality in the proposed community, and times when the presence of a true relationship of communion between men and women can be discerned, with an enriching interaction and mutual giving.

The subjection of women to masculine models was expressed in many ways. There was, as we have seen, the adoption of rules written for men, as well as imitation of their pattern of life. There was direction and often interference on the part of ecclesiastics in the internal life of, first, the female monasteries and then the religious Congregations. Above all, there was the scant consideration throughout the whole of society towards women who, in order to win acceptance and assert themselves, were forced to assume 'masculine' attitudes. In this respect we need only reread the beginnings of female monastic life to appreciate immediately the inevitable comparison with men that women were obliged to accept. Sarah, one of the desert *ammas*, replied to two hermits who were belittling her because she was a woman: 'According to nature I am a woman, but not according to my thought.'[42] To prove her worth she was forced to present herself as thinking in a masculine way, without the possibility of being respected and esteemed for the intuitive and affective dimensions that are typically feminine. 'She said again to the brethren: "It is I who am a man, you who are women."'[43]

We shall encounter the invitation to be 'men' and assume 'masculine' attitudes throughout the course of the religious life, on the lips of all the foundresses, even when they are women of outstanding personality, like Teresa of Avila. The cultural conditioning is such that in order to be truly a nun or a Religious, woman is forced to call herself 'man'! The feminine section of the *Vitae Patrum* (*Lives of the Fathers*) preserves the account of many women who, in order to pursue the monastic ideal, pretended to be men and went to live in a male community.

It was difficult, therefore, for women to express their choice of monastic and community life in a feminine way. Yet, compared with the woman living in a family, the Religious enjoyed great freedom. In a convent she had a space of her own for the development of her personality, in which she could live as other than simply dependent on man and his sexual and social demands. She could organize her life and that of the community herself. She had access to the benefits of culture. In 'double monasteries' she could exert her influence on the male community, even in the role of Superior.

Nevertheless, the feminine element remained essentially subordinate and marginal. If it was normal for men to found convents for women, the opposite was rare. St Bridget of Sweden was perhaps one of the first instances and remained the last until our own day, when a Mother Speranza or a Mother Teresa of Calcutta have founded a community for men alongside their female community. Yet even today the new communities, the new monastic experiments, and the various movements generally, are being created and inspired by men. It is a sign of prophetic novelty that a woman should have founded the Focolare Movement, an ecclesial organism whose members include, besides lay men and women, a large number of priests and Religious of both sexes who share the spirituality of the Movement, together with quite a few bishops who are 'friends'. Not only that, but the Statutes lay down that the president of the Movement should always be a woman.[44]

Today, at a time when women are finally allowed to express themselves with greater freedom, precisely as women, the female religious community is also called to rediscover its own forms of communion, new expressions of living out unity that will bear witness to what is characteristically feminine.

In his apostolic letter *Mulieris dignitatem*, John Paul II has defined the specific quality of being a woman, setting it within the reality of love. It is in woman that 'the order of love in the created world of people finds soil to put down its first root'. If 'love is an ontological and ethical necessity for people', the very heart of interpersonal relationships, then woman's vocation can only be completely understood on the basis of the primacy of love.

> The dignity of woman is measured by the order of love ... Woman is she who receives love in order to love in her turn ... In this wide and varied context, woman represents a particular value both as a human being and, at the same time, a real and particular individual because of her womanliness ... The dignity of woman is intimately connected with the love she receives because she is a woman and also with the love she gives in her turn. (§§29-30)

Speaking later of Mary, in the apostolic letter Redemptoris Mater, the Pope traces some of the typically feminine characteristics of this dimension of love:

> Womanliness stands in a unique relationship to the Mother of the Redeemer ... In the light of Mary, the Church finds reflected on the face of woman a beauty which mirrors the most sublime sentiments of which the human heart is capable: the totality of love as self-offering; the strength which is able to sustain the greatest sufferings; unbounded faithfulness and unwearying industry; the ability to combine penetrating intuition with words of support and encouragement. (§46)

Chiara Lubich, a woman of today who is, as we have seen, at the head of a vast movement, echoes the Pope's words when she writes that woman must affirm, in the way in which only she can, the value and primacy of love compared to all other gifts, compared to all other elements that go to make up our religion, including the very high honour conferred on those who are called to priesthood. Love is the most important thing ... It is through supernatural love, and for love and with love that a woman - whose very being is already fashioned with that natural love that makes her capable of every sacrifice - can find her own place in the Church. Minister of love as indeed she is, womankind continues throughout the centuries as she does today, to keep Mary's presence alive in the Church.[45]

Women can play an essential part in the evangelical plan of proclaiming the Good News. They 'can especially perform this task through the greatest of charisms, the charism of charity'.[46]

In the light of this new reading of the feminine vocation, we can understand better the unique relationship between two eminent representatives of female and male communities: Scholastica and Benedict. Scholastica left no literary remains; Benedict, on the other hand, left a Rule and his Life was written by Gregory the Great. In one way, Benedict's superiority is obvious: his Rule has guided generations of monks and nuns. And yet, in another way, the one episode involving Scholastica that has been preserved reveals her superiority over her brother.

Gregory the Great recounts that after being together in 'holy conversation', the moment of parting arrived for the brother and sister. Scholastica begged Benedict to stay longer but was unable to persuade him. So she turned to prayer and suddenly a storm burst which prevented Benedict from leaving the house to return to his monastery. 'You see,' Scholastica explained, 'I begged you and you refused my request. I begged my Lord and he listened to me.' So the two of them 'stayed up all night and filled their souls with holy talk, sharing their experience of the spiritual life'. Gregory comments:

By this story I have tried to show that he wanted something but could not get it. Certainly, from the Venerable Father's point of view, what he wanted was for the sky to remain as serene as it had been when he had come down; but contrary to his wishes, he was confronted with a miracle extracted from the divine omnipotence by the heart of a woman. Nor is it at all surprising that on this occasion a woman, anxious to go on talking with her brother, had greater power than he did, because, according to the John's teaching, 'God is love', and it was therefore very right that the more loving of the two should have been the more powerful.[47]

Scholastica did not display literary, organizational or legislative superiority. Instead, in line with her femininity, she showed a greater love. Scholastica could love more than Benedict. And this would undoubtedly have had a very particular influence on the fraternal life she lived with her sisters. Yet not a trace of this has remained in the documentary sources; written by men, they are more interested in the masculine values of juridical order than in the more feminine values of love. This episode provides a parable which sums up the history of female religious life.

At a time when the Religious who make up the female communities are discovering these dimensions of love and expressing them freely and radically, the female community is increasingly acquiring its own specific role in the Church as the icon of the presence of love. If it is true that 'God entrusts man to woman in a special way' (MD 30), it will perhaps be no less true that the female community has its own contribution to make to the Church as a whole, including the male religious community. Faced with the danger that what is essentially human could disappear from man, 'our time looks for the manifestation of that "genius" of woman which ensures sensitivity in mankind in every circumstance - simply by being human! ... Then the truth will be fulfilled that "the greatest is charity" (1 Cor 13:13)' (MD 30).

NOTES

1. The following works provide a starting point for the study of the presence of women in the religious life: L. de Candido, 'La donna nel monachesimo. Storia e interpretazione', *Servitium* (1976); J. Gribomont, 'Monachesimo femminile', DIP V, 1706-7; E. S. Severius, 'Monastero doppio', DIP VI, 51-2; M. P. Giudici, *La donna consacrata verso la sua identità. Tra memoria e profezia* (Turin-Leumann: LDC, 1982); S. Hilpisch and E. Pasztor, 'Il monachesimo femminile', in *Dall'eremo al cenobio. La civiltà monastica in Italia dalle origini all'età di Dante* (Milan: Scheiwiller, 1987) pp. 153-80; A. de Vogüé, 'Sanctimoniales (300-700 après J-C)', *Claretianum* 29 (1989), pp. 199-237; *La donna religiosa in una Chiesa-comunione* (Rome: Rogate, 1990).
2. *The Lausiac History*, 59.
3. Pasztor, loc. cit., p. 165.
4. Cf. Letters 7 and 8, quoted by Pasztor, ibid., pp. 174-5.

5. 'Il monachesimo femminile nei secoli XII e XIII', in *Movimento religioso femminile e francescanesimo nel secolo XIII* (Assisi: 1980), pp. 63-99.
6. 'Clausura', *DIP* I, 1165-83.
7. Cf. H. Jedin, *History of the Church* (ET vol. 4, New York: 1982), pp. 426-31.
8. Mansi 28, 386-94.
9. 'Epistola L', *PL* 145, 731-48.
10. F. Raurell, 'Chiara o il francescanesimo al femminile. Presupposti metodologici', *Laurentianum* 31 (1990), pp. 4-5.
11. C. Militello, 'Chiara e il "femminile"', *Laurentianum* 31 (1990), p. 65.
12. *Testament*, 37.
13. Cf. Militello, op. cit., p. 65.
14. *Rule* IV, 22.
15. Ibid., IV, 13.
16. Ibid., X, 6-7.
17. Ibid., X, 11-14.
18. Cf. J.-F. Godet, 'Claire et la vie feminine. Symboles de la femme dans ses Écrits', *Laurentianum* 31 (1990), pp. 148-75.
19. Cf. B. Dassa, *La fondazione di S. Angela Merici come prima forma di vita consacrata a Dio nel mondo* (Brescia: 1967); I. Mariani, E. Tarolli and M. Seynaeve, *Angela Merici. Contributi per una biografia* (Milan: Ancora, 1986). In English, see Philip Caraman's biography, *Saint Angela* (London: 1963).
20. *Regola*, Proemio, in Santa Angela Merici, *Regola, Ricordi, Legati* (Brescia: Queriniana, 1975), p. 7.
21. Ibid., Prologo, p. 13.
22. *Testamento spirituale*, Decimo legato, p. 113.
23. Ibid., Ottavo legato, p. 109.
24. Ibid., Decimo legato, p. 113.
25. *Ultimo ricordo*, p. 93.
26. *Testamento spirituale*, Decimo legato, pp. 113-15.
27. Ibid., p. 113.
28. *Terzo ricordo*, p. 77.
29. *Testamento spirituale*, Ultimo legato, p. 115.
30. *Ratio Instituti* (1616), in *Maria Ward e il suo Istituto* (Rome: 1968), p. 27. For the story of Mary Ward and her Institute, see J. Grisar, *Mary Wards Institut vor römischen Kongregation* (Rome: 1962).
31. 'Informatio de Jesuitissis ad Apostolicam Sedem per Rev. Dominicum Gulielmum Harisonum...', in J. Grisar, *Die ersten Anklagen in Rom gegen das institut Maria Wards* (1662) (Rome: 1959).
32. Cf. A. Vernaschi, *Una istituzione originale: le Figlie della Carità di S. Vincenzo de' Paoli* (Rome: 1967).
33. *Entretien* 56, *Correspondence, entretiens, documents*, ed. P. Coste, vol. IX, p. 662.
34. Ibid., vol. IX, p. 658.
35. Ibid., vol. X, pp. 661-2.
36. *Nella Chiesa al servizio dei poveri. Tutto il pensiero di S. Luisa de Marillac esposto con le sue parole* (Rome: Ed. Vincenziane, 1978), p. 236.

37. Ibid., p. 238.
38. Ibid., pp. 236-7.
39. Ibid., pp. 239-54.
40. See the powerful reconstruction of the birth and development of female Congregations in France by C. Langlois, *Le catholicisme au féminin. Les congregations français à supérieure générale au XIXe siècle* (Paris: Cerf, 1984). Cf. also Ch. Molette, *Guide aux sources de l'Histoire des Congrégations féminines françaises de vie active* (Paris: 1974).
41. A careful analysis, quoting many significant texts, can be found in O. Arnold, *Le corps et l'âme. La vie des religieuses au XIXe siècle* (Paris: Seuil, 1984).
42. *Vita e Detti dei Madri del deserto*, vol. II, p. 191; in English, Benedicta Ward SLG, *The Sayings of the Desert Fathers* (London: Mowbray, 1975), p. 230, no. 4.
43. Ward, p. 230, no. 9.
44. Cf. C. Lubich's interview with Franca Zambonini, *A Life for Unity* (London: New City, 1994), pp. 142-3.
45. Ibid., pp. 152-5.
46. Ibid.
47. *Life of St Benedict*, 33.

PART THREE

Theological Reflection

1 The Trinitarian Mystery
The Trinity as archetype of community

As we have studied the self-understanding of communities, we have found along the way explicit references to the unity of the Trinity as the type and basis of koinonia in the religious community. The unity of the Twelve around Jesus and the unity which made the first Christians at Jerusalem of one heart and soul among themselves refers back to a still deeper unity manifested in these communities and at the same time transcending them: the koinonia of the Trinity. Beyond the many experiments in religious community, beyond the prototype and normative communities of Christ's disciples and the Christians at Jerusalem, is the trinitarian archetype, the divine agape, the ineffable communion of Persons. Every Christian community is a 'sacrament of God's agape',[1] a place where the life of the triune Godhead is mirrored, shared and lived. That is its deepest nature and at the same time its innermost vocation.

Augustine's contribution was shown to be particularly important here, because of the theological interpretation he was able to give of his own experience of community. Contemplating the work of the Spirit of Pentecost, who 'of many souls and many hearts ... made one soul and one heart', he could ascend to the Trinity and there gaze upon the result of the unity effected by the same Spirit. If, as he wrote, the Spirit, *pax unitatis*, made many people one heart and one soul,

> we believe that, all the more, in the peace of God which passes all understanding, the Father, the Son and the Holy Spirit are not three gods but one God; this unity is as much superior to that formed by the one soul and one heart among the first Christians as the peace which passes all understanding [the Holy Spirit] is superior to the peace possessed by all those first faithful, who were one soul and heart reaching out to God.[2]

The Augustinian monastic community, in continuity with the Jerusalem experience, appeared as an icon of the Trinity, recognized as deriving from it and sharing in its mystery of unity.

The appeal to the Trinity as the archetype of community recurs several times along the path taken by the religious life, even if the theme was not always handled with the depth and centrality it deserved. St Vincent de Paul, for example, said this to the Daughters of Charity:

> You see, my daughters, just as God is one alone in himself, and there are three Persons in him, without the Father being greater than the Son or the Son than the Holy Spirit, so the Daughters of Charity, who have to be the image of the Most Holy Trinity, although they are many are nevertheless of one heart and one soul ... Thus you will make this Company a copy of the Most Holy Trinity. In this way your Company will represent the unity of the Sacred Trinity.[3]

Today, the Church's growth in understanding of its dimension of mystery, in particular as *Ecclesia de Trinitate*, helps us to understand better the mystical and trinitarian dimensions of the religious community as well. Every form of community in the Church in fact derives the depth of its own being from the *trinitarian community*, through the Trinity's communication of itself and the mystery of its unity. Christian unity is founded on the trinitarian life, shared with the faithful through their incorporation into Christ. An understanding of the relationship between the religious community and the Trinity can therefore only come through an understanding of the relationship between the Church and the Trinity, because the religious community shares in the larger ecclesial community and expresses it in a particular way.

The Council's reflection on the religious life moves in this direction. The whole of chapter 6 of *Lumen Gentium* presents the religious life as a component part of the mystery of the Church. Recovered as a living part of the *Ecclesia de Trinitate*, the consecrated life was rediscovered as deriving from the very mystery of the Trinity. This way of life, according to the teaching of the Council Fathers, is born out of the love of God as 'that precious gift of divine grace given to some by the Father' (LG 42c); it constitutes 'an abiding re-enactment in the Church of the form of life which the Son of God made his own when he came into the world' (LG 44c); it lives in docility to the Holy Spirit, 'for the increase of the holiness of the Church, to the greater glory of the one and undivided Trinity which in Christ and through Christ is the source and origin of all holiness' (LG 47).

In recent years, following the Council's indications, an attempt has been made to review the whole aim of the religious life on the basis of the mystery of the Trinity. This process has hardly begun and has not yet borne its anticipated fruits, but nevertheless it does afford a glimpse of the potential fruitfulness of this new line of reflection. The trinitarian mystery in fact affects the consecrated life in all its aspects: consecration, communion and mission.[4]

Consecration, as a radical expression of baptism, places the Religious in a direct relationship with the trinitarian God. *Perfectae caritatis* had already seen consecration in trinitarian terms when it pointed to the Father as the source of the call, the Son as the one to be followed, and the Holy Spirit as the one who prompts a person to live increasingly for Christ and the Church (cf. 1c). Going more deeply into the teaching of the Council, John Paul II has written that consecration 'creates a new bond between man and the Triune God, in Jesus Christ' and produces in the consecrated person 'the joy of belonging exclusively to God, of being a special possession of the Blessed Trinity, Father, Son and Holy Spirit'.[5] The Code of Canon Law itself sums up the trinitarian orientation of consecration in the following words: 'Consecrated life, through the profession of the evangelical counsels, is a form of life by which the faithful, following Christ more closely beneath the action of the Holy Spirit, dedicate themselves wholly to the God they love supremely' (Canon 573.1).

Similarly, the dimensions of apostolate and diakonia in religious communities, though varying greatly according to their different charisms, are in continuity with the Trinity's going out from itself, the ecstasy of its self-giving love which places it at the service of human beings. The community opens itself in its turn and continues the mission entrusted by the Father to the Son and fulfilled in the Spirit, by giving itself to its particular form of ministry in order to bring the whole person and all people to the fulfilment of their vocation: to live in the Trinity.

However, reference to the Trinity becomes particularly pressing (and fertile in its results) in connection with the koinonia aspect of community. We can therefore begin our reflection with the Second Vatican Council, where the Church gave a more conscious expression to its own connection with the Trinity.

The Trinity as the Origin and Source of Communion

The increased awareness of the mystery of the Church and' the Holy Spirit, which has, in certain aspects, characterized Christian life and theology in our century, inevitably brought with it a deeper awareness of the trinitarian mystery.[6] The Church, as an icon of the Trinity, could not contemplate its nature and mystery without returning to the source of its being. The same can be said of the rediscovery of the Spirit. He 'works' for the Father and the Son, and therefore establishing a new relationship with the Spirit means finding oneself again in the Trinity. By making us cry 'Abba' and bringing us to confess that 'Jesus is Lord', he leads us into the mystery of communion with the Three.

The third main trend of contemporary Christian thinking is concerned with the mystery of the Crucified God and a deeper understanding of the paschal event. This reality, like those of ecclesiology and pneumatology, ends in contemplation of the trinitarian mystery, which the paschal mystery manifests and communicates. 'To think of the Cross is to speak of the Trinity.'[7]

This rediscovery of the Trinity as the horizon of Christian life and even Christian thought characterizes today's ecclesial experience and awareness. We are living an existential rediscovery of the God of Jesus Christ, the One-in-Three God. Christianity as it used to be lived ran the risk of an amorphous flattening and a faceless God. Some years ago it could still be said that 'If the doctrine of the Trinity were to be suppressed as false, most religious literature could remain almost unchanged'.[8] For all their orthodox profession of faith in the Trinity, Christians are in practice virtually 'monotheists' in their religious life.[9] Kant's words about the uselessness of the Trinity were unfortunately only too true for many Christians. 'Taken literally, it is absolutely impossible to draw anything practical from the doctrine of the Trinity, even if it could be considered comprehensible, much less if it is realized that it transcends every concept of ours.'[10]

The Second Vatican Council made the face of the God of Jesus Christ shine out afresh and initiated a rich period of doctrinal reflection which has increasingly devoted its attention on the trinitarian mystery. The ecclesiology of *Lumen Gentium* is already trinitarian. In its first chapter it states the theme of *Ecclesia in Trinitate*, recalling the celebrated expression of Cyprian: 'The universal Church is seen to be "a people brought into unity from the unity of the Father, the Son and the Holy Spirit"' (LG 4). One of the greatest commentators has written:

> The subtle word play of the original is almost untranslatable: *de unitate ...* plebs *adunata*. The Latin preposition '*de*' evokes simultaneously the ideas of imitation and participation; it is 'starting from' this unity between the divine Hypostases that the 'unification' of the people extends. Uniting themselves, the people share in another Unity; thus for St Cyprian the unity of the Church is no longer intelligible without that of the Trinity.[11]

At other times the Council spoke of the Church-Trinity relationship as constituting the very being of the Church. Its origin is trinitarian; we read in *Gaudium et spes* of the Church 'proceeding from the love of the eternal Father ... founded by Christ in time and gathered into one by the Holy Spirit' (no. 40). Its model and its principle are trinitarian, as *Unitatis redintegratio* states in another important text: 'The highest exemplar and source of this mystery [of the Church] is the unity, in the Trinity of Persons, of one God, the Father and the Son in the Holy Spirit' (no. 2f). The result of its journey through history is trinitarian:

> The Church prays and likewise labours so that into the People of God, the Body of the Lord and the Temple of the Holy Spirit, may pass the fullness of the whole world, and that in Christ, the head of all things, all honour and glory may be rendered to the Creator, the Father of the universe. (LG 17)

If Cyprian, in the text quoted from *Lumen Gentium*, had laid more emphasis on the unity than the plurality, the Council took the trinitarian reference further by looking more at the dynamics of the individual Persons. The opening chapters 2-4 of both *Lumen Gentium* and *Ad gentes* show the Church as the actual fulfilment in history of the Father's plan, accomplished in the Son and interiorized by the Spirit. Each of the Persons is considered individually. In the background is the prologue to the Epistle to the Ephesians, in which the author presents each of the Persons at the beginning of the economy of salvation (cf. Eph. 1:3-10). Giving themselves, they bring the Church to birth.

Communicating himself in Christ and the Spirit, God reveals himself as what he is most intimately: Love. To contemplate the way in which he has given himself in Christ is to understand love: 'By this we know love, that he laid down his life for us' (1 John 3:16). If he reveals himself as love by giving himself, it is because in himself he is already self-giving love, mutual giving, communion, Trinity (cf. 1 John 4:8, 16): the 'economic' Trinity (that is, acting in history) enables us to know the 'immanent' Trinity (the Trinity in its inner life). Conversely, we can say that because God is Love in himself, God reveals himself to human beings as love.

Thus the Trinity forms a life of love radically orientated to opening itself, spreading itself outside itself - because, according to the familiar Scholastic axiom, by its very nature Good spreads itself around - in order to create new nuclei of unity sharing in that same reality of communion, that same life of love which fills the existence of the Trinity.

This is already evident on the level of creation. Creation, with humanity at its summit, reveals in itself the imprint of God as communion, God as Trinity. Revelation 'shows us that the very heart of existence, the heart of reality, the origin and so the form of everything, is love, the sense of interpersonal community. The heart of being is a communion of persons ... The nature of being is communion.'[12] The mark of the Trinity is impressed everywhere.

This appears even more obviously true on the level of the economy of salvation. The Church, willed by the Father, appears as the creation of the Son, always renewed by the Spirit. It is

> the work of the Blessed Trinity. As man was made in the image of God and in his knowledge and love reflects the divine activity, so the Church which represents Jesus Christ must be the manifestation, in time, of the life of the Trinity. There is an epiphany of God the Creator through man, and there is an epiphany of God One and Three through Christ and his Church: 'As the Father sent me, even so I send you' (John 20:21).[13]

A Family of Brothers United in the Same Father

The initiative in the plan of salvation came from the Father as the 'source of love'. It is he who decreed 'to raise men to participation in his divine life' (cf. LG 2; AG 2). Since the divine life is trinitarian life, he calls human beings to participate in it not as individuals but together, as members of his one family. In fact we read in *Ad gentes* that 'It pleased

God', precisely as Father, 'to call men to share in his life and not merely singly, without any bond between them, but he formed them into a people, in which his children who had been scattered were gathered together' (no. 2). The Father has a precise design of his own:

> the extension of trinitarian life itself to the whole of humanity. Through Christ the Father wills to associate us with the relationships of filiation and spiration proper to the trinitarian life. He wills to give birth to his Son again in every human being, to breathe his Spirit into them and to unite all human beings with one another in the closest communion in order that they may all be one, as the Father and the Son are one in the same Spirit of love.[14]

In the generation of the Son we too are made sons and daughters, and that is what we truly are.[15] Thanks to his 'great love' (1 John 3:1) we can call him 'Father' (Luke 11:2). In fact the relationship of being made a son or daughter establishes a closer and more innate bond than that created by being physical offspring, to the extent that, as Nicolas Cabasilas wrote, Christians born of the mysteries are more children of God than they are children of their parents. Francis of Assisi has helped us become aware that at the moment when we call God Father and recognize ourselves as his sons and daughters, we declare and recognize ourselves as brothers and sisters of one another. If we are children of one and the same Father, we are brothers and sisters to one another. This is the basis of the universal brotherhood expressed by every individual community.

The greatest joy we can give to God is precisely that of presenting ourselves to him as a united family. We cannot come before him at his altar if we have something against our brother (or sister) (cf. Matt. 5:23-4). Our offering is not acceptable to him if it is not made in unity with our brethren.

The religious life has often reaffirmed the reality of only one Father. Inspired by the words of Jesus, 'Call no man your father on earth, for you have one Father, who is in heaven', it has emphasized the reality of brotherhood: 'You are all brethren' (Matt. 23:9, 8). We think immediately of Basil, Augustine, Francis... Even where an abbot (abbas) appears at the centre of a community, the name of father is given him because 'he is believed to act in the place of Christ'. The abbot is called father 'not because he demands these titles, but for the honour and love of Christ'.[16] For the rest, everyone in the community must consider themselves equal before the Father.

Made One in Christ Jesus

If the initiative in the plan of salvation - to gather all people in the unity of the Trinity to form the family of God's children - comes from the Father as the 'source of love', it is realized in the mission of the Son, come to reassemble this family. As the high priest prophesied, he 'should die ... to gather into one the children of God who are scattered abroad' (John 11:52). Our divine sonship is possible in the Son. He is the mediator of the divine life. The Trinity communicates its life through him.

The Council, referring to the work of Christ, once again interprets the divine plan in terms of unity. 'In order to establish a relationship of peace and communion with himself, and in order to bring about brotherly union among men, and they sinners, God decided to enter into the history of mankind in a new and definitive manner, by sending his own Son in human flesh' (AG 3). The Father's purpose is always the same: to make, or remake, human beings into brothers and sisters by associating them with himself and so enabling them to become sons and daughters in him and with him. 'It is the [Church]', we read in *Lumen Gentium* (no. 6),

> whom Christ 'loved and for whom he delivered himself up that he might sanctify her' (Eph. 5:26). It is she whom he unites to himself by an unbreakable alliance, and whom he constantly 'nourishes and cherishes' (Eph. 5:29). It is she whom, once purified, he willed to be joined to himself, subject in love and fidelity (cf. Eph. 5:24), and whom, finally, he filled with heavenly gifts for all eternity, in order that we may know the love of God and of Christ for us, a love which surpasses all understanding.

The divine life flows first of all into Christ as the 'firstborn of all creation'. 'For in him the whole fullness of deity dwells bodily.' Through him it reaches us in our turn and we are all made partakers in this 'fullness of life in him' (Col. 2:9). Therefore Christ can fill the Church with his gifts, 'that she may tend to and arrive at all the fullness of God' (LG 7). Through Christ the divine life, the trinitarian life, reaches the

Church which, entering into communion with Christ, is immersed in the life of the Trinity. Baptism is the same, a sharing in Christ's death and resurrection which is immersion in the Trinity (cf. Matt. 28:19) and the basis of a new sharing in God's very nature (cf. 2 Pet. 1:4). Likewise the Eucharist is a communion in the Body and Blood of Christ which makes it possible to enter into communion with the Trinity (cf. UR 15).

At the heart of this transmission of life, mediated by the sacraments and assimilation into Christ, is the paschal event. Here Jesus reveals and imparts the mystery of the Trinity; here he destroys what is negative in human beings and accomplishes the work of salvation; here in his death he enables the Father to meet with humanity, with people who are once again his sons and daughters; here he gives the Spirit and creates the new community which begins the recapitulation of the whole universe in God. In the paschal mystery Christ brings us to birth in this new life, 'a divine grain of wheat that withers and dies to give us the life of God's children'.[17] Here the old nature has been crucified with him and died with him in his death. Here, out of his resurrection, is born the new nature which for Paul is not only the individual become Christ, but all people become Christ, the whole Christ. It is the irruption of the life of the Trinity into human history, an event which establishes and bears the Church to which that life is imparted. At the same time the mystery of Christ's death and resurrection offers humanity the possibility of returning to the Trinity. The heavens are once again open and we are called to ascend with Christ to the right hand of the Father.

Thus the fruit of redemption is the breaking in upon us of the life of Christ, Christ himself. The Spirit conforms us to Christ and, grafted into Christ, we are brought into relationship with the Father in order to become partakers in the divine life, trinitarian koinonia. It is this sharing in the trinitarian agape which makes ecclesial koinonia possible.

If the fruit of this family relationship with the Father is that the religious community has the appearance of a family of brothers and sisters, the fruit of the relationship with Christ is that it appears to be a body transcending divisions: 'There is neither Jew nor Greek, there is neither slave nor free, there is neither male nor female'. The unity between those who make up the community seems strong enough to make them all 'one in Christ Jesus' (Gal. 3:28). Because it is one in Christ, the community will be able to have 'one heart and one soul'. If no one in the family of God should allow himself to be called father, in the community of Jesus no one can be called 'teacher', 'for you have one master [teacher], the Christ' (Matt. 23:10). The members of Jesus' community are all disciples, held together in unity by the one Teacher. Impossible not to recall here Benedict's *schola Dominici servitii* (school of the Lord's service)!

In the Koinonia of the Holy Spirit

The Father's initiative and the Son's work find their completion in the sending of the Spirit, who works from within and by interiorizing the work of salvation gives it reality (cf. AG 4; LG 4). In the paschal event Christ, the bearer of the Spirit, becomes the giver of his Spirit. He opens the way for the spirit by pouring it out on humanity. The 'glory' he received from the Father, which makes him Son and binds him to the Father, he passes on to his own so that they can enter into the trinitarian communion: 'The glory which thou hast given me I have given to them, that they may be one even as we are one' (John 17:22).

As we know, in the Latin tradition the Spirit is seen as *nexus amoris*, the bond of love between the Father and the Son (Bonaventure) and, in the Son, between creatures and the Father. When he comes, the *nexus amoris*, he creates the same bond of love between the faithful, making himself the source of ecclesial communion, continually sustaining and refreshing it. As the day of Pentecost in Jerusalem showed, koinonia is in fact the work of the Spirit. As the inmost life of God, he is gift and love become a Person. It was Augustine who deepened this doctrine, which was to remain classic in the West: 'The Holy Spirit is communion, friendship, charity, unity, gift.'[18]

When the Spirit comes he brings love as a gift, which makes communion possible. Indeed, he is himself the love of God given and poured out in the human heart (cf. Rom. 5:5). Love is of the Spirit (cf. Rom. 15:30; Col. 1:8). The love which the Spirit pours out in the human heart becomes the gift of self to the brethren, until they are drawn into the mutuality of love according to the Lord's command, even to unity, according to the Lord's last wish.

As St Thomas Aquinas has in fact acutely explained, united in this with the tradition of the East, the Holy Spirit himself, as the Person given, is the bond of love. 'In God', he explains, there is a twofold unity, that of the divine nature and that of Love, which is the Holy Spirit. We have to reproduce this unity which exists in God. Therefore it is not enough for us all to have, by grace, the same divine life which makes us partakers in the divine nature. We must also be united by love with God and one another, in the personal Love which is the Holy Spirit.[19]

The Holy Spirit, then, is at work in the Church. He builds it up (cf. 1 Cor. 3:16; Eph. 2:22), renews it by his gifts (cf. 1 Cor. 12:7-11), unifies it so that all believers are one in Christ (cf. Gal. 3:28). The one Spirit forms the one Body by assimilating every Christian into Christ (cf. Eph. 4:4; 1 Cor. 12:8-9; Rom. 12;6-7).

In this way the community of believers enters into the circuit of that very relationship of agape which connects the Father and the Son (cf. John 14:22ff., 31; 15:9-10; 17:26). The Spirit, the Father and the Son's principle of unity, becomes the principle of unity within the Church, as Augustine again reminds us. The Father and the Son 'willed that we should be united with one another and with them through him who is their communion. They have brought us together into unity by that gift which is common to them both, that is, the Holy Spirit, God and the gift of God.'[20] 'So becoming a Christian,' as Cardinal Ratzinger writes, commenting on Augustine's thought,

> means becoming 'communio', penetrating therefore into the Spirit's essential mode of being ... The paradoxical property [of the Spirit] - according to St Augustine - is that of being 'communio', of being, in his ultimate identity as a Person, wholly in the movement of unity. It follows that 'spiritual' must always and essentially imply 'unifying' and 'communicating'.[21]

Inspired by the Spirit, the community is united as a living spiritual temple. Augustine said of the first Christians, as prototypes of his own monastic community, that 'they had certainly become temples of God, not simply as individuals but a temple of God together. They had become, in other words, a place sacred to the Lord ... a single place for the Lord.'[22] To the religious community, the Spirit transmits his characteristic stamp of freedom which, while it unites people, also distinguishes them in the variety of the gifts which each receives and shares. Thus the dynamism of the Spirit prevents unity becoming an anonymous standardization and amorphous levelling. The individual members enjoy the freedom of the Spirit, each maturing according to the design prepared for him or her by God and at the same time establishing harmonious relationships of mutual communion. The Spirit, ever new, brings his creativity as a gift to the community, preventing it from becoming repetitive or bogged down in a lethal inactivity. Finally, he who is the 'ecstasy' or opening out of the Trinity also continues to effect the expansion of unity within the community. Thanks to the Spirit, the community does not close in on itself but communicates its life in missionary openness and involves the realities it encounters in that process of unification into which it has itself been drawn by the Spirit.

The three divine Persons introduce us into their life. The unity of the Trinity lays the foundations of the unity of the Church. Through the initiative of the Father and the work of the Son, extended by the Spirit and put into practice in the preaching of the apostles and the mediation of the sacraments, we are grafted into that unity and live in and by it. It is God as Trinity who imparts himself to us and draws us into his own life.

Involved in the Dynamics of the Trinity

Sharing in the life of the Trinity means sharing in its very dynamics of love. The mission of the Son prolongs his eternal generation in history, just as the mission of the Spirit prolongs and manifests his eternal sending forth. The Second Vatican Council sought to show the prolonging of the divine procession of the Word and the Spirit in the Church as a sort of historical unfolding of the trinitarian mystery. The divine and eternal processions of the Son and the Spirit appear as the terms of what is possible, the models and eternal grounds for the Church as the completion of all creation, into which it is called to be eternally integrated.

Receiving its own unity from the unity of the Father, the Son and the Spirit, the Church is, so to speak, eternally generated with the Son and sent out with the Spirit, the Son and Spirit who are sent to the Church and who, in the Church, proceed from the Father. The Church can become the sacrament of salvation because it is a mystery which bears the fundamental mystery, that of the redeeming Trinity.[23] As the Council affirms, in this way that sharing in the koinonia of the Trinity to which every believer is called ends up as a deeper ecclesial communion. 'The closer their union with the Father, the Word and the Spirit, the more deeply and easily will they [the faithful] be able to grow in mutual brotherly love' (UR 7).

Precisely because it makes possible the koinonia of the Church, the koinonia of the Trinity is also the model for its accomplishment. The conciliar texts again:

> The Lord Jesus, when praying to the Father 'that they may all be one ... even as we are one' (Jn. 17:21-2), has opened up new horizons closed to human reason by implying that there is a certain parallel between the union existing among the divine persons and the union of the sons of God in truth and love.[24]

The Church finds in the *perichoresis* (or reciprocal existence) of the Trinity the very dynamics of trinitarian love, the most sublime analogy of its own life of communion and the model of relations between the faithful. The unity of the Trinity, which is the source and foundation of the community, at the same time appears as its divine model.

We therefore need to consider the *perichoresis* of the divine Persons in order to understand the mutual knowledge that should be amongst us, the mutual welcome, belonging and love. De Margerie writes:

> Christ invites us to believe in the relationship of mutual indwelling between himself and the Father, in order that we may later come to know them by sight, or at least in their mystical anticipation (cf. John 14:11, 20), that is, through both the exercise of the mutual indwelling of unitive charity among Christians and between them on the one hand and the Father and the Son on the other (cf. John 17:21). The exercise of imperfect created mutual indwelling and the inter-subjectivity of love therefore constitute, for the New Testament, the conditions for the full disclosure to sight of the perfect uncreated mutual indwelling and the inter-subjectivity of the Father and the Son in the Spirit.[25]

The *perichoresis* of the Persons, as lived in the Trinity - mutual giving and welcome to and of each other - remains the archetype of our unity. Yet we, as human beings, cannot penetrate one another as the divine Persons do. Sharing in the divine life, however, enables God to penetrate us and make us one. Sharing in his love makes possible the exchange of mutual love which mysteriously makes us be in one another.[26] And it is precisely mutual love which is the most perfect accomplishment of trinitarian and ecclesial life, the newness of the paschal life to which Christ calls us: 'A new commandment I give to you, that you love one another; even as I have loved you, that you also love one another' (John 13:34). To love one another in Christ, in the same measure that he does, is to live the trinitarian love on earth, grafted both individually and together into God's own life of love. Mutual love is therefore the life of the trinitarian *perichoresis* communicated to human beings, the law which governs the very relationships between the Persons of the Trinity. The new commandment can in fact be seen as the translation into human language of the inter-trinitarian *perichoresis* and koinonia. Accordingly, this proves to be the law of life for the messianic people of the Church, the icon of the Trinity (cf. LG 9b). Piero Coda has written thus on this subject:

> Human beings are enabled by grace to live in their mutual relationships a life which translates into history the very reciprocal life of the Trinity. 'On earth as it is in heaven.' A human being, redeemed and divinized, can henceforward love another human being as Christ has loved him, because Christ lives in one who loves, and the same Christ lives in the other person loved by him. Their mutual love is divinized, it is trinitarian. It is Christ in me who loves Christ in you, and this mutual love is the Love of Christ, it is the Holy Spirit. Between the two who love one another in this way, with the love of Christ, the presence of a Third is established - in a way analogous to what happens in the Blessed Trinity, where the Father and the Son love one another in the Holy Spirit - a Third who is the Risen Christ himself, present in the strength and light of his Spirit.[27]

That is what is in the prayer that Christ addresses to the Father: 'I in them and thou in me'. In the paschal event - in which we have a share by the Word and sacraments - he introduces us into his own relationship of love of the Son for the Father. This relationship with the Trinity makes possible a second relationship, between Christians themselves: 'That they also may be in us'.

> As in the relationship between the Father and the individual Christian it is Christ who acts as centre and mediator, bringing about an increasingly full communion of the human person with God, so it is Christ again who acts as centre and mediator in the relationship

of love between two or more believers who love one another in his same love, because at that moment the same Christ, present in both Christians by grace, is the principle of their love. 'There will be one Christ,' St Augustine comments, 'loving himself.'[28]

The communion of the Trinity is the radical and constructive basis of the communion which exists between believers and gives life to every Christian community. The Christian vocation becomes a vocation to unity: 'There is one body and one Spirit, just as you were called to the one hope that belongs to your call, one Lord, one faith, one baptism, one God and Father of us all, who is above all and through all and in all' (Eph. 4:4-6). 'You were called in the one body' (Col. 3:15). The circulation of grace between the Father, the Risen Christ and the Spirit of Pentecost, which makes the Church live as a divine reality and imparts theological life to each individual, allows and incites communion between all believers as brothers and sisters in one family and witnesses to that eschatological communion which will come about when the ecclesial community reaches its fulfilment in perfect unity with the unity of the Trinity.[29] Thus the Church appears as 'a sacrament or sign and instrument of intimate union with God and the unity of the whole human race' (LG 1).

The Church is on its way to the Trinity from which it was born and whose life of agape it shares. The Church's aim and end in its pilgrimage to the Trinity is represented by the contemplation of 'God one and three clearly as he is' (cf. LG 49). The religious community tries to put itself at the forefront of this movement. Addressing Religious specifically, *Lumen Gentium* invites every consecrated person to take

> earnest care to preserve and excel still more in the life in which God has called him [or her], for the increase of the holiness of the Church, to the greater glory of the one and undivided Trinity, which in Christ and through Christ is the source and origin of all holiness. (LG 47)

In one of his best-known pages, de Lubac has written:

> God has not created us in order that we should remain within the limits of our nature or live a solitary life; he has created us to be brought, together, into the heart of his trinitarian life. Jesus Christ offered himself in sacrifice so that we might be one in this unity of the divine Persons ... There is a place in which, already on this

earth, this meeting of all in the Trinity begins. There is a family of God, the mysterious extension of the Trinity in time, which not only prepares us for this life of unity and gives us a sure guarantee of it but makes us partakers in it already. It is the only society which is fully 'open', the only one in line with our deepest yearnings, the place where we can finally attain our full scope. 'A people gathered together in the unity of the Father and the Son and the Holy Spirit' - that is the Church. 'It is full of the Trinity.'[30]

Thus the Church, and within it the religious community, originates in the Trinity. It is structured in its likeness and moves towards the trinitarian fulfilment of history. The Trinity shapes its life, articulates its structures, and awaits it at the end.

NOTES

1. Tillard, *Davanti a Dio e per il mondo*, p. 233 (E.T. *Before God and the World*).
2. *Letters* 238, 2, 16.
3. *Perfezione evangelica* (Rome: 1967), pp. 197-8.
4. Cf. A. Ablondi, 'Dalla Trinità alla comunità', *Consacrazione e Servizio* 28 (1979), n. 10, pp. 7-17; G. Cabra, *Breve meditazione sui voti* (Brescia 1983); X. Pikaza, 'Trinidad', in *Diccionario Teológico de la Vida Consagrada* (Madrid: 1989), pp. 1758-77; idem., 'En comunidad: Como la familia del Dios-Trinidad', *Vida Religiosa* 66 (1989), pp. 57-66; N. Silanes, 'Trinidad y vida consagrada', *Comunidades* 17 (1989), no. 66-7, pp. 47-65 (this whole number of the review is devoted to a bibliography of 'Trinity and consecrated life').
5. *Redemptor Hominis*, 7, 8. So, for example, the formula of oblation of the Oblates of Mary Immaculate begins: 'In the name of Our Lord Jesus Christ, in the presence of the Blessed Trinity...' In a liturgical context again, in the *Rite of Consecration of Virgins*, we read the following words addressed to the people about to be consecrated: 'The Comforter Spirit ... today through our ministry consecrates you with a new spiritual anointing and by a new title dedicates you to the holiness of the Father; while raising you to the dignity of brides of Christ, He unites you with an indissoluble bond to His Son' (*Ordo consecrationis virginum*, n. 29; E.T. *The Rite of Consecration to a Life of Virginity* does not bring out this trinitarian aspect so clearly).
6. A rich bibliography testifies to this deeper appreciation of the trinitarian dimension of the mystery of the Church. Here we offer only some of the most important studies: M. Philipon, 'La Santissima Trinità e la Chiesa', in *La Chiesa del Vaticano II*, ed G. Barauna (Florence: Vallecchi, 1965), pp. 329-50; B. de Margerie, *La Trinité chrétienne dans l'histoire* (Paris: 1975), especially pp. 303-31; idem., 'Réflexion sur la Trinité economique et

immanente. Relations humaines et relations divines', *Esprit et Vie* 90 (1980), pp. 177-84, 209-18; N. Silanes, *La Iglesia de la Trinidad en el Vaticano II. Estudio genético-teológico* (Salamanca: 1981); B. Forte, *La Chiesa icona della Trinità. Breve ecclesiologia* (Brescia: Queriniana, 1984); P. Cipollone, *Studio sulla spiritualità trinitaria nei capitoli I-VII della 'Lumen gentium'* (Ed. 'Pro Sanctitate'; Rome: 1986); P. Coda, 'Per una ontologia trinitaria della carità', *Lateranum*, n.s. 51 (1988), pp. 60-77.

7.   B. Forte, 'La Trinità: Storia di Dio nella storia dell'uomo', in *Trinità, vita di Dio progetto dell'uomo* (Rome: Città Nuova, 1987), p. 113.

8.   K. Rahner, *Mysterium Salutis*, 3 (Brescia: Queriniana, 1969), p. 404.

9.   Idem., *Saggi teologici* (Rome: Paoline, 1965), p. 591.

10.   *Il conflitto delle facoltà* (Genoa 1953), p. 47.

11.   Mgr Philips, *La Chiesa e il suo mistero nel Concilio Vaticano II* (Milan: Jaca Book, 1968), p. 87.

12.   J. Daniélou, *Trinità e mistero dell'esistenza* (Brescia: 1969), p. 37.

13.   *Il mistero della Chiesa e dell'Eucaristia alla luce del mistero della SS. Trinità* (The Monaco Document of the Catholic-Orthodox Dialogue, 1982).

14.   R. Latourelle, *Teologia della rivelazione* (Assisi: 1970), pp. 512-13.

15.   Paul speaks of 'adoptive' sonship, a term used in secular speech. This word, *huiothesia*, needs to be understood in its etymological sense; the Christian is 'constituted a son'. 'When God makes a human being his child, he acts not juridically but divinely, or like a creator' (F.-X. Durrwell, *Le Père. Dieu en son mystère*, [Paris: 1988], p. 85).

16.   *Rule of St Benedict*, 63.13.

17.   C. Lubich, *Tutti siano uno* (Rome: 1968), p. 88.

18.   *De Trinitate*, VI, 5, 7.

19.   *In Johannem*, 17, 26.

20.   *Sermo*, 71, 12, 18.

21.   'Lo Spirito Santo come "communio"', in *La riscoperta dello Spirito. Esperienza e teologia dello Spirito Santo* (Milan: 1977), p. 254.

22.   *Exp. in Ps.* 131, 5.

23.   Cf. de Margerie, *La Trinité chrétienne dans l'histoire*, pp. 307-8. 'The love of the Father and of the Son in the unity of the Holy Spirit', we read in an ecumenical declaration, 'is the source and end of the unity which God, Father, Son and Holy Spirit, willed amongst all human beings and in the whole of creation. We believe that we are partakers in this unity within the Church of Jesus Christ who was before everything and by whom everything exists. In Him alone, destined by the Father to be the Head of the Body, the Church possesses that true unity which the Holy Spirit revealed on the day of Pentecost' (Declaration of the Ecumenical Council of Churches, New Delhi Congress 1961).

24.   GS 24c. *Unitatis redingratio* also emphasizes not so much the unity of nature as the bond of the interpersonal unity of Father and Son in the Holy Spirit: 'Of this mystery [of the Church] the supreme model and principle is the unity in the Trinity of the Persons of one God, the Father and the Son in the Holy Spirit' (no. 2f).

25. De Margerie, op. cit. p. 246.
26. Cf. M. Cerini, 'Trinità e Chiesa: una riflessione teologica a partire dall'esperienza di "Gesù in mezzo"', *Nuova Umanità* 5 (Rome: 1983), no. 30, pp. 105-8.
27. P. Coda, *La Chiesa, profezia dell'umanità compiuta*, pp. 93-4.
28. P. Coda, '"Non prego solo per questi"', in *Il testamento di Gesù* (Rome: 1985), p. 242.
29. Cf. C. Rocchetta, 'La comunione, dono dello Spirito alla Chiesa', *Presenza Pastorale* 52 (1982), p. 25.
30. H. de Lubac, *Meditazioni sulla Chiesa* (Milan: 1968) pp. 292-3 (E.T., *The Splendour of the Church* [London: 1956], pp. 174-5).

2 The Paschal Mystery
The risen Lord as the life of the community in the power of the Spirit

We have just seen how ecclesial koinonia is based on sharing in the divine koinonia and how the paschal event is the way between the koinonia of the Trinity and that of the Church.

In fact, the history of the Church's origins shows that the humanity born of Christ is a reconciled, reunited humanity. Luke presents the community at Jerusalem to us as the first realization of the life of the Trinity on earth. The whole book of Acts, as the book of the Church, is the story of the progressive expansion of unity as a characteristic feature of the new humanity. At Jerusalem, unity is reconstructed among everyone in one soul and one heart. Communion appears as a fundamental and constituent element of Christian existence. Human harmony, an original fact of humanity subsequently torn apart by selfishness, jealousy and mutual lack of understanding - the fruit of the disunity with God caused by sin - is re-established in the new unity effected by Christ.

Paul explicitly connects the fraternal koinonia typical of the Christian community with redemption. Through his preaching of the good news, the Apostle makes it known that if we are now no longer foreigners and enemies, we owe it to the fact that Christ has reconciled us 'in his body of flesh by his death' (Col. 1:22).

> For he is our peace, who has made us both one, and has broken down the dividing wall of hostility, by abolishing in his flesh the law of commandments and ordinances, that he might create in himself one new man in place of the two, so making peace, and might reconcile us both to God in one body through the cross, thereby bringing the hostility to an end. (Eph. 2:14-16)

In the mystery of his death and resurrection, Christ recreated the unity shattered by sin: the unity of human beings with the Father and, consequently, among themselves. Reconciliation with God (cf. 2 Cor. 5:18-21) produces fraternal reconciliation.

On the cross Christ recapitulated all things (cf. Eph. 1:10). The reality of the incarnation and the radicality of the 'descent' meant that the Son of God could assume all that is human and share in our history and all its connotations of drama and sin. As a result, in his 'ascension' he could draw everything with him and so become the 'fullness' or *pleroma*, because everything belonged to him (cf. Eph. 4:7-10). The cross is at the heart of this movement of Christ because it was precisely there, on the cross, that he finally established his deep relationship of unity with humanity. In his exaltation on the cross - which is at once death, resurrection and return to the Father - he draws everyone to himself (cf. John 12:32), making them all one among themselves. The Fathers and mystics interpreted the mystery enacted there in terms of a bridal mysticism between Christ as Bridegroom and the Church as bride.

Grafted on to Christ by baptism, which initiates us into the mystery of his death and resurrection and imparts it to us, we form his body. Communion in Christ ends up as the communion of the Church. Communion is therefore the outcome of Christ's redemptive work; in reconciling us with God he has reconciled us with each other.

In a Church which is communion, the fruit of the paschal mystery, the religious community appears as an eloquent sign of all that Christ's Passover achieved. In its consecration, inclusion in Christ becomes radicalized. In fact, religious consecration is, as the Second Vatican Council taught, a continuation and radicalization of baptismal consecration. The religious life simply 'desires to derive still more abundant fruit from the grace of ... baptism' (LG 44a). It appears wholly centred on the paschal mystery, as a life of radical following of Christ and sharing the same destiny. On this topic, the SCRSI document which summarizes the *Essential elements of the Church's teaching on Religious Life* says: 'Religious consecration establishes a particular communion between the Religious and God, and, in him, between the members of a particular Institute. This communion is the fundamental element which creates the unity of the religious family.' After listing the sociological factors which contribute to building up and reinforcing unity, it goes on to say that 'its foundation is, however, the communion in Christ established by the original charism. Community takes root in religious consecration itself' (no. 18).

Since the religious community is a paschal community, we shall be able to appreciate more deeply the profound mystery that inspires it if we continue and deepen our study of the paschal event. In particular, we shall try to discern two aspects of it: Jesus' humbling of himself (kenosis) on the cross, and his presence as the Risen One.

Kenosis as the Revelation of Otherness and the Relationship of Unity

For contemporary theology, the paschal event is the privileged place for understanding the mystery of the Trinity.[1] As we have observed before, God fully reveals himself in it as distinct and united Persons and imparts himself to humanity made Church. The religious community, therefore, like every other expression of unity in the Church, must continually reimmerse itself in the mystery of Christ dying on the cross in order to enter, through it, into the dynamism of koinonia.

The death of Christ on the cross unlocks the understanding of the mystery of God as a relationship of love and at the same time shows the driving force of that love. We have already, in the previous chapter, dwelt on the relationships within the Trinity which are the basis and model of relationships in the Church. But we have not yet gone deeper into how the relationships came into being within the Trinity and, consequently, within the human community. Now it is precisely in the light of the paschal mystery that the agape of the Trinity, as a structure of mutuality, shows its particular 'kenotic' character. The christological kenosis reveals the dynamics of the trinitarian agape, so that we sense that the moment of kenosis is implicit and inherent in the very concept of agape.

The interpretation of the *Mysterium Paschale*, repeatedly offered by von Balthasar and now assumed by contemporary theology, is that 'the ultimate presupposition of kenosis is the altruism of the Persons (as pure relations) in the life of love between the Trinity'.

Jesus showed the means and the measure of love, the only love that he can live - the love of the Trinity - on the cross where 'he emptied himself' (Phil. 2:7). He lived the experience of emptying out, kenosis, to the point of being tested by abandonment by the Father, expressed in the cry 'My God, my God, why hast thou forsaken me?' (Mark 15:34).[2] In this cry the Trinity reveals and shares itself. It means Jesus' separation from the Father. It is the translation into human terms of the relationship between the Son and the Father which exists within the Trinity. Jesus' separation from the Father refers back to the eternal generation of the Son which the Father effects in himself. The Father makes the Son other than himself in a generation of love which is infinite joy. Transposed to earth, the otherness that results from generation is suffered by Jesus' humanity as a painful abandonment that echoes, assumes and consumes the abandonment and distance from God into which humanity has been thrown by sin. In his cry on the cross Jesus

> reveals to us how the trinitarian mystery of divine *Agape* can be understood. It is by giving himself and taking this gift of himself to the utmost depths of abandonment and death that the person of the incarnate Word realizes his identity in unity with the Father.[3]

In a valuable document, the International Theological Commission has made its own this interpretation of the mystery of Jesus' abandonment on the cross. It states that 'the Son's distancing of himself from the Father in his kenotic emptying' and his lived experience of abandonment are 'the characteristic aspect, in the economy of redemption, of the (extreme) distinction between the Persons of the Blessed Trinity, who are otherwise perfectly united in the identity of one and the same nature and an infinite love.'[4]

The mutuality or *perichoresis* of the Trinity, revealed in the paschal event, shows itself as crossed by a dynamic 'not-being', the meeting-point between a unity and distinction which have a shared origin. Relative and relational 'not-being', as the dynamic of self-giving mutual love, is thus an inner part of being and as such is brought about by freedom. Sergei Bulgakov explains:

> Love possesses itself in the other, exists only by identifying itself with the other; it is as if it did not exist in itself; yet in this not existing all the power of its existence is revealed, to the extent that the other exists in it and life is realized in the other.[5]

When we turn to the Trinity, we discover with surprise that the 'not' seems to create otherness. Each of the Three 'is not' the other. This is a 'not' which does not belong to the absolute Being which is God, but to its unfolding in three Persons. Each of the Three is wholly given to the others; he is himself by 'not-being' in himself but in the others; and he is himself because he is restored by the others to himself, in mutuality. M. Cerini explains the love of the Word within the Trinity as an infinite emptiness of Self, a total gift of Self as Word to the Father, an absolute nothing which nevertheless *is love*, and therefore *is*. It is eternally the Son; it is response to that total gift of Self - that infinite emptiness - which is the Father, who first gives the whole of Himself. It might be said that it empties itself, obliterates itself - for on earth giving all includes 'losing', 'emptiness' - but instead it is, because it *is love*; and it is the Father, who eternally begets the Son. And from their mutual unconditional love proceeds the Holy Spirit, Love made a Person ... It is the paradox of love, which *is not*, does not exist of itself, and therefore is: is love.[6]

Jesus therefore shows us that the true dynamism of love, in which human beings find the fulfilment of their personal being, is by its nature crossed by a moment of 'death', of 'self-giving', of 'the loss of one's own life'. A moment of kenosis, therefore. To illustrate the dynamics of the mystery about to be accomplished, Jesus declared in the Gospel of John (10:17): 'For this reason the Father loves me, because I lay down my life, that I may take it again.' In order to find his life again in the resurrection and the fullness of his glorious body which will contain the totality of the new creation, he must deliver it up, lose it. The recognition of otherness and complete mutuality as unity in distinction presupposes the ability to 'lose oneself in order to find oneself again' (cf. Luke 9:25; John 15:13; 10:17-18).

In its profound dynamism, the paschal mystery thus reveals to us that love has a moment of 'not-being', the prelude to a new fullness of being which transcends itself. In fact, Jesus' radical gift of self also coincides with the gift of the Spirit. Jesus crucified 'hands over' the Spirit (cf. John 19:30). The moment of kenosis, or emptying out of self and 'not-being', is accomplished in the gift of the Spirit.

If Christ's kenosis reveals the presence of that relative 'not-being' which constitutes the otherness within the Trinity and makes possible that relationship of *perichoresis* in the freedom of the Three which is the basis of unity and distinction, then kenosis must also be the law of the community born out of the paschal event. The kenotic component of the paschal event establishes and defines the community.

We have already said that the trinitarian law is translated into the human situation by the commandment of mutual love: 'Love one another, even as I have loved you' (John 13:34; cf. 15:12, 17). If this reflects the trinitarian dynamic, we should also find in it the characteristic 'not-being'. The kenotic element is in fact present in the new commandment, indicated by that phrase 'as I have loved you'. 'Love one another' means *perichoresis* among the members of the community. 'As I have loved you' indicates the form of its mutual relations. Jesus loved us to the point of giving his life for his friends, he loved us to the extreme limit of death, death on a cross (cf. John 13:1), to the point of losing his own identity, of 'not being', in the loss of his relationship with the Father. 'Yes, Jesus crucified and forsaken is the way of loving our neighbours. His death on the cross, forsaken, is the highest, divine, heroic lesson from Jesus about what love is.'[7]

Jesus not only gives himself as a model, he also offers the possibility of loving as he loved. In fact he transmits the same love with which he loved. If it is true that the Christian life is the continuation of Christ's life in Christians, our charity is not just an imitation of his but, more deeply, a sharing and prolonging of it. We can love in a Christian way only through and in Jesus.

As well as proposing a model to be imitated, the 'as' of the new commandment can indeed also be understood in the causal sense of 'because'. Love one another *because* I love you; by loving you I impart my love to you and therefore the ability to love. The 'as' of the new commandment refers to another 'as': '*As* the Father has loved me, so have I loved you; abide in my love' (John 15:9). So Jesus has loved us with the same love with which he and the Father love each other, thus making us capable of an analogous relationship of love among ourselves. Fraternal love is made possible by the love with which Christ loves us.

It is significant that the two declarations of the new commandment enclose the discourse on the vine and its branches (cf. John 15.1-7) and the statement of the downward movement of agape (cf. John 15:9). It is the one divine agape which in the Spirit unites the Father and the Son, the Son and the sons (and daughters), and the offspring - in the Son - with the Father and each another. It is not, of course, a question of a love identical to that of Jesus, or as holy, but 'of a love of the same quality or the same nature'. The 'as' of the commandment does not in fact 'indicate a simple comparison, a more or less distant analogy or a superficial resemblance ... but a profound conformity, because the example of Jesus is both the norm of love and its basis'. It is a question, in short, of 'a pregnant theological meaning; imitation is similarity, prolongation and assimilation: "as" the Father loves Jesus, so Jesus loves believers (cf. John 15:9; 17:23)'.[8] Consequently Jesus can ask the Father for the fullness of his unity with the Father to be realized among the disciples: 'That they may all be one, even *as* thou, Father, art in me, and I in thee, that they also may be (one) in us' (John 17:21).

Taking up these word's of St John's Gospel, Chiara Lubich has written: 'Only Christ can make two *one*, because his love, which nullifies the self (a love infused in us by the Holy Spirit) enables us to enter into the depths of others' hearts.' In one who 'nullifies himself' and between two who are united with each other by nullifying themselves in one another by love, 'Christ lives again and, in Christ, the Father'. This unity, Chiara Lubich continues, demands a love for one's brethren which 'nullifies self' in order that Christ may live in everyone, and all may be more equal and distinctive as a result of their unity. The mystery of the Trinity lives again where 'the Three live by uniting themselves in their very nature, Love, and in uniting (making themselves nothing) they find themselves again'. 'When Jesus is among us, we are *one* and we are *three*, each equal to the one.'[9]

We shall return later to the demands involved in this nullifying and the concrete dynamic of community which derives from it. For the present we shall remain on the level of theology in order to study a further element of the paschal event just mentioned: the Risen Christ who lives in the community.

The Presence of the Risen Lord

Having 'lost' his life in the course of making himself nothing, Jesus 'found it again', glorious and spiritualized; the Lord, the risen Jesus, is the Spirit (cf. 2 Cor. 3:17). Henceforward he lives a new kind of presence among his disciples; he is present in the Spirit in the community he brought into being.

As he promised, Christ is present in his Church: 'Lo, I am with you always, to the close of the age' (Matt. 28:20).

> The Church is now the real and eschatological presence of the victorious and definitive divine will of grace, established in the world by God in the person of Christ. The Church is the enduring presence of that first sacramental word, which is Christ in the world effecting what it expresses.[10]

Naturally, this presence of his is expressed in many ways, as the Council's Constitution on the Liturgy emphasized, for example, and Paul VI's Encyclical *Mysterium fidei* developed at greater length. Christ is present in the liturgical assembly, in his Word, in the sacraments, in his ministers... If the emphasis in this variety of presences has usually been laid on the eucharistic presence, this should not be to the detriment of the others. 'This presence', Paul VI wrote, referring to the eucharistic presence, 'is called "real" not by exclusion, as if the others were not "real", but by antonomasia'.[11] Rather than being an entity isolated from the other modes of presence, the purpose of the eucharist is to deepen the presence of Christ in the community and each of its members. The purpose of the Word, the sacrament and the action of the Spirit is to make the community the permanent place of Christ's presence. Present day theology, from the Council onwards, has rediscovered the manifold nature of that presence.

Deeper study of the reality of the local church, and the Church as the mystery of communion, has particularly emphasized the presence of the Risen Lord among the faithful assembled in his name, in accordance with Jesus' promise: 'Where two or three are gathered in my name, there am I in the midst of them.'[12] This is the rediscovery of Christ present in the local church, the concrete presence of the universal Church. More concretely still, it is the rediscovery of Christ present not only in each individual local church in the sense of a diocese or a parish, but in each 'cell' of Christianity. Since Christ is present even where there are only 'two or three', then even in the smallest expression of unity, there is the Church. As Odo Casel wrote, this does not mean that

> the one Church is fragmented into a plurality of individual communities, nor that the multiplicity of individual churches, united, together form the one Church. The Church is only one, wherever it appears; it is completely whole and divine even where only two or three are gathered in the name of Christ.[13]

A commentator on Matthew notes that

> In miniature, the Church is everywhere, present where two or three are gathered in the name of the Lord. That is a community around Christ and in Christ. The Church is universally there where the community of all the faithful meets around Christ.[14]

However, we must recognize that this kind of presence, which is particularly appropriate for defining the nature of the religious community, has usually been restricted, in theological understanding, to the setting of the liturgy and worship, as if its connection was exclusively with the moment in which the Christian community meets to pray and celebrate the sacraments.(15) The Second Vatican Council shed fresh light on the real presence of Christ in the liturgical assembly (cf. SC 7), but did not confine itself to this kind of presence. It considered that the presence of Jesus promised in Matt. 18:20 is also realized in the setting of the apostolate (cf. AA 18). Nor is this presence seen as limited to Catholics; the presence of 'Jesus in the midst' can also be established among Christians of another denomination (cf. UR 8). This agrees with exegetical studies which conclude that 'the risen Jesus promises his presence to every meeting (held on account of, or for, his name) regardless of its type or size'.(16)

The Council could therefore come to regard this presence as typical of the religious community. 'A community gathered together as a true family in the Lord's name enjoys his presence, through the love of God which is poured into their hearts by the Holy Spirit' (PC 15).

In his well-known commentary on *Perfectae caritatis*, Tillard has emphasized the wealth contained in this text, which makes clear the mysterious reality of the presence of the Lord amongst religious, the relation between this presence and mutual charity, and the ecclesial dimension which the community finds it takes on. He wrote:

> Number 15 [of *Perfectae caritatis*] seems to us one of the cardinal points of the whole Decree, one of the places where the spirit of the Council stands out most clearly, and the essentially ecclesial dimension of the religious life can be perceived most vividly. Founded on the Eucharist and the word of God, the community is not simply the sum total of a number of Christians searching for personal perfection, each on his [or her] own account; but in its fraternal life it is the sign and proclamation of the great *koinonia* of charity which, in the Son, the Father wills to establish among human beings. We believe that we are not exaggerating the value of this section when we say that its editors have rendered an inestimable service to the religious life, and indirectly to the whole Church of God, by emphasizing the quality of mystery in the very being of the community.

In fact, as Tillard writes further on,

> the common life is the realization of the fraternal koinonia of all, through the personal presence of the Lord Jesus. It follows that in the world it is the announcement of Christ's coming. Showing fraternal charity, mutual respect, and the desire to bear one another's burdens are nothing less than the translation into human action of the profound and mysterious reality of the unity of life with the Father in Jesus which is established by baptism and rooted in the Eucharist, and which all, by their profession, want to bring to its fullness.[17]

The Council only brought back into focus an experience which had always figured in the history of the religious life, even if it had not perhaps been studied as systematically and deeply as it is today. The monastery has several times been regarded as the place of Christ's presence in the midst of his disciples. For example, we read in Theodore Balsamon: 'Since it has been said by the mouth of God, "where two or three are gathered in my name, there am I in their midst", at least three people are necessary for the foundation of an institution which goes by the name of a monastery.'[18] Basil refers several times to the text of Matt. 18:20 in his *Asketicon*. John, Bishop of Antioch, in his turn defines the monastery as follows:

> Perhaps you do not know what a monastery is? It is a completely sacred house, perhaps erected in the name of Christ God, with paintings of Him, His miracles and His divine sufferings in the sacred precincts. In the church there are the sacred books and precious sacred furnishings. There is the holy community of those who for God have renounced the world and what is in it, and themselves. They are close to God, they listen to Him, sing day and night, and chant psalms ... And they have Him always in their midst, in accordance with His most certain and divine promise: 'For where there are two or three gathered in my name,' he said, 'there am I in their midst.'[19]

Particularly forceful in this respect are the words that Angela Merici addressed to the women who watched over her consecrated virgins:

> Take special care that they are united and of one will, as we read of the Apostles and the other Christians in the primitive Church ... And endeavour to be so yourselves with all your daughters,

because the more united you are, the more will Jesus Christ be in your midst as father and good shepherd.[20]

The last word I say to you, entreating you even with my blood, is that you will all agree, united together in one heart and one will. Be bound to one another by the bond of charity, esteeming one another, helping one another, bearing with one another in Jesus Christ. For if you try to be like this, without any doubt the Lord God will be in your midst.[21]

This last text not only confirms the view of the community as the place where the Risen Christ is present, but also brings out the particular nature of that presence. It demands the constructive contribution of those who make up the community, a concrete and radical attitude of mutual love, in order to create an atmosphere of communion and unity. Having the presence of the Risen Lord requires, in fact, being assembled 'in his name'. Any sort of meeting is not enough. The presence of the Risen Christ in the community, Yves Congar has written, is 'a presence of covenant, in which God has pledged himself with the promise to be active, in his grace, in the operations of the Church, once the conditions of the covenant have been satisfied and its structures respected'.[22] These conditions are precisely fraternal communion, coming together 'in his name'. This is particularly appropriate to the religious community, which is indeed united in the name of Jesus, to live by following him and in obedience to his word, especially the commandment of mutual love.

The religious community, then, is a place in which Christ makes himself present and the Church is made visible; an authentic place of following where the experience of the Twelve and the disciples around the Master is continued. He himself makes himself present among those whom he has called and consecrated to himself, forming them into a community. He himself lives in their midst and makes himself their koinonia.

As we have mentioned before, love between the members of the community is not merely an ethical obligation. Rather, it is the fruit of sharing the divine love itself. The mutual love within the community is the very love of Christ loving. He is the 'I' who loves and the 'Thou' who receives the love, just as 'the Son of God incarnate, present in his human community as "I" and "Thou", also forms a "we" in it'. On the basis of this theological nature of charity, J. Galot can affirm the ontological reality of the presence promised by Jesus:

> We need to recognize the full significance of Jesus' affirmation: 'Where two or three are gathered in my name, there am I in the midst of them' (Matt. 18:20). If we interpret this statement simply as a moral presence of Christ in every meeting, we shall fail to understand its deep meaning ... This presence retains all its reality. It is an ontological presence.[23]

M. Zago, the Superior General of the Oblates of Mary Immaculate, seems to me to have succeeded in effectively synthesizing the twofold dimension of this presence - the covenantal and the ontological. Commenting on the Rule of his Institute, which presents the community of the Apostles with Jesus as the model for its life, he explains:

> It is not a question of a purely exterior model but of the realization of reality itself. Even if the model is realized in an analogous way, it remains none the less real. Christ calls us, brings us together and is present. We follow him and become his fellow workers in and through the community, because Christ makes himself present in it: 'Where two or three are gathered in my name, there am I in the midst of them' (Matt. 18:20). Holiness and mission come through the community not because it is a means in itself but because Christ makes himself present in and through it. Certainly, this presence is not effected by a sacramental word as in the Eucharist, but by our Christian way of living itself. Constitution 37 provides us with the theological key and indicates to us how the mission-community can be realized in an experiential way: 'To the extent that unity of spirit and heart grows among the Oblates, so far will they bear witness to people that Jesus lives in their midst and brings about their unity in order to send them out to proclaim his Kingdom.'(24)

Other forms of the common life emphasize the same reality. Madeleine Delbrêl writes thus, in a text with the significant title of *On the birth of small lay communities*:

> 'Where two or three are gathered in my name, there am I in the midst of them.' To live in community is to express a kind of sacrament for the world. It is a guarantee of the presence of Jesus. The common life lived in a spirit of total charity is an essential spark for lighting a fire to warm those around us ... The witness of a single

person, whether he likes it or not, bears only his signature. The witness of a community, if it is faithful, bears the signature of Christ.[25]

Speaking earlier of the focolare, we saw that Chiara Lubich emphasized the ontological reality of the presence of Christ in its midst and the personal character of this presence. Her charism has enabled her to make a notable contribution to bringing out this presence of the Risen Christ in the community and making its nature better appreciated. In some verses written for Christmas, she emphasizes once again how real the presence of Jesus is in the midst of his own. It is the same Jesus who was present between Mary and Joseph at Bethlehem:

> 'Where two or three are gathered
> in my name, there am I
> in the midst of them.'
> In their midst exactly
> as two thousand years ago
> in the midst of Mary and Joseph.
> Only that his presence,
> though real, is spiritual.
> Jesus does not like remaining just in tabernacles.
> His desire is to be amongst people
> and share with them thoughts, plans,
> worries, joys...
> He came to earth for this as well:
> to give us the opportunity of having him
> among us always to bring the warmth,
> the hope, the light, the harmony
> which every Christmas brings.[26]

Going more deeply into this type of presence, Chiara Lubich explains that it is real but not local. To say that 'Jesus is in our midst' means all and each of us being penetrated by the reality of Christ and therefore made one by him and in him. 'When two souls meet in the name of Christ, Christ is born between them, that is, *in them* and, maintaining this unity, we can say with sincerity: "It is no longer I who live but Christ lives in me".'[27]

Aware of the reality of that presence, the religious community can experience its countless fruits. The presence of the risen Lord in the community is in fact an active presence. The SCRSI document on *The Contemplative Dimension of the Religious Life*, addressed to all Religious, men and women, repeats that 'the religious community is in itself a theological reality, an object of contemplation, "a true family in the Lord's name" (PC 15)' and points out the first fundamental consequence. If the community is the place of God's presence, then it is 'of its nature, the place where it should be particularly possible to attain the experience of God in its fullness and communicate it to others. Mutual fraternal acceptance, in charity, contributes to "the creation of a favourable setting for the progress of each person" (ET 39).'[28] Because the Lord himself is present among the members of the community, they can attain to holiness.

The action of Jesus in the midst of a religious community actually favours the 'progress of each person' in many ways. Christ present in his community operates first of all on the illuminative level. Just as he became present again among the community when he placed himself between the two on the way to Emmaus, so he continues to explain the meaning of the scriptures and set hearts ablaze. This illuminating activity can be seen at various levels. When the truths of faith and Christian life are made the purpose of communion and gathered in the unity of people who love one another and are enlightened by the Spirit whom the Risen Christ shares with his own, then they are seen in depth, gathered from within, attained with the kind of knowledge which comes from wisdom and experience. For the two on the way to Emmaus, the presentation of the scriptures had the effect of setting their hearts ablaze. It was therefore a loving penetration of the mystery. The life of mutual love, which makes people live in God and share in his life, in its turn enables them to discover, as if by an inborn ability, things as God sees and wills them.[29] The presence of the Lord among his own gathered in his name actually brings with it the entire presence of the Trinity and enables them to live in the trinitarian way. Spiritual life, liturgical life, the life of prayer, the reality of the Church, in a word all the deepest and most substantial components of the life of Religious, are interiorized and become living and effective realities.

This applies particularly to the knowledge, rediscovery and acting out of the specific charism of the Institute.[30] As this is of its nature a communal grace, it must be guarded, understood and studied more deeply precisely by the community as such, and can only be perceived and lived in its integrity within a dynamic of unity.

The presence of the Risen Christ also becomes a guarantee of light for that communal discernment which many today so urgently desire. The community has the task of evaluating its own way of life, pastoral choices and decisions to be taken, and for this Christ himself makes himself the interpreter of the Father's design for the whole community, through his illuminative action.

Finally, by his presence in the community he enlightens consciences at the personal level. The presence of the Lord, it has been said, is like a 'loudspeaker of Jesus in each soul', which 'amplifies his voice within us and makes us better able to understand (and so to live) the "new man" in us'.[31] What God asks of each one is seen better in unity, and people are more ready to conform to his will. There is a more immediate perception of defects to be eliminated and steps forward and choices to be made.

As well as being illuminative, the Master's action in his community is directed towards strengthening the will so that what has been perceived can be accomplished. It gives courage (*parrhesia*), strength to set out on the path of holiness and confront the difficulties inherent in spiritual growth: external contradictions, interior trials, discouragements. It infuses joy and brings peace even amid the most difficult situations. As John Chrysostom wrote, commenting on the verse in Proverbs (18:19), 'A brother helped by a brother is like a strong city': 'Great is the strength which comes from being together, because charity grows when we are together and united, and if charity grows, the reality of God [amongst us] also necessarily grows.'[32] These words also afford a glimpse of the aspect of protection against evil. The Lord, present among united brethren, defends them from temptation, danger and adversity.

These are only some expressions, however, of what is accomplished by the Lord present in the community. We could say something about the life of prayer; is it not he who becomes prayer to the Father among those who pray? We could also talk about material sustenance; did not Jesus tell us to seek the Kingdom of God first of all, in the assurance that when we do, all the rest will come as well? But 'the Kingdom of God is in the midst of you' (Luke 17:21). It is he, therefore, made present and living in the community, who attracts the Father's providence. And again, is it not he who spreads light so that all who come into contact with the community are impressed by the witness of its life? We could go on, but, finally, the life of unity enables every member of the community to live and grow in all aspects of life.

Moreover - and here we come to another effect of the Lord living in the community - the community does not live for itself. Christ opens it out and gives it an attitude of service. He makes it an instrument of his diakonia and his witness to new life and sends it out to proclaim and share the mystery of its salvation. The Risen Christ who lives in the community makes it a witness to his resurrection. As the Risen Christ sent the apostles out over the whole world on the day of his ascension and the Spirit brought the first Christian community out from the Cenacle on the day of Pentecost, so every religious community, as an authentic spirit-filled community of the Risen Christ, is sent out into the world and appears, by its very nature, intrinsically apostolic.

The Lord present in the midst of his own shapes every aspect of the community's life. All the Religious is left to do is to live in mutual love, that love Christ infuses when he gives his own Spirit. 'As the Father and the Son, loving one another, emit (like two pieces of wood crossed and burning) a single flame, the Holy Spirit', so we, loving one another like them, and 'burning like as many pieces of wood placed on top of each other, by our total death release a single flame, the Holy Spirit, the Spirit of the Risen Christ in our midst'.[33]

This brings us to the final point in our contemplation of the paschal mystery: the Spirit given to his community by the Risen Christ. The gift of the Spirit is in fact an intrinsic component of the paschal mystery. Death, resurrection and the sending of the Spirit are one mystery, which for us takes on historical form as a succession of moments in time.

Charity, the Gift of the Spirit

The passage from *Perfectae caritatis* that we have already read (no. 15) made a close connection between the reality of charity, the Spirit, and the presence of the Risen Christ in the religious community: 'A community gathered together as a true family in the Lord's name enjoys *his presence* through the *love of God* which is poured into their hearts by the Holy Spirit.'

The community possesses charity as a gift brought by the Spirit. Charity in its turn allows the conditions to be created for the Lord to be effectively present. It ensures that the community will not be a haphazard assembly of people but a gathering 'in the name of Jesus'. This process assumes that the Spirit is sent to the community. And it is that action which Christ accomplishes as the culminating moment of the paschal event: he sends the Spirit. In this way the Risen Christ puts himself at the beginning of the community, because he sends it the Spirit who transmits the divine agape. He also puts himself at its end, not only by being present in it as the fruit of mutual love but also by enabling the community consciously to 'enjoy' his presence. By undergoing the ascesis involved in mutual love - remember what is meant by kenosis - the community is called to enter into the mystical dimension and experience in itself the presence of the Risen Christ.

So we come back to the starting point in our reflection on community: God is love. The life which the Risen Christ shares by sending the Spirit is the very life of the God of love; it is agape. We have truly been made 'partakers in the divine nature' (2 Pet. 1:4).

If religious consecration is the radicalization of baptism, it is a life of charity lived to the full. In baptism we were actually given the Holy Spirit in whom the Father and the Son love one another and human beings. 'You will be baptized in the Holy Spirit,' Jesus had said before his ascension (Acts 1:5; 11:16). Baptism or 'immersion' in the Spirit means that the Spirit permeates us totally, to the very roots of our being, so that Paul can say that in baptism 'all were made to drink of one Spirit' (1 Cor. 12:13). The Holy Spirit, given to us by Christ who died on the cross and rose again, is the principle of the new life in him; and the love of God, that with which God loves, is poured out in our hearts. Baptism has united us with Christ dead and risen, with that act of freedom through which he loved us to the utmost by giving his life for us, that outstanding charity in which he has somehow been fixed by his death.

The religious community is called to relive fully that baptismal reality. By the power of the Spirit of the Risen Christ, it lives relationships founded on a love whose origin is not human but divine (cf. Rom. 5:5; 1 Thess. 4:9; 1 John 4:7). It lives by God's gift. Thanks only to this theological charity, we can fulfil the new commandment of mutual love. Thanks only to this gift from on high, community can be formed, community seen as a set of loving relationships modelled on the relationships of the Trinity.

So we can appreciate the reason for John Paul II's exhortation to Religious in *Redemptoris donum*, in which he invites them to live their religious vocation consistently, as a particular sharing in the love of God. After declaring that consecration and the profession of the evangelical counsels 'are a particular *witness of love*', he continues:

> It was just in this way that the Apostle prayed in his Epistle to the Philippians: 'May your love abound more and more...' (Phil. 1:9-11). In virtue of Christ's redemption, 'God's love has been poured into our hearts through the Holy Spirit which has been given to us' (Rom. 5:5). Unceasingly I beg the Holy Spirit to grant each of you, man or woman, 'in accordance with each one's special gift' (cf. 1 Cor. 7:7), to bear a particular witness to this love. In a manner worthy of your vocation, may 'the law of the Spirit of life in Christ Jesus...' conquer in you, that law which has 'set us free from the law of sin and death' (Rom. 8:2). Live, then, this new life to the full extent of your vocation and also to the full extent of the various gifts of God which correspond to the vocation of the individual religious families ... It is precisely this witness of love that the world of today and humanity need. They need your witness to the redemption, in the same way that it is conveyed in profession of the evangelical counsels. (No. 14)

What makes a community is not a house, a certain number of people, a shared structure, or participation in common acts. These are elements which can if necessary express the mutual communion which has been achieved, and at the same time they can be the means of realizing it, but they do not create it. What creates the community is the mutual love between all its members, a love which, following the example of Christ's love, is ready to give its life in a real kenosis; the presence of the Risen Lord; and the Spirit who gives life to it so that it can share in the love of the Trinity.

NOTES

1. Precise references will be found in two studies by P. Coda: *Evento pasquale*. *Trinità e storia* (Rome 1984); and 'Per una ontologia trinitaria della carità. Una riflessione di carattere introduttivo', *Lateranum*, n.s. 51 (1985), pp. 60-77.

2. Cf. G. Rossé, *Il grido di Gesù in croce* (Rome: Città Nuova, 1984); L. Caza, *'Mon Dieu, mon Dieu, pourquoi m'as-tu abandonné?' comme Bonne Nouvelle de Jésus Christ, Fils de Dieu, comme Bonne Nouvelle de Dieu pour la multitude* (Montreal and Paris:1989); M. Cerini, *Dio Amore nell'esperienza e nel pensiero di Chiara Lubich* (Rome: Città Nuova, 1991), pp. 51-73.

3. Coda, 'Per una ontologia trinitaria della carità', p. 73.

4. International Theological Commission, *Some Questions Concerning Christology* (EV 7, 683).

5. 'Il Paraclito', *EDB* (Bologna: 1971), p. 396.

6. Cerini, op. cit., p. 63.

7. C. Lubich, *The Secret of Unity* (London: New City, 1997), p. 94.

8. *Agapè dans le Nouveau Testament*, III (Paris: 1959), pp. 161-74. Spicq emphasizes that the term *kathos* ('as') denotes the nature itself and is stronger than other similar conjunctions such as *hos, hosper, hoste*, etc., which can also mean 'as'.

9. Quoted by Cerini, op. cit., pp. 57-8.

10. K. Rahner, *Chiesa e Sacramenti* (Brescia: Queriniana, 1969), p. 20.

11. *Mysterium fidei, Acta Apostolicae Sedis* 57 (1965), 762.

12. Matt. 18:20. Cf. J. M. Povilus, *La presenza di Gesù tra i suoi nella teologia di oggi* (Rome: Città Nuova, 1977); G. Rossé, *Gesù in mezzo: Mt 18,20 nell'esegesi contemporanea* (Rome: Città Nuova, 1972).

13. O. Casel, *Il mistero dell'Ecclesia* (Città Nuova, Rome 1966), p. 159.

14. C. Gutzwiller, *Cristo nel Vangelo di Matteo* (Città Nuova, Rome 1969), p. 228.

15. A further setting in which theological reflection has located this presence of the Risen Christ is a conciliar session or other analogous ecclesial gatherings.

16. Rossé, *Gesù in mezzo*, p. 138.

17. 'Le grandi leggi del rinnovamento', in *Il rinnovamento della vita religiosa* (Vallecchi, Florence 1968), pp. 124-8.

18. *In can. XVII, Conc. oecum. VII*, PG 137, 974.

19. *De monast. laic. non trad.*, PG 132, 1134.

20. *Decimo legato*, in *Regola, Ricordi, Legati* (Brescia: Queriniana, 1975), p. 113.

21. *Ultimo ricordo*, ibid., p. 93.

22. 'Note sul Concilio come assemblea e sulla conciliarità fondamentale della Chiesa', in *Orizzonti attuali della teologia*, II (Rome: 1967), pp. 170-4.

23. *La Persona di Cristo* (Assisi: 1970), pp. 99-101.

24. 'Community', *Vie Oblate Life* 48 (1988), pp. 9-10.

25. *Comunità secondo il Vangelo* (Brescia: Morcelliana, 1976), p. 35.

26. Quoted in Povilus, *'Gesù in mezzo' nel pensiero di Chiara Lubich* (Rome: Città Nuova, 1981), p. 53.
27. Quoted in Povilus, op. cit., p. 57.
28. N. 15, EV 7, 522.
29. See the interesting remarks on this subject made by G. Mura, 'Ermeneutica e "Gesù in mezzo": Emmaus', *Nuova Umanità* no. 30 (November-December 1983), pp. 71-85.
30. I have developed this aspect in 'Indicazioni metodologiche per l'ermeneutica del carisma dei fondatori', *Claretianum* 30 (1990), pp. 5-47.
31. C. Lubich, *Diario 1964-65* (Rome 1985), p. 16.
32. *In Ep. ad Hebr.*, 10, 25, *Hom.* 19.1.
33. C. Lubich, quoted in Cerini, op. cit., p. 88.

3 The Gift of Unity
The theological components of community

Born of God's love and made partaker, through the paschal event, in the life of the Trinity itself, the theological dimension of the community is constantly nourished by God himself. It is nourished from on high by the gift of the Word, the Eucharist and the sacramental presence of brothers and sisters. The very members of the first church at Jerusalem lived by these divine realities: 'They devoted themselves to the apostles' teaching and fellowship. to the breaking of bread and the prayers' (Acts 2:42).

Nourished by the Word, the Eucharist and fraternal communion, the religious community is also established in its deepest reality and can become what it is called to be: a privileged place of Christ's presence. The Second Vatican Council has written about this:

> Common life, in prayer and the sharing of the same spirit (Acts 2:42), should be constant, after the example of the early Church, in which the company of believers were of one heart and soul. It should be nourished by the teaching of the Gospel and by the sacred liturgy, especially by the Eucharist. (PC 15)

Community continues to reveal itself, in its 'downward' dimension, as a gift from on high, the fruit of the love of God who constantly communicates himself to it.

Unity in the Word of God and in the 'Word' of Charism

A single call brings the members of the community together and unites them with one another. Christ's summons, 'Come, follow me', continues to make itself heard in the heart of men and women called to the religious life. This summons gathers different people into the same community just as, when it sounded for the first time on Lake Genesareth, it brought into being the group that was to follow Jesus closely. The Word continues to show all its intrinsic power to call together, its ability to create communities, peoples, unity.

Of old the community of the people of Israel began with a call, that of Abraham, and it was formed as such by the Word of God received at Sinai (cf. Exod. 24:7-8). Likewise, the new people of God, represented by the Twelve, the symbol of the twelve tribes of the new Israel, was born from a call. Called personally by name, one by one, the apostles found themselves together behind the same Master. The Church in its turn was born from hearing the word of Peter, who shared the event of the Word made flesh and his history amongst us (cf. Acts 2:41). Every Christian community is always born and grows by receiving the Word (cf. 1 Thess. 1:5-10). Acts describes the 'journey' of the Word which, wherever it arrives, gives birth to the Church. The Church is a 'convocation': a common call which God addresses to several people. United in the name of Jesus, in his word, in him the Word, they are united amongst themselves by his presence (cf. Matt. 18:20) to the point of becoming a single reality in Christ.

The whole of the New Testament shows the dynamics through which the word of Christ built up the community. As the 'word of salvation' (Acts 13:26), the 'word of life' (Phil. 2:16), the Word gives birth to the new life in those who are baptized. Baptism is actually a 'washing of water with the word' (Eph. 5:26). Christians are 'born anew, not of perishable seed but of imperishable, through the living and abiding word of God' (1 Pet. 1:23). God 'of his own will ... brought us forth by the word of truth' (Jas. 1:18).

Brought to birth by the Word, the Church continues to grow, nourished by the Word; the growth of the Church, according to the Acts of the Apostles, is identified with the very growth of the Word (cf. 6:7; 12:24; 19:20). The Word nourishes and unifies it, so that the faithful are brought to unity of thought, to having the same thought as Christ (cf. 1 Cor. 2:16). In fact, Christ, through his Word which is also himself, communicates himself to each person, making all one. This is the unity of faith. The Church is actually 'one body, one spirit' because 'one faith' lives in it (Eph. 4:5). Consequently Paul requires the faithful at Corinth to agree among themselves, 'that there may be no dissensions among you, but that you be united in the same mind and the same judgement' (1 Cor. 1:10). It is in fact necessary that 'we all attain to the unity of the faith and of the knowledge of the Son of God' (Eph. 4:13). Faith is thus not only the principle of personal existence; it is the first principle of unity between people and unity for the Church as a whole.

The religious community undergoes a similar process.[1] It is formed as the result of a call and a particular 'word' which realizes the Word of the Gospel in a specific charismatic identity.

The community is born, above all, of Christ's call, which reflects the eternal love of the Father.[2] We have already seen how the apostles immediately found themselves with others in their personal path of following. It is the same for men and women Religious: vocation is transformed into *con*-vocation. The religious vocation, in continuity with the vocation of Jesus' first disciples, leads people to follow, together, the same Master and so to form a community of life with him and amongst themselves. For the most part a completely mixed group, they have no other motive for their mutual attraction but their common call to follow. The religious community is not elective (people do not choose one another because they share particular human affinities) but elected (people are chosen and called by God). It reflects completely the identity of the new family of the children of God, the family identified by Jesus as those who do the will of his Father (cf. Mark 3:34-5). It is not born out of a human plan, the outcome of human initiative, but from a divine plan derived from the Father's will revealed by Christ's word.

When we consider the community as the result of a response to a common call and the common doing of the will of God together, we can understand the fundamental role played in it by obedience. This is seen to serve the receiving of the Word and the complete doing of the Father's will revealed in the Word. The vow of obedience is most intelligible from the perspective of the unity to which the community is called. It is a way of receiving and doing fully the will of the Father, and so arriving at the formation of one mind and unity in the community.

In the religious life the Word which gives birth to unity has a particular face. In fact, the call to follow usually comes about through the mediation of a charism given to a founder or foundress, which is put into action in a particular religious family. The founder and the Institute become mediators of the Word which calls together and unites.

The ultimate origin and foundation of the charism of the Institute is in the Word incarnate who reveals and speaks himself through the founder or foundress, who appears as the 'word' of the one Word, 'word' of the Word, a particular aspect of the totality of the Gospel. The action of the Spirit of revelation and truth, who teaches 'all truth' and recalls Jesus' words (cf. John 14:24-6; 16:13), leads the founders into a deep existential understanding of a particular evangelical 'word' and through it opens the understanding of the scriptures to them (cf. Luke 24:45). In the light of that particular evangelical dimension, which may be a mystery of Christ's life, a specific word of his, or several elements of the Gospel together, the Spirit enables them to read the entire Gospel in such a way that they reach a particular synthesis of their own and, vice versa, they find the whole Gospel collected in their particular 'word' so that it becomes the centre and key for their understanding of the Gospel. The charism given to the founders, even before it is a concrete response to the Church through a specific work, appears as an ability to read the whole Christian mystery in the light of one of its aspects. It is a concrete method of living the Gospel. There are many possible ways of reading and incarnating the Gospel, because the riches of Christ are unfathomable and inexhaustible (cf. Eph. 3:8) and his love surpasses all knowledge (cf. Eph. 3:19) since the fullness of the Godhead truly dwells in him (cf. Col. 2:10).

With their experience of life and their teaching, and through the religious family they bring into being, founders and foundresses become a 'living exegesis' of the Word of God. When we think about them and their work, we understand the Gospel in a new way, because they are able to translate it into life. Religious families thus appear as a kind of new incarnation of the Word in one of his words. The Council's Constitution on Revelation notes this particular type of living exegesis. In the Church, in fact, the progressive understanding of the Gospel comes about through 'the experience given by a deeper understanding of spiritual things' (DV 8), as well as by study and the teaching of the Magisterium. The Spirit leads the founders through a particular experiential journey into exactly such an understanding of the mystery.[3]

Unity in the Church comes from interior adherence to the Word of Christ, in faith, and requires assiduous perseverance to assimilate the teaching of the Apostles to whom Jesus entrusted the Gospel. In the same way, the religious community finds its own unity in receiving the charism which brought it into being and remaining faithful to it. A whole 'spiritual patrimony' is entrusted to the community, which contains the 'evangelical word' as it was understood and lived by the founder and subsequently put into practice by succeeding generations. The Council issued an invitation to rediscovery: 'the spirit and aims of each founder should be faithfully accepted and retained, as indeed should each institute's sound traditions, for all of these constitute the patrimony of an institute' (PC 2b). The conciliar and post-conciliar Magisterium has vigorously emphasized the worth of these elements which establish every individual religious family. In documents relating to the religious life such words as spirit, gift, function, purpose, inspiration, intention, charism, mission, character, identity and nature constantly recur, with the addition at every turn of the term 'proper' or 'own' to indicate that the identity of every Institute consists of a particular way, suggested by the Spirit, of following and imitating Christ in a dimension of his mystery.[4]

Thus even before dealing with exterior forms of uniformity and regularity, the unity of the community has to be constantly sought in shared reference to its particular charism, as it was imparted by the founder and guarded and developed throughout the Institute's life (cf. MR 11). Possession of a common heritage, a spiritual patrimony, may be a cohesive sociological factor; but even more than that, it is a spiritual element in that cohesion. It is understandable, therefore, why the conciliar and post-conciliar Magisterium has devoted so much of the renewal of the religious life to the task of revealing the authenticity and richness of the particular charism, 'in order', as Paul VI asked of Religious, ' to make your sources flow with renewed vigour and freshness' (ET 51).

Unity in the Eucharist

The second gift offered to the community to enable it to fulfil its vocation as koinonia in the trinitarian koinonia is the Eucharist. As a paschal sacrament, it introduces us into the Trinity and provides a share in the trinitarian agape. By the Eucharist, as the Council teaches, the faithful 'have access to God the Father through the Son, the Word made flesh who suffered and was glorified, in the outpouring of the Holy Spirit. And so ... they enter into communion with the most holy Trinity' (UR 15).

Nourished by the same Eucharist, Christians 'manifest in a concrete way that unity of the People of God which this holy sacrament aptly signifies and admirably realizes' (LG 11). The Eucharist achieves a universal communion without limits of time or space. Every eucharistic celebration brings together all the members of the Church, yesterday's as well as today's, in the unity of the one Body of Christ, the Lord of time and space.

The first Christians at Jerusalem were assiduous in the 'breaking of bread' and this made them all of one heart and one soul. In fact, 'Because there is one bread, we who are many are one body, for we all partake of the one bread' (1 Cor. 10:17).

The divine life which Jesus came to bring to earth, and which is imparted to us in baptism, attains its fullness precisely in the Eucharist. Here Christ gives himself as food to nourish us with his own life. He had come in order that we might have life and have it in abundance. In the Eucharist he has become the bread of life, the bread which gives life by restoring our life to the point of making it divine.

By the Eucharist Christ wills to transform not only the individual believer who communicates with him, but all humanity, even in its physical dimension, and ultimately to involve the cosmos itself in this unity. Eating at the table of life is not for the solitary individual. Jesus gave a precise structure to the action that enables his bread of life to be transmitted: a supper, a meeting of brothers, as in a family, around the same table. The function of the Eucharist is to communicate life to several people at the same time, and so to form the Church. It creates not just the new person but the new people as well, gathered and restored by the same bread. Christians have always understood and experienced that 'the Eucharist makes the Church'. The *Didache* reproduces a eucharistic prayer of about AD 50 which formulates the theme which later became classic and was constantly taken up again by the tradition: 'As this broken bread, once dispersed over the hills, was brought together and became one loaf, so may thy Church be brought together from the ends of the earth into thy kingdom' (9.4). This was the direction in which eucharistic catechesis developed from the Fathers to the present day. John Chrysostom, commenting on St Paul's First Epistle to the Corinthians, took up the image of the bread formed by many ears of corn:

> What is this bread in fact? The body of Christ. And what do those who communicate become? The body of Christ: not many bodies but a single body! In fact, as the bread, made out of many grains, is so united that the grains can no longer be seen ... so we are closely united with one another in Christ.[5]

John of Damascus wrote that the Eucharist 'is called communion and it truly is that, because by it we communicate and are united with Christ'.[6] Albert the Great summed up the teaching of the Fathers as follows:

> As bread, the matter of this sacrament, is made one from many grains, which communicate to one another the whole of their content and permeate one another, so the true body of Christ is made of many drops of the blood of our nature ... mingled with one another, and thus many faithful ... united in love and communicating with Christ the head, mystically form the one body of Christ ... and therefore this sacrament leads us to establish a communion of all our possessions, temporal and spiritual.[7]

And again:

> The outward form of this sacrament signifies communion, which means the union of many in one, that is, in bread and wine; for the bread is made from many grains and the wine from many grapes.[8]

> By the very fact that [Christ] unites everyone in himself, he unites them with each other. For if several things are united with a third, they are also united with one another.[9]

Thomas Aquinas, a disciple of Albert the Great, wrote that the Eucharist 'is the sacrament of the Church's unity'[10] because 'the unity of the mystical Body is produced by the real body, received sacramentally'.[11] 'The real effect (res) of this sacrament is the unity of the mystical Body'[12] and 'charity, considered not only in its habitus but also in its exercise'.[13]

In our own day Paul VI declared with firm conviction that the Eucharist was willed by Christ in order that

> from being strangers, scattered and indifferent to one another, we may become united, equals and friends; it is given to us so that from being an unfeeling and selfish crowd, people divided amongst themselves and mutually hostile, we may become a people, a true people, believing and loving, of one heart and one soul.[14]

'The Eucharist', the Italian bishops have written,

> is the force which shapes the community and increases its ability to love; it makes the community a house that welcomes everyone, the village fountain that offers its springs of water to all, as Pope John loved to say. In it, all diversity is reconciled in harmony, every

beseeching voice receives a hearing, every need finds someone to bend over it with love. Meeting, openness, and celebration are its distinguishing marks.[15]

The koinonia of the Church actually finds its sign and cause in the Eucharist. Nourished by the one bread, we have the same life and form the same body. The Eucharist is communion in Christ with our brethren. By uniting Christians through the Eucharist with himself and one another in a single body which is his own, Christ gives life to the Church in its deepest essence as the body of Christ, fraternity, unity, life, communion with God.

The Council reiterates this traditional aspect of the Eucharist in some of its principal texts: 'In the sacrament of the eucharistic bread, the unity of believers, who form one body in Christ ... is both expressed and brought about' (LG 3); 'we are taken up into communion with him and with one another' (LG 7). The eucharistic prayers confirm this: 'To us who are nourished with the body and blood of your Son give the fullness of the Holy Spirit, that we may become in Christ one body and one spirit'.[16]

Thus the Council can say: 'It is not possible for a Christian community to be built up without having as its root and pivot the celebration of the Blessed Eucharist, so any education tending to form community spirit must start from it' (PO 6).

The Eucharist, by transforming believers into Christ, gives them the opportunity to carry out fully the 'new commandment'. They can love *as* Christ loved, to the extent of identifying himself with each one of them, and it is he himself who loves in them. It was not by chance that Jesus gave the new commandment while he was giving the Eucharist. The fulfilment of the commandment of love is made possible in the sacrament of love. John Paul II writes on this topic:

Eucharistic worship forms the soul of all Christian life. If Christian life is actually expressed in the fulfilment of the greatest commandment, that is, the love of God and neighbour, this love finds its proper source in the Blessed Sacrament, which is commonly called the sacrament of love ... The Eucharist signifies this charity and therefore calls it to mind, makes it present, and at the same time realizes it ... Not only do we know love but we ourselves begin to love. We enter upon the way of love and make progress in it ... The authentic meaning of the Eucharist becomes, of itself, a school of active love of neighbour.[17]

A community within the great community of the Church, the religious community in its turn lives by the Eucharist. As we read in *Evangelica testificatio* (no. 48), 'Your communities, since they are united in Christ's name, naturally have as their centre the Eucharist, "the Sacrament of love, the sign of unity and the bond of charity" (SC 47).'

The whole of the consecrated life can be seen as eucharistic life.[18] Consecration has an intrinsic eucharistic structure; the Council interprets it as an oblation closely associated with the eucharistic sacrifice (cf. LG 45c). In the same way, the apostolic dimension of the religious life finds it own point of reference in the dynamism of the Eucharist; it follows the pattern of the gift which, in the Eucharist, Christ makes of himself for the salvation of the world. While bringing out these aspects, the conciliar and post-conciliar Magisterium, in its treatment of the relationship between the Eucharist and the religious life, prefers to concentrate on the communal dimension. It is the Eucharist that provides the opportunity to make the community a true family in which unity is fully achieved.

The religious community actually has its source in the Eucharist and finds there its basis and starting-point for a dynamic development of its own being and koinonia. Thus we read in the conciliar documents: 'The celebration of the Eucharist and intense participation in it as "the source and summit of the Christian life" (LG 11), form the indispensable and inspiring centre of the contemplative dimension of every religious community.'[19] 'Common life, in prayer and the sharing of the same spirit (Acts 2:42), should be constant ... nourished by the teaching of the Gospel and by the sacred liturgy, especially by the Eucharist' (LG 15). It is understandable, in the light of these principles, why the request is repeatedly made that there should always be an oratory with the Eucharist in a religious house. 'The real presence of the Lord Jesus in the Eucharist, devoutly reserved and adored, will be for them a living sign of a communion which is built up every day in charity.'[20] In the community the reservation of the Eucharist 'expresses and at the same time makes real that which must be the principal mission of every religious family' (ET 48).

The Brother or Sister as Sacrament of God's Love

Equally with the Word and the Eucharist, our brother or sister is given to us as the mediator of God's love. In addition to the hearing of God's Word and the breaking of bread, the characteristic feature of the first Christian community was its living of koinonia, the relationships with brothers and sisters. How could communion be lived without brethren? Trinitarian koinonia is the relationship between the three divine Persons. To live according to the Trinity, the religious community needs a multiplicity of people. Brothers and sisters are the concrete opportunity and the indispensable necessity for living the commandment of mutual love which, by its very definition, needs to be reciprocal. Our brother or sister is the opportunity to make Christ present among us.

Let us recall how well Augustine grasped the reality of brotherhood in its precise theological definition, when he wrote in his Rule: 'Live, all of you, of one mind and in concord and, in yourselves, mutually honour the God whose Temple you are.'[21] Francis also perceived his brothers as a gift from God, as he declares in his *Testament*: 'The Lord gave me brethren.'[22] Celano relates Francis' joy when he received his first companion as a gift from the Lord: 'It appeared to him that the Lord was caring for him, by giving him the companion - Bernard - whom everyone needs, and a faithful friend.'[23]

Brothers and sisters become a sacrament of Christ. Even before they are the object of our love, they are an expression of God's love for us. They are for us the presence of Christ.

We need to refer to the mystery of the incarnation and the 'sacramentality' of Christ. John helps our reflection on this point. The Gnostic believes he can attain to the transcendent God by raising himself above the world through his own efforts in contemplation and ascetic purification. The prologue of John's Gospel (1:18) clearly rejects such a claim: 'No one has ever seen God; the only Son, who is in the bosom of the Father, he has made him known.' By introducing his gospel in this way, John presents the life of the Son as an epiphany of God's love made present in the world. It is therefore in the Son Jesus made flesh that we have to seek the Father. 'He who has seen me has seen the Father', Jesus himself will say (John 14:9). As his signs reveal, behind Jesus the love of the Father is dynamically present.

Jesus extends the same process of incarnation to his brethren. As it is impossible to disregard the humanity of Christ in the journey to the

Father and the life of the Trinity, so too it is impossible to avoid brothers and sisters, because Christ identified himself with the Apostles, with all the faithful and, even more, with every human being. Anyone who receives Christ's envoy receives Christ himself (cf. Matt. 10:40; John 13:20), and anyone who listens to him or despises him listens to or despises Christ (cf. Luke 10:16). At the same time, anyone who welcomes a disciple of Christ, whoever he or she may be, welcomes Christ himself because he identifies himself with every one of the 'little ones' (cf. Luke 9:46-8). To Saul, persecuting Christians, Jesus says: 'Why do you persecute me? ... I am Jesus, whom you are persecuting' (Acts 9:4-5). Strong in this experience, Paul knows that there is no longer Jew or Greek, slave or free man, man or woman in any Christian, because 'Christ is all in all' (Col. 3:11), just as it is no longer he, Paul, who lives but Christ in him (cf. Gal. 2:20). Agreeing with the Synoptics and Paul, John also regards the deepest reality of every Christian as being Christ who 'dwells' in them (cf. John 6:56) and 'is' in him permanently (cf. 15:5, 7). This is the deep reality of the 'I' of Jesus in them (cf. 17:23). And, finally, Jesus is present in every human being. He identifies himself with whoever is in need, whether it is the hungry, the thirsty, the stranger, the naked, the ill or those in prison. Whatever we do for them is done for him (cf. Matt. 25:31-46).

Henceforward it is no longer possible to love God without our brothers and sisters as intermediaries. If John could write in the prologue of his gospel that 'No one has ever seen God; the only Son, who is in the bosom of the Father, he has made him known' (1:18), he can write with equal consistency in his First Epistle: 'No man has ever seen God; if we love one another, God abides in us and his love is perfected in us' (1 John 4:12). No one has ever seen God, yet he reaches us and allows himself to be reached through Christ as intermediary and through our brothers and sisters in him. In this way we have access to the fullness and perfection of his love.

So the grace of community can be understood in this way: here our brothers and sisters, God's gift, are constantly present to us and through them the love of God reaches us, enfolds us, and leads us into his own love.

The religious community is not only the outcome of particular social factors or the personal initiative of several people. It is willed by God. It is he who takes the initiative in its formation and makes known how it can be realized. The person reconciled with God receives God's own love and therefore the ability to establish trinitarian relationships on earth. 'The religious community is, in itself, a theological reality, an object of contemplation; as a "family united in the name of the Lord" it is by its very nature the place where the experience of God must be attainable in its fullness and communicable to others' (DC 15). Receiving the life of the Trinity in this way, united around Christ and inspired by his Spirit, the community becomes a way of return to the Trinity. Born of the Trinity, it returns to it.

NOTES

1. Cf. S. Blanco Pacheco, 'La comunidad religiosa convocada por la palabra', in *Urgidos por la Palabra. Fundamentación bíblica de la Vida Religiosa* (Madrid: Publ. Claretianas, 1989), pp. 139-59.
2. The meditation offered to Religious by John Paul II in *Redemptionis donum* (3-6) provides a stimulating text on vocation as a call of love.
3. For deeper study I refer the reader to what I have written in *I fondatori uomini dello Spirito*, pp. 219-21.
4. Cf. F. Ciardi, 'Note sulla dottrina dei religiosi nei documenti post-conciliari', *Claretianum* 26 (1986), pp. 302-6; S.-M. Alonso, 'El patrimonio espiritual de un instituto religioso', *Claretianum* 30 (1990), pp. 49-67.
5. *In 1 Cor. hom.*, 23, 2.
6. *De fide orth.*, IV, 13, PG 94, 1154.
7. *In Jo.*, 6, 64.
8. *De eccles. hierarch.*, 3, 2.
9. *IV Sent.*, d.8, a.11.
10. *Super Ev. Ioannis*, c.6, lect. VI.
11. *S. Th.*, III, q.82, a.2 ad 3; cf. q.73, a.4.
12. Ibid., III, q.73, a.3.
13. Ibid., III, q.79, a.4.
14. *Insegnamenti di Paolo VI* (Vatican Polyglot Press: 1966), III, p. 358.
15. ECC 28.
16. Eucharistic Prayer III. 'By communion in the Body and Blood of Christ may the Holy Spirit unite us in one body' (Eucharistic Prayer II).
17. *Dominicae Coenae*, 5-6.
18. The relationship between consecrated life, community and Eucharist occurs particularly frequently in theological reflection at the present time: A. Aparcio Rodriguez, 'La Eucaristía en nuestros textos constitucionales', *Vida Religiosa* 62 (1987), pp. 61-71; J. M. de Miguel, 'Eucaristía y Vida Religiosa', *Comunidades* 15 (1987), table of contents no. 59; H. A. Pedro, 'Eucarisita, centro e culmine di ogni comunità', *Vita Consacrata* 26 (1990),

pp. 18-29; J. C. R. García Paredes, 'Contemplando la Eucaristía con nuestros fundadores', *Vida religiosa* 62 (1987), pp. 41-61; M. Gesteira Garza, 'La Eucaristía y la vida religiosa', *Vida Religiosa* 62 (1987), pp. 11-27; J. Luzarraga, 'El mensaje de la Eucaristía para la vida consagrada según el N.T.', *Manresa* 57 (1985), pp. 335-62; V. Muñiz, 'La celebracíon litúrgica en la edificacíon de la comunidad', *Comunidadea* 15 (1987), pp. 223-32; R. F. O'Toole, 'What the Lord's Supper can mean for Religious', *Review for Religious* 44 (1985), pp. 237-49; M. Pfister, 'Eucharist. Celebration for community', *Review for Religious* 25 (1986), pp. 25-35; J. M. R. Tillard, 'L'Eucharistie et la fraternité', *Nouvelle Revue Théologique* 91 (1969), pp. 113-35; S. Wood, 'The Eucharist: Heart of religious community', *Review for Religious* 46 (1987), pp. 178-86.

19. SCRSI, *Dimensione contemplativa della vita religiosa*, 8.
20. Ibid., 15.
21. *Rule*, 9.
22. *Testament*, 16.
23. *1 Celano*, 24.

4 'Ecstasy' of Love
The evangelistic dimension of community

The unity which the Trinity imparts to the community does not stop just with the community. It is not only an 'intensive' unity, understood as progressive growth in communion among its members. It is also an 'extensive' unity, a unity called to radiate and expand in a 'catholic' dimension. The unity which God imparts is able to involve others in the dynamics of communion. The purpose of the Father, 'that they may all be one', embraces all human beings in Christ, through the Spirit.

The Holy Spirit, the bond of unity in the Trinity, is the 'ecstasy' of the divine Persons because he 'opens' them to creation and the work of incarnation and redemption. In the same way, the unity of the community, the fruit of the same Spirit, becomes an authentic possibility for the community of 'ecstasy' towards the world. The life of the community is not a narcissistic turning in on itself, but an openness to the outside in order to communicate to everyone the gift received and involve everyone in the dynamics of unity. The life of the community expresses itself, therefore, in service, *diakonia*, witness and proclamation. The Risen Christ who lives in the community and imparts his Spirit to it, makes it a witness to his resurrection. As the Risen Christ sent his community out into all the world and the Spirit drove the first Christian community out from the Cenacle, so every religious community, made a truly spiritual community by the Risen Christ, is drawn out into the world; it is intrinsically, by its very nature, apostolic.

Reference to the community of the apostles, and that of Jerusalem, will once again be obligatory.

Jesus actually united the Twelve around himself and formed them into a community in order to send them out to proclaim the Good News of the Kingdom he inaugurated: 'Follow me and I will make you fishers of human beings', he had said to them at the time of their call (Mark 1:17). And to Peter in particular, in his role of guide to the other apostles, he said: 'Henceforth you will be catching human beings' (Luke 5:10). Later, on the mountain, Jesus 'appointed twelve ... to be with him, and to be sent out to preach' (Mark 3:15). The community of the Twelve, therefore, did not live for itself, as Jesus did not live for himself. The Twelve are with Jesus to become his envoys and witnesses. The apostolic community is a community of envoys, a community wholly dedicated to the Kingdom of God. By its adherence to Jesus, it reveals the advent of the new world and the demands it makes on everyone. By its unity it testifies to the very reality of God, the unity of love amongst the three divine Persons.

The community at Jerusalem continued the experience of the Twelve and the mandate entrusted to them by Jesus. Its life, nourished by the Word, the Eucharist, koinonia and prayer, possesses a great power of attraction and witness, as we can see at the end of the description of its common life in the first and third 'summaries' in Acts. The first Christians had 'favour with all the people. And the Lord added to their number [literally, "to their being one"] day by day those who were being saved' (Acts 2:47); 'the people held them in high honour. And more than ever believers were added to the Lord, multitudes both of men and women' (Acts 5:13-14). The description in the first 'summary' also specifies how the word, the sharing, the common prayer and the Eucharist were experienced: all was performed 'with glad and generous hearts' (2:46). The simplicity and joy of the community life are signs of the presence and action of the Risen Christ. Bearing witness to the risen Lord was not only by words but also by the quality of community life.[1]

This is a constant to be found throughout the New Testament: 'Let your light so shine before men that they may see your good works and give glory to your Father who is in heaven' (Matt. 5:16; 'Do all things without grumbling or questioning, that you may be blameless and innocent, children of God without blemish ... you shine as lights in the world' (Phil. 2:14-25); 'Maintain good conduct among the Gentiles, so that ... they may see your good deeds and glorify God on the day of visitation' (1 Pet. 2:12). The Gospel of John in particular closely connects the witness of unity and evangelical proclamation: 'May they also be [one] in us, so that the world may believe that thou hast sent me' (17:21); 'May they become perfectly one, so that the world may know that thou hast sent me' (17:23). It is precisely this dimension of unity that characterizes today's evangelization.

Communion is Missionary

Until a few years ago, evangelization based itself on the missionary mandate in Matthew (28:19-20): 'Go therefore and make disciples of all nations, baptizing them in the name of the Father and of the Son and of the Holy Spirit, teaching them to observe all that I have commanded you.' The main emphasis was laid on the word to be proclaimed.

Today greater prominence is given to what is called John's missionary mandate, recognized in Jesus' prayer to the Father from which we have just read about the relationship between unity and faith in Christ: 'May they also be [one] in us, so that the world may believe that thou hast sent me' (17:21); 'May they become perfectly one, so that the world may know that thou hast sent me' (17:23).

Presenting these two models of evangelization, Tillard writes about witness:

> [This type of] evangelization, attested in the New Testament, is more communal. It may be described as the option of the evangelist John. Its emphasis is not on a movement *ad extra* but rather on the internal quality of the ecclesial community itself. Such a community must be 'loveable', that is, it must manifest the truth of its liturgical prayer by the very quality of its evangelical life; it must manifest the renewing power of the Gospel by its mutual fraternal help and the seriousness of its engagement with the great human problems. That is the meaning of the expressions 'May they all be one' and 'Love one another' in the Johannine tradition. It is also the style of some short texts included in the first chapters of the Acts of the Apostles. In this type of evangelization the transmission of the faith is effected by a sort of contagion.[2]

The Matthean and Johannine missionary mandates should not be placed in antithesis. They are two equally evangelical dimensions, inseparable from one another. The word must find its support in the witness to unity of the community which proclaims it; and the witness of the life must be able to make itself word in order to declare explicitly the faith which inspires it.

The community must be able to show the truth of Christ's work. While it says in words that Christ died to reconcile human beings to God and each other and to give life to a new humanity, it ought to show this truth through its way of life. The community ought to show in itself the truthfulness of the reconciliation and unity brought about by Christ. The word must be borne out by witness to unity. Paul VI wrote in *Evangelii nuntiandi* (no. 77):

> The power of evangelization will be very much diminished if those who proclaim the Gospel are divided amongst themselves by so many kinds of disunity ... The Lord's spiritual testament tells us that unity amongst his followers is not only the proof that we are his, but also that he is the envoy of the Father, the criterion of credibility for Christians and for Christ himself. As evangelizers we have to offer to Christ's faithful the image, not of people divided and separated by quarrels which do not edify at all, but of people who are mature in their faith, able to be at ease togéther and above practical tensions by virtue of their common, sincere and disinterested quest for truth. Yes, the success of evangelization is undoubtedly bound up with the witness to unity given by the Church.

John Paul II has expressed this same conviction with great effectiveness in *Christifideles laici* (no. 32):

> Communion begets communion and assumes, essentially, the features of a missionary communion ... Communion and mission are deeply connected, they penetrate one another and imply one another, to the point that communion represents at the same time both the source and the outcome of mission, communion is missionary and mission is for communion.

The rediscovery and appreciation of the Johannine missionary mandate meets the needs of people today. In fact, as *Redemptoris missio* reminds us, taking up the message of *Evangelii nuntiandi*, 'Contemporary humanity believes more in witnesses than in teachers, more in experience than in doctrine, more in life and facts than in theories' (no. 42). But the Johannine mandate particularly answers to the very nature of the message which the Church is called to proclaim: A God who is Trinity, living the communion of love and seeking to impart his own life of communion to all humanity. The Church is called to work to build up the Kingdom of God, which is modelled on the mutual immanence of the three divine Persons.

Confronted with today's disillusioned humanity, which has rejected God - or rather the distorted images of a God who is paternalistic, a *deus ex machina*, or the opponent of human beings - the 'new evangelization' is called to renewed courage to proclaim a 'new' God, or the true face of God. This is a God who is love, relationship, dialogue and communion, and at the same time he is a God who, precisely because he is love, can come to meet human beings and share everything they have, even suffering, sin and death. This is a God who makes human beings free like himself, divinizing them and giving them the capacity for new relationships with other human beings who have again become brothers and sisters, to the point at which they are enabled to live on earth the life of the Trinity itself. Jesus' mission, as we have seen, is in fact precisely to bring the Trinity to earth and earth into the Trinity or, as we read in *Redemptoris missio*, 'to bestow a share in the communion that exists between the Father and the Son' (no. 23).

The aim of the missionary proclamation, then, is a continuation of Christ's mission, the achievement of trinitarian koinonia among human beings. 'That which we have seen and heard', those who evangelize should be able to say, 'we proclaim also to you, so that you may have fellowship [communion] with us; and our fellowship [communion] is with the Father and with his Son Jesus Christ' (1 John 1:3). Men and women Religious, like all Christians, are taken into the dynamic of the Trinity ('our communion is with the Father and with his son Jesus Christ') and are called to introduce all the men and women to whom they are sent into that same dynamic of communion ('so that you may have communion with us').

How can a message whose very nature is communion be credible if it is not proclaimed by a community? The community has to be the subject of evangelization. 'Proclamation is never a personal activity' (RM 45). The community is the most adequate subject for proclaiming the advent of the new family of God's children. If the Kingdom of God we are called to announce was wholly interior and private, an exclusively personal relationship with God, as liberal theology wanted it to be, all we would need to have would be some individual experience of God to communicate. But if the Kingdom of God is the gathering of his children around the one Father, the formation of the new people of God accomplished in the blood of Christ and brought about by the Holy Spirit, then it must be proclaimed by a community or someone who speaks on behalf of the community. Actual experience of the life of unity, trinitarian koinonia and the koinonia of the Church, is essential if it is the known and the lived which has to be communicated.

'People are missionaries first of all because they are like the Church, which lives unity in love deeply, before being missionaries by what they say or do' (RM 23).

The need for witness is also related to the very nature of the Good News. Even before it is truth, it is life, and life is communicated through life. The Christian message is experiential, existential, vital. Of its very nature it demands an initiation which is not an explanation but an introduction, through life, into the mystery itself.[3]

Only to the extent that people are able to live the mystery of Christ, his word and his relationship to the Father of love and total self-giving, will the cross, the proclamation of his mystery, be credible. The proclamation of Christ always presupposes the experience of Christ. As John teaches, we can proclaim only what we have contemplated. People are authoritative when it is life that speaks, when there is no dissonance between what is said and what is lived. If the spoken word is founded on the Word and is the outcome of living the Word, then speaking it will be authoritative. It will possess spiritual force, the power of witness, of having experienced the values spoken about, pursued them and lived them joyously. Jesus had words of eternal life because he was the Word. Before proclaiming the Word, we have to live it, let ourselves be evangelized by the Word, in order to be the Word. We have to be able to say with Paul: 'We have the mind of Christ' (1 Cor. 2:16)

The experience of communion with Christ and communion amongst themselves enabled the Twelve to go and evangelize. The same experience of communion was lived in Jerusalem. Jerusalem, understood as the place of koinonia, is therefore the 'base camp' of every apostle and every proclaimer of the Gospel, the hinterland of life which makes the word effective.

The Apostolic Dimension of the Religious Life

In this dynamism of the Church the religious community is called to play a very particular role. The Council emphatically underlined the eminently apostolic nature of the religious life *per se*. It forms an integral and inalienable part of the Church's life and mission (cf. LG 43b; PC 5a). The evangelical counsels in fact 'unite those who practise them to the Church and her mystery in a special way' (LG 44). Consecration is in itself orientated to mission (cf. PC 8; RD 15; EE 12). 'Religious', declares *Evangelii nuntiandi*, 'find in the consecrated life a privileged means for effective evangelization.' The document *Mutuae relationes* is largely devoted to this theme, as is *Religiosi e promozione umana*. Again, the documents of the Magisterium lay particular emphasis on witness to the transcendent God loved above everything as one of the greatest specific contributions that Religious are called to make to evangelization (cf. LG 31.44c). *Evangelica testificatio*, in particular, shows how the secularized world needs the witness and active presence of Religious to be provoked into authenticity (cf. 3.51-2).

In line with what we have learnt about the characteristics of present-day evangelization, it is again the element of *community* which gives the typical apostolate of Religious its very particular tone. Because of the communal nature of the charism of every Institute, men and women Religious exercise their apostolate in community and through the community (cf. EE 25-7).

The community as such is shown to be particularly effective in meeting the aims of the apostolate. 'The unity of the brethren', we read in *Perfectae caritatis* (no. 15), 'is a symbol of the coming of Christ (cf. Jn. 13:35; 17:21) and is a source of great apostolic power.' Furthermore, the life of unity that has grown up within the community is itself evangelization. The community, even before it speaks, actually says Christ by its very presence. In fact it contains the Risen Lord in its own unity and it is he who radiates light, touches hearts and converts those who come into contact with the community or with its members who are always and everywhere its expression.

'Indeed, the success of evangelization certainly depends on the witness to unity given by the Church' (RM 77). Religious take their place at the heart of this witness as a particularly eloquent and expressive sign of the Church's unity (cf. RPU 24-5; RD 15). Even a deeply missionary Institute like the Oblates of Mary Immaculate can affirm that 'community life for us Oblates is not only necessary for the mission but is itself mission, and at the same time a hallmark of mission in the Church'.[4] The following was written by its Superior General, Fr Fernand Jetté:

> The more we are united among ourselves, in authentic communities ... the more fruit our apostolate of evangelization will bear, fruit which remains ... We must be able to build up authentic,

evangelized communities amongst ourselves which will then become evangelizing communities.'[5]

It is not possible to bring everyone to unity and so build up the Kingdom of God if the community which evangelizes is not already united.

The request made by the Council for 'a common growth in unity ... to give the Church greater credibility' in 'a world which is becoming more unified every day' (GS 24) concerns Religious first and foremost. They feel particularly sensitive to these appeals for the building of a united world and, within a Church which is communion, they feel qualified, by virtue of their vocation, to bear notable witness to the reality of unity.

> In the Church as an ecclesial community and in the world, Religious, as experts in communion, are called to be witnesses to and craftsmen of that plan for communion which according to God is the summit of human history ... They actually bear witness to all their brethren in the faith, in a world which is often deeply divided, that it is possible to share possessions, fraternal affection, a way of life and activity. This ability comes from their acceptance of the invitation to follow Christ the Lord more freely and closely, that Christ who was sent by the Father as the firstborn among many brothers to institute a new fraternal communion by the gift of his Spirit. (RPU 24)

For a New Charismatic Creativity

The ways in which both men and women Religious bear their witness to the Kingdom and share in the mission of Christ and the Church, are as many as the charisms which have been entrusted to them. Because of Religious, the Church appears equipped for every good work (cf. PC 1). The founders started out from their original synthesis of spirituality and the incarnation of the words of the Gospel which the Spirit led them to experience. This enabled them to discern the needs of their times and respond to them over a broad spectrum of action. The newness of their evangelical life was also expressed in novel forms of apostolate in all sectors and expressions of human life. They carried out a wide-ranging evangelization which was able to care for the whole of human nature and all human beings and showed the various faces of Christ, who comes to meet actual human beings. It is Christ who lives again through the different religious families, 'in contemplation on the mountain, or proclaiming the kingdom of God to the multitudes, or healing the sick and maimed and converting sinners to a good life, or blessing children and doing good to all men, always in obedience to the will of the Father who sent him' (LG 46). The religious life becomes diaconal and apostolic service.

This expresses itself in a witness to the reality of God's love for human beings, which is able to care for the sick, prisoners, the poor, orphans and the handicapped, as well as opening up new frontiers in the field of teaching, catechesis and pastoral activity. Religious have constantly taken their place in the forefront of evangelization, from the time that Augustine and his monks set out for England, to the penetration of China and the New World, and even the Arctic missions among the Eskimos. 'But who does not esteem the immense contribution they have made and continue to make to evangelization?' wrote Paul VI in admiration.

> Because of their religious consecration they are *par excellence* ready and free to leave everything and go to proclaim the Gospel to the ends of the earth. They are enterprising, and their apostolate is often marked by an originality and ingenuity which compel admiration. They are generous, they are often to be found at the frontier posts of mission, and they take the greatest risks with their health and life itself. Yes indeed, the Church owes them much.[6]

On the other hand, the religious life today cannot stand still looking complacently at the glories of the past. It is called to undertake a courageous renewal, as the Magisterium constantly requests, in order to continue offering its proper charismatic contribution to what John Paul II has called the 'new evangelization'. The new evangelization in fact demands a new ability to understand present-day society and undertake new initiatives that will reach today's humanity and meet their expectations in an intelligible and appropriate language. What we read in the document *Mutuae relationes* is still an authentic challenge to the religious life: 'In these times of ours Religious are asked in a particular way for that same charismatic, lively and ingeniously authentic inventiveness which shone so brilliantly in their founders' (no. 23). The document asks for present-day requirements to be met with the same 'apostolic diligence in devising new, ingenious and courageous ecclesial experiments', in obedience to the Holy Spirit 'who is by nature creative'. In fact, the charismatic nature of the religious life accords extremely well with 'a fertile alacrity of inventiveness and enterprise' (no. 19).

John Paul II addressed a similar invitation to the Religious of Latin America:

> Just as they did in their own times, your founders would put their best apostolic energies at Christ's service in our days as well, together with their deep ecclesial sense, the creativity of their pastoral initiatives, their love for the poor from which so many undertakings for the Church sprang. The same generosity and self-denial which impelled the founders must move you, their spiritual sons, to keep alive the charisms which, by the same power of the Spirit which produces them, continue to enrich and adapt themselves, without losing their authentic character, in order to be at the service of the Church and complete the setting up of his Kingdom ... Therefore, to the extent that you Religious are faithful to your charism, you will be given the power of apostolic creativity to guide you in the preaching and inculturation of the Gospel.[7]

How are we to respond to this pressing request of the Church? John Paul II himself offers an approach to a solution in his encyclical on mission.

> The renewed enthusiasm for the mission *ad gentes* (though the same can be said of evangelization in general) calls for holy missionaries. It is not enough to renew pastoral methods, or better organize and co-ordinate ecclesial forces, or research the biblical and theological bases of faith more thoroughly; it is necessary to stir up a new 'ardour for sanctity' among missionaries and in the whole Christian community. (RM 90)

By now we are aware that the holiness of the religious community is formed above all by participation in the very holiness of God, the Trinity, who communicates himself to it through the presence of the risen Lord giving his Spirit. The way to holiness, and therefore the new way for evangelization, will have to be sought in this direction.

Chiara Lubich, with her usual characteristic vision of the community as a place where 'Jesus in the midst' is present, had in 1960 already offered an inspiring prophetic interpretation of evangelization which dealt with this theme of holiness:

In the saints, at the most varied periods, in the most diverse personalities, in the most dissimilar places and customs, it is always Christ who returns to the midst of his people to bring them again an echo of his words ... The saint is a word of God spoken to *that* period ... Today also the world is in need of its saint.

But what will today's saint need to be like, she wondered, to be able to respond to the immense challenges of today's society? Perhaps today a saint is not enough, and Christ himself needs to place himself at the head of humanity, united in 'an unbreakable unity'. Today we need 'a community of human beings united in the name of the Saint of saints'. Today's saint is Jesus present in the community of all who are united in his name.[8]

He himself, through the community, makes himself present again among men and women, to communicate his own life to them. The more the community is like this, the more alive the presence of Christ will be in it. Consequently, the specific ministry will demonstrate a new, unhoped-for effectiveness and fruitfulness, because it will be Christ himself performing his own action through it. It will be he, through the community that he shapes, who proclaims the Kingdom of God, heals the sick, converts sinners, and accomplishes every good work. Thus once again the religious life speaks of God by its living.

Moreover, the risen Jesus, present in those who are united in his name, continues to give his Spirit to the community, that Spirit who was the source of the Institute's charism. Because the founders and foundresses were docile to the Spirit's guidance, they were able to be creative and in their prophetic dimension respond to the times and to the needs and expectations of their contemporaries. In the same way, it will be under the guidance of the same Spirit, given to the community that lives in unity, that the Religious of today, men and women, will also regain the charismatic dynamisms of their vocation, the ability to read the signs of the times, and ways of answering them. The charismatic renewal of the Institute will also spring from the life of the community.

NOTES

1. Cf. M. Dumais, 'La communauté missionnaire dans l'Église primitive', *Vie Oblate Life* 49 (1990), pp. 129-45.
2. J. M. R. Tillard, 'Dos modos de evangelizar', *Vida Religiosa* 69 (1990), pp. 324-5.
3. Cf. M. Zago, 'La nuova evangelizzazione nel pensiero di Giovanni Paolo II', in *La nuova evangelizzazione e i religiosi* (Rome: Città Nuova, 1991), pp. 73-80.
4. *Missionari nell'oggi del mondo*. Final document of the 1986 General Chapter, no. 109.
5. *Lettres aux Oblats de Marie Immaculée* (Rome: 1985), pp. 218-19.
6. EN 69. For the missionary contribution to the religious life, see Enrico di Santa Maria, 'Il servizio missionario della vita religiosa', in *Spiritualità della missione* (Rome: Teresianum, 1986), pp. 145-63; J. Rigal, *Il coraggio della missione* (Cinisello Balsamo: Paoline, 1987), pp. 139-70.
7. *Los caminos del Evangelio*, Apostolic Letter to the men and women Religious of Latin America on the occasion of the Fifth Centenary of the Evangelization of the New World, 29 June 1990, nos. 26 and 28.
8. 'Il santo di oggi', in *Pensieri* (Rome: 1961), pp. 117-21. Cf. *L'azione apostolica dei religiosi* (various authors; Milan: 1980); E. Vigano, 'Il Carattere ecclesiale della spiritualità religiosa apostolica', *Vita Consacrata* 19 (1983), pp. 648-73; *Vita religiosa apostolica* (UISG document with a commentary; Bologna: EDB 1985); S. M. Gonzales Silva, *La vida religiosa apostólica* (Madrid: Publ. Claretianas, 1985); A. Bandera, 'Comunidad religiosa y misiones', *La Vida Sobrenatural* 66 (1986), pp. 71-83; M. Azevedo, 'Vita religiosa ed evangelizzazione del mondo contemporaneo', *Vita Consacrata* 22 (1986), pp. 745-57; S. Recchi, 'Consacrazione e missione' *Vita Consacrata* 23 (1987), pp. 546-52; X. Pikaza, 'The public and witness dimension of religious life', *Review for Religious* 46 (1987), pp. 661-73; J. C. R. García, 'Misión', in *Diccionario Teológico de la Vida Consagrada* (Madrid: Publ. Claretianas, 1989), 1096-1123; J. Tuñi, 'Testimonio', ibid., 1722-37; S. Raponi, 'Integrazione tra apostolato e vita religiosa', *Vita Consacrata* XXVI (1990), pp. 176-86; *La nuova evangelizzazione e i religiosi* (various authors; Rome: Città Nuova, 1991).

5 Sign of the Communion of Saints

The religious community in the community of the Church

The reflection by the Pachomians, Basil, Augustine and others who initiated the different forms of community on the experience of their own communities, as well as the theological reflection in which we have engaged up to this point, have drawn liberally and repeatedly on the doctrine of the koinonia of the Church. It is natural, therefore, to ask to what extent the different forms of religious community experience communion in a way which is original compared to that of the Church as a whole, and what new element the religious community contributes, in comparison with other expressions of ecclesial community such as the family and the parish.

It is not clear, from the central text of Vatican II on the religious community (no. 15 of *Perfectae caritatis*), what specifically distinguishes the religious community from other Christian communities. All the biblical references which enrich this text can be applied to every form of communion in the Church. Some may find this a cause for regret, but on the other hand we can immediately deduce from this fact the positive consequence that the religious community is, fundamentally and before all else, a *Christian community*.

The Ecclesiality of the Religious Community

Picking up on the intuition of primitive monasticism, contemporary theology strongly emphasizes the ecclesial dimension of the religious life, particularly that of the community.[1] To understand all the depths of the religious community, it has to be placed within Christian koinonia. 'The koinonia which must be realized in the monastery', writes Marsili in his lapidary style, 'is no other than, nor inferior to or different from, that which Scripture in the New Testament sets before us as the soul and inner reality of the ecclesial community.'[2]

On the other hand, this is the vision which has been restored to us by the Second Vatican Council. *Lumen Gentium* presents the religious life as 'a gift of God which the Church has received from her Lord' (LG 43a). It belongs, therefore, to the very life of the Church, as one type of response to the call to holiness which Christ addresses to the whole people of God. The evangelical counsels 'unite those who practise them to the Church and her mystery in a special way' (LG 44b), so that the state of life 'which is constituted by the profession of the evangelical counsels, while not entering into the hierarchical structure of the Church, belongs undeniably to her life and holiness' (LG 44d). Paul VI, that great interpreter of the Council, was aware of that ecclesial dimension and so could write about those whom he called 'exceptional witnesses to the transcendence of the love of Christ', that without their concrete sign 'there would be a danger that the charity which animates the entire Church would grow cold, that the salvific paradox of the Gospel would be blunted, and that the "salt" of faith would lose its savour in a world undergoing secularization' (ET 3).

Still speaking of religious consecration, Paul VI emphasizes in this same document (*Evangelica testificatio*) that it is effected in the Church through both the ministers who receive it and the Christian community 'whose love recognizes, welcomes, sustains and embraces those who within it make an offering of themselves as a living sign' (ET 7). Mother Church's attitude of loving welcome in her recognition of men and women Religious as authentic sons and daughters could not have been better expressed.

Being part of the Church and sharing in its mystery, the religious community lives by the one ecclesial koinonia in its double dimension of communion with God One-in-Three and with the brethren. Yet there are different ways of living the one ecclesial communion. The way koinonia is lived is different in a family, a religious community, a parish, an association or a diocese. The way in which communion is lived between the local churches is different again.

The one 'communion' can be lived in different 'communities'. In this connection, the Italian Bishops' Conference has given a clear description of these two realities, distinct yet intrinsically related:

> When we speak of 'communion' we think of that gift of the Holy Spirit by which the human person is no longer alone or distant from God but is called to belong to the same communion which binds Father, Son and Holy Spirit to one another, and rejoices to find everywhere, especially in those who believe in Christ, brethren

with whom he shares the profound mystery of his relationship with God ... When we speak of 'ecclesial community' we think of a concrete form of association which springs from communion; in it the faithful receive, live and transmit the gift of communion ... [In the ecclesial community] communion is constituted on the basis of visible and stable relationships which bind the faithful to one another in their common profession of faith ... [Consequently the community] enjoys as many visible structures and tools through which the message and grace of Jesus, the incarnate Son of God, are transmitted to men and women. The community does not, through its concrete decisions and its limits, restrict the breadth and depth of communion but neither does it exhaust it; it is like a sacrament of it, that is, the manifestation and the instrument which reveal it as present in the history of humanity.[3]

Marsili, referring to the religious community and the use of the word 'koinonia' to indicate its deepest nature, wrote equally clearly:

If we wish to justify the recovery of the word 'koinonia', I would say that while today *community* is a factual situation at the level of statistics, koinonia is *communion*, that is, the dynamic element which is always in the process of becoming and which forms the community.[4]

What then is the specific form in the Church in which the religious community lives the common ecclesial koinonia and how does it fit itself into organic unity with the other ecclesial expressions of community?

The answer to this question would take us far beyond the task we have set ourselves in this book. It actually involves defining the theological status of the whole idea of the religious life. Nevertheless, while keeping to the limited field of reflecting on the community as a place of communion, we shall try to present some of the lines of thought proposed by various writers.

Elements which Characterize the Religious Community

First of all, we can put together some specific notes which give the religious community a particular identity within the ecclesial community. These can be summed up under four headings: consecration, charismatic nature, the common life, and the grace of being together.

The primary characteristic of the religious community is the fact that it is a *community of consecrated people*. It is not by chance that *Perfectae caritatis* puts the description of the community (no. 15) immediately after what is said about the vows (nos. 12-14). More particularly, the fact that the discussion of community follows immediately after the vow of obedience has led some writers to regard the religious community as the outcome of obedience, or at least to emphasize the close interdependence between obedience and community. Lozano, for example, writes that obedience 'or the shared listening to the Word and the communal fulfilment of the divine will is the very root of community life'.[5]

In any case, the religious community is composed of people who have built their lives around the evangelical counsels as a particular way for perfecting charity. The vows spring from charity, as a response of love to a call of love, and their purpose is the full attainment of charity. Consecration therefore constitutes a particularly fertile 'humus' for life in common. The common life becomes a quest for perfect charity, in mutual love, which is characteristic of the religious life and expressed in the vows. The three evangelical counsels, lived in the common life, are given their character by the community and at the same time give the community its character.[6] Some authors have spoken directly of a specific counsel of unity, as important as the classic triad, which would shape the life of consecration.[7]

A second characteristic feature of the religious community comes from its being a *charismatic community*. This springs from a common call to share the same charism with other brothers and sisters. At the root of every religious family is the particular experience of the founder or foundress. The members of the community identify themselves with his or her ideal of life to the point of being united in what is often seen as a particular 'family' relationship of communion with one another. What actually creates the community is the particular charism received from the founder and shared by his or her companions, which leads them to establish the same kind of life and live the evangelical counsels in the same way. All the members are united amongst themselves by their common relationship with the founder and still more with his or her charism. In its corporate responsibility for the patrimony of the Institute, the religious community takes on the concrete appearance of a particular religious family. In virtue of the charism it has received, it assumes its own specific physiognomy in the Church.

A third factor which enables the religious family to put ecclesial communion into practice in a particular way is *life in common*.[8] So obvious in itself, this is perhaps the dimension least emphasized by the Council and post-conciliar theology, which had quite different preoccupations about the religious life. In fact, they needed to distance themselves from a certain canonical conception of the common life which saw the community above all in the light of the kind of determinate *physical* regulations which were formulated by the 1917 Code of Canon Law. Because of this, the conciliar documents on the religious life prefer to speak in terms of communion or fraternity rather than community life, a term which recalled precisely those rules and regulations which, because they lacked the breath of communion, had been in danger of degenerating into legalism. In an authoritative commentary on *Perfectae caritatis* which illustrates the situation of a large part of the religious life, we read:

> Juridical prescriptions have gained the upper hand over the spontaneity of charity ... The *community* has become a juridical entity rather than a translation of the *communion of charity* ... In the end, will it be possible to reverse the present order and set the life of *fraternal communion* above the *juridical community*? To shake off an excessively rigid framework and allow *fraternity truly* to live?[9]

In fact, 'concentrating the attention of the common life on organization and disciplinary measures had impoverished the life of the community both in itself and in its relations *ad extra*.'[10] In the same way, identifying the problem of the relationship between the religious community and the ecclesial community with the question of exemption has on occasion impeded reflection on juridical questions.

Nevertheless, we need to distinguish between 'life in communion' or fraternity which, because it is proper to the whole Church, is proper to all the consecrated, and 'life in common' , which is typical of Religious. It is a problem, for example, for the Secular Institutes that when the conciliar and post-conciliar documents speak of consecration, they identify communion with life in common. It was John Paul II who drew the distinction clearly: 'Community life is an essential element, not of consecrated life as such but of the religious form of this consecration. God has called Religious to become holy and to work in community.'[11] Secular Institutes, although they live in communion, are not necessarily called to live in common.

A further distinction has to be made between the common life itself and the concrete and particular structures of the common life, which have to be defined in accordance with the nature and mission of the Institute. These, far from contradicting or stifling the charism, must rather form its appropriate setting and enable it to be defined and developed in the most fitting ways.

Thus the religious community offers ecclesial communion a specific pattern of its own, making it visible, concentrating it, as it were, in a stable common life. On this subject, Tillard writes that the seed of brotherhood sown by Christ

> is scattered here and there in the universe of humanity. Its effects are often veiled by the fact that the manifold daily tasks of Christians oblige them to separate in order to be leaven in the dough. Only the Sunday assembly is able to signify its reality more intensely. The [religious] *community*, by a special way of life, aims to make this actual presence more alive and more continually visible. It therefore has to be *a sign of the ecclesial communion which is the gift of the Father made in Jesus and his Spirit.*[12]

A fourth characteristic of the religious community is concerned with how the relationships between its members are established. They differ from those found in other forms of community. Lucas Gutierrez explains this as follows:

> We must say that the religious life leads to a different 'koinonia of grace', precisely because when it affirms the community as a concept it leaves natural communities on one side, even when they are raised to the level of grace, in order to affirm the one community of grace, the one fraternity of God's children, in such a way that the basis of interpersonal relationships in the religious community contains none of the elements that build up the natural community.[13]

Lozano also pursues this train of thought:

> The appropriate way in which the religious community can be the Church is entirely particular. In fact, unlike the family or, in a different way, the parish, it is not a pre-existent human reality which receives the faith in order to raise itself. Its sole *raison d'être* is precisely to be the Church, because in it the human reality is created by faith; people gather in it to develop, together, a Christian way of life and it is in this evangelical context that relationships between

people are established. Like the family, the religious community takes the Church as far as a shared life but, unlike the family, the religious community exists simply to be the Church. And this achievement is the fruit of making the condition of discipleship into a concrete way of life characteristic of the religious life, by actively renouncing the creation of one's own family and the search for personal development within the power structures of secular society. The members of these communities want only to be disciples and to form groups of disciples.[14]

The religious community therefore possesses a particular identity of its own in the ecclesial communion because it is composed of people consecrated by vows, its specific charism gives it particular features of its own, it practises a concrete and stable common life, and it does not possess any prior human bonds - relations between its members are motivated only by the call of grace.

The Religious Community in Communion with other Communities

From the point of view of communion, every kind of ecclesial community has the same theological nature and expresses the fundamental unity which connects all Christian vocations. They are all inspired and supported by the identical koinonia. In this sense, for all the perceived diversity and multiplicity of vocations, it is impossible to speak of the superiority of one form *vis-à-vis* another. The one koinonia is realized in different forms of community, which give rise to a wonderful variety of experiences of communion.

While we can emphasize the substantial unity of the varied manifestations of the one communion, we should not fail to applaud and value the charismatic diversity of the communities which express the one koinonia, a diversity which is just as much willed by God. If the religious community can be characterized like this, it is legitimate to ask about its situation with regard to the Church as a whole. Does it have a particular role of its own, proper to it as a religious community? There is a variety of answers to this question on the ecclesiological status of the religious community, depending, of course, on the different theologies of the religious life.

For some writers, the religious community has a merely functional value in terms of either personal sanctification or greater apostolic effectiveness. Tillard has called these concepts of community 'utilitarian' and 'pragmatic'. Without loading these terms with negative connotations, such an understanding of community does appear incomplete and inadequate.[15]

Unquestionably, the religious community is a place where the perfection of charity can be attained, and therefore a privileged place of holiness, and we shall be returning to this aspect. Equally obvious is the apostolic potential of the religious community, and we have already considered this. However, the emphasis on community as a means to holiness, which is so marked in some monastic communities, runs the risk of leaving the mystery-dimension of koinonia in the background. The result is the same when the community is seen only as an instrument of mission. Some female communities inspired by the Jesuits, for example, express this instrumental aspect in the following words:

> The priority in our religious life is mission. The value of the apostolate prevails over the value of 'being together'. We did not enter religious life to live in a particular community but in an apostolic body and in history ... Being sent out is an essential component of the apostolic community.[16]

If these fundamental aspects of the religious community were made absolutes, the community would lose its character as the place of God's presence and sharing in the koinonia of the Trinity and become something merely instrumental. To us this view of the community seems reductionist and an inadequate basis for an ecclesiological status of its own.

Another way of understanding the relation between the religious community and the other expressions of ecclesial communion has been to see it as different forms of the one following of Christ.

Starting from the evangelical inspiration at the source of the monastic and religious life, we first of all questioned the legitimacy of the reference by religious communities to the group of disciples who followed Jesus. When men and women Religious claim to be in perfect continuity with the experience of the primitive community of the Twelve around Jesus, is this appropriation justified, when the following of Christ is the point of reference and paradigm for the whole of the new

Israel? If all Christians are called to reflect the community of those who follow Jesus, why should the religious community claim this model as its own particular prototype?

To begin with, we need to note that reference to the community of the Twelve did not arise in the history of the religious life as a contrast to the ordinary Christian way of life but as a simple desire to live the Christian life in all its integrity. If those who followed Jesus are a model for every Christian, Religious have looked for inspiration precisely in their own experience as Christians. At the same time, there are undeniably different means of realizing the one act of following. The Second Vatican Council, while applying the following of Christ to all Christians, indicated a particular type of following for Religious. All Christians are called to follow Jesus: 'The forms and tasks of life are many but holiness is one - that sanctity which is cultivated by all who ... follow Christ, poor, humble and cross-bearing, that they may deserve to be partakers of his glory' (LG 41a). Nevertheless, 'From the very beginning of the Church there were men and women who set out to follow Christ with greater liberty, and to imitate him more closely' (PC 1b).

Von Balthasar has tried to explain the distinction of vocations within the Church by starting from the diversity of practice in the one following of Christ. He notes that concentric circles were formed around Jesus of people who joined him on a decreasing scale of closeness. Jesus did not ask everyone to follow him physically. There were different forms of belonging, more or less closely, to his circle. He may ask everyone to adopt an unambiguous position towards himself as a person and his proclamation of salvation, but he does not ask everyone to become his direct collaborator in proclaiming the Kingdom by leaving everything and putting themselves wholly at his disposal for missionary journeying. All are called to 'enter into the Kingdom' and live its radical demands. Not all are called to 'walk behind Jesus'. Jesus calls only some to this type of following and only to these does he state particular requirements.

However, the group of people that Jesus assembled to be with him in a permanent way was not segregated from the rest of the disciples. Jesus did not create an élite. Those who followed him were called in order to become a sign of the new Israel. The account of the apostles' vocation is not directly related to the fundamental call to newness of life which Jesus addresses to all when, for example, he proclaims 'I am the light of the world; he who *follows me* will not walk in darkness, but will have the light of life' (John 8:12). The vocation of the apostles is not concerned with that 'being *called* out of darkness into his marvellous light' (1 Pet. 2:9) by which Christians are established in their being. The vocation of the apostles to follow Jesus does not show the 'vertical' dimension between the Church and the world but a new 'horizontal' distinction within the Church itself.

To explain this 'horizontal' division further, von Balthasar produces an interpretation of his own that is in some respects questionable, but nevertheless attractive and stimulating. He analyses the movement created around Jesus and shows the different ways in which the same call was worked out in the Church. Some, after receiving salvation, were invited to 'go', to return in newness of life to their own normal environment of work and activity and there to bear witness to the new life received. Others were invited instead to 'come'.

> Thus the *movement* of the two groups is *exactly opposite*. The disciples come to Jesus on the basis of an urgent, almost stereotypical, invitation, 'Come!', which is the opposite of the 'Go!' with which Jesus dismisses those who are not called. On the basis of this 'Come!', 'Come and see', 'Come and follow me', the disciples from then on were with Jesus, they were sent a distance away from him and then 'returned to [him] and told him all that they had done and taught' (Mark 6:30). On the other hand, the masses, moving away from the world in which they live, approached the Lord and after their meeting with him were sent back to their places in the world. Both forms of meeting, both circular movements, complete each other but in such a way that the journey by the masses to meet the Lord is a search to have needs met, and his dismissal signifies healing and the grace to carry on their future life in the world. The sending out of the disciples into the world, on the other hand, takes place only at the Lord's bidding and in his interests, and their return to him signifies a return to their true and proper place.[17]

According to von Balthasar, for some of the disciples 'being in the world' is the result of a mission received from Jesus and it becomes the setting in which to exercise their Christian calling. For others there is an invitation to be with the Master constantly and share every aspect of his life.

The 'horizontal division' within the people of God which this writer proposes would give the religious community a clear ecclesiastical status. Nevertheless the division seems too pronounced, leading inevitably to Religious being regarded as on a 'higher' level than the laity, who remain on a 'lower' level. The scheme outlined by von Balthasar does, however, offer some fundamental approaches to an understanding of the religious community.

One such approach concerns the deepest identity which, as we have already seen, comes from constant reference to the apostolic community. The religious community arises out of the interior desire stirred up by the Spirit in some Christians who feel drawn to leave their normal environment actually, with all that that means, not to imitate slavishly what was done by the men and women who 'followed Jesus', but to live in their own day their radical attachment to the person of Jesus. It is the call to realize visibly and existentially the experience of those who walked after Jesus on the roads of Palestine and to live, here and now, the future age in which the Lamb will be 'followed' wherever he goes (cf. Rev. 14:4).

The community of the apostles is thus the prototype and constant model for the religious form of community. The apostles are seen as those who left everything (including material possessions) to follow Jesus, accompanying him physically through the various stages of his ministry, giving all their time to his concerns, entrusting themselves completely to his word, and reaching a particularly intimate level of relationship with him, unlike others such as Mary, Martha, Lazarus, Nicodemus and Zacchaeus who, while giving total allegiance to Jesus and his word, continued to lead a 'normal' life in their own homes. The origin and character of the religious community derive from the intention to relive the experience of the apostles to the point of physically leaving profession, family and country in order to lead an 'apostolic life'.

Another approach offered by von Balthasar concerns the relation of the religious community to the other components of the People of God. It presents itself as a sign. It is this second aspect, which has not perhaps been sufficiently developed, that is increasingly emerging in contemporary reflection on the ecclesiological status of the religious community as the aspect which best expresses its identity.

In fact, reflection on the nature of the religious community is moving in the direction of the symbolic, parabolic or sacramental dimensions of the religious life. This is the perspective that today commands the greatest consensus and best seems to correspond to the unitary vision of the People of God.

An enquiry conducted by the review *Vida Religiosa* among some of Europe's best-known theologians revealed a common convergence of emphasis among thinkers from very different backgrounds regarding this point of view on the religious life.[18] The religious life possesses 'the pronounced character of a sign' (Pannenberg); it is 'a radical symbol of following' (Metz); 'a sign of the kingdom of God in the midst of the world' (Fries); 'an outline of the Kingdom' (Matura); 'an existential sign of messianic hope' (Moltmann); 'a prophetic alternative' (Sölle); 'a prophetic state open to the signs of the times' (Chenu); 'an instrument of Christ's presence in the world' (Alszeghy); it consists in 'living in the sight of others, in an exemplary way, the radicality of Christian faith' (Greinacher); it is 'a living reminder of eschatology' (Durrwell); 'a cipher [in the sense of a symbol in a coded message] of the whole ecclesial community' (Forte); 'a witness to a service that is supremely liberating' (Dianich); 'a record of the faith on which the Church is built' (Tillard); 'the restlessness and liveliness of the Church's stability' (Martina).

So the religious life has the nature of a symbol, a sign, a parable.[19] Like an icon, it tells the whole People of God what the Church is called to be in terms of holiness and following Christ even to the point of total conformity with him in a definitive sharing in the mystery of the divine life. It seems to be the radicalization of the deepest needs of the evangelical life. Finally, to use the words of *Mutuae relationes*, the religious life appears as 'a particular way of sharing in the sacramental nature of the People of God' (MR 10).

If the religious life is seen as the radicalization of Christian life, then the religious community is the radicalization of ecclesial koinonia, a place where this appears in its full significance. This interpretation is proposed effectively and insistently by Tillard and followed by many others: 'Religious ... belong to the varied group of believers who aim to make the koinonia which is the very foundation of the Church of God more intense, more unbroken and therefore more visible.'(20) The apostolic community, writes Tillard again, represents a plan for Christian life that aims at transposing into the Church's present situation the radical option of the community of those who 'followed Jesus'. In fact, it is not a question of choosing moral imitation of Christ - the ideal of every Christian life (cf. 1 Cor. 11:1; John 13:15; 1 John 2:6; 1 Pet. 2:21) - but of entering, to the best of one's ability, on the typical journey of the apostolic group, surrendering to the profound action of the person and words of Jesus.[21]

The religious community, therefore, has to be placed in the varied group of those among the faithful who 'aim to make the koinonia which is the very foundation of the Church of God more intense, more unbroken and therefore more visible.'[22]

Continuing in the same vein, Bruno Secondin runs through the statements of the Council which place the religious life at the centre of the Church's mystery and concludes that

Religious are ... within the 'Church as communion', inasmuch as they are 'moved by the Spirit', the principle of unity in communion (LG 12), and aim at making the reality of koinonia more intense, unbroken and visible, and reap greater fruit from it ... the religious community proclaims by its whole being that the present is pregnant with the future, the beginnings of the Kingdom are here *already* ... If it wants to be a mystery of communion in the Church which is holy koinonia, the religious community must reproduce and revive its most typical features with remarkable precision.[23]

In particular, its faith, expectation, invocation, following, devout listening to the Word, remembering of Easter and life according to the Spirit must shine out.[24]

The religious community reveals to the Church its most profound *raison d'être*: to follow Christ freely and radically in order to enjoy his presence, share his paschal journey and gain intimacy with the Father through him. And to put itself again with him at the service of all humanity, in order to bind everyone into the true and definitive glorified Body of Christ.[25]

'What then is the religious community?' asks Aubry, again following this line of thought.

It is the Church made real in a kind of significant summary. They are the baptized people who, called by a singular privilege of grace, separate themselves from the 'world', that is, from the usual conditions of life, family, professional and civic, to come together and live the mystery of the Church *permanently, publicly and officially ...* Religious communities polarize the life of the Church ... In brief, every religious community is like a permanent 'sacrament' of the Church, that is, a visible sign of its present and future mystery, and a sign which is effective to the extent that the community already potentially realizes this mystery.[26]

For all the diversity of interpretation in the descriptions and forms of the presence and meaning of the religious community, we can discern a substantial convergence in considering it as a special and effective sign of unity. It is called to express the One Church's life of unity, as if it were a particular concentration or summary of unity, and to proclaim it afresh with a exceptionally forceful witness. The Church as communion finds one of its typical expressions in the religious community.

In the wider ecclesial community, the religious community takes on the character of an 'icon', a place where people meet the active presence of the Risen Christ and the trinitarian koinonia he imparts. In it, the presence of the risen Lord and his Spirit can actually be constantly 'enjoyed' (cf. PC 15). At the same time, it also possesses the character of an 'epiphany'; it shows the Church what it is and what it ought to be.

The Religious Community, Reminder and Prophetic Sign of Unity

As an effective sign of unity and communion, the religious community can contribute powerfully to the renewal and perennial youth of the Church.

In the Church's history, renewal has often begun with a new realization of God's plan for communion, and this has especially been the result of recurrent new expressions of the charisms, in many cases fulfilled in particular forms of the religious life. The preferred source of inspiration for such a plan has been the evangelical koinonia lived in the primitive Church in Jerusalem. Bori, in his study of the early Church, has shown that it can be said that the memory of the Church in its beginnings, and particularly the description of its life according to the Acts of the Apostles, has always been a model, an example, an ideal (on occasions a myth) in the course of the Church's history. Particularly at critical periods and decisive turning-points, the idea of a reform which looks to the 'ecclesiae primitivae forma' [the form of the primitive Church], the possibility of a return to the old, the beginnings, has again been put forward with renewed vigour. From the monastic movements to the Gregorian reform, from the Protestant Reformation to the latest, most complex post-conciliar developments in the Catholic world, the texts of Acts have been a stimulus, a provocation and a principle of crisis in the Christian conscience in the dilemma between the eternal absolute validity of the ideal and the continual need to express it in history.[27]

This theme of 'return to the beginnings', understood not in a nostalgic or archaeological sense but as a confrontation with the Christian message in its purest form and a drawing on its sources for concrete expression in the present time, is precisely the task that every religious community sets itself at its birth.[28]

The religious community therefore possesses a specific vocation of its own within the Church, to be a *reminder* of the primitive community, and a *charismatic and prophetic realization* of its future definitive fulfilment.

As a *reminder* of the community of the Twelve around Jesus and the community brought into being by the apostles in Jerusalem, the religious community sets itself the task of once again making present that experience which is always a paradigm. It does this by following - perhaps even literally - the same way, leaving everything, living together, sharing material possessions, a particular unity of will and intention ... It sets itself before the Church as a place that bears witness to the historical koinonia of the Gospel. If the Church as a whole is called to live the original koinonia, the religious community is a particular crystallization of it, a place where the process of communion is permanently and pre-eminently carried out. Here Christian koinonia is seen in its most demanding and stable form.

The reminder of the initial koinonia made by the religious community is not an academic evocation but an existential proclamation before the whole Christian community of its real possibility and, at the same time, its radical demands. The religious community should be able to say by its very existence: Our 'beginnings' are not remote, confined to the past, nor are they the announcement of Utopia for the future. The koinonia made possible by the Paschal event and inaugurated by Pentecost, is a present reality which can be experienced and is made visible in the religious community. The reminder becomes an appeal, addressed to the whole Church, to live in accordance with its nature and be communion. At the same time it proclaims its feasibility.

In the history of the religious community, the memory of the beginnings acquires a rich and varied *charismatic realization*. The multiplicity of religious communities is an enrichment for the Church on its journey towards unity. The adjustment that the religious community has been able to make, by a special thrust of the Spirit, in the variety of the forms of common life, according to times and cultures, actually shows the legitimate plurality that the one koinonia can assume in the life of the Church and of peoples. Every century is called to reinterpret and adapt the Christian message, which never becomes atrophied and always can and must be an adequate response to new cultural and social demands.

Finally, within the Church the religious community is a *prophecy* of its accomplished koinonia, when there will be only one flock around the one Shepherd, and all the children of God will be seated at the same table as a family no longer united by the ties of flesh and blood but by divine parenthood. The religious community is not actually assembled by the spontaneous choice of its members but by God's free call, and it is not bound together by blood relationships like the human family but only by theological charity. Because of its communal element, the 'eschatological' dimension of the religious life becomes a proclamation and anticipation of that communion of saints which the whole Church is called to live in its fullness in the new heaven and the new earth.

So that its presence as a sign within the Church may be abundantly clear, the religious community has to preserve its presence as a living part of the local church. As Secondin has emphasized, 'the specific space and the theological function of the religious community' can best be identified when it starts from the theology of the local church. Without this concrete incarnation of the radical choice for the Kingdom in a specific history and a determinate place, it is difficult for the religious community to become an effective sign. The international organization of religious Institutes, with decisions and plans which suffer from being 'perspectives on distant operational centres', must not run counter to humble local needs. Otherwise, 'there is the risk of appearing splendid atoms, living for themselves'.

If the insertion is authentic, the mutual relationship between the religious community and the local church becomes fertile for both of them. A community that belongs to an international Institute has the advantage of not being enclosed within 'the narrow world of a town or city, and this freedom from provincialism is certainly a benefit for the local church. Yet the religious community is a *sign* above all to the extent that it shines with reality and sensitivity towards the real Church, and journeys in its company.'

> If it takes being rooted in a particular context seriously, the community will be a living body and not an island in the local church. At the same time, however, the religious community, because of its connections and relations with a larger community, must help the local church to know, make its own and love the evangelical values which have matured elsewhere. And also help the local church to offer its own authentic values to the dialogue between all the Churches.

It is a question of a productive dialectic between insertion and connection.[29]

The religious community does not exhaust its function as a prophetic sign within the Catholic Church alone. It stretches out towards the realization of unity between the Churches and, further still, between religions. Even more, it reaches out towards the unification of all humanity. For years now there has been a dialogue in progress between many Catholic monastic communities and the monastic life of the Orthodox Church. In the evangelical Churches the birth of new forms of monastic community is marked by a strong ecumenical tendency. Interconfessional monastic communities are asserting themselves. Thus religious communities - in the various Churches - are taking the lead in the path towards unity, a unity which they already anticipate at the level of a common choice of the evangelical life, prayer and fraternal communion. In the dialogue between world religions as well, monastic communities are in every case at the forefront. Meetings, conferences and the exchange of experiences are being multiplied between the monastic forms of the different religions. There are in fact a variety of points of contact and numerous common expressions of monastic religion.

The religious community presses still further ahead. Its vocation is to be a sign of the realization of human beings as such, and their deepest call to go out from themselves in 'ecstasy' in relationship with other human beings and, with them, to transcend themselves in a communion which draws on the divine and leads to the communion of the Trinity.

Human beings can in fact only fulfil themselves as people in communion. What better than a religious community to reveal this truth and this possibility to humanity today? Human beings feel an attraction to communion with others, an attraction which seems to be continually impeded by an inability to overcome the relationship of *homo homini lupus* [human beings as wolves to each other]. In view of this, the religious community is called to show itself as the existential possibility of peaceful and fraternal life together - a possibility, therefore, of the integral and harmonious growth of people in their individuality and their serene capacity for relationship. Was not the Benedictine community of old the place where people of different cultures, such as Latins and barbarians, met and fused? Was it not a place for brotherly fellowship between the learned and the illiterate, the poor and the rich, nobles and plebeians? And are not many of today's communities, especially those belonging to international Institutes, the affirmation in miniature that unity between peoples, races and social classes is possible?

Moreover, the religious community is not a place where communion happens without strife and without cost. This too reveals a message of hope for many other human social groups. The community is made up of people who generally differ from each other in temperament, tastes and attitudes, yet in spite of not being together in the name of friendship, natural mutual attraction or sympathy, they are able to live in unity. Every religious community is an 'elect' community, brought together and established by a call of God, not a human will. It is not 'elective', that is to say, not the result of a mutual choice by its members on the grounds of affinity, friendship, affection or feeling, even if these elements can be - and usually are - present in a community as the fruit of a life of authentic Christian love. This communal mix reflects the differences in many other kinds of human society, such as the environments of work and school, even the family itself when it is no longer bound together by affection or feeling. Furthermore, the members of a religious community, like all human beings, experience the signs of sin in themselves and the roots of selfishness it has left in the hearts of all living people. Their community is always the fruit of conversion and victory over selfishness.

Men and women Religious can thus, by virtue of their experience, teach how to live in a unity which does not depend on spontaneous relationships or even mutual attraction, and may indeed involve a sense of mutual repulsion. If the religious community lives according to its vocation, motivated by all the typical connotations of theological charity (universality, freedom, service, sacrifice, readiness for self-offering ...), then it will be able to testify that relationships are somehow possible. There is an obvious authenticity when religious communities give the message of hope in this way to a world desperately searching for relationships and often having to live instead with separations and divorce within the family, tensions and an atmosphere of conflict at work, racism and abuse of power in social areas...

The religious community's vocation is to show itself as reconciled humanity, demonstrating the ways and types of reconciliation and the practical dynamics of a relationship that is increasingly free, authentic and deep, that makes people fully themselves and leads to the greatest and most personal unity - the unity of the Trinity to which we are in fact called and which is the norm for relationships. In this sense, the religious community puts itself into the bondage of concord and peace as a *prophecy of fulfilled humanity* and the *eschatological sign* of the new people who will inhabit the new heavens and the new earth. Thus the religious community can become what it is called to be:

> Communion open to the local church, the universal Church, the whole human family; not, therefore, a group closed up in its spiritual self-sufficiency but a concrete koinonia, organically inserted in the universal, Christian and human koinonia.[30]

Men and women Religious can indeed declare by their life that God's plan for humanity, revealed in Jesus Christ, is not a Utopia - unity is possible. By their common life they can testify that relationships are somehow possible, that Christ has truly opened the way to a new social order. The Oblates of Mary Immaculate, confronted with this prophetic invitation, have said to themselves: 'Christ wills that, by living together in spite of the inevitable difficulties, we show that his love and his Spirit are stronger than all the forces of disintegration.'[31]

NOTES

1. Cf. J. M. R. Tillard, *I religiosi nel cuore della Chiesa* (Brescia: Queriniana, 1968); id., 'La comunità religiosa luogo della "sequela"', in *Davanti a Dio e per il mondo*, pp. 206-92; J. Cambier, 'Il senso ecclesiale della vita comunitaria', in *Per una presenza viva dei religiosi nella Chiesa e nel mondo* (Turin: LDC, 1970), pp. 555-88; B. Neunheuser, 'L'esenzione, segno di missione carismatica', *Religiosi e Vescovi Oggi* 1 (1973), pp. 27-42; M. A. Asiain, *La vida religiosa en la Iglesia. Contribución a una eclesiologia de la vida religiosa* (Salamanca: Secretariado Trinitario, 1977); B. Secondin, 'Comunità religiosa e comunione ecclesiale', in *Vita comunitaria* (Milan: Ancora, 1979), pp. 45-80.

2. S. Marsili, 'L'abate nella koinonia del monastero', in *Figura e funzione dell'autorità nella comunità religiosa* (Alba: Paoline, 1978), p. 281.

3. *Comunione e comunità*, Pastoral plan for the 80s of the Italian Bishops' Conference, nos. 14-15.

4. Marsili, op. cit., p. 280.

5. Lozano, *La sequela di Cristo*, p. 241.

6. Even before the Council the communal significance of the vows was being emphasized: cf. R. Carpentier, 'Aspetti comunitari dei voti e delle osservanze', in *Vita di comunità* (Turin: Marietti, 1962), pp. 169-94 (the French original dates from 1956).

7. This is the position of, for example, S. Wisse and J. Beyer.

8. On this aspect it is essential to refer to the study by G. Geeroms, *La vie fraternelee en commun dans la vie religieuse du Concile au Côde* (De Gijzegem: ASBL des Soeurs de S. Vincent de Paul, 1989).

9. Tillard, *Il rinnovamento della vita religiosa*, p. 131.

10. Secondin, op. cit., p. 59.

11. To the consecrated, Madrid, 2 November 1982.

12. Tillard, *Il rinnovamento...*, p. 129.

13. *Teología sistemática de la vida religiosa* (Madrid: Publ. Claretianas, 1976), pp. 394-5.

14. Lozano, op. cit., pp. 240-1.

15. 'La mystère de la communauté', *Vie des Communautées Religieuses* 24 (1966), pp. 98-112.

16. 'Le rôle de la supérieure locale dans les communautés féminines ignatiennes', *Vie Consacrée* 62 (1990), p. 273.

17. *Gli stati di vita del cristiano* (Milan: Jaca Book, 1985), pp. 123-4.

18. 'Teólogos europeos ante de la vida religiosa', *Vida Religiosa* 60 (1986), pp. 401-68.
19. For a first bibliographical survey, cf. M. Diez Presa, 'La vida religiosa, realidad-signo transcendente, profético, salvífico', *Vida Religiosa* 68 (1990), pp. 116-21.
20. *Davanti a Dio e per il mondo*, p. 233.
21. Ibid., p. 179.
22. 'Comunità', DIP, II, 1371.
23. Secondin, op. cit., p. 49.
24. Cf. ibid., p. 62.
25. Ibid., p. 68.
26. *Teologia della vita religiosa* (Leumann: LDC, 1988), pp. 54-7.
27. Bori, *Chiesa primitiva*, p. 11.
28. I refer to what I have written before on this subject: *I fondatori uomini dello Spirito*, pp. 297-303.
29. Cf. Secondin, op. cit., pp. 53, 60-1, 75.
30. R. Hale, 'La koinonia aperta della vita monastica', *Vita Monastica* n. 126 (1976), p. 128.
31. *La communauté*, p. 12.

PART FOUR

The Daily Journey

1 Community as Duty and Commitment

The anthropological dimension of community

We have seen how the community is born from on high, as the fruit of the gift of trinitarian koinonia imparted through the paschal mystery. The Trinity itself, sharing its own life, becomes present in the community with the Risen Christ and his Spirit, and nourishes it with the Word, the Eucharist, agape and the mediation of the brethren.

But the religious community is also a commitment, a duty and a vocation. The love received demands to be lived, even if it is the very gift received that makes the response possible. Reached and transformed by the reality of the love of God, the religious community can now travel the way that leads back to God and become a privileged place for the exercise of charity, where it is possible to love according to nature, that is, the divine nature of God's sons and daughters., In this way, although the community is wholly the work of God, it seems to be the work of its members themselves, who are called to live the trinitarian life they are given and consistently build up their common life in the likeness of the One-in-Three.

The community has an anthropological, as well as a theological dimension: it is built up by the positive action of the 'new' people God calls to form it. The members of the community are called to prove and display the koinonia received, in mutual love.

Having contemplated the theological dimension of the community, we can now go on in this fourth part to study some aspects of its anthropological dimension. We shall see that the religious community is a place in which, in an active response, the gift of the divine agape is lived so that people can develop fully and the unity of the Trinity can be attained in the communion between all the members of the community.

The Community As a Place of Personal Growth

The religious community, in its anthropological dimension, seems to be the work of the people who make it up and to exist for their benefit. Basil has already demonstrated that the social dimension of human beings is naturally presupposed when the community is formed, and is the way in which the human reality of its members will be fully exercised.

Men and women are in fact constitutionally called to communion. In his teaching as pope, John Paul II has constantly emphasized this social dimension of people. Analysing the accounts of the creation of man and woman, the Pope writes that 'humanity means being called to interpersonal communion'. Commenting on *Gaudium et spes* no. 24, he says even more explicitly:

> Human beings - both men and women - are the only beings among all the creatures of the visible world whom God the Creator 'desired for himself'; they are, therefore, persons. Being a person means tending towards the realization of self (the conciliar text speaks of 'finding oneself'), which can only be accomplished 'by a sincere gift of self'.

Of course, John Paul II cannot avoid pointing to 'God himself as Trinity, as a communion of Persons' as the source and model to which men and women must constantly look for the interpretation of being a person. It follows that 'to say that human beings are created in the image and likeness of God means that human beings are also called to exist "for" others, to become a gift' (MD 7).

We know that this concept of the person is typically Christian and how it became part of the common cultural heritage, from its beginnings in the theological reflection on the two great mysteries of the Trinity and the Incarnation carried out during the first centuries of Christianity. In patristic tradition, the person transcends both nature and the individual and, as relationship, openness to others and welcome of them, is itself communion.[1]

The rediscovery of the relationship of communion with others as an essential and irreplaceable element in becoming fully human coincides with a whole trend in the anthropological sciences and philosophy itself. The human sciences today are giving increasing prominence to the social dimension of human beings. Cartesian individualism, which regarded the human being as a self-sufficient consciousness, has given way to a more global understanding of human beings, an appreciation of their structure as beings of dialogue and interpersonal activity, beings who fulfil themselves in meeting with others. Personalism in particular has developed a concept of the person which offers a valid contribution to the relation between the gift of self in communion and personal growth.

Starting from a Christian base, modern personalism has taken its place as an alternative to liberal individualism and Marxist collectivism, and has reasserted the fundamentally communal dimension of human beings. 'The person', maintains Emmanuel Mounier, 'only exists in relation to others, only knows himself because of others and only finds himself in others.'[2] In this vein, the then Cardinal Karol Wojtyla emphasized the importance of relationships for the realization of the individual: 'The communion of the "we" is that form of the human plural in which the person is realized to the greatest degree as subject.'[3] Only in relationship with others do human beings become truly persons, that is to say, they realize themselves fully as human persons and attain to their full vocation which calls them to be in the image and likeness of a God who of his nature is a relationship of love. Unless they live in a relationship of love, therefore, human beings will never be what they are called to be. 'Love', Mounier writes again, 'is not added to the person as something extra, a luxury; without love the person does not exist ... without love people do not reach the point of being persons.'[4] For the person, love is the very possibility of being: 'I exist only so far as I exist for others ... To be means to love.'[5] The Cartesian *cogito* is overturned by loving, which provides the possibility of realizing a person's being, saving it from being condemned to remain 'being', an individual who atrophies because it cannot transcend itself. So the I-Thou relationship is presented not only as essential to both for mutual formation but as the very possibility of being persons and therefore capable of transcendence.[6]

This line of thought appears consistent with the vocation of human beings, who are called to communion with God. As God is 'Persons-in-communion', so human beings are called to personhood, to personhood as communion. They are called to pass from being individuals to being persons, opening up their individuality in relationship with others. With convincing insight, G. M. Zanghí has described this passage as the 'pasch' to which every human being is called:

If individualism is necessity, personhood is freedom. If individualism is inequality, personhood is equality, not by a levelling but by acceptance of totality in diversity. If individualism is analysis, personhood is synthesis ... If individualism is, then, 'the unique in a point', personhood is the expansion (liberation!) of this point, without robbing it of individuality, until it comprehends the totality of points; it is 'the communion of points'.[7]

Taking this reasoning on to a more strictly Christian level, Bulgakov wrote that

ecclesial love, in the likeness of the Blessed Trinity, overcomes the self-centredness which breeds singularity, with the power of the whole, and penetrates into the soul as a higher reality ... The person finds a higher centre in place of his own, and instead of being ex-centric and selfish, becomes con-centric with the whole.[8]

The Council made this awakening to the social dimension of every human being its own; in *Gaudium et spes* (no. 12) we read that 'by his innermost nature man is a social being; and if he does not enter into relations with others he can neither live nor develop his gifts'. In this context the Council states clearly the 'communitarian nature of man's vocation' in the 'design of God' (GS 24), a vocation which finds its perfection and fulfilment in Jesus, who brought the law of brotherly love (cf. GS 32).

Jesus' new commandment is not, then, something extrinsic to humanity, juxtaposed or imposed from above. It springs from the inmost structure of the human race and unfolds its intrinsic possibilities, enabling it to fulfil itself totally both as humanity and as individual people. The messianic people have as their law the new precept, to love as Christ himself loved us (cf. LG 9), because this is the law through which all humanity can reach its original identity. The Word of God, the Council affirms again,

reveals to us that 'God is love' (1 John 4:8) and at the same time teaches that the fundamental law of human perfection, and consequently of the transformation of the world, is the new commandment of love. He assures those who trust in the charity of God that the way of love is open to all men and that the effort to establish a universal brotherhood will not be in vain. (GS 38)

The pedagogic implications of this new ecclesiological position are immediately obvious. The human sciences tell us that human beings cannot succeed in becoming persons except through relationship. Revelation in its turn teaches us that Christians will only reach that goal by living the trinitarian relationship with their brothers and sisters. As members of a Church which has the mission to be a sacrament, 'a sign and instrument, that is, of communion with God and of unity among all men' (LG 1), Christians are called to be, by their nature, people of communion and can only become such in communion, experienced and lived communion.

The Italian Bishops' Conference, in its document on preparation for the ministerial priesthood, applies this principle to the formation of seminarians, stating what it is careful to call a 'very general law of divine pedagogy': 'The ecclesial nature of faith demands that it should be a community which educates by its lived witness, so that each member may benefit, in mutual witness, from an atmosphere of Christian life.'[9] And the Council document on the contemplative dimension of the religious life, reminds all Religious that

> the religious community is in itself a theological reality, an object of contemplation, 'gathered together as a true family in the Lord's name' (PC 15) and, of its nature, the place where it should be possible, in a particular way, to attain the experience of God in its fullness and communicate it to others. Mutual fraternal acceptance, in charity, contributes to creating 'surroundings which are favourable to the spiritual progress of each member of the community' (ET 39).[10]

The life of communion appears as the normal, indeed necessary, setting in which the call of both individuals and groups to the perfection of charity can grow and mature. Moreover, it fosters the quest for God not only in ourselves but also among us, so that the religious community is not only an instrument of holiness but the very place of holiness.

Towards a Community Spirituality

All this has immediate consequences for the way in which community life is lived. It cannot be taken for granted, in fact, that because a community life is being lived, the process of human and spiritual growth will be communitarian. Spiritual life can easily be individualistic even in community. The religious community can be a place where everyone goes their own way, alone. Community does not always, in practice, mean communion.

Shortly before his death, Karl Rahner spoke of spirituality in the Church of the future and singled out 'fraternal communion in the Spirit as the peculiar and essential element of tomorrow's spirituality'. The novelty of the spirituality of the future will actually be 'fraternal communion in which it will be possible to have the same fundamental experience of the Spirit'. With deep humility Rahner recognized, however, that

> we who are older have often had only a marginal experience of this phenomenon ... We who are older have been spiritually individualists, because of our background and our formation ... If there is an experience of the Spirit to be had in common, generally regarded as such, and so desired and lived, it is clearly the experience of the first Pentecost in the Church, an event - it must be presumed - which was certainly not the casual meeting of a number of individualistic mystics but the experience of the Spirit by the community ... I think that in a spirituality of the future the element of fraternal spiritual communion, a spirituality lived together, may play a more determinate part and that slowly and decisively it will be necessary to continue along that road.[11]

If many, like Rahner, do not know which road to take for an authentic journey to communion, it is perhaps because much of spirituality has been understood and lived as an individualistic path towards God. The individual concept of the spiritual life, which has predominated in the history of the Church and was emphasized by the advent of Humanism and the Renaissance, originated mainly in contemplation of the Trinity dwelling in the redeemed and justified soul. If attention is concentrated on the presence of the Trinity in the individual, the spiritual path will normally tend towards mystic union with the Persons living in the soul.

In fact, for all the extraordinary variety in the experiences of the mystics and the teachings of the spiritual masters, tradition has mapped out a path which remains fundamentally individual. The search for God leads the human being inward. The guiding thought of Christian anthropology has been - more or less consciously - Jesus' promise: 'If a man loves me, he will keep my word, and my Father will love him, and we will come to him and make our home with him' (John 14:23). The person in Christ is a dwelling place of the Trinity. The mutual immanence of Christ and the Christian ends up as the whole Trinity indwelling the soul of the divinized person.[12] The call to share in the life of the Trinity has thus led Christian tradition almost exclusively to centre the work of holiness on the deepening of this inner personal relationship with the God who dwells in the soul of the righteous. The way to God is, then, a way inwards and it accords privileged status to solitude and silence.

If this individual way inwards to the dwelling of the Trinity created the great mystics, we know that historically it also ran the risk of causing deviations towards positions that can hardly still be called Christian. We have already seen that absorption in the quest for God *in interiore homine* [in the inner man] led to a gradual estrangement from fellow-Christians, almost to the point of rejecting them. We need only recall once more the first of the sayings of Abba Arsenius, in which he states the condition for salvation as 'flee from men and you will be saved'.[13] And in another of his sayings: 'I cannot live with God and with men ... I cannot leave God to be with men.'[14] *Fuga mundi* leads to *fuga hominis*, and then to *fuga fratris*. Even when we leave the desert and turn, for example, to the invaluable book *The Imitation of Christ*, we find similar teachings:

> The greatest Saints avoided the society of men, when they could, and rather chose to serve God in solitude. A wise man said: Every time I went among men, I returned home less of a man ... It is easier to remain withdrawn at home than succeed in guarding yourself when you go out ... But God and his angels draw near to him who draws away from his friends and acquaintances.[15]

We were able to appreciate the positive aspect of this concept of the spiritual life when we considered it as a parable of the radical choice of God. It is a fact that theological and spiritual reflection have usually given a privileged status to the time of the individual above that of the social and communal. When theological reflection seeks the created image of the Trinity, for example, it prefers to apply it to a single person rather than to a social or ecclesial relationship. Augustine, Bonaventure and Thomas Aquinas, in particular, together with many others, regard redeemed and divinized man as sharing in the trinitarian nature in himself, in the mutual relationship of his own spiritual faculties (memory, intellect and will) enhanced by grace. Therefore they find the trinitarian analogy in the unity of the interior faculties of the individual person rather than among people united in ecclesial communion. The latest representative of this rich tradition of thought, in terms of time, is the Christian philosopher M. Federico Sciacca, who calls 'the intelligent being'

> uni-trinitarian in the sense that his uni-trinitarian being is an image of, or has a certain imperfect analogy to, God One-in-Three; man is a being, and each man is *one*, triadic and at the same time trinitarian in what he has that is analogous to the divine Trinity, which in itself is a mystery revealed by God and as such a gift of faith.[16]

An example of a predominantly individual concept of the spiritual life which is the result of this theological outlook can be found in the figurative interpretation of certain gospel texts, when it is not wholly contradictory. An example is Christ's promise to be present among people united in his name (cf. Matt. 18:20). For some ancient authors, Origen initially but also Cassian, Ambrose and Jerome, the 'two or three' united in the name of Jesus are not so much the disciples as the parts of the soul or the human make-up reunited in interior harmony.[17] Such an interpretation extended even to Catherine of Siena, who paraphrased Christ's words as follows: 'When these three virtues and powers of the soul [memory, intellect and will] are gathered together, I am in their midst by grace.'[18]

Another, much more important, example is that of the privatization, in spiritual terms, of communal images such as the building and the plantation, the new man growing to the full stature of Christ, and bridal union with Christ - all images which in Scripture are referred in the first place to the Church. In these cases, 'the collective aim is original and cannot be analysed as a broadening of the laws of individual growth. If they have to be compared, the relationship will be reversed: the individual process copies, with some variants, the scheme of the communal history of salvation.'[19] The Church is the growing body of Christ, the people of God on their journey, the bride uniting herself to her Bridegroom. Precisely because Christians live and grow in and with the Church, they will live the very dynamisms and stages of their maturing with it and in unity with all its other members.

In spite of its basic tendency to individualize the way of holiness, tradition, as we have seen frequently with regard to the historical understanding of the religious community, also offers us pointers towards opening out the way of holiness to communitarian dimensions. However, these aspects have not, in the history of spirituality, been studied sufficiently thoroughly and have not actually given rise to collective or communitarian spiritual itineraries.

Analysing the history of Christian thought, von Balthasar has shown the full effect of philosophy's failure to give intersubjectivity a central place in its reflections. Anchored in Greek thought, Christian theology has not been able to develop fully all the dimensions of the mystery of charity offered by revelation. Two of its fundamental characteristics have been particularly studied: its divine origin as a sharing in the love of the Trinity, and its function in uniting God and human beings. Because of this twofold character of charity, patristic and scholastic theology was able to go more deeply into the ontology of created being, redeemed and divinized in its vertical relationship to God. Thus Christian thought has always seen an analogy of the Trinity in created beings and has tried to build up a corresponding anthropology on this basis. On the other hand, there has not been such thorough study of the consequences at the intersubjective level of sharing in the divine life, even if there have been some attempts to develop a trinitarian ontology on these lines.

Today we are witnessing a transition from an intra-subjective to an inter-subjective analogy of the Trinity, even if, as has been rightly observed,

the operation requires due attention and a correct appreciation of the analogical tool, and must base itself, without any one-sidedness, on the positive elements that the previous approach had yielded. The intrasubjective trinitarian analogy is called, in fact, to give a dimension of depth (in the ontological sense) to the intersubjective.[20]

Being towards another (ecstasy) respects and indeed fosters being in self (enstasy) in a way analogous to what happens in the divine Persons.[21]

The new horizons of theology are also opening the way to new possibilities of understanding the spiritual journey. If the reflections of the first councils centred on Christ, and the Council of Trent interested itself in the justification of sinful humanity, the Second Vatican Council directs its attention to the Church as the mystical Body of Christ, a people gathered together in the bond of the Trinity's love, and

> modifies the scheme of spirituality and pastoral theology in an ecclesial sense. The salvation and perfection of one's own soul, on which preachers and spiritual writers had laid so much emphasis, is set free from individualistic preoccupations, to be inserted into the broader context of the divine plan ... [The Council] feels the need to develop a spirituality centred on ecumenical reconciliation and to live intensely the bonds of evangelical fraternity, to the extent of forming a community on the pattern of the primitive community described as the ideal in the Acts of the Apostles.[22]

The Holy Spirit is steering away from the individual journey towards the centre of the soul where the Trinity dwells, towards a communitarian way which rediscovers union between brethren as the place where the Trinity is present. For this new way, the way of growth for the individual, finds the gift of self to others completely indispensable (we can recall the quotation from *Gaudium et spes* no. 24). Souls have moved away from fleeing from the brethren in order to go to God, and have set themselves to search for their brethren in order to go to God with them, or rather to find God in mutual unity.

Prompted by the Spirit, contemporary theology is bringing out the ecclesiological themes of koinonia - the mystical Body, the people of God, the *Ecclesia de Trinitate* (the Church of the Trinity) - so as to open up the way for new communal spiritual itineraries.

The community dimension is thus becoming one of the strongest and most marked characteristics of contemporary spirituality. The following has been written in this regard:

> Contemporary spiritual movements are all seeking to put into practice a *spirituality lived together*, which emphasizes fraternal community in the Spirit as its essential element. It is a need to live together the values of the Gospel, more or less following the example of the first community at Jerusalem, in order to build up an authentic spiritual life of a communitarian kind, open to the experience of God.[23]

We can glimpse the revolutionary implications of this transition from a predominantly individualistic spirituality to a communitarian, or better, trinitarian spirituality. As Chiara Lubich writes, offering a typical example of this new orientation:

> Ours is a way of going to God by way of other human beings. We go to God through human beings, indeed together with human beings, together with our brethren. Thus a noticeably collective way. And in this collective way individuals also find their personal perfection. It is as if people who seek God in themselves in other spiritualities are standing in a garden full of flowers but looking at and admiring only one flower. They admire, love and adore God in themselves. It seems to us that God is asking us to look at many flowers, because God is or can be present in other people as well. And as I ought to love God in myself - when I am alone - so I ought to love him in my brother or sister when they are with me. Then I shall not love flight from the world as much as the quest for Christ in the world; I shall love not only solitude but also company; not only silence but also the spoken word. And when love for Christ in my brother or sister is mutual, we live in our meeting according to the model of the Trinity, the two of us like the Father and the Son, and the Holy Spirit coming in between us with his gifts as the soul of the mystical Body. When Jesus is the motive for brethren meeting, they become one as God is one, but they are not alone, any more than God is alone, although he is one, because he is Love. When we meet in this way, Christ's words are fulfilled: 'Where two or three are united in my name, I am in the midst of them' (Matt. 18:20). The risen Lord is there. It is this Christ whom we must always possess or, better, by whom we must increasingly be possessed. He is the holiness of the group and of each individual person.[24]

In Search of Brethren

In a spirituality which thrives on trinitarian ecclesiology, therefore, brethren are not to be avoided but sought out; they are not a distraction but part of building that unity which contains God. Given by God, they become simultaneously a sacrament for reaching God. The relationship of love for a brother or sister becomes a means and an expression of loving God and being introduced into the koinonia of the Trinity.

If it is true that John, the theologian of agape, sees love as essentially coming down from above, it is also true that he repeatedly calls it 'the commandment'. Indeed, in his Gospel, and even more clearly in the Epistles, the commandments (*entolai*) are reduced to the commandment (*entole*) of fraternal charity. We may recall that for the Hebrew mind, the Law (commandments) is often regarded as 'the way of (towards) the Lord'. So fraternal love, a sign of having been reached by the love of God, also becomes an expression of love for God and a means of reaching him.

James regards fraternal love quite simply as worship paid to God. 'Religion that is pure and undefiled before God and the Father is this: to visit orphans and widows in their affliction, and to keep oneself unstained from the world' (1:27). To speak of religion here, the apostle uses a term (*threskeia*) which, apart from this passage, is found only twice in the New Testament. It means religion as cult and observance (cf. Acts 26:5; Col. 2:15). The apostle is therefore affirming that compassion shown to brothers in need is a worship or cult (*threskeia*) pleasing to God. Fraternal love has a cultic, liturgical value. His thinking here is in line with those texts of Matthew in which Christ affirms that everything done to someone poor (cf. Matt. 25:40-5) or a disciple (cf. Matt. 10:40-2) is done to him. It is significant that the first of these texts makes love for the poor the very object of the Last Judgement: 'Enter into the Kingdom ... Depart from me...' People are justified by fraternal love. In religions, people are usually just or unjust according to their observance or non-observance of the rites and practices of their particular religion. In the parable of the Pharisee and the publican, too, the former feels justified by the fact that he fulfils the ethical and ritual commandments of fasting and tithes (cf. Luke 18:11-12). Christ, in his description of the Last Judgement, makes no mention of ritual observance - only of fraternal love. Service of brethren becomes service rendered to Christ.

In defence of religious communities devoted to works of charity, Thomas Aquinas used one of these texts (Matt. 25:40) as a basis for his conclusion that '*obsequia proximis facta, in quantum ad deum referuntur, dicuntur esse sacrificia quaedam*' ('Acts of love for a neighbour performed for the love of God are, according to Christ's words, in a certain sense cultic).[25]

Unlike other religions, human relationships are the centre of Christian religious practice, a privileged expression of our relationship with God. Consequently, human relationships are taken by Christ as the proper expression of worship paid to God. The Eucharist itself, as the central act of Christian worship, consists in a meeting of brothers and sisters, and it is in the context of such a meeting that communion with Christ is obtained. Christ gives himself in the Supper to brothers and sisters who are together. The Eucharist as a sacrament, with its circular structure of communion, can only be understood in the context of an incarnational religion which has made human relationships the sacrament of meeting with God. Thus we come back to the intimate connection and mutual penetration of agape, koinonia, *ecclesia*, *Eucharistia*.

We have already pointed out the implications of the realism of the mystery of the incarnation and the 'sacramentality' of Christ. As God reaches us in Christ and Christ reaches us through the mediation of our brother or sister, so, in reverse, we communicate with Christ through them. We go to God through the humanity of Christ, but Christ has taught us that we go to him through our brethren. God cannot be directly seen, John reminds us; we can, however, be in loving communion with him through loving communion with our brothers and sisters (cf. 1 John 4:12). To a religion of pure transcendence, John opposes one of grace; instead of a solitary search for God, he proposes a community life in which the experience of God as Love can be found.

Fraternal agape is not only *signum*, that is, a demonstration of our having been reached by God's love (the descending movement: our brother or sister as a gift of God); it is also *sacramentum*, in the sense of a way of access to God (the ascending movement: the brother or sister as sacrament for meeting God). The neighbour becomes a sacrament, *sacramentum proximi*; it is precisely a question of the *sacramentum Ecclesiae*, the fundamental sign of meeting with Christ.

The Centrality of Love

It is easy, therefore, to understand the call to love our brother and sister which is constantly addressed to Christians throughout the New Testament. Only in loving is the human vocation fully realized, and the potential in every individual fulfilled in their *pasch*, passover, to personal completeness. Loving is the true way to be Christian, to build up 'Church-koinonia', to approach God the One-in-Three in unity, as a people.

Moreover, it seems clear that love is proved and reaches its fullness when it goes out to a brother or sister and involves him or her in that same dynamic of love until it becomes the mutuality which alone reflects completely the trinitarian nature of agape: 'If we love one another, God abides in us and his love is perfected in us' (1 John 4:12). Loving one another is the condition attached to reaching God, possessing him and fully living his life of agape.

As the great Christian tradition has clearly understood, the dilemma of loving either God or our neighbour is solved at its root. For Basil, the question of the twofold commandment is resolved in a single identical love. Consequently,

> it is by means of the first commandment that the second is fulfilled; and through the second, one goes back again to the first. He who loves the Lord also, as a result, loves his neighbour ... Then in his turn, he who loves his neighbour satisfies love for God, because the Lord accepts that kindness as given to him.[26]

For Augustine, 'there is no surer stairway for reaching the love of God than the love of human beings for one another'.[27] If the love of God is commanded first, love of neighbour has to be followed first.

> Love of God is the first to be commanded; love of neighbour the first which needs to be practised. When the Lord pronounces the two precepts of love, he does not command you first to love your neighbour and then to love God but puts God first and then neighbour. But since you do not as yet see God, you will merit to see him by loving your neighbour. By loving your neighbour you make your eye pure so that it will be able to see God.[28]

Gregory the Great writes in his turn:

> There are two precepts of love, namely love of God and love of neighbour. From love of God is born love of neighbour; and love of neighbour nourishes love of God. For he who neglects love of God is quite incapable of loving his neighbour. And we can make greater progress in the love of God if, in the bosom of his love, we are first given the milk of love for our neighbour ... Thus in the soil of our heart [God] has planted first the root of love for him, and then, like leaves, love for brethren has developed. And John again

attests that the love of God should be joined to love of neighbour when he says: 'He who does not love his brother whom he has seen, cannot love God whom he has not seen'.[29]

Thomas Aquinas summed it up when he said that the act by which the neighbour and God are loved is of the same species: *'idem specie actus est quo diligitur Deus et quo diligitur proximus. Et propter hoc habitus caritatis non solum se extendit ad dilectionem Dei, sed etiam ad dilectionem proximi.'*[30]

The relationship between human beings becomes the existential space for the gift of God. The relationship with God

> is always first on the level of being; it is always and only in God that I meet others, it is in his openness towards me (by which I exist) that I can open myself to others. On the level of existent reality, however, it is the second; it is through openness to others that I achieve an openness to God in which I mature through openness to others.[31]

Love for other people becomes, even from the existential point of view, the highway for Christian growth. The brother or sister becomes the concrete 'way' for reaching God, as well as a tool for testing the spiritual path (cf. 1 John 4:12, 20). The Christian's way consists, in fact, in 'walking in love' (Eph. 5:2); indeed, as Paul again says, love is 'the better way' (1 Cor. 12:31). Charity is indeed the complete fulfilment of the law (cf. Rom. 13:10), the bond of perfection (cf. Col. 3:14). And it is by love for our brethren that we pass from death to life (cf. 1 John 3:14).

We are talking here about the rudiments, the ABC, of the Gospel. Yet the practice of charity progressively enlarges the soul and gives the person concerned the characteristic features of love described by Paul. The person trained in charity becomes patient and kind, 'is not jealous or boastful ... is not arrogant or rude ... does not insist on [his] own way ... is not irritable or resentful ... does not rejoice at wrong, but rejoices in the right. Love bears all things, believes all things, hopes all things, endures all things' (1 Cor. 13:4-7).

The person who shows the effects of charity described here has now reached maturity, complete self-dominion, balance and magnanimity, has overcome self-centredness and become, with Christ, 'the perfect human' in self-giving; he or she no longer lives for him or herself but for the building up of the Church, and is wholly dedicated to the Kingdom of God. Someone who is 'made charity' in this way will remain for ever, as charity remains for ever (cf. 1 Cor. 13:8).

The religious community appears more clearly now as not so much a place which makes recollection and the individual way to God possible, but rather the place where charity can be practised, which offers the opportunity for constant communion with brethren. Here the radical gift of self is required, and the total openness which alone makes full personal maturity possible. Brothers or sisters are deliberately sought so that mutual love can be lived with them. The community then becomes the place of God's presence, in which God can be experienced and the presence of the Risen Christ and the fruits of his Spirit *enjoyed*. It will be a fertile soil or 'humus' for continual growth and maturing until all together attain the full stature of Christ, a prophetic sign of how the communion of saints lives, a centre which irradiates the evangelical life.

We can now read the whole of the second part of no. 15 of *Perfectae caritatis* and appreciate all its depth:

> Religious, as members of Christ, should live together as brothers and should give pride of place to one another in esteem, carrying one another's burdens. A community gathered together as a true family in the Lord's name enjoys his presence, through the love of God which is poured into their hearts by the Holy Spirit. For love sums up the law and is the bond which makes us perfect; by it we know that we have crossed over from death to life. Indeed, the unity of the brethren is a symbol of the coming of Christ and is a source of great apostolic power.

NOTES

1. Cf. G. M. Zanghí, 'Poche riflessioni su la persona', *Nuova Umanità*, n. 7 (Jan-Feb 1980), pp. 9-19.
2. *La communication*, p. 453, quoted by M. Richard, *Studi sul pensiero contemporaneo. Le grandi correnti* (Rome: 1979), p. 138.
3. *Der Streit um den Menschen* (Kevelaer: 1979), p. 54.
4. *Révolution personnaliste et communautaire* (Paris: Montaigne, 1936), p. 193.
5. *Le personnalisme* in *Oeuvres*, III, p. 453.
6. Cf. A. Danesi, *Unità e pluralità. Mounier e il ritorno alla persona* (Rome: Città Nuova, 1984), p. 100.
7. G. M. Zanghí, 'Prospettive per una cultura cristiana in Europa oggi', *Nuova Umanità* 13 (1991), n. 73, p. 83.
8. S. Bulgakov, *Il Paraclito* (Bologna: 1971), p. 450.
9. *La preparazione al sacerdozio ministeriale. Orientamenti e norme* (Rome: 1972), p. 109.
10. No. 15, *Enchiridion Vaticanum*, 7, 522.
11. 'Elementi di spiritualità nella Chiesa del futuro' in *Problemi e prospettive di spiritualità*, ed. T. Goffi and B. Secondin (Brescia: 1983), pp. 440-1.
12. For a succinct presentation of the classic view of Christian anthropology, as well as the transition to a 'trinitarian anthropology', cf. P. Coda, 'La Chiesa profezia dell'umanità compiuta. Abbozzo di antropologia trinitaria', in *La Chiesa salvezza dell'uomo*, vol. 1 (Rome: 1984), pp. 77-112.
13. *The Sayings of the Desert Fathers*, trans. Benedicta Ward SLG (London: Mowbray, 1975), p. 9, no. 1.
14. Ibid., p. 11, no. 13.
15. I, XX, 1-6.
16. *Ontologia triadica e trinitaria. Discorso metafisico teologico* (Milan: 1973), p. 99.
17. Origen, *In Matth.*, 14, 3; Cassian, *Conferences*, 12, 11, 1; Paulinus, *Ep.* 36, 4; Ambrose, *In Luc.*, 7, 192-3; Jerome, *In Matth.*, 3.
18. *Dialogue*, ed. G. Cavallini (Rome: 1968) c. LIX, p. 121.
19. F. Ruiz Salvador, *Caminos del Espíritu* (Madrid: 1978), p. 420.
20. P. Coda, *Evento pasquale. Trinità e storia* (Rome: Città Nuova, 1984), p. 172.
21. Ibid., p. 170.
22. S. de Fiores, 'Spiritualità contemporanea', in *Nuovo Dizionario di Spiritualità* (Rome: Paoline, 1978), p. 1535.
23. Giovanna della Croce, 'Linee di forza della spiritualità contemporanea', *Rivista di Vita Spirituale* 39 (1985), p. 551. On the emergence of the communitarian aspect in spirituality, cf. J. Castellano Cervera, 'Tendenze emergenti dalla riflessione teologica contemporanea. Prospettive attuali della teologia spirituale', *Nuova Umanità* 5 (1983), n. 30, pp. 57-70; K. Rahner, 'Elementi di spiritualità nella Chiesa del futuro', in *Problemi e prospettive di spiritualità* (Brescia: Queriniana, 1983), pp. 433-43; J. García Rojo, 'Decididos a caminar juntos', *Revista de Espiritualidad* 38 (1979), pp. 335-56. For the modern movements: B. Secondin, 'Movimenti comunitari',

in *Problemi e prospettive di spiritualità*, pp. 389-408; J. Povilus, 'Considerazioni su una esperienza comunitaria di Dio-Trinità oggi', in *Il Dio di Gesù Cristo* (Rome: Città Nuova, 1982), pp. 275-82; K. Hemmerle, *Vie per l'unità. Tracce di un cammino teologico e spirituale* (Rome: Città Nuova, 1985).

24. Talk given to the 'Bishop friends of the Movement', Rocca di Papa 10.2.1984.
25. *Summa Theologiae*, II-II, q. 188, a. 2.
26. *The Ascetic Works of Saint Basil*, trans. W. K. L. Clarke (London: 1925), p. 158.
27. *De Moribus Ecclesiae Catholicae* I, 26.48.
28. *In Joannem*, 17, 8.
29. *Moralia*, PL 75, 780-1.
30. *Summa Theologiae*, II-II, q. 25, a. 1.
31. Zanghí, *Prospettive*, pp. 81-2.

2 The Concreteness of Love
How to build up the community

If our brother and sister are the 'sacrament' of meeting with Christ, if love is the Christian's 'way', if in the mutuality of love there is the possibility of experiencing the trinitarian God, then the community is the privileged place for living the Christian vocation in all its fullness.

But how are we to love? What concrete practice is required of the members of a religious community in order that it may arrive at being what it is called to be? Rather than deal exhaustively with the pedagogy of charity, we would like simply to indicate some paths which can be travelled in trying to look at the actual source of agape. If we are children of a God who is Love, we cannot help resembling him as well, especially in the exercise of love.

The Practice of Charity

Directing their gaze to God as Love, each member of the community feels called to that basic attitude of going out of self towards the other. It is a question, as we have seen, of the *pasch* or passover from individual to person, or the exodus from self-centredness to self-giving, the passage from being for oneself to being for others. Born for communion, human beings are in fact blocked in their relationships because of sin. The devil, by definition, is division and his work is to break relationships. Redemption, on the other hand, is the work which Christ accomplishes to free human beings from the many divisions and splits which are part of human life in relation to God, brethren, nature, and the self, and so to restore freedom to them in the full communion of love.

The initiators of the different religious communities always felt the resistance of human nature, marked by sin, to the building up of authentic relationships in love. We have seen how vehemently they hurled themselves against those who created divisions within the community. The breaking of unity is in fact the greatest sin, the sin which creates the greatest resemblance to the devil, just as building up unity brings people closer to the God of unity and love. It is the makers of peace who will actually be called children of God! (Matt. 5:9). When founders and foundresses wish to warn against disunity within the community they draw liberally on the lists of sins found in the Pauline writings. These are lists which denounce human selfishness, turning back on self, and all the negative attitudes which impede the building up of the life of communion. Here is a list of these sins in alphabetical order, as they occur in Paul's letters: anger, arrogance, blasphemy, cleverness in wrongdoing, cruelty, deceit, discord, disobedience, drunkenness, foolish talk, fraud, gluttony, gossiping, greed, homosexuality, hostility towards God, idolatry, immorality, indifference, infidelity, insubordination, jealousy, licentiousness, lust, magic, malice, murder, obscenity, pederasty, perversion, pride, quarrelling, sectarianism, slander, stupidity, selfish ambition, theft and vanity.[1] It is striking that all the sins listed by Paul have some connection with relationships within the community; they are impediments to communion and at the same time the fruit of disunity.

When people join a community they must realize that they are coming from this environment of sin and that everyone's heart harbours the evils which corrode communion. Ours are communities of sinners, just as the Church is holy but composed of sinners. It is clear, then, that to arrive at koinonia it is necessary to pass through *metanoia*.

It was not by chance that in monasticism, conversion, baptism and entry into the community were often combined in a single act. Hence also the recurrent theme of monastic profession as a 'second baptism'.[2] You cannot enter upon life in common without conversion, without having purified your heart from the selfishness rooted there in the most diverse forms and appearances.

These words 'metanoia', 'conversion', must be taken in their original meaning. 'Metanoia' means a change of outlook, or reasoning with a new and higher logic. It is a question of being able to think according to God and not according to human beings (cf. Mark 8:33). God always thinks thoughts of peace (cf. Jer. 29:11). It is a matter of entering into the evangelical logic of love for enemies, giving your cloak to anyone who asks for your tunic, turning the other cheek, and giving freely without expecting any return. Etymologically, 'conversion' means the reversal of estrangement: from the self-centred direction to the altruistic, from seeing everything from your own standpoint to living for others, from greed for possessions to generosity towards all.

It is the same Paul who, after listing the works of the flesh, lists the fruit of the Spirit, which are born in the 'new man' as the result of conversion. As the former destroyed relationships, so these latter are related to communion: 'But the fruit of the Spirit is love, joy, peace, patience, kindness, goodness, faithfulness, gentleness, self-control ... those who belong to Christ Jesus have crucified the flesh with its passions and desires. If we live by the Spirit, let us also walk by the Spirit' (Gal. 5:22-25). After listing sins against unity, he writes again: 'You were washed, you were sanctified, you were justified in the name of the Lord Jesus Christ and in the Spirit of our God' (1 Cor. 6:11).

'Now', he writes, still in a context of contrasting the before and after of conversion, 'you have put off the old nature with its practices and have put on the new nature.' Then Paul once again describes the distinguishing characteristics of the new nature:

> Put on then as God's chosen ones, holy and beloved, compassion, kindness, lowliness, meekness, and patience, forbearing one another and, if one has a complaint against another, forgiving each other; as the Lord has forgiven you, so you also must forgive. And above all these put on love, which binds everything together in perfect harmony. And let the peace of Christ rule in your hearts, to which indeed you were called in the one body. And be thankful. Let the word of Christ dwell in you richly, teach and admonish one another in all wisdom, and sing psalms and hymns and spiritual songs with thankfulness in your hearts to God. And whatever you do, in word or deed, do everything in the name of the Lord Jesus, giving thanks to God the Father through him. (Col. 3:9-17)

The characteristics of the new nature are identified with the means needed to build up the community: a person who has the new nature is one who is capable of creating communion.

It can be dangerous to look at the mystical aspect of community without taking into account the selfish tendency present in each one of its members, and without considering the need for a right and proper continual conversion. Direct comparison between the models of community and the concrete situation of one's particular community might breed frustration and disappointment. On the one hand, there is a vision of light, on the other, the awareness of harsh reality, in which it is possible to experience coldness, lack of understanding, failure and division. Therefore the intrinsic unity of the paschal mystery in its twofold dimension of death and resurrection can never be sufficiently emphasized. The mystery of life can only be lived with the mystery of death, just as death for love cannot fail to lead to the fullness of life.

Metanoia, the deep inner conversion brought about in each person by Christ and his Spirit in baptism and ratified in religious profession, needs to be renewed constantly every day.

Together with this permanent attitude of conversion, building up community demands a particular attitude of faith, or the ability always to see the other with new eyes. This is a question of an authentic attitude of faith because we have to recognize the true presence of Christ in the people God puts beside us in the journey of discipleship. This is one expression of metanoia, a change in a person's way of seeing and thinking. It is this faith which makes us go beyond a purely human evaluation of the members of the community, with its temptation to stop at the negative aspects which inevitably emerge. Prolonged living together leads to the discovery of the defects of others as well as their gifts. Furthermore, since the members of the community do not choose one another, there can even be groundless antipathies. With the passing of time, we acquire a negative view of someone else that no longer takes account of the divine living in them or their vocation as a child of God. Then distrust makes its appearance, or the conviction that the other person can never change. We no longer hold them in esteem, we have no more faith in the possibility of their 'resurrection'; a veil seems to have come down over our eyes. That is why we need an attitude of faith, which can always look with new eyes and always be ready to believe and trust others. Rather than feeling judged, everyone needs to feel accepted and loved just as they are. And it is this surrounding warmth that will soften a particular awkwardness, give light to understand how much needs to be changed in our own life, and so on.

When a brother or sister is seen constantly in this supernatural light, and appreciated as a 'sacrament' of meeting with God, this produces a form of relationship expressed in concrete love. Metanoia is translated into diakonia, and thus building community begins 'from below', in an 'upward movement'.

The connotations of this love are endless. Love is in fact like a diamond, it has a thousand facets. Precisely because of this, love has to be able to show itself in a myriad of ways. The hymn to charity in the First Letter to the Corinthians (ch. 13) shows us how love has to clothe itself, according to circumstances, in patience, meekness, kindness, self-effacement, humility, respect, disinterestedness, gentleness, forgiveness, justice, truth, mercy, trust, hope and tolerance. Charity is the fulfilling of the Law; it includes all the other virtues and expresses itself through them.

These varied expressions of love must show themselves not so much - and not only - in life's solemn moments and occasions but also, and especially, in the simplicity of daily fraternal living, rich in humanity and made up of little things. The way to build up community quickly and solidly is to live those words of the Gospel which immediately produce in us a positive attitude of service to the brother or sister put beside us by the Lord. 'As you did it to one of the least of these my brethren, you did it to me' (Matt. 25:40); 'Love your neighbour as yourself' (Matt. 22:39); and so on. These words place us in an immediate and concrete situation of giving, they impel us to go out of ourselves in constant service of others, in a positive attitude of self-offering that will prevent us giving in to self.

The Word of God brings out some concrete forms of self-giving which are characteristic of love.

First of all, *serving*. This is Jesus' own first teaching on how to love. He 'came not to be served but to serve, and to give his life as a ransom for many' (Matt. 20:28) and consummated his ultimate love on the cross. Shortly before he died, he had given visible expression to the concreteness of love by washing his disciples' feet and inviting them to do the same: 'You also ought to wash one another's feet' (John 13:14).

Service demands an attitude of humility. 'Be humble', recommends the letter of Peter when it speaks about how to live out mutual love (cf. 1 Pet. 3:8). According to the Lord's constant teaching, it is a matter of putting yourself in the last place. When the sons of Zebedee asked for the first place, the Master answered: 'You know that the rulers of the Gentiles lord it over them, and their great men exercise authority over them. It shall not be so among you; but whoever is great among you must be your servant' (Matt. 20:25-7). To the disciples with ambitions for primacy, Jesus declares: 'If anyone would be first, he must be last of all and servant of all' (Mark 9:35).

The evangelical way of presenting yourself to others is in an attitude of humility and real service. A community will grow in love on condition that each member washes the feet of the others in the difficulties of everyday life, the ordinariness of small gestures and the hidden silence which does not expect recognition: 'Do not let your left hand know what your right hand is doing' (Matt. 6:3). But serving your brother or sister - not making them serve you! What this is all about is pure gift, expressed in the most common community tasks, those very ordinary activities ranging from keeping the house clean to creating a festive atmosphere in a moment of recreation, from creatively enlivening community prayer to being the first to share experiences during a meeting. Service means something concrete, something done, something costly. What comes to mind immediately is a mother who does not spare herself, who gives herself from morning to night as if it was the most normal thing in the world. Even to her children and her husband, it seems normal, like a service owing to them. That is the way to love in community, where everyone is called to be the mother of others in a service that is constant, real, daily and concrete. Service is not a pretence, a *do ut des* ('I give so that you can give to me in return'); it is a free concern for others, for the community. The servant and the slave are forced to perform their tasks by need or circumstances. The Christian who serves follows Christ's example not by force but impelled and motivated by love.

A second aspect of love is *welcoming*, which leads to accepting others and identifying with them to the point of making their anxieties, sufferings, joys, preoccupations and successes your own. Love is oblivious of self and wholly taken up with others. The others are welcomed and loved as they are and not as we would like them to be. We have to reject the temptation to want others in our image and likeness or according to our own tastes. Rather, it is a question of being able to rejoice in the diversity, wealth and complementarity of gifts, as the founders of communities taught us when they recalled the Pauline image of the one body with its different limbs and organs.

In order to understand others and welcome them in their individuality, as a gift, we have to enter into their interior world and see with their eyes, feel with their feelings, share their very life and everything that is theirs. It is Paul's invitation to become a Greek with the Greeks, a Jew with Jews, weak with the weak - the invitation to become everything to everyone (cf. 1 Cor. 9:19-23). It is to rejoice with those who rejoice and mourn with those who mourn, and to have the same feelings for each other (cf. Rom. 12:5). Here too it is a matter of a typically paschal dimension. On the cross Jesus went to the furthest limit in 'becoming everything to everyone', sharing all that is ours: he who knew nothing of sin became sin for us (2 Cor. 5:21), experienced our separation from the Father (cf. Mark 15:34), submitted to our very death (cf. Phil. 2:6-8). On the model of Christ's sharing, ours is not simply a matter of 'feeling with' others, but a real 'bearing one another's burdens' (cf. Gal. 6:2).

Welcoming means not pretending, and having patience, 'resorting to temporary compromise just so that the common journey is not disrupted'[3] in the conviction that the less perfect in unity is better than the more perfect in disunity. It means being able to wait for others whose pace of maturing is slower than ours, or who do not grow with the speed we would like to impose on the community's progress.

Welcoming also means being able to love with the heart. Love for your brother or sister is not in fact a Platonic love. Peter invites us to love one another 'sincerely as brothers', 'earnestly from the heart' (1 Pet. 1:22). This is an entire love that can make people 'share in the joy and sorrow of others' and inspired by 'love of the brethren' (1 Pet. 3:8-9). Love between the members of one and the same religious community cannot be expressed in a depersonalized relationship of rarefied courtesy. The gift of self and the following of Christ do not mortify feeling; rather, they make it blossom in all its glory, purified from ambiguity and selfishness and enhancing a person's gifts.

Welcoming further implies an ability to listen, in order that others may feel thoroughly understood. Love knows how to be silent and listen. Knowing how to listen is not easy. When others are speaking, it is often tempting to interrupt them because you have already understood, or you are thinking about the answer or what you will have to say when it is your turn. But knowing how to listen is a capacity for silence, an interior emptiness, and a receptivity that is wholly loving. Only in this way will the other person feel completely listened to, and completely able to express their own needs and expose their doubts or plans. The capacity to listen is both the most elementary and the highest form of intellectual 'midwifery'. And it is one of the most precious gifts we can make to another person. In a community we need to be able to 'waste time' in order to listen. Welcoming also means allowing ourselves to be welcomed, since loving means being able to let yourself be loved.

A third attitude typical of love, which again can be found in the paschal mystery where love is explained, is that it is *freely given*. We are in fact children of a Father who loved us first (cf. John 4:19). 'God shows his love for us in that while we were yet sinners Christ died for us ... For if while we were enemies we were reconciled to God by the death of his Son, much more, now that we are reconciled, shall we be saved by his life' (Rom. 5:8-10). Love always takes the initiative in loving, after the example of the divine agape. In a community someone has to be the first to move, to love, to decide to make a fresh start with relationships when they have been damaged, without demanding anything from others. In order to love, you cannot wait for others to love. The first step is always up to each one of us! We could paraphrase 1 John 4:10 as 'In this is love, not that others should love us, but that we should love others'.

This is perhaps the purest form of love, because it is the most disinterested. It is a love that does not seek its own ends but only the good of others, a love which does not lay down conditions beforehand ('I will love you if...') but loves because that is the nature of love. It is a love that can endure even the lack of understanding, perhaps even the insults or derision, which are possible within a community. Those who have understood the value of koinonia will try everything to obtain it, and their sole object is to build up the common good, not their own interests; they look to this, not to themselves. The temptation in community life is in fact to demand to be loved, to wait for others to deal with situations, to expect someone else to take the first step in rebuilding relationships that have been compromised. Love, on the other hand, loves spontaneously, loves first, without making any demand. It finds its motivation for loving in love itself.

Another feature of love, indispensable for building up the community, is *universality*. Love loves everyone, without exception or preference. Everyone! This word is repeated several times by Jesus precisely in the context of the paschal event: 'When I am lifted up from the earth, I will draw *all men* to myself' (John 12:32); 'Father, may they *all* be one' (John 17:21). Religious will have to train themselves to serve, welcome, and love spontaneously each one of their brothers or sisters in the community, leaving on one side the inevitable preferences or antipathies.

Again, love is full of thoughtfulness and lavishes attention on other people. It is *benevolent*, that is, it wishes others well and interests itself as much in others as in itself, in all the events of their life from physical health to sanctification. If God asks for an account of the other members of the community with the question 'Where is your brother?', you cannot answer 'Am I my brother's keeper?' (Gen. 4:9). It is precisely *we* who *are* the keepers of our brothers and sisters. It is exactly because we are members of the same body that we cannot ignore our brother, not even for the sake of holiness.

Teaching Methods for the Life of Unity

These and other similar attitudes of love are fundamental for the birth and development of communion. Communion demands that everyone should be able to put love into practice, first of all by deeds, always ready to make a fresh start. It demands that everyone should live in love, without dependence. If we lean on one another, when one falls the others fall too! Rather, community life requires that when one falls, another will be ready to offer support him and lift him or her up again. Full communion presupposes that everyone is mature and has a sense of identity, just as, at the same time, the life of communion enables everyone to mature in their own personality.

However, these aspects of love, as we have described them so far, do not yet, strictly speaking, constitute the life of unity. Community is born only when love is mutual, or when the love that each offers to the others is reciprocated and love answers love. Trinitarian koinonia is, in fact, mutual love. If the love of one of the divine Persons was not returned by the others, there would be no One-in-Three. Similarly, Jesus did not express the new commandment as the 'golden rule' of not doing to others what you do not want done to you, or as an invitation to love others as yourself. The new commandment implies mutuality: love 'one another'. If the religious community is to be a *Christian* community, it must of necesssity live the new commandment: the love which inspires it must be mutual.

Mutual love, like the love in practice of which we have just spoken, requires its own route and its special tools.

I think we need first of all to declare explicitly to one another our common will to walk together following the same Master. Often we assume this, simply because we all find ourselves in the same community. Yet sometimes there is a risk that we may be trusting in mere assumptions, and possibly deluding ourselves. A certain timidity or shyness about supernatural things, human respect, or being trained in reticence about the interior life often prevent us from remembering the reason why we are living together. There is a risk that we can walk behind the same Master for years on end, in the same community, without ever exchanging a word with one another about our journey.

When the founders and their companions began the common life, they agreed explicitly on a common way of discipleship. As successors to the founders, the members of the community are also called to show one another their common will to follow. They need to tell one another, repeatedly, the common aim that the Spirit has communicated to each and to all, so that together they can go more deeply into their vocation, taking advantage particularly of special moments such as retreats, community meetings and times of prayer, but also perhaps of fixed times of shared relaxation. They need to learn to look at one another and say to one another with simplicity and truth: 'We are walking together with the same Person. We share the same ideal. We are living for the same cause. Together we want to fulfil Jesus' commandment; we cannot, in fact, live by ourselves because to love "one another" we need "one and another"; both of us are necessary, indeed indispensable. Therefore I love you *as* Christ loved you. And I, the other replies - and this is mutuality - I too love you *as* Christ loved you.'

What, we may now ask, are the teaching methods needed for learning how to keep this mutual love, and therefore unity, always alive so that the presence of the Lord may always be living and tangible in the community?

In accordance with what we have just said, one of these fundamental elements is *sharing* our experiences. It is a question of being able to give what God is doing within and around each one of us: the steps forward we make, the fruits of our apostolate, as well as our doubts and difficulties. Nothing is ours and everything has to be passed on, so that it can all circulate. We are all invited by the Word of God to put our gifts generously at the service of others (cf. 1 Pet. 4:10).

> Since amongst brothers we do not choose one another but accept one another, there is no true brotherhood if we do not agree to enter into our brother's life and consent for him to enter into ours. Without this sharing of life, brotherhood will remain no more than a sign of genealogical belonging, with no interest to anyone.[4]

In order to justify the attitude of reserve about the interior life, a persistent spiritual tradition continues to quote a text from the book of Tobit which says that it is good to keep the king's affairs hidden. Yet these words, in Hebrew literary convention, are only meant to reinforce the second part of the verse (systematically and inexplicably passed over in silence), which instead invites communication of the gifts received: 'It is good to guard the secret of a king, but gloriously to reveal the works of God' (Tob. 12:7).

We need to eliminate false ideas which confuse sharing experiences with exhibitionism, an outburst of feelings, and useless talk of self. To understand accurately and profoundly what is meant by sharing one's spiritual progress and experiences in the evangelical life, we must look at the Father who speaks the Word, at Mary who sings her Magnificat, at Paul who constantly opens himself to the recipients of his letters. Mary can tell of the great things done in her by the Almighty. Paul tells everything about himself: his conversion, the way of an apostle, even his deepest experiences such as being taken up to the third heaven and his mystical relationship with Christ; he also reveals his tormented anxieties at the thought of his people who do not accept the revelation of Christ, and his own weaknesses and trials, the thorn in his flesh. Then Paul invites his faithful to do the same, with a view to mutual help and improvement: 'Mend your ways, heed my appeal, agree with one another' (2 Cor. 13:11); 'teach and admonish one another in all wisdom' (Col. 3:16). The Epistle to the Hebrews is equally explicit: 'Let us consider how to stir up one another to love and good works ... encouraging one another' (Heb. 10:24-5).

This sharing or communion encourages the achievement of that unity of soul and thought to which Paul invites his communities. From his faithful he demands a single thought, the same feelings, agreement, harmony, and community of spirit (cf. Phil. 1:27; 2:2; 4:2; 2 Cor. 13:11; 12:16; 15:5).

Thinking the same thing does not mean that all Christians must have the same ideas and opinions. We see this clearly in Rom. 15:5-6, where Paul does not ask the 'strong' or the 'weak' to renounce their outlook, but to behave in such a way that such legitimate plurality will not harm their deep unity of spirit which comes from their sharing one faith.[5]

However, it is important to be able to understand other people thoroughly and take into account their inner logic and the motives which lead them to act in a certain way. This can only be attained through deep mutual openness.

When this happens, there is a mutual enrichment of all the members of the community; they rejoice in the wealth of their complementary outlooks and different feelings. Complementarity is also noticeable in the variety of gifts which each contributes to the common life. This, among other things, banishes jealousy and envy, because everyone is led to rejoice in the good of others, in the conviction that, precisely because of their communion, that good belongs equally to them. Others are no longer seen as antagonists if their gifts are shared. Thus we are set free from the little compensations which all human beings continually seek, freed for a serene openness to others, until we reach complete interior liberty.

Communion eliminates suspicion and negative judgements. The fact that people do not feel judged and assessed on the basis of possible mistakes fosters communion. This is only possible to the extent that there is an atmosphere of simplicity and sincerity. Mutual trust is needed.

Here we see another indispensable element: *mutual forgiveness*. The mistakes of others have to be taken into account, and therefore people must be ready, in accordance with the rule Jesus gave to his community, to forgive seventy times seven (cf. Matt. 10:21). Forgiveness also implies not constraining others in rigid moulds of our own. Love believes in the possibility of others' renewal, it hopes for their resurrection, because love, 'believing all things, hoping all things, enduring all things' (1 Cor. 13:7), restores trust.

The ability to see daily with new eyes of which we spoke previously, to see with that look of faith which discerns a child of God in the person beside us, is born out of this mutual forgiveness. 'Do not let the sun go down on your anger' (Eph. 4.26) is an imperative which the whole community must make its own. Everyone must be able to count on the forgiveness of the others. When mutual forgiveness circulates in the community, its members can express themselves naturally and spontaneously. Love does not judge. The very fact of beginning a fresh day knowing that you are not assessed on the basis of yesterday's mistake gives everyone a new zest and a new hope. When people do not feel judged they can move freely and gain greater self-confidence because they know that even if they make a mistake they will not be shown up and ostracised. Rather, the community is encouraging and appreciative, and everyone can blossom to the full, according to their own personality - quite the opposite of uniformity and levelling.

The attitude of mutual compassion must not be confused with a desire for peace that seeks a quiet life, the result of tacit compromise or a fear of arousing the sensitivities of others which is fear of provoking conflict. 'In religious houses,' it has been written, 'the members can refuse to face certain truths, and to spare one another they often choose the way of condoning silence, compromise or ambiguous "prudence" and "meekness".'[6] So the sharing of experiences and compassionate mutual acceptance must be integrated with that teaching method, that indispensable spur to the dynamic of growth: appraisal, both personal and communal.

Personal appraisal, in the form of conversation, counsel, or spiritual direction, is an acquired component of the spiritual journey. It continues to be extremely important because it is there that we find the dynamics of unity mentioned earlier, together with the fruits of that light which the presence of Jesus typically sheds among people united in his name. In personal conversation, unlike sharing between all the members of the community, we can share particular trials or special moments of the spiritual way which may not be appropriate to tell to everyone. At this level it is easier to remove difficulties, check interior progress and appraise our spiritual life in depth.

Tradition also offers a community appraisal, the 'Chapter of faults' or similar structures. There is today, perhaps, a need for a broader and more flexible framework. The whole community, for example, under the wise guidance of its superior, could carry out at fixed times and in suitable forms a calm and positive examination of each member, to bring out the lights and shadows. In this way the possibly negative aspects of people will be noticed and together the community can suggest and look for ways of solving them. In the same way, the positive elements will be indicated so that they can increase. Does not Paul invite us to teach and instruct one another with all wisdom (cf. Col. 3:16)? It is a question of rediscovering the tools of fraternal correction and mutual support. We are each of us called, in fact, to seek the good of others and care for others as we do for ourselves. The practice of mutual love requires the ability to spur ourselves on in a constant pressing towards holiness without consenting to compromises, breaks or slackening. When mutual love in the community reaches this level of concreteness, the way of formation is assured.

Then the community, following Paul's invitation to 'love one another with brotherly affection' (Rom. 12:10), will be revealed as a true community of brothers or sisters. The religious community must reach the point of reflecting the life of a family in which people love one another 'sincerely as brothers', 'earnestly from the heart'. It is a question, however, of a very particular family, united not by human motives but by supernatural bonds, having been 'born anew, not of perishable seed but of imperishable, through the living and abiding word of God' (1 Pet. 1:23).[7]

Thus we can welcome the exhortation in Peter's Epistle: 'Finally, all of you, have unity of spirit, sympathy, love of the brethren, a tender heart and a humble mind. Do not return evil for evil or reviling for reviling; but on the contrary, bless' (1 Pet. 3:8-9).

The Measure of Love

Mutual love, as we have already seen, requires a radical love. Love in the community must possess the measure of Christ's love, which implies the complete gift of self, to the point of giving your life. If Jesus loved us to the point of death, 'we ought to lay down our lives for the brethren' (1 John 3:16). Koinonia is a Utopia if it is not formed by people who can rise to being 'one'.

Here we have to draw out all the consequences of the concept of the person, which is itself (*enstasis*) in *ecstasis* to another. 'It is only in renouncing its own possession', Lossky wrote, 'and giving itself freely, in ceasing to exist for itself that the person finds full expression.'[8] To understand the person thoroughly, we know that we have to mount to the Trinity and draw out the consequences of the dynamics of its life, which consists entirely in the capacity of the Persons to 'not-be' in giving, an 'ecstasy' of love.

In the mystery of his abandonment on the cross, and his death, Jesus revealed the trinitarian dynamics of love by showing love's radicalness. There he stripped himself of everything with the utmost generosity. The mystery of his annihilating himself is a mystery of giving.

His love is an oblation, total gift. Christ is bread given, blood poured out: 'Take, eat; this is my body which is *given* for you'; 'drink this all of you; this is my blood which is *shed* for you'. In the mystery of his cross, made present now in the Eucharist, he descends into the abyss of 'not-being' to give his 'being' totally. Thus he continues the Father's act of loving oblation: 'God so loved the world that he gave his only Son' (John 3:16).

Love is therefore the gift of self. It is going out of self in order to enter into another, to live increasingly in the beloved. Love, John was to say, is recognized precisely by this offering of self to the beloved: 'By this we know love, that he laid down his life for us' (1 John 3:16). By travelling this road, Christ created the new people. He thus becomes the model for all who want to build up unity with their brethren.

In the light of the mystery of his abandonment and death on the cross, the vows that Religious take then acquire all their significance for the community. In a religious community, consecrated chastity is indispensable for entering into communion with others and maintaining unity. In fact, it makes it possible to love with a true love, with a pure and whole heart. Through it, the heart is purified from the craving to possess and appropriate others, or restrict and limit love. Rather, chastity enlarges love so that it is for everyone. Purifying the heart to make it free to love will at times be seen as a genuine dying, a concrete fulfilment of the evangelical 'hating one's own life' (John 12:25), because it extends right to the abolition of a natural family of one's own, 'mother and wife and children and brothers and sisters' (Luke 14:26), as the necessary way to establish the community as a new family born not of flesh and blood but of the will of God. On the cross Jesus showed all the radicalness of this way. He did not rely on any help, human, spiritual or divine. The disciples had left him. He detached his mother from him by giving her to John. Even the Father seemed to forsake him. This is the model for everyone who has to purify their heart in order to attain a love which embraces the universe.

Like consecrated chastity, poverty is also an indispensable condition for community life. As an act of love it is simultaneously an emptying of self and a giving of self, expressed in putting one's material and spiritual possessions in common. When people are themselves rich, there is no possibility of a genuine meeting with others. To love another brother we need to become so poor in spirit that we possess nothing but love. And love is empty of self. For love to be concrete, to the extent of sharing completely all that one has and is, it needs a permanent and emotional detachment from everything, a detachment given definite form in the sincere and radical giving of possessions and gifts. On the cross Jesus teaches us the most absolute detachment from everything. He is the perfect model of the poor in spirit. He divests himself of everything and gives body, blood, soul and divinity: the model for everyone who is called to the total gift of self and the complete sharing of all their possessions.

For unity in the community to be complete, the members need, finally, to give all their own feelings, plans and wills, so that together they may discover the very will of God, who unifies them all. This is the way of obedience, which is ready to renounce its own will in order to embrace to the full that of God. On the cross Jesus accepted and carried out the Father's will in perfect obedience, even if this meant total darkness and cost him his life. And he is the model of all who have to live obedience to the point of overcoming the test of absurdity or lack of relationship with superiors.

The way to koinonia, begun in metanoia and expressed in diakonia, must thus pass through kenosis[9]. Following the road travelled by its Master, the community cannot escape from the fundamental evangelical law: 'Whoever would save his life will lose it, and whoever loses his life for my sake will find it' (Matt. 16:25). In predominantly individual spiritualities, this law of the gospel has given rise to many forms of ascesis such as silence, withdrawal into solitude, penance, vigils, fasting... In a communal spirituality it can offer another range of ascetic forms, born out of the exercise of mutual love. In mutual love, one person has to make room for another, in an emptiness which is the cancelling out of self because everything has been given, extremely and radically. It is a matter of cancelling out the self in order to receive others with their desires and thoughts, sorrows and joys; an emptying out which is both the effect of the gift of self to the other and an availability to receive the other; forgetting self is the fruit of being attentive to someone else. Without 'dying' for one another and 'giving our life' for one another, there can be no communion.

If the structure of the new commandment has the sign of death in it, it also possesses its fruit, which is precisely new life, unity, the pneumatic presence of the risen Lord. We die to ourselves to give life to the Risen

Christ in the midst of the community. We die to multiplicity to give life to unity and thus rediscover distinction and the wealth of diversity.

Once again, we verify the truth of 'on earth as it is in heaven'. Because God is one and is love, he is Trinity. Because in the community its members are 'perfected in unity', everyone regains their own innermost personality. Because Religious have lost their own personalities in order to put on that of Christ, in unity, Christ takes on the personality of the Religious and makes all the elements of their purified persons his own, expressing himself with their sensitivity, their gifts, their feelings, their creativity and their interior riches.

The community thus sets itself up as a school that specializes in the perfecting of charity, a crucible in which the soul is purified and the spiritual self refined to the point of full conformity with the crucified Christ in his greatest expression of love. Perhaps there is nothing better than the intense inner activity provoked by living in mutual love to enable us to reach the deepest experience of Christ and say with truth: 'I know nothing among you except Jesus Christ and him crucified' (1 Cor. 2:2). Then and only then shall we truthfully be able to say: 'We know and believe in love' (1 John 4:16).

NOTES

1. Cf. Rom. 1:29-31; 13:13; 1 Cor. 5:10-11; 6:9-10; 2 Cor. 12:20-1; Gal. 5:19-21; Col. 3:5-8. Cf. J. Navone, *Dono di sé e comunione. La Trinità e l'umana realizzazione* (Assisi: Cittadella, 1990), pp. 64-8.
2. C. Palmés, 'Bautismo', in *Diccionario Teológico de la Vida Consagrada* (Madrid: Publ. Claretianas 1989), pp. 89-104.
3. De Fiores, *Spiritualità contemporanea*, p. 1536.
4. *Dizionario francescano*, pp. 624-5.
5. Dupont, 'L'unione tra i primi cristiani', in *Nuovi studi sugli Atti degli Apostoli*, p. 285.
6. M. van Tente, *Nuove comunità*, DIP, VI, 481.
7. For the community as a family, see X. Pikaza, 'La vida religiosa como familia', *Nova et Vetera* 11 (1986), pp. 209-25; F. Sbaffoni, 'La comunità religiosa come vera famiglia', *Rivista di Ascetica e Mistica* 54 (1985), pp. 108-26.
8. *The Mystical Theology of the Eastern Church*, p. 124.
9. Cf. Navone, op. cit., pp. 62-77.

Conclusion

The route we have travelled now seems clear; we see it unfolding in the context of the broad curve of salvation. Its beginning was in the creation itself, when God, forming human beings in his image and likeness, created them for communion. God the creator has actually revealed himself as Love, Trinity, Communion. Our road ends in the perfected unity of the end of time, when everything will be recapitulated in Christ and Christ himself will be subject to the Father, so that God will be all in all. Jesus' prayer to the Father, 'May they be one in us', will thus find its complete fulfilment.

Situated between these two extremes of the parabola are the human adventure and the divine adventure: human sin which has broken every kind of relationship; and the mystery of Jesus, the Word of God who becomes flesh. Christ comes to reconstitute the family of God's children, torn apart by sin, and to bring human beings back to unity.

He began to carry out the mission entrusted to him by the Father by gathering round him apostles and disciples, the beginning of the new people and a living parable of the reconciled human family. To them he entrusted the new commandment of mutual love, as the realization on earth of the life of the Trinity. 'Love one another as I have loved you' became the law of life for the messianic people of the Church, the icon of the Trinity.

During his last supper with his disciples, before his passion, death and resurrection, Jesus instituted the Eucharist which, by making us share in the one bread and the one cup, enables us to realize mutual love on the model and in the measure of his own love; and he turned to the Father to ask him for the unity of all humanity, grafted into the unity of the Trinity.

Then he entrusted himself to the Father's will and in the paschal mystery accomplished that unity which he had taught his disciples to live and for which he had asked the Father. Lifted up between heaven and earth, he drew everyone to himself, destroyed the wall of separation between peoples, and brought about reconciliation with God and between human beings, making all of them one. Thus the paschal mystery reveals the way to build up unity. Only if the grain of wheat falls into the ground and dies can it bear fruit. Here love reaches its ultimate expression, to the point of giving its life. The definitive revelation of the dynamics of the trinitarian mystery is disclosed, which is a mystery of love, made of the gift of self and mutual welcome, in the perichoresis of the Persons. It is the archetype of our unity. Thus we too are called to love one another to the point of giving our lives for each other.

The coming of the Holy Spirit, the first gift to the faithful, realized the unity brought about by Christ. Poured out on the disciples gathered in the Cenacle, it made the Church visible, characterized from its first moment as communion. The Spirit of Pentecost in Jerusalem reconstituted the unity of the human race which had been broken at Babel. So the life of the first Christians, the prototype of every Christian community, indeed of the Church itself, appears as koinonia and unity of one heart and one soul.

Ever since, throughout the course of its history, the Church has become increasingly aware of being the Body of Christ, the temple of the Spirit, the sacrament of the innermost union of the human race, communion, icon of the Trinity, until today, when the Second Vatican Council has perhaps brought out the dimensions of this mystery as never before.

Consecrated life has, from its birth, grasped the inner nature of Christianity. After the eremetic life had asserted the primacy of God - who asks to be loved with the whole heart, soul and strength - and the radicalness and demands of following Christ, cenobitism began increasingly to emphasize the dimension of communion.

The community of the first Christians at Jerusalem became the prototype for the first monastic communities. Further inspirational models emerged subsequently, such as the prophetic communities of the Old Testament and the family at Nazareth. But it was particularly the itinerant community of the disciples and apostles who followed Jesus that became increasingly the source of inspiration for later religious communities. Underlying these models we can discern the archetype of every form of community: the life of unity of the Persons of the Most Holy Trinity.

The different sources of inspiration have produced different forms of community. Some emphasize the ascetic element, others fraternity, others the dimension of ministry, and yet others apostolic service.

Always present at their birth is the charismatic action of the Spirit. He leads into all truth and from age to age introduces a particular understanding of the Word of God and reveals new dimensions of the unfathomable mystery of Christ. He who delves into the human heart raises up men and women who, illumined by the light of the Gospel, and made sensitive to the signs of the times, give life to new religious communities and consequently to new ways of realizing the one communion, in a diversity of ministries and communities. The common life takes on a particular appearance according to the mission of the individual Institutes. So today we can admire the 'wonderful variety' of religious families which enrich the Church and equip it for every good work.

For all the variety of their forms, religious communities exhibit a profound unity by virtue of their common origin. One and the same Spirit is at work in the multiplicity of their charisms (cf. 1 Cor. 12:11). United in their common charismatic origin, they are also united in their common identification with the one Christ. In fact, they appear as different expressions of the identical mystery of Christ and the identical Gospel. All of them are following the one Christ, even if their ways and styles are different. The Lord and his Spirit are present in them: 'A community gathered together as a true family in the Lord's name enjoys his presence, through the love of God which is poured into their hearts by the Holy Spirit' (PC 15).

In spite of all the variety of their ministries, religious communities are united in pursuing the same goal: every charism is given for the building up of the Body of Christ (cf. LG 45). Anyone who proclaims the Gospel does so in order to bring human beings to unity between themselves and with God. Those who live in contemplation and prayer do so to achieve this same unity. Those who care for the sick do so in order to introduce people to this objective of unity, as do those who teach... Everything converges on one point and has one purpose: the building up of the Body of Christ. Inspired by the Risen Lord living in them and communicating his own Spirit to them, religious communities expand their communion in an extraordinary range of service, diakonia, witness and proclamation, according to their individual charisms. They become a proclamation of the unity achieved by Christ, a prophetic sign of the humanity that will inhabit the new earth, leaven in the lump so that all may enter and be part of Christ's plan of unity: 'That they may all be one'.

Thus it becomes inconceivable that a particular ministry should be exercised other than in communion with all other ministries. A single community or a single Institute on its own cannot carry out this divine plan. All communities have to be united in realizing it, in spite of the variety of their charisms. The document *Religious and human promotion* reminds us that 'the common vocation of Christians to union with God and between human beings for the salvation of the world must be considered even before the diversity of gifts and ministries' (no. 20). Indeed, gifts and ministries are for the sake of that union. We might say that every community, every charism, every spirituality is inspired by koinonia and targeted on koinonia.

The same unity which must inspire relations between religious communities is needed for all the other vocations in the Church, so that they can be a witness to the whole world of the unity of the new people of God. Men and women Religious cannot be fully themselves and carry out their task if they are not in full communion with laypeople, presbyters and bishops. The Church is actually one in the variety of its vocations and charisms, and every vocation is a gift to others, every charism gives light to others. Only by communicating the gifts of the Spirit can the people of God succeed in releasing the extraordinary charismatic potential which enriches it and is leading history towards the fullness of the new heavens and the new earth.

Unity widens out further to the need for communion with other Churches, and to dialogue with believers of all religions, so that all together may enter into dialogue with the non-believing world and so, starting from our unity in Christ, draw all human beings into the great design of building a united world.

The religious community is rediscovering itself as one expression of the great ecclesial koinonia – an inalienable expression. Born of koinonia, it will be increasingly itself in proportion to how far it lives from koinonia and for koinonia.

Selected Bibliography

Only titles relating to Religious community from a theological and spiritual perspective are listed. Other basic articles of books of a historical nature, or dealing with the theology of the Religious life and theology in general, are cited *en passant* in the text. (Some English works added by translator.)

ABLONDI A., Dalla Trinita allà comunità, *Consacrazione e Servizio*, 28 (1979), n. 10, pp. 7-17

AGUILAR F., Attuazione comunitaria dei consigli evangelici, *Vita Consacrata*, 8 (1972), pp.545-56.

ALAIZ A., *Los testigos de la fraternidad. Dimensión comunitaria de la vida religiosa*, Madrid: 1973.
La comunidad religiosa profecía de la nueva humanidad, Madrid: 1991.

ALDAZABAL J., Los religiosos, comunidad orante, *Phase* 26 (1986), pp.231-45.

ALONSO S.M., *La utopía de la vida religiosa. Reflexiones desde la fé*, Madrid: 1982.
La vida consagrada. Sintesis teólogica, Madrid: 1980.

ANDRES GUTIERREZ DJ., 'La vida común religiosa', *Apollinaris*, 50 (1977), pp. 119-48.

ARANGUREN I., 'La comunión cenobítica, *Cistercium*, 23 (1971), pp. 247-258.

ARBUCKLE G., *Strategies for Growth in Religious Life*, Slough: 1986.
Out of Chaos, Refounding Religious Congregations, London: 1988.
Grieving for a Change. A Spirituality for refounding Gospel Communities, London: 1991.

ARBUCKLE G., and FLEMING D., *Religious Life: Rebirth through Conversion*, Slough: 1991.

ARRONDO J.L., Nuevo planteamiento de la comunidad religiosa, *Revista de Espiritualidad*, 47 (1988), pp. 603-30.

ASIAIN M.A., En busca de la renovación de nuestra vida comunitaria, *Vida Religiosa*, 38 (1975), pp. 405-20.

BARROSSE T., Religious Community and the Primitive Church, *Review for Religious*, 25 (1966), pp. 971-85.

BEHA H.M., *Living Community*, Milwaukee, Wisconsin: 1967.
'Towards a Theology of Community', *Review for Religious*, 24 (1965), pp. 735-743.
'Contemplative Community - Solitude Community', *Ibid.*, 38 (1979), pp. 78-90.

BISIGNANO S., 'La formazione comunitaria nella vita religiosa apostolica', *Vita Consacrata*, 22 (1986), pp. 420-30.

BLACKFRIARS DOMINICANS of, the, Oxford (1950-1951), a series of books on the Religious life:
1. *Religious Sisters.*
2. *Vocation.*
3. *Obedience.*
4. *Poverty.*
5. *Chastity.*
6. *The Doctrinal Instruction of Religious Sisters.*
7. *The Direction of Nuns.*
8. *Common Life.*

BLANCO PACHECO S., 'La comunidad de los pacificos', *Vida Religiosa'*, 60 (1986), pp. 245-59.
La comunidad religiosa convocada por la Palabra, in Urgidos por la Palabra. Fundamentos biblicos de la Vida Religiosa, Madrid: 1989, pp. 139-59.

BOFF M.L., 'La evolución de la vida religiosa en el movimiento de eclesiogénesis', *Vida Religiosa*, 62 (1987), pp. 404-8.

BONHOEFFER D., *La vita comune*, Brescia: 1969

BOURDEAU G., 'La théologie de la vie religieuse depuis Vatican II: une thélologie ou des opinions', *La Vie des Communautes Religieuses*, 44 (1986), pp. 90-101.

BOYD R, 'The Prayer of the Community', *The Way*, 10 (1970), pp. 220-29.

BRACKEN J., 'Community and Religious Life: A Question of Interpretation', *Review for Religious*, 31 (1972), pp. 732-41.

BUTLER, C., *Ways of Christian Life: Old Spirituality for Modern Men*, London: 1932.

CABRA P.G., *Comunità religiosa e vocazione*, Rome: 1983.

CARBONE V., *La comunità religiosa*, Vatican City: 1975.

CASTAÑEDA R, 'Fondamenti biblici della comunità apostolica', *Consacrazione e Servizio*, 34 (1985), n. 1, pp. 7-21; n. 2, pp. 7-20; n. 3,pp. 14-23; n.4, pp. 7-17.

CIARDI F., 'Un cammino per la dilatazione della comunione', *Consacrazione e Servizio*, 28 (1979), n. 11, pp. 11-32.

    L'apporto della comunità nel cammino spirituale, La guida spirituale nella Vita Religiosa, Rome: 1986, pp. 109-42.

    'La comunita religiosa segno di speranza', *Vita Consacrata*, 25 (1989), pp. 216-26.

CODINA MAS P., 'La pertenencia, factor de cohesión en la comunidad religiosa', *Vida Religiosa*, 42 (1977), pp. 147-59.

COLLI C., *Vivere in comunione. Per una spiritualita della vita comunitaria*, Bologna: 1978.

    'Comunità religiosa come mistero di comunione', *Consacrazione e Servizio*, 34 (1985), n. 10, pp. 14-24.

    'Come creare comunità-comunione', *Consacrazione e Servizio*, 34 (1985), n. 12, pp. 7-14.

COVENTRY, J., et al., *Religious Life Today*, Tenbury Wells (no date).

CRIPPA L., 'Per stimare e vivere il mistero della vita comune', *Vita Consacrata*, 19 (1983), pp. 137-46.

DE CANDIDO L., *Fraternità, Nuovo Dizionario di Spiritualita*, Rome: 1979, pp. 674-88.

    'Esperti di comunione. Monaci, frati ed altri', *Servitium*, 20 (1986), pp. 345-69.

DEL BURGO L., 'La comunidad religiosa, signo elocuente de liberación', *Revista de Espiritualidad*, 44 (1985), pp. 467-91.

DE MIGUEL J. M., Eucaristía y Vida Religiosa, *Comunidades*, 15 (1987), fichero de materias n. 59.

DE PEDRO H. A., 'Eucaristia, centro e culmine di ogni comunita', *Vita Consacrata*, 26 (1990), pp. 18-29.

DELPLANQUE B., 'La vie en communion', *La Vie Spirituelle, Supplement*, 21 (1968), pp. 303-39.

DIANICH S.,' Comunita', *Nuovo Dizionario di Teología*, Paoline, Alba, 1977, pp. 148-65.

DIEZ M., 'Comunion', *Diccionario Teológico de la Vida Consagrada*, cit., pp. 317-27.

DIEZ PRESA M., 'La vida religiosa, realidad-signo trascendente, profético, salvifico', *Vida Religiosa*, 68 (1990), pp. 116-21.

DUBAY T., *Ecclesial Women. Towards a Theology of the Religious State*, Staten Island: 1970.

DUCHARME A., *Discerniment spiritual et délibération communautaire*, Conférence Religieuse Canadienne, Ottawa: 1974.

Une dynamique communautaire de la foi. La communauté religieuse, Montreal: 1982.

'Tâche personnelle et mission communautaire', *La Vie des Communautés Religieuses*, 44 (1986), pp. 230-44.

Sister EDNA MARY, *The Religious Life*, London: 1968.

FARICY, R., *The End of the Religious Life*, Minneapolis: 1983.

FARICY, R., and BLackborrow, S., *The Healing of the Religious Life*, Great Wakering, Essex (no date).

FERNANDEZ P., 'La comunidad de vida consagrada', *Teología Espiritual*, 24 (1980), pp. 53-78.

FERNANDEZ SANZ G., 'La vida religiosa como parabola', *Vida Religiosa*, 68 (1990), pp.122-31.

FIAND, B., *Living the Vision: Religious Vows in an Age of Change*, New York: 1990.

FINKLER P., *Unificación de la vida en la comunidad religiosa*, Madrid: 1982.

FITZGERALD W.F.P., 'Why Community?', *Supplement to Doctrine and Life*, 8 (1970), pp. 19-25.

FLEMING, D. (ed.), *Religious Life at the Crossroads*, New York: 1985.

FORTE B., 'Signos de recuerdo, comunión y esperanza. Religiosos en la Iglesia según el Vaticano II, *Vida Religiosa*, 68 (1990), pp.132-40.

FRANCIS M., *A Right To Be Merry*, London: 1957. *Marginals*, Chicago: 1967.

FUERTES BILDARRAZ J.B., 'La "vida fraterna en común" de los religiosos y su trayectoria histórico-jurídica', *Apollinaris*, 55 (1982), pp. 532-68.

'Vita religiosa: de communione in communitate', *Commentarium pro Religiosis et Missionariis*, 65 (1984), pp. 23-75.

FUSTER S., 'La vida comunitaria como reflejo del misterio trinitario', *Teologia Espiritual*, 29 (1985), pp. 297-313.

GALOT J., 'La stima vicendevole in comunità', *Vita Consacrata*, 16 (1980), pp. 265-74.

GALOT J., 'L'impegno all'amore fraterno nella comunità', *Vita Consacrata*, 22 (1986), pp. 12-25.

'La condivisione nella comunità', *Vita Consacrata*, 22 (1986) 101-16.

'Una prospettiva illimitata di carità', *Vita Consacrata*, 22 (1986), pp. 272-86.

'Il perdono reciproco nella comunità', *Vita Consacrata*, 22 (1986), pp. 733-44, 833-43.

'Il superamento della carita', *Vita Consacrata*, 25 (1989), pp.101-15, 437-50.

'Il grande amore fraterno', *Vita Consacrata*, 26 (1990), pp. 1-17.

GAMBINO V., *Comunità religiosa, comunità di persone*, Brescia: 1968.

'La dimensione comunitaria o di "Koinonia" della vita religiosa', *Per una presenza viva dei religiosi nella Chiesa e nel mondo*, Turin: 1970, pp. 555-88.

GARCIA J.M., *Hogar y taller: Seguimiento de Jesús y comunidad religiosa*, Santander: 1985.

GARCIA PAREDES J.C.R, 'Seguir a Cristo en comunidad', *Vida Religiosa*, 48 (1980), pp. 52-63.

'La comunidad que nace de la Cruz', *Vida Religiosa*, 58 (1985), pp. 353-64.

GEEROMS G., *La vie fraternelle en commun dans la vie religieuse du Concile au Côde*, Rome: 1989.

GESTEIRA GARZA M., 'La Eucaristia y la vida religiosa', *Vida Religiosa*, 62 (1987), pp. 11-27.

GEYJ.-C., *La vie religieuse, memoire évangelique de l'Église*, Paris: 1987.

GIARDINI F., 'Una vita esclusivamente consacrata alla SS.ma Trinità', *Vita Consacrata*, 22 (1986), 630-38, 721-32, 817-32.

GIRARDI O. G., 'Vita religiosa, III. Nella Chiesa comunione, i religiosi testimoni e artefici di comunione', *Vita Consacrata*, 17 (1981), pp. 437-55.

GIUSTETTI M., (ed.) *Comunione e comunità. Koinônia*, Casale Monferrato: 1981.

GLEASON R., *To Live in Christ: Nature and Grace in the Religious Life*, Dublin: 1962.

The Restless Religious, Dayton, Ohio: 1968.

GRASSO G., 'Comunione', *Dizionario di Teologia Interdisciplinare*, I, Turin 1977, pp. 536-48.

GRAZLANO R, *La trasformazione della vita comunitaria religiosa nel tempo dell'aggiornamento*. Part of a dissertation in the Pontifical Gregorian University, Rome: 1985.

GRIEGER P., *Costruzione della persona e vita comunitaria*, Milan: 1981.

La comunità religiosa, comunità di persone, Milan: 1987.

GUERRERO J.M., 'Los religiosos ¿signos creibles de una alternativa nueva?', *Vida Religiosa*, 42 (1977), pp. 223 -35.

'La fraternità è possibile', *Consacrazione e Servizio*, 37 (1988), n. 12, pp. 19-27.

La utopía de la comunidad religiosa, Santiago: 1990.

GUTIERREZ L., *Teología sistemática de la vida religiosa*, Madrid: 1976.

HILLMAN E., 'Religious Community', *Religious Life Review* (*Supplement to Doctrine and Life*), 30 (1991), n. 146, pp. 3-10.

HINNEBUSCH P., *Religious Life a Living Liturgy*, New York: 1965.

HUYGHE G., *Tensions and Change: The Problems of Religious Orders Today*, London: 1965.

HUYGHE G., and others, *Religious Orders in the Modern World. A Symposium*, London: 1965.

JOHN PAUL II, Pope, *Challenge or Crisis*, Texts by, ed. Seamus O'Byrne, Dublin: 1987.

Speaks to Religious: Principal Allocutions and Letters (6 vols), (ed.) Jean Beyer, Leeds (no date).

LECLERCQ, J. *The Religious Vocation*, English translation, Dublin: 1955.

LEDDY M.J., *Reweaving Religious Life. Beyond the Liberal Model*. Mystic, Connecticut: 1990.

LINDEMANN K., 'Toward a Definition of Community', *Review for Religious*, 29 (1970), pp. 833-42.

LOPEZ R., *La vida comunitaria elemento principal en la renovación de la vida religiosa*, Bilbao: 1976.

LOPEZ S., 'La fraternidad primer agente de evangelizacion', *Selecciones de Franciscanismo*, 11 (1982), pp. 33-48.

LOUF A., 'Vivre en communauté fraternelle', *Vie Consacrée*, 56 (1984), pp. 135-52.

LOZANO J.M., *La sequela di Cristo. Teologia storico-sistematica della vita religiosa*,Milan: 1981.

LUZARRAGA J., 'El mensaje de la Eucaristía para la vida consagrada según el N.T.', *Manresa*, 57 (1985), pp. 335-362.

MACCISE C., 'Fraternidad', *Diccionario Teológico de la Vida Consagrada*, pp. 741-56.

MACKRELL G., *Thoughts for Religious*, Slough: 1984.

MALATESTA E., 'Aiuto fraterno reciproco nella comunione con Gesú (Riflessione sulla lavanda dei piedi, Gv 13, 1-20)', *Vita Consacrata*, 13 (1977), pp. 159-69.

MARTINEZ P., 'Formas de comunicación espiritual', *Vida Religiosa*, 48 (1980), pp. 448-64.

MASCOLO A., *La fraternité chrétienne chez les religieux et les religieuses*, Conference Religieuse Canadienne, Ottawa: 1971.

MERCATALI A., 'Comunità di vita', in *Nuovo Dizionario di Spiritualità*, S. De Fiores and T. Goffi, Rome: 1979, pp. 225-42.

MERKLE J., *Commited By Choice. Religious Life Today*, Collegeville, Minnesota: 1992.

METZ J., *Followers of Christ: The Religious Life and the Church*, London: 1978.

MOLINARI P., 'Comunidad: comunión en Cristo', *Vida Religiosa*, 35 (1973), pp. 102-109.

MOLONEY F., *Disciples and Prophetes: A Biblical Model for the Religious Life*, London: 1980.

A Life of Promise. Poverty, Chastity, Obedience, London: 1985.

MONGILLO D., I. 'La comunione di cui la vita religiosa è e deve diventare segno; II. Verso nuovi ambiti e nuovi stili di comunione; III. Per essere segno vivere la comunione', *Consacrazione e Servizio*, 34 (1985), nn. 8/9, pp. 6-22. 23-32, 33-44.

MOTTE A., *Un coeur et une âme en Dieu. La communauté religieuse*, Paris-Fribourg: 1972.

MUÑIZ V., 'La celebración litúrgica en la edificación de la comunidad, *Comunidades*', 15 (1987), pp. 223-32.

MUÑOZ R., 'Misión evangelizadora y profética de las comunidades religiosas', *Vida Religiosa*, 40 (1976), pp. 159-64.

MURPHY-O'CONNOR, J., *What is Religious Life: A critical appraisal*, Dublin (no date).

NATALI P., 'La comunità religiosa, presenza di liberazione fra gli uomini', *Consacrazione e Servizio*, 24 (1975), nn. 6-7, pp. 58-107.

NEAL, M.A., *From Nun to Sisters: An expanding vocation*, Mystic, Connecticut: 1990.

O'LEARY M., *Our Time Is Now: A Study of Some Modern Congregations and Secular Institutes*, London: 1955.

O'MURCHÚ, D., *The Prophetic Horizon of Religious Life*, London: 1989.

O'TOOLE RF., 'What the Lord's Supper Can Mean for Religious', *Review for Religious*, 44 (1985), pp. 237-49.

ORSY, M., *Open to the Spirit. Religious Life after Vatican II*, London: 1968.

PERCHENET A., *The Revival of the Religious Life and Christian Unity*, London: 1969.

PERREAULT G., 'La communauté religieuse: groupe de tâche ou de vie?', *La Vie des Communautés Religieuses*, 43 (1985), pp. 131-46.

PFISTER M., 'Eucharist. Celebration for Community', *Review for Religious*, 25 (1986), pp. 25-35.

PIKAZA X., 'La vida religiosa como familia', *Nova et Vetera*, 11 (1986), pp. 209-25.

'En comunidad: Como la familia del Dios-Trinidad', *Vida Religiosa*, 66 (1989), pp. 57-66.

Tratado de vida religiosa (Consagracion, Comunion, Mision), Madrid: 1990.

RAMBALDI G., 'Responsabilità dei religiosi nella comunione della Chiesa', *Vita Consacrata*, 22 (1986), pp. 401-19.

RAMSEY B., 'Reflections on Community', *Review for Religious*, 44 (1985), pp. 704-15.

RENNA L., 'La comunità religiosa nella comunità locale', *Carmelus*, 27 (1980), pp. 3-25.

RUEDA B., *Apología y desmitización de la vida común*, Madrid: 1970.

Progetto comunitario, Milan: 1978.

Nuovi orizzonti per il progetto di vita comunitario, Milan: 1981.

SANCHEZ MIELGO G., 'La vivencia comunitaria del Evangelio', *Teología Espiritual*, 29 (1985), pp. 275-95.

SANTANER M.A., 'Vie religieuse et vie de communauté', *La Vie Spirituelle*, 115 (1966), pp. 154-67.

'Vie de communauté et mission, *La Vie des Communautés Religieuses*, 30 (1972), pp. 139-51.

'La Vie fraternelle dans les communautés religieuses chretiennes', *La Vie des Communautés Religieuses*, 32 (1974), pp. 130- 48.

SBAFFONI E, 'La comunità religiosa come vera famiglia', *Rivista di Ascetica e Mistica*, 54 (1985), pp. 108-26.

SCHLECK, C., 'The Mystery and Holiness of Community Life', *Review for Religious*, 25 (1966), pp. 621-68.

SCHNEIDER S., *New Wineskins: Re-imagining Religious Life Today*, New York: 1986.

SECONDIN B., 'Vita in comune, vita in comunione', *Vita religiosa. Bilancio e prospettive*, Rome: 1976, pp. 200-41.

SHAUGHNESSY E J., 'Reflections on the nature of Community', *Review for Religious*, 28 (1969), pp. 277-90.

SILANES N., 'Trinidad y vida consagrada', *Comunidades*, 17 (1989), nn. 66-7, pp. 47-67.

STANLEY D., *Faith and Religious Life - A New Testament Perpective*, New York: 1971.

STEINBERG D., (ed.), *The Future of Religious Life*, Collegeville: 1990.

SUAREZ G.G., 'La comunidad religiosa en el magisterio contemporaneo de la Iglesia', *Teología Espiritual*, 17 (1973), pp. 261-82.

TERRINONI U., 'La comunione, dono e conquista', *Vita Consacrata*, 26 (1990), pp. 30-9.

TILLARD J.M.R., Le Mystère de la communauté', *La Vie des Communautes Religieuses*, 24 (1966), pp. 98-112.

'Le grandi leggi del rinnovamento della Vita Religiosa', *Il rinnovamento della Vita Religiosa*, Florence: 1968, pp. 63-133.

'L'Eucharistie et la fraternité', *Nouvelle Revue Théologique*, 91 (1969), pp. 113-35.

'La communauté religieuse', *Nouvelle Revue Théologique*, 94 (1972), pp. 488-519; 95 (1973), pp. 150-87.

'La comunità religiosa luogo della sequela di Cristo', *Davanti a Dio e per il mondo*, Rome: 1975, pp. 206-92.

TIMIADIS E., *Vivere la comunità. Il carisma della vita comune*, Turin: 1978.

'El monacato como "koinonia"', *Vida Religiosa*, 66 (1989), pp. 203-10.

TISSERAND E., *Famille ou communautè? Que peut-on mettre en commun?* Paris: 1976.

TRAPET M. A., *Pour l'avenir des nouvelles communautés dans l'Église*, Paris: 1987.

VALDERRABANO OPRDEIG J.F., 'La vida de comunidad, elemento integrante de la vida religiosa apostolica', *Testimonio*, n. 89 (1985), pp. 45-51.

VALLES C.G., *Viviendo juntos*, Santander: 1985.

VANIER J., *La comunità luogo del perdono e della festa*, Milan: 1980.

VARIOUS AUTHORS, 'Comunidad', *Diccionario Teológico de la Vida Consagrada*, Madrid: 1989, pp. 263-317.

'Comunidad, profecía permanente', *Vida Religiosa*, 63 (1988), pp. 3-64.

'Comunidad-parábola en una sociedad burguesa', *Vida Religiosa*, 64 (1988).

'Comunita', *Dizionario degli Istituti di Perfezione*, II, Rome: 1975, 1366-82.

'Dinámica de la comunidad religiosa', *Confer*, 13 (1974), pp. 341-435.

'El discernimiento comunitario', *Vita Religiosa*, 38 (1975), pp. 235-45.

'Enviados desde la comunidad', *Testimonio*, 121 (1990).

'Eucaristía, centro de la comunidad', *Vida Religiosa*, 62 (1987), pp. 3-80.

La comunità religiosa, Alma Roma, Rome (no date).

La comunità, Vicenza: 1978.

La Eucarestía en la vida de la relgiosa, Madrid: 1971.

'Nuove comunità,' *Dizionario degli Istituti di Perfezione*, VI, Rome: 1980, 479-87.

'Piccole comunità', *ibid.*

Vita comunitaria (Studies published by the *Claretianum* Institute of Theology of the Religious Life), Milan: 1979.

Vita comunitaria Esperienze e valutazioni, Padua: 1971.

VIARD C., *Vie religieuse, communion et mission*, Paris: 1988.

WENZEL K., 'Expectations of Community Along Life's Journey', *Review for Religious*, 44 (1985), pp. 815-28.

WOOD S., 'The Eucharist: Heart of Religious Community', *Review for Religious*, 46 (1987), pp. 178-86.

ZIGROSSI A., *Presenza di Cristo nella comunità consacrata*, Milan: 1973.